Social Exclusion and Inner City Europe

Social Exclusion and Inner City Europe

Regulating Urban Regeneration

S. P. Mangen

University of London
School of Economics & Political Science

First published 2004 by
PALGRAVE MACMILLAN
Houndmills, Basingstoke, Hampshire RG21 6XS and
175 Fifth Avenue, New York, N.Y. 10010
Companies and representatives throughout the world

PALGRAVE MACMILLAN is the global academic imprint of the Palgrave Macmillan division of St. Martin's Press, LLC and of Palgrave Macmillan Ltd. Macmillan® is a registered trademark in the United States, United Kingdom and other countries. Palgrave is a registered trademark in the European Union and other countries.

ISBN 1–4039–0567–3 hardback

This book is printed on paper suitable for recycling and made from fully managed and sustained forest sources.

A catalogue record for this book is available from the British Library.

Library of Congress Cataloging-in-Publication Data
Mangen, Stephen P.
    Social exclusion and inner city Europe : regulating urban regeneration /
S. P. Mangen.
        p. cm.
    Includes bibliographical references and index.
    ISBN 1–4039–0567–3
    1. Urban renewal—Europe. 2. Urban policy—Europe. 3. Inner cities—
Europe. 4. Marginality, Social—Europe. I. Title.

HT178.E8M35 2004
307.3′416′094—dc22
                                                                    2003070194

10   9   8   7   6   5   4   3   2   1
13 12 11 10 09 08 07 06 05 04

Transferred to Digital Printing 2005

To Mum

Contents

Preface   viii

Part I   Mapping the Inner City

1 Inner City Europe: Socio-Economic Change and National
   Policy Responses   3

2 Cities and their Inner Cities: Transformation and Governance   44

Part II   Inner City Regeneration Strategies

3 Regenerating the Physical Structure   83

4 Extending the Policy Remit: Socio-Economic Interventions   116

5 The Impacts of Regeneration   154

Part III   Evolving Regeneration Regimes

6 Inner City Regeneration: Mainstreaming the EU's Urban Agenda   177

7 The Inner City: Regulating Regeneration, Combating
   Social Exclusion   194

Appendix: Statistical Audit   208

Bibliography   216

Index   254

Preface

The objective of this project is to present cross-sectoral, thematic case studies addressing the broad regeneration agenda that has been evolving in a sample of inner cities in the largest EU states. Being only five in number, as ports, the cities were selected for their shared economic heritage and transformation challenges. Policy analysis is largely focussed on process and output factors and is contextualised within the different national institutional arrangements, ideologies and traditions of state intervention. The nascent EU-level remit also forms an important component.

The case study approach was adopted on the grounds that the policy area forms a relatively tight action arena which is reasonably susceptible to ready cross-national comparison. The data collected incorporate qualitative and quantitative material at neighbourhood, city, sub-regional and national scales. Essentially a single-person exercise, the analysis of social and demographic change utilised small-area statistical indicators. Policy evolution drew on an extensive range of 'elite interviews' with local politicians, public officials, the voluntary sector and representatives of neighbourhood movements. Above all, I relied heavily on an examination of a critical mass of 'grey literature' and other documentation with a limited, largely local circulation. Internet-derived material was also selectively consulted. Contrary to the pressures imposed by the rapid 'safari-trip' view-and-tell tactic, this was a long-term project with three rounds of research conducted over a dozen years. This permitted the collection of a vast array of information deriving from the mid-1970s to the present time and, thereby, facilitating a measure of sensitivity to interpretation of policy dynamism in a field where evolution may extend over a long cycle.

Funding for different phases of this research came from the University of London, London School of Economics and the Nuffield Foundation. Latterly, a grant from the ESRC enables a resource database to be constructed. This is available to researchers and practitioners via the Council's Survey Archive at the University of Essex.

Citation of those who have collaborated in a wide-ranging and lengthy project like this is always invidious. But, I would particularly like to thank Michael Parkinson, now at John Moores University, Liverpool, Loredana Seassaro of the University of Genoa, Nuria Fernández of the Gabinet d'Estudis Socials, Barcelona, André Donzel, now at the CNRS-LAMES, Aix-en-Provence and Jens Dangschat, now at the Technical University of Vienna for all their help in orientation and 'snowballing'. Over the years, several students studying for the MSc European Social Policy at the LSE helped me with data management and processing. Especial mention needs to be made of Vicky Davies for helping create the NUD*IST qualitative data base, and to Martien Kuitenbrouwer, Teresa Lenzi, Pedro Gallo and Roman Romero-Ortuño. Finally, my hearty thanks go to John Hyden for the excellent task he performed in proofreading.

Part I
Mapping the Inner City

1
Inner City Europe: Socio-Economic Change and National Policy Responses

To provide an initial orientation, a range of problems presenting in the inner city are reviewed in this introductory chapter, setting the context for discussion of the respective policy responses adopted in the last quarter of the past century in the five largest EU states. The countries examined include two 'early instigators' in the field (France and the UK), an 'average initiator' (Germany) and two countries where national innovation only gathered pace in the 1990s (Spain and Italy). For each country, a case study is selected: port cities having experienced what Dangschat and Ossenbrügge (1990) pithily termed the transformation 'from the ship to the chip' (Barcelona, Genoa, Hamburg, Liverpool and Marseilles).

Whilst in each city the inner core is a prime (though not unique) locus of socio-economic problems, the conceptual and functional equivalence of the 'inner city' is problematic, given that there may be considerable cross-national variation in the functions central areas perform. There is, then, a danger of conceptual stretching, not least in assumptions of the extent that it represents a consolidated political issue. Even within one cultural sphere, the concept as a spatial expression of reduced life chances is for Keith and Rogers (1991, p. 6) 'theoretically chaotic', and not necessarily an indication of an excluded space. In German the term *Innenstadt* also embraces the central business district and issue emergence is frequently driven by concerns about its expansion into adjacent, often desirable residential areas. The Italian *centro storico* and the Spanish *casco antiguo* have largely been conceived in terms of architectural priorities, with the aim of promoting the cultural image of the town. The attention of French political actors has typically been diverted away from the *vieux quartiers* to the *quartiers chauds*, some of which may be located centrally but, more often, are peripheral social housing estates (Mangen, 1992).

In large European cities, core localities harbour multiple functions and, in some, depending on the time of day, multiple users. Spatial specialisation of

3

users and uses 'in propinquity' is a feature determining the distinct character of each inner city. That being said, it is possible to point to significant commonalities To be sure, some of these attributes are replicated elsewhere: primarily in social housing estates on the urban fringe with which, as a result of re-housing policies, there may be close social linkages with inner neighbourhoods, or, in some cities, they may be more dispersed (Robson, 1988; OECD, 1998). Nonetheless, they do tend to exist in a unique and oft-times spatially concentrated combination in the inner city. Thus, these generally higher-density areas contain some of the worst and certainly the oldest housing stock, mostly in the owner-occupied or privately rented sector. In many countries this is supplied in small units sometimes with shared basic amenities and inhabited by single-person households. Yet, better quality accommodation has been targeted for conversion into commercial premises or gentrification, with the result that the increasingly richer and more politically articulate incomer progressively lives cheek by jowl with the growingly poorer and politically marginalised, something which has long been a feature of the southern inner city but which is more of a novelty in the north. Many neighbourhoods have witnessed a chronic and socially selective population loss with 'white flight' of family-forming households to the suburbs, resulting in an ageing or 'twin peak' demographic profile of residents combined with a large percentage of ethnic minorities or recent immigrants, increasingly of irregular status, seeking their first point of access to whatever housing is available and thereby putting pressure on demand for ever-scarcer cheap accommodation. Low educational attainment, below average investment in social and public services with resulting poor access, environmental pollution, heavy traffic and heavy noise volumes, particularly in the narrow streets of the southern historic cores, can be added to the list. To these must be added macro-scale economic restructuring and the profound changes in local labour markets as a result of tertiarisation, both of which have limited job opportunities for the unskilled. Finally, many cities record high propensities of opportunistic street crime, often exacerbated by poor street lighting, trade in illicit drugs and prostitution, raising pronounced fears of victimisation among residents. All these issues are discussed further in subsequent chapters.

Attributes of the European inner city

The sampled countries are at different stages in elaborating comprehensive strategic policies for the inner city: in general, despite the appalling state of some of the housing stock, the Mediterranean countries can be crudely regarded as 'laggards' as can Germany, although in the latter case this was primarily due to the later onset of de-industrialisation and its impact on major cities. Large tracts of the inner core were abandoned in the immediate post-war decades socially, politically and economically, when many of its residents were re-housed in the urban periphery. The official neglect implicitly derived from the notion that these were 'backward' spaces that were productive only of various manifestations of social pathology (MacGregor, 1990) – whether this was articulated in Anglo-Saxon discourse on the underclass or, more neutrally, in continental terms of 'marginalisation'. In the Anglophone world the notion of the 'inner city' first gained currency in the 1960s, some years before finding a place on the urban agenda in Britain later in the decade, after displacing earlier concepts such as 'twilight zones'. In general, the socio-economic dimensions of rehabilitation gained ground only in the 1970s as the recession bit deep; in most Continental countries this change of policy focus was delayed at least a decade, thus privileging a narrow agenda centred on the urban fabric which was particularly characteristic of the Mediterranean countries (European Commission, 1992).

Nonetheless, despite time lags, policy evolution since the Second World War has broadly followed a similar path: emergency post-war reconstruction was replaced by mass demolition and reconstruction on the periphery, a phase lasting at least until the late 1960s. In turn, relevant policy was monopolised by a concern for the physical rehabilitation of the existing stock, in some cases from the late 1960s but primarily in the 1970s. This was to varying degrees complemented by subsequent innovations in using a 'social dimension' as a response to the growing acceptance of the problem of 'urban exclusion' that required a more serious engagement with structural determinants. Solutions favoured by European politicians in the embrace of a regeneration-led rather than a narrow renewal agenda varied internally and cross-nationally, although Furbey (1999) detects in what he terms the regeneration 'metaphor' a confused agenda that nonetheless bears essential hallmarks of organic solidarity associated with conservative interpretations of social exclusion.

Influenced in part by the nascent EU policy line, a converging, more commercially oriented and longer-term economic strategic agenda evolved in the 1990s in the face of perceived transition pains due to globalisation. Albeit still in inchoate form, what has emerged is an approach to the fate of the post-Fordist European city that is dependent on a multi-faceted developmental strategy aiming at the regeneration of sub-regional economies to exploit 'glocalised' potential. In this the inner city is re-invested with much image-building economic and social capacity – even as the fulcrum for launching 'salvation activism' (Seassaro, 1991).

The cumulative effect is that key actors are at pains to present the contemporary policy context as more tightly input–outcome focussed or 'joined up'. In these new accumulation regimes the inner areas become a niche asset (Mayer, 1995). Their lot in the past quarter century was to be the locus of a proliferation of *grands projets*. Le Galès and Harding (1998) point to the contradiction that in espousing the benefits of niche position cities have curiously opted for remarkably similar projects. Thus, in the present case studies, the success of the earlier Baltimore waterfront regeneration has encouraged port cities to direct attention to their disused dockyards which have been transformed into tourist, cultural or conference centres as a sign of 'commodification' of prestige leisure in prime urban sites (Bianchini *et al.*, 1990; Mellor, 1997). Whilst projects like these may help restore a sense of identity and pride among the local populace (Hutchinson, 2000), they also have been risk-laden (see Chapter 2); nor can one ignore the frequent complaint that there has been little positive 'trickle-down' effect for adjacent residents, either in terms of quality employment creation or local use of such facilities (Griffiths, 1993). On the contrary, there have often been displacement pressures, with regard not only to housing but also the disappearance of cheaper commercial outlets, as 'mega-stores' relocate elsewhere to serve those with greater purchasing power and private transport (Thomas & Bromley, 2000).

In the past three decades, then, greater specialisation of social uses of distinct inner neighbourhoods has come about through spatial segregation which has deepened as a product of policy accumulation (or, indeed, neglect) and market forces. The early works of Castells and Godard (1974) in France and Ferras (1977) in Spain, despite criticism of being too simplistic and location-specific, chronicle the chronicity of renovation–displacement interactions. Indeed, White (1984) records how segregation historically has a long and intimate pedigree: not only by neighbourhood, but also by storey within the same building, occupation of front of house or a back annex, and so forth. But, despite this dynamic of urban polarisation, there is a certain stability among the areas that are 'losers': throughout Europe even rich metropolitan cities contain intransigent 'pockets of poverty' (see, for example, Mayor of London, 2002). The lack of ability to escape urban social exclusion is further demonstrated, for instance, by an official 'small area' deprivation index for England and Wales which indicated that, between 1981 and 1991, only 6 of the 36 most affected areas had been replaced in the league table (Burton & Boddy, 1995).

In any comparison of the degree and speed of segregation, 'retrievability' and displacement, the relative competitive strength of each city in the new European economic order is a vital catalyst. The distribution of housing tenure is also a critical factor, given that partnership between the public and private purses has become increasingly commonplace. Retrievability in the short term is the essential factor in determining the gap between 'rent' and 'value', the latter indicating that prevailing land prices are below an assessment by attracted investors of potential prices, arising from upgrading or a change of property use (Van Weesep & Musterd, 1991). Whilst major public-led urban projects affect this trade-off, pressures on reinvestment in the inner core, in the most propitious situations, have been most acute where reliance on commercial interests is greatest; these have accelerated processes of gentrification and, in many cities, gradual expansion of the central business district. In the case studies to be reviewed, speculative pressures are most apparent in Hamburg and Barcelona, both having relatively successfully negotiated the transition to the tertiary economy, and least in Marseilles and Liverpool, where planning incentives have met with less success in limiting economic and social flight from the core and where much housing reinvestment in central areas has required direct public intervention or heavy subsidies.

National policy trajectories and inner city regeneration

The nature and tradition of an area approach to social planning varies considerably among these five countries: France and the UK have been stronger on such targeted compensation, most notably, perhaps, in the field of education compensation and housing rehabilitation. Spain also is a median instigator. On the other hand – beyond physical regeneration – Italian constitutional stipulations were given as reasons for abandoning early attempts at area targeting in favour of spatial de-specification of client-oriented social policies. Reasons cited have been general equity but also – mindful of its fascist past – fears that such interventions might reinforce stigma. For much of the period under investigation Germany also placed more emphasis on across-the-board measures for much the same reasons.

By the early 1980s, however, the OECD (1983) was reporting a converging expanded approach to urban policy, at least among innovator countries, embracing not only housing and land-use measures, but also economic development, employment support and attempts to tailor general social policies to new exigencies. Two factors seem critical. One is the early recognition by some governments of the irreversibility of economic transformation, which had hit large cities hardest. Thus, due to the early onset of economic decline and the associated welfare state 'crisis', the UK was the first Western European country to initiate a dedicated programme for the inner city, in part a product of policy dissemination from the USA. In comparison, continental political parties, particularly of the centre-left, initially failed to appreciate the full implications of economic change which was impacting at various speeds on their industrial bases. This was still a period in which emerging problems were presented as new risks associated with 'social exclusion' undermining the post-war welfare *acquis*.

The other factor concentrating political minds lay in the growing urban protest movements and – in particular in Britain and France – the outbreak of riots at various points in the decade (Robson, 1988). The new presidency of Mitterand was mindful that it derived much of its electoral support in precisely the sorts of areas that were affected, and demanded a prompt and sympathetic response. Although not as severe as those contemporaneously in the UK, they provoked a major policy innovation in the form of an area-based social regeneration programme, the *Développement Social des Quartiers*, in peripheral social housing and older neighbourhood (Green & Booth, 1995; Anderson & Vieillard-Baron, 2000).

Riots in 1990 in French large estates prompted the government to establish local *maisons de justice* to take a tougher line on crime, and they were also accompanied by a new urban programme (*Grands Projets Urbains*) and the creation of 'sub-prefects', state-appointed administrators to manage urban policy locally. Further riots, a year later, accelerated the signing of what would be over 200 'urban contracts' extending over the whole of the country, rather than in narrowly selected areas (Dauge, 1991; Condro & Vitale, 2001). In comparison, its Tory counterpart in Britain had more room for manoeuvre. The 1981 Scarman report into the riots privileged a conservative linkage between unemployment, hostility on the part of segments of urban youth to the police and delinquency. Signally, given the location of the riots, and unlike the interpretation *outre Manche*, the 'institutional racism' card was downplayed (Lawless, 1989). Thus, in Britain, the riots of 1980 and 1981 were seized on as an opportunity for a long-term modernising enterprise that would critically revise pre-existing relations between central and local government, embracing ever-wider notions of partnership – 'treatment by participation' as Moore (1997) coined it. The urban development corporations, initially in the London and Liverpool docklands, circumvented the competences of local government and eagerly pursued a commercially-driven target-led agenda; significantly, they and the enterprise zones legislated in 1980 set in train an enduring and fundamental change of priorities at national level.

Wider contextual developments also played their part in redrawing boundaries for the governance of urban policy. This arose from the changing state–market–community nexus that called into question the effectiveness of central and local governments to manage risks associated with new socio-economic conditions (Castells, 1989). As Le Galès (1998) sees it, the search was on to re-regulate state competences in the search for polycentric and multi-level governance. Although this would necessarily relate to contextual specificities, governments looked for lessons for the homeland of innovations elsewhere. Principally these took the form of streamlining vertical coordination among existing tiers of public authority, as well as attempts in some states to design new sub-regional approaches for stimulating urban economies and the growing embrace – in some countries initially falteringly – of horizontal partnership. For Mayer (1995) the central underpinning dynamic was an attempt at efficient mobilisation in favour of an increasingly privatised approach to economic development. The outcome in Northern Europe, at least, is that for much of the period under investigation, effort was expended in integrating policy better to coordinate mainstream and area-targeted interventions, and to refine the delivery of cross-sectoral approaches embracing a wider range of actors (Parkinson, 1998a).

As for vertical coordination, during the 1980s Britain was alone in re-centralising competence, heralding in a period of deteriorating relations between the central government of the New Right and municipalities of a different persuasion. Reigning in the independent actions of local government became one of the hallmarks of the Thatcher era. For both legal and funding reasons sustained inroads into the powers of local authorities directly or indirectly affected their ability independently to initiate extensive urban regeneration, although later central policy reforms went some way to restoring a more salient role (see below). Admittedly, the lower tiers in other countries were also experiencing constraints on freedom of action, although generally for largely fiscal reasons. Whilst in France much of the impetus for urban economic regeneration remained with the mayors of the larger cities (Healey *et al.*, 1995), nonetheless, in a context of growing budgetary constraints, state funding through contracts proved a major lifeline for the local public purse. In comparison, the German federal system protected the sphere of action of each tier and, in fact, immediately after Unification (achieved in 1990), the states and their local authorities were largely left to their own devices in terms of funding urban regeneration. Only in the late 1990s did the federal government reassume the role of overarching stimulus by means of a dedicated funding programme. In both Italy and Spain, the regional tier in the early years of its full implementation was criticised for being too intrusively *dirigiste*, to the detriment of the scope of the municipalities to develop their own planning capacities. Spanish municipalities were therefore 'pinched' in their scope for action and, in the case of the larger authorities, this provoked chronic tension between city councils and regional governments (see Chapter 2 for the example of Barcelona). In Italy, a similar situation was aggravated by the lengthy delays, on the part of Rome, in approving or updating local plans. To make matters worse, for Jodogne (1991), the Italian regions lacked effective planning mechanisms, and one coping strategy has been to divert energies to legislating in order to constrain lower-tier government.

In operationalising horizontal partnerships 'conservative corporatist' welfare regimes have traditionally prioritised the subsidiarity principle which affords a prime role to the state-subsidised voluntary sector (Esping-Andersen, 1990) or partly municipal-owned joint enterprises. To the privileging of the voluntary agencies – something enacted also in Britain in the past quarter of a century – has come an identification of private commerce as an essential partner in 'new urban governance'. Drawing on developmental lessons from Latin America, for example, local communities have been nominated as key resources of social capital, elevating their role from mere consultation to that of active stakeholders (Amin & Thrift, 1995; Healey, 1998). In the new policy mix, therefore, the public sector is increasingly one set of actors amongst many: a coordinating facilitator in a fragmenting policy arena, or a short-term intervener to correct market failures (Davoudi, 1995; Le Galès & Harding, 1998). Here, new public management styles have the aim of engaging and sustaining public and private agencies acting in tandem (but also at times in competition) effectively determining the emerging political bargaining and funding cultures.

France

Under De Gaulle, France was regarded as a model for its sub-regional development policies based on 'growth poles', developed within the wider framework of medium-term national plans – which remain a feature of the French approach to governance. His presidency also saw the first attempts at metropolitan administration. In the early 1960s Lyon was to be a pioneer in rehabilitating its old sector through a joint public–private regeneration agency. The first legislation for area-based regeneration was passed, although rebuilding still held the greater sway (Emms, 1990).

Important policy landmarks followed in the 1970s which set the basis for an evolving urban agenda. In social housing, the 1977 *Habitat et Vie Sociale* programme, originally mostly targeting large peripheral estates, signally provided for investment not only in the physical fabric but also in social dimensions. Yet, less positively, deficiencies in community partnership were to be recorded and the funding viability of proposals for housing agencies (HLMs) overrode the interests of tenants, not least in the new rents set (Donzel, 1993). A year later, funding for an ad hoc partnership, for private sector housing improvement, importantly created a longer-term arena of engagement between the state, municipal and private sectors through joint public–private companies (*societés mixtes* – a favoured French solution to the supply of urban services, see Lorrain [1992]). The renewed funding and administrative environment promised landlords flexibility and streamlining of decision-making and permitted rent control on upgraded properties, whilst tenants were also offered a measure of security. That the approach was not entirely robust is evidenced in outcomes reviewed by Punter (1981) who noted that deprived municipalities were disadvantaged by the requirement to share costs, and administration proved difficult in inner city areas characterised by complex multiple ownership; inadequate funding also created problems for poorer owners and voluntary agencies. And, although a preliminary evaluation of the neighbourhood's social composition was required, this was undermined by the neglect of how this interacted with economic trends and by the absence of a plan for more extensive city-wide regeneration.

Winchester (1993) complains that the various programmes of this period were monopolised by private developers to the neglect of effective neighbourhood participation, and made only a small dent into the stock in need of rehabilitation, particularly in the private sector. To make matters worse, their scale of operation swiftly declined. On the other hand, Punter (1981) is more sanguine: despite deficiencies, she assesses the cumulative outcome of policies as paving the way for a progressive revision of urban governance, incorporating the newly established regions and municipalities into a contractual engagement, whilst also delegating a major role in rehabilitation to the private sector. This policy pathway would be further exploited from the early 1980s.

The election of Mitterand in 1981 was to be a key event in policy evolution. For one, decentralisation – the first major administrative reform since Napoleon – would have a central impact. Although if it was to disappoint the left wing of his party by watering down commitments to radical forms of self-administration – Mény (1984) insisting that it was more a re-invigoration of elite decision-making – it did revise the framework of urban governance by redistributing competences among the various tiers of public authorities and provided a basis for medium-term state–regional 'contracts', announced in 1982. Equally – and within his broad agenda for across-the-board social reform, made the more urgent by urban riots prior to his election – Mitterand set in train a broad stream of strategies, extending into new concerns such as urban delinquency. A year into his office, a high-profile commission was created with the remit of overseeing a substantial national programme for the neighbourhood regeneration (*Développement Social des Quartiers – DSQ*) that prescribed a multi-dimensional and integrated approach. Together with its successor it rapidly expanded, encapsulating well over 500 localities by the early 1990s, funding being contributed by the government, municipalities, housing and social agencies. It was to be the heart of French urban policy in his first term (Condro & Vitale, 2001). In addition, a collaborative 'interministerial' approach to employment and the social rehabilitation of 'at risk' youth was adopted. In 1983 the *Banlieue 89* project was instigated for social and educational measures on estates in the educational priority areas. As a result of these policies urban grants, as a proportion of local authority revenues, increased significantly in the first 3 years of the presidency, especially in municipalities controlled by the left (Wolman *et al.*, 1992). Moreover, during much of the decade there was an evolving focus on urban economic development, though Keating (1991) doubts that, at least initially, it amounted to much beyond bailing out endangered businesses.

Despite some neo-liberal realignment, the incoming 'cohabiting' government of the right, from 1986, did not fundamentally change regeneration policies. Indeed, contrary to exhortations for narrower targeting, the DSQ programme was expanded to more localities, which continued after Mitterand's re-election in 1988, prior to the major policy review at the end of the decade. Despite criticisms of evaluative and participatory deficiencies, Tricart (1991) speculates that the more successful schemes were operating in left-run small- or medium-size cities.

Significantly, the socialists' return to government triggered extensive reforms, in line with the cross-party concerns about growing social exclusion, one resolution being the introduction of a second-generation social assistance scheme based on contractual engagement of recipients for participation in inclusion measures: the *Revenu Minimum d'Insertion (RMI)*. Intended as a major departure, Mitterand announced that, henceforth, 5-year urban contracts (*Contrats de Ville*) would be concluded directly between municipalities and the state, whilst also retaining state–region collaboration for certain matters. They were to build on the experiences of the first round of contracts involving the three tiers of government in 1984 and, at least in their pilot phase, were to target funding on 13 cities before being extended throughout the country. The DSQ projects were incorporated within their envelope and were afforded a more comprehensive, city-focussed, approach through a revision of the programme establishing the *Développement Social Urbain* (*DSU*). The DSUs aimed at strengthening vertical and horizontal partnership in an attempt to redress what had been increasingly judged as a disjointed and too small-scale a framework to deliver effective outcomes (Jessen & Neumann, 1999). Expanding the number of beneficiary localities the DSUs mainstreamed what had been the rather experimental nature of their predecessor (Le Galès & Mawson, 1994). In addition, a high-ranking 'inter-ministerial delegation' was formed to promote organisational and funding reform and coordination which would engage all major actors; another would address race relations. Municipalities were also awarded competences to promote a wider economic development strategy.

In a comparative investigation, Leroy (1990) judges France as the only state by the turn of the 1980s to have a truly national integrative approach. Yet, Keating (1991) is among those who compare targeted funding streams on both sides of the Channel at the turn of the decade and finds that for France wanting, although it was underpinned by a somewhat greater maintenance of mainstream outlays. Nevertheless, difficulties among local authorities in producing matched funding was compounded by the fact that some central allocations were not new money and, in practice, dedicated budgets were diverted to finance routine responsibilities (Dauge, 1991; Body-Gendrot, 2000b). Donzel (1993), whilst conceding that major central fiscal commitments would necessarily incur greater scrutiny by government, questions how compatible this was with the ongoing decentralisation agenda. And, finally, in spite of intentions, Green and Booth (1995) are sceptical that the renewed contract model did actually represent the radical break with existing policies that was claimed.

At a time of a renewed bout of riots, the proliferation of reforms from 1990 onwards, on the administrative front, bears comparison with the funding innovations of British Conservatives in the same period. Mitterand, in 1990, created a ministry for cities and urban affairs (*Ministère de la Ville*) – the portfolio being held by the ill-fated Tapie, more famous as manager of the Marseilles OM football club – as a demonstration of the determination of the state to commit itself to the breaking of the cycle of urban social exclusion. This engagement was to be assisted by the appointment in 1991 of the 'sub-prefects' in the 13 most deprived *départements*. A sub-regional developmental element was to be further stimulated by the conclusion of 'city charters', which in the event met with mixed fortunes (Sallez, 1998). The renewed policy line was also to be prosecuted through a centrally imposed attempt at 'equalising' regulation from richer to poorer local authorities. In the event, this would not survive the change of government to the right in 1993. To this was added legislation aiming for a more balanced spatial distribution of social housing to temper urban polarisation and to facilitate the access of the most deprived. Further rioting in 1991 infused the general policy line with a stronger economic regenerative element, though it stopped short of affirmative action in employment creation. However, Parkinson (1998a) notes that enduring priorities remained largely social in ambition, due in some part to rivalries among the central bureaucracy.

With the change of government to the right in 1993, policy effort in the field was dispersed. Owing to its emblematic liberal socialism, the new administration of the right demoted the urban portfolio, the inter-ministerial delegation no longer directly answering to the prime minister. Instead, much of the remit was subsumed within the Social Affairs ministry, whilst associated social control functions were repatriated to the Justice brief where the minister concerned was keen to present a tough image on illegal immigration. The new round of *Contrats de Ville* offered a greater pooling of funding by moves towards integration of the very many different pots of public money. This, and later policies adopted by this government, produced a doubling of central allocations. There were aspirations for a more targeted, longer-term DSU approach, although by the mid-1990s the proliferation of nominations resulted in about 1300 neighbourhoods being beneficiaries in one way or another (Sallez, 1998). Nonetheless, the contracts did continue efforts to consolidate horizontal collaboration with non-statutory actors, and improved concertation among statutory agencies. The system of 'sub-prefects' was extended, as was the role of the mayors in directing policy.

Beyond the contracts, evidence of concentration of investment was exemplified in 1994 by the identification of a dozen of the most deprived neighbourhoods in the country as *Grands Projets Urbains* (GPUs) to which up to one quarter of all available funding was to be directed. For Parkinson (1998a) the GPUs represented a harder-edge approach – similar to the Urban Development Corporations adopted a decade earlier in Britain. By emphasising larger-scale medium to long-term physical regeneration, they contrasted with a more social dimension favoured in policies associated with the *Contrats*. Matched funding was a requirement – something which proved a constraint in the poorer cities and caused delays in implementation (Musterd & de Winter, 1998). Furthermore, as the projects were intended to be implemented through a refined, centrally designed agenda, there were accusations that they amounted to an unambiguous re-centralisation of policy direction (Sallez, 1998). However, in the face of opposition, the government did concede a local model of public–private partnership. Further targeting was to be achieved by special state-funded 4-year planning programmes for de-industrialising north-eastern départements.

Several commentators have attempted an evaluation of urban policies pursued under left and right governments during Mitterand's presidency. Policy had evolved from a narrow small-area focus to a broader design, more integrated at the end of this period with economic objectives. Models of participation had also matured. In part, this policy evolution was a response, not only to the riots, but also to the rising urban electoral appeal of the far right *Front National.* The French agenda, too, also helped to form and was in turn informed by EU-level initiatives, particularly in regard to the pursuit of sustainable development. Yet, equally, the highly productive output had resulted in a confusing complex of agencies and projects in operation in the same field. Accordingly, as an official report of 1993 complained, the arena was rendered non-transparent in the public's eyes. Subsidies targeted on poor areas were modest, given the volume of real need, with complex regulations and perverse outcomes. Heavy administration and intransigent bureaucratic rivalries were indicted, which could hardly have been helped by the downgrading of urban policy competences in 1993. Engagement of the private sector was marginal, particularly compared to what was then happening in Britain (e.g. Le Galès & Mawson, 1994; Anderson & Vieillard-Baron, 2000).

The new Chirac presidency provided an opportunity for further policy re-launching. The conservative government, in 1996, instituted a 3-year *Pacte de Relance pour la Ville* announced by Gaudin, in his capacity as minister (his other function being the new mayor of Marseilles). Amid a flurry of rhetoric about an urban 'Marshall Plan', the pact again stressed the need for closer ministerial integration and the importance of a more robust economic dimension, largely private investment-led. Key reforms were to follow rapidly: 700 *zones urbaines sensibles* were selected from the pool of 1300 neighbourhoods already in receipt of funding from existing programmes and, of these, 350 areas were earmarked for *redynamisation urbaine*, in part through tax exemptions. Similar in many respects to British enterprise zones, over 40 tightly circumscribed *zones franches* (*ZFUs*) were chosen from those localities with the highest unemployment and lowest level of qualifications. These zones aimed to stimulate inward investment by small firms through the most generous level of tax and social security levy exemptions available until 2000, the ultimate goal being the creation of 100,000 net jobs. They co-existed with other schemes also dispensing various tax concessions for job creation (OECD, 1998). Guiding policy direction was an expressed desire to remedy the comparative marginal role that the private sector had played in the urban contracts. Yet these measures, too, were to be criticised in practice for enhancing the role of the central state. This was particularly the case in the exercise of nomination rights, rather than a stronger reliance on competitive tendering, something which, it was argued, dissipated the potential for refined targeting (Parkinson, 1998a; Sallez, 1998).

The change of government to the left, in 1997, again led to some redirection of priorities. However, the ambition of adopting more across-the-board and city-wide initiatives was maintained which continued a measure of displacement of reliance on a strong small-area focus. Equally – and reflecting the contemporary agenda in other EU states – a greater emphasis was placed on integrating urban security, employment promotion and social integration into one framework. However, a dedicated urban ministry was not restored but, in line with the enhancing of the economic dimension, responsibilities were entrusted to the employment portfolio, to complement the transferring of more competences to the local level.

An important official report *Demain La Ville* of 1998 moved this agenda forward by advocating a substantial budget increase and by examining the quality of urban governance, particularly with regard to comparative remits of 'sub-prefects', and lower-tier councils. Previous ineffective legislation was replaced by renewed stipulations in 1999 to eradicate institutional fragmentation through the creation of new metropolitan agglomerations (Donzel, 2001). The funding periods for the *Contrats de Ville* were extended to correspond with those of the regional contracts and, with an eye to securing EU monies, to be broadly in line with the Structural Fund cycle. Further interventions for educational priority areas were specified (Mangin & Panerai, 1999). On the other hand, the planned phasing out of the *zones franches* in 2002, following critical evaluations of their performance and, in particular, the high cost of net jobs added, did not go ahead after the incoming government of the right overturned the decision. The programme was, in fact, expanded once consultations with the European Commission concerning possible violations of competition law had been completed.

Legislation in 2000 (*Loi sur la Solidarité et le Renouvellement Urbain – SRU*) stipulated the revision of the GPU programme with a stronger focus on comprehensive measures for strategic regeneration, although many of the existing projects, being long term, were guaranteed longevity. With the irresistible temptation to rename – this time *Grands Projets de Ville (GPV)* – 50 localities were to benefit from increased earmarked funding within the framework of the *Contrats de Ville* with an expectation that some, like their predecessor GPUs, could operate for up to 15 years (Anderson & Vieillard-Baron, 2000). Among others, one aim of the law was to achieve a greater social mix and spatial distribution of social housing throughout the country through the setting up of minimum provision thresholds. This will be an enormous task, since many HLM estates were heavily segregated, not least in ethnic terms (Edou, 1998). The new *Contrats de Ville*, to run from 2000 to 2006, have become the sole envelope for urban policy, in comparison with past versions and, in one way or other, will intervene in areas that contain just over 10 per cent of the total population.

Proposals announced in 2003 aim to advance this agenda by reserving a global allocation of 30 billion euros between 2004 and 2008 for extensive investment in regeneration, which will be disbursed through a single budget. Also there will be an agency for urban renovation incorporating the principal national actors. As a general measure – and with a view to completing the outstanding upgrading of older housing in the inner cities – action is to be taken to clarify what is often the complex legal situation of accommodation in shared ownership (*co-propriété*). This will include imposing new obligations on owners, with increased default options in terms of compulsory purchase. More specifically, the national programmes for deprived neighbourhoods – the *zones urbaines sensibles* – which had numbered about 100 in the early 1980s *DSQ* projects mushroomed to some 750 now (and to incorporate a population of 6 million) and will concentrate investment on the most degraded, reflecting preferences in contemporary neighbourhood renewal actions in Britain (see below). A national observatory is to be established to assist in this task. Among the objectives is major housing and infrastructural rehabilitation and a resolution of the problem of the large amount of vacant properties. Another is the creation of up to 100,000 new jobs over 5 years, in part through the extension of the ZFUs to new locations (current information is available at www.ville.gouv.fr).

Since the *Habitat et Vie Sociale* projects of the late 1970s, France has been regarded as a leader in policy innovation; certainly, the French experience is central to the Europeanisation of urban policy (see Chapter 6). The republican notion of contract has been a growing impulse since the early 1980s in attempts to re-engage the state, its agents at all levels and a range of social and economic actors in an integrated implementation arena. It is true that for much of the study period, as Parkinson (1998a) remarks, there was consistent criticism that the series of *Contrats* tended to operate in parallel rather than in tandem with much allied effort dependent on a multiplicity of co-existing funding budgets. However, there has been a discernible move away from original agendas largely informed by social concerns, to those that are more overarching and more firmly commercial and economic in ambition, with the purpose of securing sustainability. Equally, the scale of operation both in terms of geography and time horizons – as in many countries – has reaffirmed a centrality for the level of the conurbation, going some way to displacing the more ad hoc, short-term 'welfarist' approach detectable in many small-area programmes.

All these trends have made the policy arena much more complex, with inevitable consequences for effective evaluation. The issue of race has never been far below the surface in terms of whose interests are really being served. At one extreme, the *Front National* in the presidential campaign of 2002 indicted the cumulative distributional consequences of policy as favouring immigrants and neglecting the 'native French'. For this party, the net outcome amounted to a chronic waste of money, with successive contracts merely exacerbating a two-speed society. Other critics have been moderate in tone. Nonetheless, there has, for example, been concern that the complexity of funding and administering this policy arena has been hindered by the lack of a dedicated ministry for much of the period, despite the efforts to address matters of governance at lower level (e.g. Condro & Vitale, 2001). There has also been the accusation that the 'contract culture' negates decentralisation policies by reinforcing the influence of national government which has all too often spread funding too thinly (e.g. Hall & Mawson, 1999). Deficiencies of horizontal partnership have been cited – particularly, by international comparison, the marginal involvement of commercial actors and many communities, as well as a fuller embrace of the third sector (e.g. OECD, 1998). Within the tiers of government, impediments to a sustainable across-the-board approach, for some, have been tolerated for too long – the education ministry has chronically resisted full incorporation, for example, and the engagement of police authorities needs to be reinforced as, too, that of authorities in the départements which are competent in crucially related areas such as the social services and the management of the RMI (Anderson & Vieillard-Baron, 2000).

Germany

The urgency of post-war reconstruction dictated that new building was the primary urban agenda in West Germany before the 1980s. The federal government's role was largely confined to sponsoring 'experimental model programmes' and providing the legislative basis for implementation by lower tiers (Froessler, 1994). Under Brandt's progressive social platform measures were enacted in 1971 for joint federal-state action on rehabilitation (*Stadtbauförderungsgesetz*) although mass demolition continued, provoking a widespread squatter protest movement (Kunze & Schubert, 2001). However, there were stipulations about a 'social plan' with community consultation and certain options to guarantee the rights of existing residents, which, as Pfotenhauer (2000) notes, drew on best practice elsewhere, for example, in Bologna (see below). By the mid-1970s the scene was set for an acceleration of cost-sharing between the tiers of pubic administration and for the engagement of private property owners through a variety of subsidies within multi-annual funding programmes. Policy output accelerated thereafter with the establishment of long-term housing investment plans in 1977, followed a year later by intervention in the field of housing modernisation and energy conservation.

This is not to say that outcomes were always as desired. Bureaucratic compartmentalisation stymied effective administrative and funding coordination at local level. The requirement for matched funding also penalised municipalities with a lower tax base which, to reduce financial burdens, often veered away from housing in the worst state. Futhermore, the possibilities for protecting original tenants was not taken up everywhere. Community participation was in the event restricted and socially skewed and the assumption that, for the most part, rehabilitation costs would sooner or later filter through into rents resulted in considerable resident displacement.

All in all then, the social distributional effects were regressive (Marcuse, 1982; Leutner, 1990).

In the early 1980s, extra federal efforts were conceded: in 1983, modest 'seedbed' federal funding first became available for a 'model programme' to rehabilitate which, 2 years later, was extended to the upgrading of post-war peripheral social housing estates. After the introduction of an extensive estates action programme in 1987, roughly half of all public expenditure on housing was allocated to the modernisation and repairs programme. Yet the sum of these efforts during the 1980s was to have undesired consequences. In many of West Germany's larger cities some rehabilitation had incurred the conversion of very small units into larger flats, thereby reducing the supply of cheaper one- or two-room accommodation at a time of growing demand for it. Moreover, the problem was to some extent exacerbated by change of use for commercial purposes. Critics such as Pfotenhauer (2000) argue that, as the decade progressed, there was growing recognition in some official quarters that the primacy of a physical agenda had stimulated the social displacement of poorer residents. Accordingly, issues of affordability and rental and other guarantees for original tenants began to gain ground. Kohl's government favoured earmarking funds to provide incentives to the private sector for investment in target areas, whilst still offering some protection to existing tenants (OECD, 1998).

Until the late 1990s and the chancellorship of Schröder there was no national area-based urban deprivation programme. However, during the 1980s – first in North Rhine Westfalia, in which the de-industrialising Ruhr area is situated, followed by Hamburg and Berlin – some states pioneered their own programmes. These comprised innovations in horizontal and vertical cooperation and community participation and were to provide the basis for the federal model, which in turn drew on the experience of the *Contrat de Ville* in France and the City Challenge in England (Alisch, 1998; Kunzmann, 1998).

As in so much of social policy, Unification was not exploited as an opportunity for innovative urban reform; rather the urgency of the situation dictated the reverse. Yet Unification did impose a new political economy of regeneration. In 1990 the task of urban regeneration was enshrined as a permanent obligation on the part of public authorities. To stimulate activity a new 3-year federal-states urban development programme was implemented in 1991, but of necessity it focussed on the urgency of problems in the new Länder. Thus, in effect, a dual funding policy ensured a massive diversion of resources to the east and, in effect, due to the growing impact of the recession on budgetary outlays, the federal programme in the west was discontinued in the following year, apart from limited annually negotiated structural aid and the research costs of experimentation with alternative forms of house construction which also extended to the needs of special groups. According to Lang (1994) the outcome was that the more innovative old Länder such as North Rhine Westfalia and Hamburg were loaded with major outstanding commitments at a time when their budgets were sorely overstretched. Most of the western states opted for small-scale interventions in the hope that cumulatively they would add up to an overall strategy. In the east, the total impact was to be an emergency upgrading of the housing stock rather than fulfilling wider regenerative ambitions. Federal subsidies for job creation were also concentrated there.

For Pfotenhauer (2000) in the first half of the 1990s, rhetoric on community participation was strong, but fiscal realities prompted public authorities to attach greater emphasis to engagement of major private investment, albeit with attempts on their part to impose a social element in approved projects. Indeed, a larger private involvement was vital in order that local authorities could secure the scarce federal funding. Notwithstanding this goal, a frequent outcome was that, apart from housing, the upgrading of flanking facilities, such as schools, fell victim to retrenchment. Furthermore, given the relatively small amount that the public purse was contributing to private rehabilitation, many developers preferred to finance projects in their entirety, in order to avoid restrictions on tenancies and rents. The effect was that property speculation was intensified, exacerbating displacement and, with it, social segregation. Reflecting both the Rio Summit of the UN and the associated *Agenda 21* as well as EU advocacy of sustainable development, a federal report in 1996 reiterated international consensus about bottom-up approaches and a widened role for NGOs. The report offered framework guidelines on general urban regeneration and the rehabilitation of social housing estates (von Petz & Schubert, 1998).

The transfer of government in 1998 to a SPD–Green coalition under Chancellor Schröder prompted a change in direction. The federal government became a more pro-active partner, not least in terms of funding. It advocated a 'joined up' multi-dimensional approach within a longer-term policy commitment which was demonstrated in the mainstreaming of the federal agenda, rather than its relegation to marginal, ad hoc projects. The revised priorities built on internal experiences such as the urban regeneration programmes of early innovators among the states and were associated with other 'new departures' of the Chancellor, such as his plans for an 'Alliance for Jobs' which was eventually announced in 1999. There was also lesson-learning especially from France, the Netherlands and the UK. In addition, EU programmes for local-area development had particular impact on those parts of Germany that had not hitherto been among the innovators in regeneration (Sauter, 2001). Finally, policy reform was also a product of the resolve of ministers at state level who, during the last phase of the Kohl chancellorship, pressed for a federal-state initiative for the most excluded neighbourhoods (Schubert, 1998a). Accordingly, the 'Social City' (*Soziale Stadt*) programme was announced to start in 1999. It marked a notable change of funding criteria. Allocations were based on population and unemployment indicators, rather than, as in the past, the overwhelming majority of outlays automatically by-passing the old states. This served the interests of the Red–Green alliance since it was here that they found their strongest electoral base. Moreover, the western Länder could readily demonstrate the cumulative effects of deprivation of funding since Unification. In the event, Kunze and Schubert (2001) calculate that the initial federal commitments allocated about 75 per cent of funds to the western states. In addition, the programme adopted the planning horizons of the new EU Structural Funding period, an important coordinating device, given that the eastern states were beneficiaries of Objective One status, and many industrially declining areas in the west received Objective Two funding.

Whilst the 5-year programme encompasses inner city areas, about 70 per cent of neighbourhoods are peripheral estates, many in the new *Länder*. Once again, federal outlays are matched by the states and the municipalities. All 16 states are participating, and it eventually has extended to some 200 projects in about 150 municipalities, although their distinctiveness varies as many have been integrated into ongoing local interventions. In addition, in each state there is a dedicated federal 'model experimental project'. The implementation route selected was to be that of local-area management with which Hamburg, among other *Länder*, had experimented in their own programmes. Equally there was a desire to seek means of promoting neighbourhood economies through exploiting the locality as a 'bottom-up' social network milieu whilst also integrating these measures within the wider sub-regional economy. As a sign of the times, great stress is laid on private-sector engagement, community participation, integrated horizontal and vertical cooperation of key agents, sustainability of regeneration, 'networking' of the selected neighbourhoods and output evaluation in terms of the integration of physical, economic and social dimensions, in which relative newcomers such as urban health services joined the agenda.

Whether the programme, in reality, represents a radical break or is substantially a continuation of past policy (but on a more extensive scale) has been the subject of considerable debate (see, for example, the collection of papers in *Jahrbuch Stadterneuerung 2000*). Initially set at roughly 200 million euro, Kuhlmann (2001) judges the annual commitment as meagre in comparison to national programmes in other EU member states (it was subsequently increased to 300 million). On the other hand he draws parallels with the UK in the approach to reducing problems of unemployment, housing and poverty, whilst there is less attention to crime or the integration of ethnic minorities. Drawing on the first 2 years of its operation, Kunze and Schubert (2001) complain of variegated success in terms of implementation. However, as Sauter (2001) concedes, one must bear in mind that, apart from the pioneer authorities, for many areas of Germany this was a new management agenda necessitating an important learning process (for recent material on the programme, visit www.sozialestadt.de).

In conclusion, during the 1990s with post-Unification pressures and those emanating from globalisation – and its 'glocalised' dimension – a city-wide planning focus to provide a sounder integration of the small-area projects was rediscovered. It was an era when participatory models increasingly gave way to wider engagement of other actors, particularly the courting of the commercial sector, although public–private partnerships by international standards remain relatively less central. But as policy has evolved in the past quarter of a century, the federal contribution – albeit rising sharply – remained a relatively minor funding source. The majority of the public purse still derives from the states and municipalities, a fact which encumbers the poorer authorities and perpetuates considerable spatial inequalities, particularly as there has been a flight of the more affluent to suburbs beyond the fiscal reach of the city. Nonetheless, it remains true that in most cities social segregation is less acute than in the UK or France, for example (Schubert, 1998a). Moreover, compared with many other EU states, the outstanding 'islands of deprivation' in the majority of cities in the old Länder tend to be both smaller in size and fewer in number (Pfotenhauer, 2000). On the other hand, for Schubert (1998a) the greater emphasis on the market and wider partnership has served to produce evermore differentiated impacts of policy, thereby compromising the ability to achieve an overall evaluation.

Italy

The urban agenda in Italy has reflected the professional domination by architects. For much of the study period this has produced a profusion of small-scale projects directed towards the urban fabric, rather than the formulation of overarching operational strategies. Central funding allocations were modest and painfully slow in disbursement, as was the state approval of town plans. Mass internal migration from the south overwhelmed the receiving cities elsewhere, with the inevitable uncontrolled growth of shanty towns. Fiscal crisis at all tiers of administration, political instability at central level and the hasty production of poorly drafted legislation requiring later supplementation by 'emergency' measures were the essential hallmarks of what has been termed the 'Italian vice' (ILRES, 1988). Preference for 'de-specification' in terms of social interventions meant that needs-targeting played a minimum role; reliance on the short term and the ad hoc pushed into the background a more determined resolution of the interests of conservation and innovation (Jodogne, 1991). Besides, planning regulations were widely ignored with little penalty, or by-passed through clientelistic decision-making (Calabi, 1984; Newman & Thornley, 1996). A further – and ongoing – major problem has been the lack of affordable housing, not helped by disjunctive policy-making arenas involving a profusion of actors both vertically and horizontally, and often competitive in motivation. It has been an environment redolent of reliance on *laisser-faire* coping strategies, critical vacuums being filled by the construction industry inevitably acting in its own interest. The chronic lack of accountability meant that the interests of local communities were increasingly sidelined, feeding community distrust of the public hand (Seassaro, 1993).

Not that the post-war period was without its exemplary models or measured rehabilitation, the best documented being that of Bologna in the 1960s where a communist-led prosperous authority, supported by the first neighbourhood councils, limited speculative redevelopment of its central residential areas by stimulating upgrading by cooperatives and small landlords, and by offering guarantees to existing tenants (White, 1984). The problem was that circumstances pertaining there did not exist widely (Caballero, 1982). Nevertheless, its evident successes and growing disenchantment with national policy prompted central governments, from the early 1970s, to regulate mass compulsory purchase and to provide some funding for rehabilitation, with the newly-formed regional authorities being awarded major competences in this field. Moreover, during this period, most cities had established some form of elected district councils with possibilities of delegation of policy responsibilities, although, in the event, their role remained mainly consultative (Punter, 1981).

Modernisation of policy followed in 1977 through the sanctioning by the regions of multi-annual housing programmes stipulating that 15 per cent of outlays be earmarked for rehabilitation. A year later, 'special' measures were enacted to extend the competences of municipalities to sponsor renovation, not only of public housing but also by extending their activity to engagement with private owners, thereby initiating the first steps towards a more formalised partnership model. Among other things, a decennial plan aimed to provide programmatic frameworks for funding regeneration of historic centres and adjacent older areas, either through public or private intervention, updating legislation passed before the war. But, as Van Hees (1991) records, a major limitation of the attempt to integrate efforts derived from the relatively small amount of funding for rehabilitation, which was too easily marginalised in the total outlays that were still largely oriented to new construction. The majority of the rehabilitated stock in the decade following these measures was social housing. Long delays in obtaining approval and the small amounts of subsidy accruing impinged most heavily on the private rented tenure. Despite the intention of moving significantly away from disparate individual upgrading, in the event much of the effort expended was at the level of individual flat units, which left the housing block or the immediate neighbourhood relatively untouched (ILRES, 1988).

The failure to ensure the maintenance of the older private rented stock was not simply due to inadequacies of rehabilitation measures. It also ensued from the unintended consequences of rent control reform, again passed in 1978. Whilst rents were regulated, the period of notice for end-of-contract was reduced. Moreover, there was no rent control in respect of a change of use of property, providing incentives for transfer to commercial premises. For these and other reasons, the law failed to stem the contraction of the private rented sector, but rather stimulated an increase in evictions or incentives on the part of landlords to let their property decay. Accordingly, the overall impression of measures adopted in the 1970s is of very modest outcomes produced in small-scale projects, and a weak engagement of private actors. Punter (1981) indicts lengthy bureaucratic procedures and resistance from powerful local property elites as seriously delaying progress in this period, citing the case of Milan as an example.

Other critics highlighted the rather narrow focus in the 1970s solely on housing in what was the limited regeneration of the inner core. This led to neglect of neighbourhood commercial activities which, although typically small-scale, were a source of ready employment for the local residents (Pannella, 1980). A respondent in the present study pointed out that where the ground floors of buildings to be renovated were commercial premises, these did not attract public subsidy, although temporary accommodation and a right of return was granted.

National attempts to consolidate the measures prescribed in 1978 followed in 1982 when, for the first time, a target was set stipulating that one-fifth of relevant public expenditure should be reserved for rehabilitation, with the possibility of funding to re-house in order to vacate older property for major works. Parallel measures, initiated by regional governments, proved more significant with the effect that, by 1985, almost half of housing investment in Liguria, for example, was devoted to residential upgrading (ILRES, 1988). Yet during the 1980s, in all, the national public purse funded less than 10 per cent of total rehabilitation costs, being particularly miserly in the case of the private sector. The arbitrary nature of disbursement meant that these limited funds failed to be employed strategically as seedbed money. Moreover, several of the respondents in the present study complained that the lengthy process of decision-making, in a period of building cost inflation, rendered the proportion of real public subsidy even less significant – prompting further delays as applicants reapplied for supplements. Nor could local sources of public expenditure make good these deficits. Reforms in 1973 and again in the 1980s failed to provide a stable funding base for the municipalities and the era was marked by the gravity of growing indebtedness (Mouritzen & Nielsen, 1992).

The European Commission (1992) judged Italian municipalities at this time as enjoying insufficient competence or funding to undertake effective urban regeneration, being subject to excessive dirigisme by both Rome and the regions. In order to improve public administration within an overall policy of reinforcing regional devolution and to achieve some integration at the sub-regional level, a policy for the creation of metropolitan authorities was announced in 1990. The intention was to subsume some of the urban and spatial roles then undertaken by the municipalities and provinces, permitting the larger conurbations to by-pass regional supervision (Newman & Thornley, 1996). The remaining functions of the municipalities and provinces were to be modernised. This agenda included a greater emphasis on community participation and the direct election of mayors; the reforms also aimed to guarantee them a measure of funding stability, although at the cost of some loss of fiscal autonomy. However, all these reforms were enacted during a period of a seriously deteriorating fiscal and political environment in Italy with the consequence that, even by the late 1990s, many had not reached full fruition (Governa & Salone, 2002). In addition to the announcement of these measures, action was instigated at the neighbourhood level for the invigoration of the district (circumscription) councils.

Central government only began to privilege a higher priority for urban regeneration in the early 1990s, a time which saw both an increase in programme output – albeit in a limited approach of individual, categorical schemes – and a change of focus towards wider infrastructural investment to complement the narrower field of housing improvement (Bramezza, 1998). Faltering moves were initiated towards a more determined effort to sustain the incorporation of the private sector in projects henceforth designed on a larger scale. As a result a series of 'complex' programmes were announced in these years. 'Integrated programmes' were initiated in 1991 aiming to stimulate local authorities to engage with private partners in a wider, more plural regeneration agenda, which would depart from the narrow confines of the traditional planning approach in order to accelerate the upgrading of the inner core where ownership crossed all three housing tenures. Implementation styles and the formation of partnerships were largely left to the discretion of the municipalities permitting a wide variation in policy lines among the cities. The lack of prescription by Rome was matched by somewhat hurried implementation.

The programmes were reinforced a year later by the additional stipulations for projects which were to be implemented cross-sectorally from the point of view of administration and resources to promote urban regeneration. Latini (1997) notes a significant change of vocabulary in that an explicit area-based vocabulary was adopted displacing one referring only to the buildings. Again, the aim is to advance a longer-term programme, by using the limited central funding to improve the integration of public and private agencies and their financial contributions. One important innovation was the ability to utilise funding for purposes other than directly related to bricks and mortar, with a primary aim of levering inward private investment.

As a further stage in advancing the cumulative agenda, and clearly influenced by emerging EU policies, sustainability of development was also becoming a more prominent issue, with innovative local programmes initiated by the city of Rome, for example. Although an associated national plan of 1993 was criticised for vagueness of ambition, it did, at least, reinforce the competitive economic advantage that many Italian cities enjoyed in terms of benefits accruing from the conservation of their historic centres. Thus, aid was allocated for the maintenance of mixed social and commercial uses in order to dispense with a narrower pre-existing preference for 'museumification' pursued without the benefit of overall strategy (Potz, 1998). This stage in national policy evolution also saw programmatic effort (the PRUs) to rehabilitate post-war social housing. This was followed in 1994 by a further national regeneration programme directly contracting municipalities to advance the progress of the 'complex' projects, with funding allocations being awarded according to explicit indicators of need (Gasparrini, 1997; Latini, 1997). In addition, many of the larger cities were independently experimenting with new managerial approaches to rehabilitation which, whilst not fully explicit public–private partnerships, were, at least, moving in that direction (Bramezza, 1998; Avarello & Ricci, 2000).

This series of measures share the hallmark of being poorly specified in terms of ordering objectives or the delivery styles to administer the 'mixed economy' of urban regeneration, particularly with regard to formations of nascent public–private partnerships. In this regard critics indicted the scarce engagement of central actors in the housing system (Avarello & Ricci, 2000). Concerns were also expressed about the effective involvement of the local communities and the deficient integration of policy with allied services sectors. It is also a fact that the programmes tended to add to the number of additional 'special' measures co-existing, but without adequate integration into, mainstream planning instruments and largely lacking a critical economic developmental approach. The 'complex' projects, for example, remained centrally controlled and, despite intentions, were in the main principally executed through construction works (OECD, 1998). Relatively superficial attention had been paid to assessing the socio-economic conditions of neighbourhoods or to initiating effective in-project monitoring. On the other hand, as already mentioned, the early 1990s also witnessed innovation by some local authorities in the direction of integrated area-based policies espousing a wider socio-economic agenda and broadening the partnership model. One source of 'seedbed' money for this purpose came from the EU's third Poverty Programme and the Urban Pilot Projects.

Urban policy output by Italian governments had never before been so voluminous as in the first 5 years of the 1990s. By 1995, therefore, the decision was adopted to reinforce targeting on the worst excesses of urban decay, by reserving 70 per cent of the earmarked budget for cities with over 300,000 population, with a secondary aim being to reaffirm policy integration through the adoption of wider partnerships. In its initial phase 76 programmes were approved (for municipalities of all sizes), although individual outlays in many cases meant that many projects had to be scaled down. About two-thirds of the programmes were directed to regenerating disused industrial land, but renewed attention was also paid to remaining semi-derelict areas within the historic core of cities.

Supplementary funding at sub-regional level in the following year identified deprived regions and those in industrial decline according to EU Structural Fund definitions. However, dedicated budgets seriously underestimated demand, and in the event less than one-third of the volume that was applied for was sanctioned, although EU funding did go some way to meeting the deficit (Latini, 1997). In addition, the accumulation of legislation was consolidated in the attempt to arrive at a unitary framework regulating relations between all tiers of government, one intention being to relax the stifling control regions exercised on detailed planning at communal level. Municipalities were encouraged to create 'mixed societies' with private enterprise for the purposes of urban regeneration, similar to their counterparts in France. These decisions were taking place in an environment where the lessons of over-reliance on the monolithic *grand projet* had been learned to the benefit of a preference for diffuse developmental projects (Campagna, 1997; Carrano, 1997).

Further innovations followed in the later years of the decade with the announcement in 1997 of neighbourhood contracts, albeit each attracting modest funding but for the first time in Italy allocated on a competitive basis. They were intended for experimental, integrated local development focussing on housing rehabilitation and the upgrading of allied facilities, as well for fostering a more formalised public–private dialogue and partnership. The 40 neighbourhood contracts oriented to social housing – involving the three principal tiers of public administration in contractual engagement – also espoused what, by now, had become an international agenda of combating urban social exclusion, in part prompted by the contemporaneous EU URBAN1 Community Initiative. Thus, the involvement of new voluntary organisations and action on youth crime, unemployment and community development were intended to feature prominently (Bricocoli, 2001). However, for the OECD (1998) the means for their effective achievement left much to be desired. In the same year EU-sponsored 'territorial employment pacts' were approved with similar ambitions but, in addition to other local private actors, the wider scanning of collaboration to include, for example, chambers of commerce, credit institutions and trade unions was required (Dematteis, Governa & Rossignolo, 1999).

Following the 1993 national plan, programmes were announced for urban regeneration and sustainable development on a city-wide or sub-regional level, culminating in the *PRUSST* programme of 1998, to complement smaller area interventions and to contribute to the formation of a European urban system. These are infrastructural plans for issues such as port development, industry, tourism and housing. The programmes are centrally funded according to a catalogue of scores prioritising different sectoral interventions; they aim to lever private funds to the amount of one-third of total investment (Moscato, 2000). Critically, operational principles such as multi-dimensionality, horizontal and vertical coordination and public–private partnership form the core of what is intended as an integrated, long-term agenda extending beyond the residential dimension of regeneration to many other policy sectors that had previously been seen as peripheral (Governa & Salone, 2002). Success depends on the long-term collaboration of local authorities and the plurality of other institutions within each specified area, and in this Seassaro (1999) finds early evidence reassuring. Nonetheless, Ricci (1999) cast doubt on its viability over the long pull, given past resistance to pool local efforts. Finally, in 2001 renewed mechanisms to afford greater autonomy of regional funding were introduced to carry forward the series of measures to improve Italian urban governance during the 1990s (current documentation is available on www.inu.it).

To conclude, for much of the period under review, at national level a strong and consistent urban policy failed to evolve, but rather a multiplicity of often conflicting planning instruments that chronically failed to constitute an effective *modus operandi* for all actors concerned and created a political domination by local instances that has, in particular, marginalised community engagement (Vinci, 2002) . Given the large number of decision-making stages, the attempt to execute innovative urban regeneration, irrespective of the scale of the project, at every turn, has had to overcome strong bureaucratic veto points at all levels of public administration. Many commentators judge these to have been more overpowering than professional planning cultures, where a long-term hegemony has been enjoyed by architects so that aesthetics of projects have tended to overwhelm their socio-economic dimensions. To these problems must be added the enduring lack of local area statistical and other intelligence. Problems appear to have been greatest in the south (Contardi, 1999; Avarello & Ricci, 2000).

One outcome was that, in many ways, Italy was dominated by private-led urban (re-) development, with the public sector dogged by rigid bureaucracy for the most part being marginalised in the process and substantially reliant on ad hoc emergency measures. In this 'bargained planning' arena democratic regulation has been compromised in favour of a significant infusion of privatisation of the system (Somma, 1999). The public and the private have each largely pursued their own distinct interventions, fuelled in part by legal obstacles to 'mixed' collaborative projects and the suspicions entertained by the left about the profit motive in urban renewal (Marcelloni, 1992).

There are clear signs of a change of approach in the accumulation of policy in the 1990s, in part stimulated by expanding EU's urban-focussed interventions. Measures in the early 1990s sought to broaden projects beyond a dominant architectural concern, embracing ideals – in intent if not always in practice – of socio-economic sustainability with the ambition of espousing a more developmental strategy with local authorities assuming a lead role as promoters. To these were added renewed action to streamline decision-making, relaxing the highly centralised and rigid bureaucratic tradition, although the chronic fiscal crisis of Italian regions and municipalities could scarcely improve the prospects of policy devolution. Moves to reinvigorate the democratic mandate have included the greater scope given to neighbourhood councils, the direct election of mayors in an attempt to strengthen their roles and infuse stability into local government, and electoral reform.

This policy output has created an increasingly complex mosaic of interventions and means that, in the new international orthodoxy of 'new public management', Italian local and central authorities have perforce needed to engage in a rapid and challenging learning process. Yet, in comparative terms, there remains something of a cultural reluctance to seek wider incorporation of non-political agents, including the local population, into policy-making processes. To be sure, such an engagement requires the generation of a significant amount of trust among all parties, something which traditionally has not been a reliable resource in the Italian polity: for one, empowering community participation requires greater preparatory groundwork than might apply elsewhere in order to establish bona fides (Bricocoli, 2001). Finally, given the unstable political relations both horizontally and vertically, the move away from comparative advantage to competitive advantage in Italian urban policy – part of a wider project to promote the 'entrepreneurial city' – could prove problematic and might, indeed, be counterproductive, since a supportive national framework has largely been absent.

Spain

Hallmarks of early urban policy in Italy were shared by Franco's Spain – and beyond. Ineffective central government policies, matched by lack of implementation at local level, pressures of mass migration to the industrialising cities in the miracle years of the 1960s, speculative developments by a construction industry exploiting public subsidies to maximise profits – often jerry-built and not infrequently illegal – paint a similar picture (Naylon, 1981; Rodríguez, 1990). Again, in the absence of a large supply of social housing for rent, affordability was a major problem for newly-formed households; for the most deprived the only resort was the shanty town (Buechler, 1983; Hooper, 1986). For many of those already housed, whilst rents were kept artificially low, there was little incentive for landlords to invest in modernisation and where they did, lack of tenancy guarantees led to substantial ejections of existing residents or sharp rent-rises, especially where public subsidies had not been involved in the rehabilitation (Lowder, 1980; Gomà & Rosetti, 1999). Accordingly, given the modicum of liberalisation of civil rights in the closing years of the regime, the situation was ripe for the first stirrings of a neighbourhood movement that would be aided and abetted by the leading Catholic charity, *Caritas*, active in many of the poorer parishes and increasingly distancing itself from the Franco establishment. The result was that, in the last throes of the dictatorship, legislation was passed to address the most urgent aspects of urban malaise, although from a narrow land-use perspective, with the particular aim of reinforcing little-used existing measures for rehabilitating historic localities (Wynne, 1984).

Although much was popularly expected of the democratic transition after Franco's death in 1975, which would impact on housing policy and urban governance, they had to vie for priority with many other pressing issues. But, at least, important pathways were set in train. In the Moncloa Pacts concluded between most of the recently legitimised national political actors in 1977, a new category of social housing for sale was introduced, with an associated construction programme. In comparison, the building effort in respect of building for rent was very modest, setting a pattern that would endure for the whole period under investigation. Political devolution to the regions and home nations was also negotiated, with principal housing and planning competences transferred to them, although implementation would be shared with the municipalities. Early action on sub-regional 'metropolitan' collaboration among the plurality of local authorities was also taken, although in the case of the Greater Barcelona it was not to be vouchsafed longevity (see Chapter 2). All these developments in public administration meant that the urban policy role of central government is subsidiary with fewer reserve powers than in other states, although Madrid has instigated some 'model' programmes (OECD, 1998). Beyond formal actors, grass-roots mobilisation to press for urban renewal of deprived neighbourhoods, offering guarantees to the existing local populace, proliferated. Whilst many activists were swiftly incorporated into the socialist party, their impact within the newly democratised municipalities under the control of the left should not be underestimated (Kenny & Knipmeyer, 1983).

Mindful of their electoral base, the socialists, elected in 1982 under González, continued with measures to regulate urban initiatives of the outgoing centre-right government. His first cabinet committed itself to a social housing construction programme of 45,000 units annually, but this was officially reduced 2 years later and the real outcome was even more modest. In 1983, a scheme for 'integrated rehabilitation areas' (ARI) was legislated with an extended system of public funding to the private sector, the level being made proportional to the salary levels of owner-occupiers. In 1985, state subsidies embraced a broader definition of 'historical buildings' to facilitate a more comprehensive approach to the planning of the inner city cores, where conservation and transformation became joint objectives. This was an important measure in cities with a core including extensive medieval and later constructions (Ibáñez, 1998). For Pol (1989) this policy output introduced a new culture of rehabilitation, albeit still too diffusely oriented largely to the level of the individual housing unit. However, it was complemented by more general social and economic infrastructural investment on the part of the municipalities, in the environment of growing conjunctural problems most acutely manifest in rising unemployment. The regions, too, were varyingly active in economic regeneration efforts, although this would have the effect of intensifying the spontaneously growing geographical inequalities. Government intervention in this field, in 1984, nominated 'zones of urgent re-industrialisation', largely in areas of declining steel, shipbuilding and port-related industries.

An important object of concern in the first González government was the constraint on housing rehabilitation posed by extremely low rent levels in the private sector. It was to be one of the areas which would bring it into conflict with *Caritas*. This Catholic national charity , also organised locally, was already complaining that the socialists were neglecting social exclusion issues and argued that whilst cheap rents meant poor housing, they did at least provide a shelter for the most deprived. Nonetheless, the government had developed a resolutely neo-liberal agenda and saw in deregulation of the rental system a speedy way to engage private landlords in the regeneration enterprise and also to unleash additional supply in this tenure. Accordingly, the Franco rent act was reformed in 1985 but only to apply to new tenancies, leaving prevailing agreements under existing stipulations and, thereby, providing every incentive for those tenants to stay put. Thus, a deeply two-tier rental regime was instigated, where non-protected rents co-existed with those controlled at peppercorn levels. Whilst the reform did increase supply, it did nothing to tackle the rehabilitation of old tenancies and, moreover, since restrictions on change of use were relaxed, there was a degree of commercial colonisation of residential areas close to city centres (Mangen, 2001).

Approaches to urban policy following EU entry in 1986 was tightly integrated into an explicit strategy for rapid modernisation, albeit at the cost of increasingly unevenly distributed benefits (Arias Goytre & Heitkamp, 2000). A revision of policy in 1987 demoted still further the future role of social housing, and within collapsing building rates in this sector almost all were allocated to units for purchase. Thus, the economic mini-boom in the years immediately after membership increased pressures on housing demand, satiated for the most part by recourse to owner-occupation for those who could afford it outright or who qualified for state subsidies to assist purchase. This latter possibility grew increasingly tighter in the later years of the 1980s, as subsidy thresholds failed to keep pace with soaring inflation of house prices with more of the stock being built for the open market. As a result, in the late 1980s, housing costs for owner-occupation rose by two-thirds, well over twice the rise in average household incomes (Alonso & Castells, 1992). Apart from the 1985 (Boyer) Act, there were no significant fiscal measures to stimulate the rented sector. Thus, for Rodríguez (1990), Spanish housing policy at the turn of the decade was markedly regressive in distributional effects: horizontally it privileged owner-occupation over renting and vertically, despite the protection of old tenancies, it tended to favour the better off over the poorer.

Following promises made by González's government during the 1989 election a further reform of rent acts was enacted but inequities substantially remained. Moreover, at the turn of the decade in too many parts of Spain, urban policy was characterised by a marked failure of administration to produce effective regeneration responses for the most deprived housing. This situation was exacerbated by rising house prices, made worse by the government's preferential treatment of the owner-occupation, almost to the total exclusion of other stock and especially the social rented sector, where new units contributed only 3 per cent of those built in 1990. There were also sharp increases in costs of building land. All in their way would have an effect on pressures to gentrify those areas of the inner core – particularly in the largest cities – that were the most easily (and profitably) retrievable with the consequent displacement of many existing residents. The cumulative effect of a growing lack of affordable housing was to reduce propensities for labour mobility, particularly among the young.

To be sure, the 1980s also saw several high-profile partnerships between central government and lower tier authorities, particularly in planning large international projects such as the Expo in Seville and the Olympic Games in Barcelona both of which took place in 1992. There were also the beginnings of integrated action for urban social exclusion and national employment creation schemes (Arias Goytre & Heitkamp, 2000). But for the rest, the lack of coordination between different levels of government did little to resolve the problems of the half a million housing units judged to be functionally ruinous, or those 2 million further units in a very bad state, to say nothing of the decaying state of the mass housing estates built on the urban periphery during the Franco era (Paniagua, 1990). For the most deprived the only source of shelter remained what it always had been: the shanty towns, still encompassing about 30,000 units (OECD, 1989).

An amendment of the 1956 planning legislation was announced in 1990 that would attempt to regulate values of developable land. These measures were consolidated in a new act in 1992 which made the preparation of a municipal urban plan compulsory for all local authorities with over 5000 population. As the older municipal plans were updated during the 1990s, they and the subsidiary neighbourhood implementation plans were increasingly targeted to the image-promoting 'entrepreneurial city'. In the meantime, however, Spain as elsewhere in the EU was experiencing a recession in house prices in the early 1990s which, at least, moderated what had been growing concerns about affordability. It was in this environment that a new 4-year housing plan was formulated, setting targets for rehabilitation of the existing stock and aiming to stimulate building in the social sector, partly to provide a fillip for the flagging construction industry but also to take action to remedy the lack of access of low-income families. At the same time, in order to increase housing supply, some local authorities were releasing municipal-owned building land at reduced prices. Yet, these efforts and the ambitions of the reform of planning legislation had limited impact in many areas of Spain. In addition, unintended policy outcomes towards the end of the housing plan, when the economy was on the upswing, were once again manifest in the volume of speculative new building above the price thresholds for subsidies, as too, the gentrification of existing stock (Nel.lo, 1998).

A further reform of rent legislation was enacted in 1994, this time to deregulate the large number of protected tenancies remaining from the Franco era. Annual rent reviews were introduced for all rented properties and limits were placed on the rights to inherit tenancies. On the other hand there were improved guarantees in respect of the minimum period of tenancy before notice could be served (Pareja & San Martín, 2002). It was hoped that the balance of measures would placate both tenant and landlord and encourage both to comply in rehabilitation efforts. To complement this series of action on the housing front, a long-term strategic plan for infrastructural investment was approved in 1994 to be in force until 2007.

Despite the endeavours of the national and sub-national authorities, the socialists on quitting office in 1996 left behind an urban planning scenario that the OECD (1998) criticised for the persistence of the lack of coordination between housing and planning aims. Decent accommodation was increasingly beyond the reach of many. New social rented housing had all but disappeared, and opportunities to rent privately were the most restricted in western Europe. Speculators supplied units where profits were greatest. Land prices amounted to up to 70 per cent of total costs in the largest cities. Finally, the outstanding task of rehabilitation of mass jerry-built housing estates which had sprung up from the 1950s onwards was enormous. Reworking OECD data for Spain and adding their own, research by Arias Goytre and Heitkamp (2000) suggests that more than one urban household in seven lived in what they judged to be areas of severe urban deprivation: 60 per cent of them in peripheral estates and the remainder in the inner city. Deprivation extended well beyond the quality of the urban fabric which – as for centuries – tended to be worse in the historic cores, but with unemployment and high rates of poor educational attainment being more prominent in the periphery.

As with so much of social policy, the new conservative government of Aznar of 1996 (to present) prosecuted broadly the same urban policy line as the socialists. Further revisions to general planning and building land regulations were adopted in 1998, as was a new multi-annual national housing plan which offered subsidies to developers of new or rehabilitated housing for rent. However, Pareja and San Martín (2002) complain of a slow implementation of the plan with indications that were hardly propitious that targets would be met (for current policy, visit www.sepes.es; www.mfom.es).

In conclusion, given that responsibility for Spanish urban policy is substantially devolved, it is inevitable that innovations in urban regeneration vary extensively in geographical terms. Certainly, cities like Barcelona and Madrid have been at the forefront of innovative projects and were among the first to engage local communities, initially in the democratic transition of the late 1970s. In general, however, since then some commentators note something of a step back from earnest attempts at community participation in favour of top-down planning in order to reinforce rapid upgrading and gentrification (e.g. Arias Goytre & Heitkamp, 2000). Finally, an ongoing project for sub-regional planning is seen by Nel.lo (1998) as an effective means to reduce the highly fragmented urban policy inputs.

United Kingdom

The UK was among the first European states to appreciate the full extent of urban decay and associated social deprivation. Direct and indirect measures were implemented during the Labour governments of the 1960s in the form of earmarked funds to assist the integration of ethnic minorities ('Section 11' money), followed by the small-area Community Development Projects, modelled on the US 'War on Poverty' (Johnson, 1999). In addition, the longer-term and mainstream Urban Programme sought to stimulate community and voluntary sector engagement as well as making overtures towards commercial development. It survived until the mid-1990s, although funding in real terms peaked much earlier (Parkinson, 1988; Robson, 1988). From the late 1960s onwards there were also specific interventions in area-based physical rehabilitation through the nomination of 'general improvement areas' in 1969 followed by 'housing action areas in 1974', both initiated by Labour, the latter affording a greater role to housing associations. These endeavours were to unleash, as Lawless (1989) notes, a rapid and bewildering proliferation of policy outputs.

A white paper on inner cities, issued by the Labour government in 1977, was influenced by the results of pilot studies and led to the reform of the Urban Programme, with a greater concern for economic regeneration and with a greater capital-intensive focus (Edwards, 1995). Equally, a nascent model of inner city partnership between the public and private sectors was to be operationalised in seven cities. Less reassuring, as several commentators of the time record (e.g. Punter, 1981), was a rushed implementation with pressures to demonstrate impacts in the very short run on the basis of what were small initial allocations in terms of total public expenditure.

New policies notably accumulated during the Conservative governments under Mrs Thatcher from 1979. As previously mentioned, riots in major cities in the early years of her premiership were to be an important trigger for action. Some of the policy basis set by Labour was retained – partnership, growing prioritisation of economic-led regeneration, pressures to demonstrate outcomes, and so forth – but in radicalised form. The output is certainly too prolific to be reviewed here, but much of it can be summarised as an unabashed push for the privatisation of urban regeneration through courting commercial interests with an accompanying demotion of local government to a subsidiary role and subject to the dictates of 'new public management'. Action on the commercial front was swiftly taken in the form of 'enterprise zones' in 1980. Based on projects in Hong Kong and the USA, they offered tax and land-use concessions to firms in relatively confined geographical areas, but for a variety of reasons they were to achieve more modest results than their models (see Lawless, 1989).

Following the outbreak of riots in several cities, including the Toxteth area of Liverpool, the Conservatives opted to by-pass local democratic control on several fronts. For one, there was the appointment of a temporary government minister for the Merseyside sub-region, assisted by a 'task force' of civil servants and an advisory group drawn from private enterprise. Furthermore, the first 'urban development corporations' (UDCs) were established in the London and Liverpool docklands in 1981. The London UDC was to be criticised for a crude alliance with the interests of the construction industry and for promoting a blatantly gentrifying agenda with limited positive trickle-down impact on the existing population. The Liverpool scheme was confined in its first phase to a relatively small area adjacent to the city centre, provoked open hostility from the city council and, in the event, demonstrated disappointing leverage investment from the private sector. On the other hand, after further riots in 1985, the number of corporations was expanded and Robson (1988), for one, argues that they should be given more credit than some critics concede. Again, pursuing the leverage agenda and drawing on American policy, 'pepper pot' urban development grants were created in 1982 with the aim of increasing the potential for employment creation in deprived urban areas. Yet, Lawless (1989) assesses that only one in three of the jobs produced was strictly new. These and other programmes, such as the 1987 'urban regeneration grants' (again escaping municipal control), were subsequently combined in an attempt at a more programmatic approach represented by the new 'city grant' announced in the 1988 report *Action for Cities*.

Besides the expansion of the UDCs, the 1985 riots produced further innovations, once again by-passing municipal control. 'City action teams' composed of high-ranking civil servants were created in the larger conurbations areas and were intended to be largely project-led and to coordinate the policies prioritised by Westminster. They were to be complemented by inner city 'task forces' of civil servants from relevant government ministries to stimulate entrepreneurialism in selected deprived local areas mostly with a high presence of ethnic minorities.

Mrs Thatcher's victory speech after her third election, in 1987, specifically named 'those inner cities' as the object of the government's urgent attention. Yet, an effective role for local government in this enterprise was to be further compromised by the reform in 1988 of local taxation (*poll tax*), the unpopularity of which ultimately contributed in no small measure to her downfall. And its role in the management of social housing was to be challenged by measures to permit other agencies to administer the stock. In the meantime, as mentioned above, a single 'city grant' – once again an American influence – was announced with a strong aim of pump-priming what otherwise could prove unprofitable regeneration projects for the private sector. As a signal to the policy line pursued by her successor in the 1990s the emphasis was laid on a strengthening of partnership and more robust developmental intervention. Importantly, one effect was to relax the limits of the sphere of action of local governments in the direction of promoting inter-municipal entrepreneurial competition that was to prove so important during the 1990s, and beyond. Accordingly, in 1989, legislation required all local councils to follow earlier pioneers by formulating local economic development plans, many offering some form of workfare and, in so doing, going some way to blurring compartmentalisation of policy arenas (Mayer, 1995). This window of opportunity for municipalities – after having spent so many demoralising years in relation to the quality of central–local relations – was to be further expanded in two major reforms of financing urban regeneration introduced by the successor government in the 1990s (discussed below).

In conclusion, there is no doubt that under Mrs Thatcher a fundamental reformulation of the regulation of urban regeneration was instigated, something that would outlive her period of office. One element of this agenda entailed the engagement of the private sector in a more central role creating greater policy space for local chambers of commerce, and new entrants such as the Confederation of British Industry and Business in the Community. Another removed part of the policy arena traditionally occupied by democratically accountable local governments. This was partly motivated by the hostile relations progressively enjoyed by her governments. However, Moore (1997) is surely right in his judgement that local authorities would have been a target, irrespective of militant reaction amongst their number, given the macroeconomic budgetary and reforming administrative agenda of the Conservatives. Thus, during the Thatcher era, they were subjected to intrusions into competences in terms of opt-outs from the control they exercised over social housing and education. In terms of funding, there was the ring-fencing of central budgetary allocations, restrictions on the ability to raise funding independently, changes in the local taxation basis and the imposition of compulsory competitive tendering in the delivery of local services. To all these must be added the pressures of management by targets. Finally, whilst dubious about the existence of wider 'society', the urban policy rhetoric embraced by the Thatcher governments was redolent of the 'community' and its values. Yet the preference for centrally led innovations, shaped by a top-down agenda and implemented by appointed bodies, reduced the scope for wide and effective public participation.

As the 1980s emerged, a number of critical reports from seemingly unlikely sources were published. Among them were those of the established Church of England which indicted the government for the impact on the inner city of what it judged to be deeply regressive distributive policies (Bowpitt, 1993). Incidentally a similar line was taken during the same period in Spain by *Caritas* to the neo-liberal predilections of the socialist government's social policies (see above). In reviewing the total urban package under Thatcher, Musterd and de Winter (1998) question whether they could seriously have represented an adequate response to the profound transformations affecting old de-industrialising cities. Indeed, Parkinson (1998b) assesses that the sum of regeneration funding in the 1980s amounted to about 2 per cent of total government expenditure and the major beneficiaries were medium and smaller cities. The Urban Programme formed a miniscule element in total public expenditures, although in general the gap between beneficiary municipalities and others did narrow. Nevertheless, the largest cities witnessed a dispersion of urban deprivation in their areas. In fact, his calculations suggest a real decrease in resources to the cities in greatest need, given that mainstream supportive funding significantly declined in the decade.

Policy accumulation meant that in the initial period of the government under Major, which assumed power in 1990, the Urban Programme was funding some 12,000 projects but most of them were on a small scale and spread over about 60 local authorities. In comparison, fewer than 100 City Grants were awarded each year (Martin & Pearce, 1995). The new administration provided a fresh opportunity to review the ongoing Conservative course of action, both with regard to horizontal and vertical partnerships, central government interventions and funding strategies. An urban regeneration agency was established in 1992, with a prime remit to stimulate private sector recycling of vacant 'brownfield' sites (Hambleton & Thomas, 1995). In 1994, integrated government offices at regional level were formed, combining most of the key ministries concerned with aspects of urban policy.

Two important funding innovations were also legislated. The first was the introduction during the early 1990s recession of 'City Challenge' which operated from 1991 until 1998. This programme represented an attempt to advance the policy pathway of partnership particularly by involving small and medium enterprise, as well as the community, and to restore greater scope for local government, albeit via competitive funding regulation. City Challenge mirrored the intention of the UDCs of the first Thatcher governments, but on a more extensive scale, in that it primarily prosecuted property-led urban renewal. But, the programme also aimed at greater reconciliation of commercial, municipal and community interests (Parkinson & Evans, 1989). With a strong focus on policy process, the model of public–private partnership explicitly advocated cross-sectoral, multi-agency collaboration and the objective of maximising private inward investment for the targeted localities (Tizot, 2001). Bidding for initial 5-year funding allocations was restricted to what was termed the 'pacemaker' Urban Partnerships, 11 localities being selected from among the 'urban priority areas'. In the second (and final) round, selection was widened with 20 areas being nominated. By the third year of operation the programme amounted to over a quarter of public expenditure for English inner cities (Oatley & Lambert, 1995).

City Challenge demonstrated the desire of the government to substitute a project-led multiplicity of separate schemes for a smaller number of more integrated cross-sectoral interventions. As such, it was an important policy evolution institutionalising formal bidding as a central pillar of urban regeneration, where the winners took all. Atkinson and Moon (1994) complain of the budgetary top-slicing constraints and the direction of monies to priorities identified by central government. Moreover many previous beneficiaries of the Urban Programme, which was being cut in real terms prior to being phased out in favour of the Urban Partnership scheme, lost out. Retrenchment also extended to 'Section 11' money (see above). Furbey (1999) detects a deliberate tactic to reconcile central regulation and growing inter-city competition by demoting still further needs-oriented planning. An explicit objective was to reward innovative, 'enabling' initiatives where short-term prospects were most propitious and, equally important, demonstrated sustainability. In the event, in the course of its operation, government could claim considerable success in terms of meeting private funding 'leverage', as well as targets relating to job creation/preservation and housing rehabilitation (Stewart, 1995; Parkinson, 1998b). Surviving only two rounds, nonetheless, it set in train a major funding reform which expanded the scope of action through integrated, across-the-board 'single regeneration budgets' (SRBs).

The SRBs, launched in 1995, merged into one budgetary package 20 urban funds, among their number those discussed above, although initially allocations to the existing commitments were retained, thereby limiting the opportunity to invest in new objectives (Stewart, 1995). On the other hand, the middle-term ambition was clear: resistant compartmentalism, short-termism, duplication of effort by parallel agencies and reliance on the small-scale were no longer to be tolerated. As stated earlier, government offices were created in each English region, bringing together ministries with urban-related remits (transport, environment, employment, trade and industry – although not incorporating health or education). They were to be responsible for disbursing the SRB according to what Hall and Mawson (1999) term tactical, 'loosely managed competition'. A broader agenda was specified: integrated action on housing, crime and policing, employment, and so forth. Building on the principles of City Challenge, reliance on the concept of 'urban priority areas' that had been selected according to some solidaristic notion of need was abandoned. It has to be said, however, that Robson's study had found a lack of fit between deprivation and per capita UPA allocations (Department of the Environment, 1994a). Instead, a more robust 'winner–loser' culture of spatial targeting was favoured (Burton & Boddy,

1995), thereby seeking to reward what was perceived as successful urban leadership and other elite engagement through a new political economy of interest intermediation.

Parkinson (1998b) records that under Major's premiership SRB funding peaked early leading to a decline in real total outlays. Despite integration of many budgets, there was criticism that some important allocations such as the housing investment programme were not included (Hall & Mawson, 1999). On the other hand the pronounced contract model of area regeneration both reflected and contributed to ongoing policy lines adopted in many member states, albeit at varying speeds.

The election of a New Labour government under Blair in 1997, campaigning for an empowering 'stakeholder society' did not immediately impact on policy pathways. Major's budgetary commitments to urban policy were to a large extent respected, as too was the enthusiastic espousal of the principles of new public management, extensive partnership and the contract culture. However, a year later, the government did respond to the criticisms that, since inception, much SRB 'new' funding was in practice already earmarked. Accordingly, within the SRB, the 'challenge fund' was increased, releasing additional money for new projects, particularly those relating to Labour's 'new deal' on unemployment and other manifestations of deprivation (Jacobs & Dutton, 2000). Henceforth, the evolution of urban regeneration policy was to be critically linked to the issue of social exclusion, a concept suspected by the Conservatives as too close to EU policies, but one which conformed to Blair's third-way agenda (Thomas & Lodge, 2000). Fundamental to this enterprise was the creation of a think tank, the *Social Exclusion Unit*. This was to be a prime actor in redrawing and coordinating the rapidly expanding urban agenda that perforce incorporated a wider scan of ministerial portfolios, most importantly perhaps education. Acting on a broad front, its recommendations have contributed to the further profusion of conditional and area-based interventions, evidencing re-investment of focus on the small-scale (Glennerster *et al.*, 1999; Amin *et al.*, 2000).

The Unit published a national strategy for neighbourhood renewal in 1998, stressing improved coordination and the need for holistic governance at the highest (cabinet) level. The ensuing 'New Deal for Communities' – a major new programme – therefore aimed to streamline partnership through enhanced local-area management and to mainstream policy, integrating it with other 'New Deal' interventions with targets extending to education, health, urban security and employment. To counter criticisms of the past SRB budgets being spread too thinly, a more intense targeting allocation was introduced. Selected 'pathfinder' neighbourhoods in the poorest areas of England were initially identified, with more to be added later (DETR, 2000). The package represented an attempt to enhance the embrace of grass-roots ideas in policy implementation. Bidding processes were changed to encourage a much longer-term funding guarantee and to dispense with the obligation fully to elaborate short-term project proposals that in reality had little chance of support (Hutchinson, 2000).

This period witnessed a plethora of initiatives in areas such as health, employment, education and even childcare (Matthews, 2001). These did not always emanate from government quarters, since other important actors were also engaged in proposing consolidating policy. For example, the key mediator for lower-tier authorities, the Local Government Association, formulated the 'New Commitment to Regeneration' in 1999 securing the close involvement of the government. It complemented ongoing official strategies by refining a sustainable and broad partnership model for capacity building. The resultant 'local strategic partnerships' were to direct regeneration efforts to a larger geographical focus than those targeting the neighbourhood level, typical of City Challenge, SRB and the New Deal for Communities. Importantly, they were to oversee the disbursement of all disposable resources for this policy field. For Russell (2001) these partnerships, which were formally adopted in later government modernising strategies (see below), raised the stakes of collaborative action by developing a longer-term perspective. However, her evaluation of their first 2 years of operation in over 20 pilot 'pathway' areas underlined the need for lengthier lead-in time for capacity-building in terms of developing trust, greater clarification of the specificities of strategy and implementation, and accountability lines.

New actors were also to enter the policy arena in this period. Despite lacking the democratic mandate for devolution of the other home nations, each region of England was bestowed with a development agency to improve planning and investment coordination in regeneration across sector and scale. The 1999 report of the government-appointed Urban Task Force was criticised for underestimating conflicting interests in the urban arena and for economic naïveté in terms of the development potential of the most deprived areas (Amin *et al.*, 2000). On the other hand, its recommendations for urban regeneration companies were adopted. To discharge their brief effectively, they are required to secure close collaboration with the public and private sectors and, particularly, with the 'local strategic partnerships'. Action was also taken to improve the status and efficiency of local authorities, in part through a 'best value' programme to modernise organisation and to compel authorities to enhance public consultation. The option of elected mayors was also legislated.

The Urban White Paper of 2000 reviewed the performance of the first phase of Labour's urban policy. For Robson and colleagues (2000) it was strong on prescribing 'nested' urban governance to harmonise multi-level interventions in one socio-economic planning blueprint. Plans were announced for expanded budgets for urban services and, within this context, the SRB, which in six annual rounds was estimated to have levered private investment at a ratio of 2:1, was to be replaced. From 2002, in its stead, a 'single programme budget' was to envelop the environment, transport, education, employment and industry portfolios, and regional development agencies were awarded greater freedoms in allocating funding (DETR, 2000). The Comprehensive Spending Review and proposals contained in the budget of 2000 announced new expenditure and fiscal subsidies to stimulate further entrepreneurial and property regeneration in the most deprived areas within a framework of increased emphasis on proven performance (Nevin & Lee, 2000).

In 2001 a new 'national strategy for neighbourhood renewal' was announced with substantial dedicated budgets to supplement the New Deal and the complex of client-oriented programmes and drawing lessons from French experiences such as the *régies des quartiers* discussed in Chapter 4. It made explicit its aim to further a multi-speed, 'joined up' agenda increasing funding to alleviate multiple manifestations of deprivation at local level for which all evidence pointed towards intransigent concentration: the poorest 10 per cent of wards contained twice the national average of means-tested benefit claimants and three times the child poverty rate. Accordingly, the principle of needs-based solidarity funding, largely discontinued by the Conservatives, was reinforced. In specific terms the strategy's overarching goal was to narrow the gap between over 80 of the poorest localities and their richer counterparts targeting a comprehensive range of socio-economic performance indicators. Central to its operationalisation was the 'pathfinder' model expanding from the initial round of areas identified to others which could demonstrate the potential of wide 'local strategic part-nerships' together with an emphasis on local neighbourhood management. Mindful of the fact that the evaluation of early rounds of the SRB had reported a disappointingly low rate of productive involvement of local communities, partnerships were required to seek their effective engagement within a long-term sustainable commitment of all 'stakeholders', the overall target being to rationalise action in the face of the vast array of new legislation. Entrusted with enabling rather than executing, these partnerships were to scrutinise mainstream policies and budgets of all the public authorities in their areas, with significant funding announced in 2003 – potentially extending for up to 15 years. Key priorities of the strategy include housing, investment in skills and business, as well as the securing of a high rate of private-sector leverage. Nine 'pathfinder' housing renewal areas were nominated in sub-regions in the English North and Midlands where demand has been chronically low.

New Labour's approach to urban regeneration in many ways summarises the key strengths and weaknesses of policy evolution in the past quarter century. It has returned to a more solidaristic basis, stronger on the community-led solutions that can be traced back to previous Labour admin-istrations. But it has retained – and in critical ways intensified – the reliance on new public management, partnership, and inter-municipal competition through targets, league tables and awards for best practice. A central position for commercial solutions has also been maintained, moving still further from mere 'welfarist' approaches (Parkinson, 1998b). The rapid policy output, characteristic of all UK governments from the 1980s, continued and newly emerging priorities have been carried forward: notably a more sustainable coordination of neighbourhood-focussed projects with those aspiring to a city-wide or sub-regional dimension (Cameron & Davoudi, 1998). Moreover, Blair's governments have restored to local authorities significantly greater scope of competence, albeit within the framework of 'strategic partnerships'.

The high level of policy output has done little to counteract accusations that the urban arena has become increasingly confused and unfathomable. Despite unitary budgets for some policy areas, the simultaneous spreading of funding too thinly among a complex profusion of small dedicated projects has not helped, nor has the considerable reorganisation and transfer of competences at central ministry level. There is still some distance to go in harmonising cross-sectoral interventions at different spatial levels, although it is early days yet to judge longer-term viability. Whilst there have been signal successes along the regeneration route, there are still too many areas where, despite considerable investment, positive outcomes have proved elusive: in this regard valuable lessons may be garnered from an ongoing study of four English localities, which aims to pinpoint why effective regeneration has been so elusive (current information on policy is available at www.odpm.gov.uk).

Conclusion

The five member states are at various points along the road of modernising the governance of urban regeneration. Some of the slower to react have clung to the idea of spontaneous 'trickle-down' effects (Atkinson, 2000b). Since the late 1970s, state-led interventions have been most prominent in France and the UK, although during the 1990s national programmes of varying scales were also implemented in Italy and Germany. In comparison, Spain retains the strongest exclusivity of devolved competence in this policy arena. Over time, reliance on state-directed solutions was prosecuted in France through the refinement of a vertical partnership between the various tiers of government. In it prominence has been afforded to the republican ideal of a contract between citizen and the state in which the public purse would be dominant. Contemporaneously, the UK government under the Conservatives espoused a progressively widened horizontal partnership formula. This was particularly strong on engagement of commercial actors and reliance on competitive bidding among local authorities for central funding which was conditional on securing private-sector 'leverage'. However, in general, irrespective of funding strategies, all five countries have progressively invested effort in forming public–private partnerships, so much so that they have achieved the status of a new orthodoxy. Conventionally they are defended in terms of extracting 'added value', sustainability and – in the best examples – empowering local communities.

As with all associated policies of the welfare state, the reform of urban regeneration policy was perforce a response to the rapid transformation of economic scenarios since the mid-1970s. This was an era of the growing fiscal crisis of the local state, albeit cross-nationally of different speeds and intensities. The result was that lower-tier authorities in many countries were progressively reliant on national seedbed or earmarked funding in order to engage in policy innovation, although frequently this was disbursed at the same time as mainstream allocations were being cut in real terms. Over the long pull, constraints imposed by 'fiscal stress' were most marked in municipalities in the UK, Spain and Italy; in comparison, constitutional guarantees and funding mechanisms ensured a less pressured time for their counterparts in Germany and France, where mayors of the major cities were also powerful national actors, although the impact of central austerity programmes there should not be underestimated. Nonetheless, within this conjunctural climate, cities – even those victims of de-industrialisation – were being repackaged as the prime locations for renewing national prosperity. Thus, in the current political rhetoric a central anchor for its achievement was municipal enterpreneurialism, which would not only be locally instigated but would also be supported by mainstream, national socio-economic policies. What became the order of the day were multi-level interventions strongly placing the whole city within its sub-regional context whilst, to varying degrees, retaining preferences for neighbourhood targeting.

Consequently, whilst the neo-liberal ideology prevalent in many EU countries discredited heavy state regulation as harking back to defunct Keynesianism, central partnership with the post-Fordist city has been viewed as indispensable for exploiting potentials emanating from a globalising economy. Simply put, urban regeneration has been evermore perceived as a primary tool of economic development and, as such, simply too important a catalyst for central government to surrender critical direction. To be sure, this policy line bears the risk of downplaying the fact that the playing field is far from level among cities and within the neighbourhoods each contains. It follows that success in terms of retrievability has been variable.

Contrary to what might have been deduced from post-Fordist imperatives, then, over the past quarter century – and to varying degrees – a re-centralisation of policy formulation at state level has evolved, within an ever-increasing profusion of typically disparate programmes. During the 1990s more attention was paid to how the effectiveness of these programmes could be improved by efforts to overcome bureaucratic compartmentalisation through the pursuit of institutionalised collaboration among central government instances. Consequently, moves towards a multi-sectoral regeneration approach have been devised. Countries such as Britain and France, at a more mature stage of policy evolution, are currently favouring greater selectivity of targeting, although the temptation to add dedicated, though relatively small-scale, projects to specific sectors within this policy area appears irresistible. As for policy implementation, within the broad boundaries and outcome targets determined by national governments, the specific style adopted has been substantially left to local resolution. This has ensured that, despite significant trends of convergence, in the 'mixed economy' of urban regeneration in the EU, diversity is still an apparent attribute.

2
Cities and their Inner Cities: Transformation and Governance

This chapter profiles socio-economic characteristics of the case study cities and introduces discussion of regeneration policy regimes, as a preliminary to later substantive analysis. To achieve this a broad range of qualitative and quantitative materials at both city and small-area level is examined for the past quarter century relating the varying fortunes of the sample. The Appendix provides definitions of the inner city study zones and data on a range of statistical indicators. As availability varies by year and policy sector, their selective incorporation here is supplemented by other materials. Then follows discussion of the overarching policy frameworks and the local political environments in which they were implemented.

As gateway cities, these European ports long enjoyed innate advantages in terms of consolidating an integrated economic base extending over a considerable hinterland and, with it, their political power. As with other industrial areas dominated by allied industries they have faced the greatest transformation shocks. In their case, however, mono-functional decline is not only a product of international competition, but also due to the growth of deregulated container ports in their own sub-regions, as a result of economic development policies pursued since the 1960s. The last 25 years have witnessed considerable divergence in the success of European port cities in transforming their economies away from a heavy dependence on related activities towards a more variegated economic base. Detail support for this observation can be derived from the multivariate analysis conducted by Cheshire (1990) of the severity of urban problems due to core–peripheral disparities associated with growing integration of EU functional sub-regions, 1971–88. To some extent, outcomes relate to the retention of a certain geographical advantage; unlike Barcelona and Hamburg, the three other cities have also faced growing cultural competition from nearby cities: Aix in respect of Marseilles, Manchester for Liverpool and Milan for Genoa. Yet, whatever the case, the impact on inner city populations has tended to be the most profound (Cheshire & Hay, 1989). In large number they owed their livelihood to adjacent docklands and dependent industries and the large companies or public sector enterprises that dominated them.

Economic transformation

The sampled cities include those which, for the first 30 years of the post-war period, were among the most prosperous in their countries (Barcelona, Hamburg and Genoa) and others (Liverpool and, to a lesser extent, Marseilles) which had already passed the high watermark of their relative prosperity. Historically, in all the cities most port activities were conducted in docks contiguous to the inner neighbourhoods and provided a major source of employment for their male populations, ensuring the wealth of the wider city, as the more opulent late-Georgian terraces of inner Liverpool testify. That is no longer the case. Thus, despite divergences in wealth, the sample shares certain commonalities. The early signs of economic transformation, which was to impact so radically on the port-related base to their economies, were, at least during the first half of the 1970s, slow to be appreciated by local political elites dominated by the left-of-centre parties. Besides, both sides of industry had long enjoyed significant privileges: the directors of the port authorities were key actors exercising much political and economic influence, whilst the heavily unionised labour force was typically protected either by generous state subsidies to the industry and/or extensive guarantees of job securities. All these factors combined to ensure a politicised management of the ports, delaying reactions to growing pressures on their viability, particularly in formulating responses to the competition of containerisation in neighbouring, newer ports (e.g. García, 1991). Finally, the ports tended to report an increase in volume of cargo trade and, in some cases, ferry and tourist traffic during the 1990s, after a dramatic decline in port and associated industry lasting two decades or longer, in the case of Liverpool. But, this did not filter through to job creation, manpower remaining a rump of what it had been in the heydays of the early post-war period (for Barcelona, see Nel.lo, 1998; Pla Estratègic, 2000; for Genoa, see Arvati, 1988; Gazzola & Carminati, 1991; for Liverpool, see Meegan, 1994; Parkinson & Russell, 1994; and for Marseilles, see Donzel, 1998; Peraldi, 2001). To some extent, the fortunes of the Port of Hamburg have been something of an exception. German Unification initially provided a fillip. And, in contrast to Liverpool, where UK membership peripheralised the port still further, the entry of Sweden and Finland to the EU expanded Hamburg's hinterland (Dangschat, 1992; Friedrichs, 1998; Berger & Schmalfeld, 1999), although plans for a large container-port in Wilhemshaven on the North Sea coast will, again, present a threat.

In contrast to the significant shared fate of their ports compensatory economic expansion has varied considerably, with Barcelona and Hamburg being the most successful in effecting the adjustment, although how this

impacts on the employment chances of their inner city workforces is
a different matter. After a comparatively late but severe industrial recession,
Barcelona was the beneficiary of an infusion of municipal-led entrepreneurial
strategy aiming at industrial reconversion, as well as exploiting the windfall
of being allocated the 1992 Olympic Games (Parkinson, 1994). As capital of
Catalonia – and the major growth pole of the *Mediterranean Arc* – it has
impressively expanded its economy, particularly in the internationalising
elements of the tertiary sector, significantly extending its commuter hinterland (Lanaspa *et al.*, 2003). As a metropolis increasingly attractive to inward
investment, it is a prime example of the potentials of what Swyngedouw
(1992) has coined *glocalisation*. With above national and EU economic
growth rates its employment base in the late 1990s was located not far off
80 per cent in the tertiary sector, although it was then beginning to show
signs of slowing down (Barcelona Economìa, 2000).

A similar injection of positive municipal entrepreneurialism was also
demonstrated in Hamburg from the 1980s. Until the re-establishment of
Berlin as the nation's capital, the city retained its primacy in the media, as
well as being an important financial centre. Services in the 1980s already
accounted for more than three-quarters of economic output at a time when
the city had lost over a quarter of its employment capacity – three times the
national average – biting hard into the local revenue base (Dangschat, 1993;
Läpple *et al.*, 1994). To be sure, the recession of the early 1990s exacerbated
the city's ability to fund the economic and social costs of substantial
in-migration from the east (Wirtschaftsbehörde, 1993). However, thereafter,
the growth in tertiarisation more than compensated losses in other sectors,
although, of course services tended to meet the employment needs of
different clientele, with many offering low income in comparison to the lost
industrial jobs: 'star' performers accounting for not far from half of the job
growth included IT, and health and social services (BAGS, 2001a).

In comparison, the remaining three cities were less fortunate. Like Liverpool, Genoa's problems arose from the fact that it housed a large number
of economic sectors in chronic decline that had been dependent on large
state industries which were increasingly being diverted to the south of the
country (Jodogne, 1991; Seassaro, 1991). Accordingly, in the 1980s 40 per cent
of its employment base was eradicated and service growth was below
national average, certainly below its nearby competitors in the north-west:
Milan and Turin, something which national legislation did little to remedy
(Monteverde, 1989; Comune di Genova, 1992a). The dominant position of
Marseilles in its region was ensured by successive public investment and
regional development policies prosecuted under de Gaulle (see Chapter 1).
However, his agenda also extended to develop a hierarchical regional
economy enhancing the status of newer ports like Fos and commercial
centres like Aix, a strategy which increased with decline in state subsidies
(Donzel, 1990, 1991). Consequently, in the 30 years up to 1990 well over

half of industrial jobs evaporated, being particularly acute after the mid-1970s (Donzel, 1998; Peraldi, 2001) and the sluggish development of the tertiary sector was an inadequate palliative. As with the other two cities in this group, employment growth, when it occurred, over-proportionally relied on the public sector and especially the municipality (Sanmarco & Morel, 1985). Nor was the hoped-for rate of tertiarisation realised. The result was that the political elite began to see the creation of the Single Market and the city's place in the hierarchy of the *Mediterranean arc* as more a threat than an opportunity.

On many counts, Liverpool's lot has been the worst of the three. Robson (1988) is among many to comment on how manufacturing veered towards a low-skills base and a reliance on branch firms all too exposed to closure when the economic climate dipped. Coming after substantial shedding of manufacturing jobs from the mid-1960s, in the 1980s alone 30 per cent were lost among the seven largest companies (Parkinson, 1988; Parkinson & Russell, 1994). Tertiarisation, where it occurred – and counter to national trends, it actually contracted during the 1970s – was heavily oriented to the low-pay sector (Liverpool City Council, 1993a). In comparison to its competitor cities, the development of small and medium enterprises, moreover, has been less firmly embedded and exposed to a high rate of relatively short survival (Best Value, 2000). In this chronic problematic environment, then, it is not surprising the workforce has been excessively reliant on public sector employment which at times has embraced over one worker in three (Liverpool City Council, 1987a). To add to its difficulties in the early 1980s the leftist city council's fractious relations with right-wing central government, as well a reputation for militant trade unionism, created a deeply negative image scarcely propitious for inward investment that proved difficult to shrug off. In any case, for too long, civic commitment to economic regeneration was half-hearted or during the 1980s pursued through strategies out of favour nationally, such as a large social housing programme: in the meantime competitor cities and especially Manchester, for long a leader in municipal entrepreneurialism, were reaping the dividends of neo-liberal developmental preferences (Parkinson, 1990). In conclusion, the proportions of the outstanding task Liverpool faces may be adduced from studies like that of Huggins (2002) who has examined competitiveness and productivity factors at small-area level and assesses that on a range of indicators more than 60 per cent of its wards are in the lowest performing quartile nationally.

As implied in the preceding discussion, there has been marked variation in the success of local labour markets to soak up unemployment. But a common feature – widely reported elsewhere – is the intransigence of pockets of long-term unemployment which in some localities is now extending to the fourth cohort.

Official rates of unemployment are particularly problematic in the southern countries where ready access to the submerged economy has the effect of inflating their volume (e.g. OECD, 1986). In Barcelona, the last quarter of the twentieth century saw sharp variations in fortune: the city unemployment rate in the mid-1980s peaked at over 20 per cent, falling below the national average in the early 1990s due to the wider 'Olympics' effect (García, 1993). After a rise due to the recession of the early 1990s affecting all EU states, rates in the late 1990s had declined to around 7 per cent and there was also an increase in female activity rates, although male unemployment and that of youth fell less sharply (Barcelona Activa, 1999). Rates for 2001 suggest a further upturn in joblessness. Hamburg's success is on similar lines, although following a somewhat different trajectory. Steadily rising unemployment until the late 1980s was oft-times above the national average, albeit not the city worst effected (Süss & Trojan, 1992). The catalyst provided by Unification was relatively short-lived and the wider European recession of the early 1990s proved a stronger impact, but healthy growth rates of the late 1990s enabled the city to recoup, with the economic activity rate being restored to its level 20 years earlier. That these encouraging trends do not, however, represent a universal remedy is exemplified by underlying persistent lower employment in certain social groups and localities. Thus, among 'foreigners' rates at times have been double the average and half of the jobless were unskilled or blue-collar workers, being most at risk of intransigent long-term unemployment (BfA, 2000). Despite the concentration of jobs there, the central city borough, Mitte, and Harburg, its deprived neighbour south of the Elbe, consistently recorded high rates (BAGS, 2001a). In the Klostertor-Hammerbrook area of the inner city, with almost half its population enumerated as 'foreign', the rate of unemployment in 2001 was almost three times the city average (see Appendix). Prognoses indicate that the situation for all these groups will be further exacerbated by the economic transformations benefiting the rest of the population, their lot made worse by the operation of insurance-based welfare transferring increasing numbers to discretionary social assistance, once earned entitlements expire (BAGS, 1997).

An estimate of real unemployment in Genoa is rendered difficult by the fact that many of the most deprived including illegal immigrants, who largely reside in the historic centre, are highly dependent on an extensive submerged economy. This, of course, is the sector most evasive of official estimates, although it undoubtedly fulfils an important welfare support for all groups excluded from insurance-based welfare. The rate of joblessness has remained above the average for the prosperous north-west. Liverpudlians have had to live for the longest period with high rates of unemployment: the city's decline and that of much of the Merseyside sub-region was progressing from the early 1960s (Turok & Edge, 1999). Accordingly, long-term unemployment has been particularly acute. Almost 40 per cent of those registered had been out of work for more than 2 years in the mid- to late 1980s, evidencing the chronic lack of aggregate demand for labour (Liverpool City

Council, 1988b). By the late 1990s those out of work for over a year still accounted for almost one-third of the total. In fact, the city has enjoyed the unenviable status of the highest unemployment of any conurbation in England since the 1950s (Parkinson & Russell, 1994). According to an official index of deprivation, by 2000, despite an increase in employment during the second half of the 1990s, Liverpool's unemployment rate was still twice the national average and three-quarters of its wards were among the most deprived 10 per cent nationally (Bailey *et al.*, 2002; Begg *et al.*, 2002; Boddy, 2002). In many respects Marseilles mirrors the fate of Liverpool. Unemployment rates have, at times, been twice the national average, with ethnic minority populations and particularly the young in the northern districts being hardest hit. In 1999, unemployment in the three central arrondissements was over half as much again as in the city as a whole, although the youth unemployment gap was much narrower.

Those inner cities

It was argued in the last chapter that European inner cities – whatever their formations – present a specific constellation of problems, albeit within what can be a wider spatial distribution of deprivation (in the British context see, for example, DETR, 2000). The sum of evidence about urban social exclusion suggests that its structuring is a function of cumulative segregative impacts of market and welfare allocative processes that determine its character over space. Musterd and de Winter (1998) attempt an admittedly speculative distinction between those countries (e.g. France and the UK) that have reacted to social segregation – particularly its ethnic dimensions – primarily through an area-targeted deprivation agenda and others (e.g. the Netherlands and Germany) in which such segregation is perceived more as a function of spatial concentration, to be resolved through dispersion.

The variation in demographic and other trends since around the mid-1970s is recorded in the Appendix and, to avoid repetition here, additional material for various points of the study period is incorporated to highlight key evolutions. The trajectories of decline of the population of the five cities and their inner cores reveal considerable differences with the lowest attrition being in Hamburg. On the other hand, there is an intimate correlation between sharp demographic and economic decline and social exclusion in Liverpool, which has been extensively examined (e.g. Parkinson, 1994). Authorities in Barcelona and Genoa made conscious efforts to reduce the high densities of their populations, particularly acute in the historic cores. Thus, both the Ciutat Vella and Centro Storico have been losing population at least since the 1970s; however, in the case of the former this has been in the context of a growth in the city as a whole, whilst overall decline has characterised the latter. Both of these cities, as centres of industry, had been the object of southern internal migration in the immediate post-war decades, followed in the case of Barcelona by returning migrant workers, initially from Latin America and subsequently the EEC (Buechler, 1983), which led to strong spatial divisions of the cities, not least according to class and, in Barcelona, linguistic competence (Lowder, 1980; Gazzola, 1982; White, 1984). The growth of Marseilles' population arose particularly from substantial Italian mass immigration. It was followed in the early 1960s by the urgency of receiving large inflows of repatriated *pieds noirs* as a result of Algerian independence, a period which has been associated with the onset of economic decline (Tulasne, 1994). In addition, like all large EU cities, the sample has been the object of substantial migration from developing countries, an issue discussed in a later section.

Finally, in terms of demography – and not least in the interests of retaining their local fiscal base – all of the cities have been minded to search for ways of tempering outflows of the affluent, either from the inner city or beyond the city boundaries, although these have been least effective (with the corollary that it has continued to be the most serious) in Liverpool. Nevertheless, such policies – a direct or indirect tactic to stimulate the gentrification of target localities – produce mixed results: many commentators point out that the more successful it is, the more pressurised the supply of cheap housing, creating serious local displacement chains which can have serious social consequences (e.g. Punter, 1981; Dangschat, 1993).

Ciutat Vella, Barcelona

The extensive historical neighbourhoods that form Ciutat Vella, on either side of the main thoroughfare, Las Ramblas, leading down from Plaça de Catalunya to the sea contain over 50,000 housing and commercial units (Serra, 1989). Despite some efforts under Franco to open up the area and subsequent rehabilitation programmes, it is still densely populated. Indeed, in the early 1980s, densities matched many in the Third World cities, some parts containing over 700 persons per hectare, although that has now been reduced to 195, the highest in the city (Barcelona Societat, 1999). High densities have not been so much the product of 'traditional' large Mediterranean families but, rather, the volume of single-person households living in very small housing units. In Ciutat Vella, the proportion of single-person households in the mid-1980s was some 75 per cent in excess of the city average, in part reflecting the excess of very elderly poor households, as well as the growing influx of single immigrants. Although not the commercial centre (that is to its north), Ciutat Vella remains the heart of regional and city administration and a locus of many cultural facilities. The immediate visible feature is its heterogeneity. Whilst in some tracts residential needs are in intense competition with commercial and tourist interests (e.g. Barri Gòtic) others like Raval, due to an image of urban insecurity, have been subject to persistent selective out-migration and a decline in commerce, particularly the night-time economy (Serra & Gausa, 1995). Evidence points to a rapid deterioration from the late 1950s with a rapid inflow of southern migrants and manifestations of marginalisation such as extensive street prostitution (Gomà & Rosetti, 1999; Valls, 2001).

Each of the four *barris* (*quarters*), currently has specific problems: serious crime, drug-trading and prostitution have tended to be more prevalent in the Barri Xino in Raval. Raval was the cradle of the industrial revolution in the city in the 19th century. But some of its areas, despite the 'Olympics effect', are still judged as beyond retrieval by private developers and as 'no-go' areas after dark, although further opening up of the area and the establishment of cultural and university facilities there was intended to ameliorate the situation. On the other hand, Casc Antic, the medieval urban extension of the city in the last two decades has been undergoing much residential upgrading, primarily by private actors. An ageing population is more marked in the most ancient part of the city, Barri Gòtic, where speculative pressures are also greatest, since it contains the principal historical buildings of the city and some of the more characterful squares: it was the first to show the signs of gentrification. Barceloneta is the most recent of the four, created in the 18th century for mariners. Being adjacent to the sea and ongoing regeneration of the littoral stemming from the Olympic Games, it too has been the object of private-sector retrieval.

Centro Storico, Genoa

> But as..., I wandered... at hazard through the tortuous byways of the city, I said to myself, not without an accent of private triumph, that here at last was something it would be almost impossible to modernise. (Henry James, *Italian Hours* (recalling Genoa's Centro Storico). New York, Grove Press, originally published 1909, p. 114).

Arguably the largest of Italian historic cores – and the 'tightest topographical tangle in the world' as Henry James called it, Centro Storico also remains one of the most dilapidated (Somma, 1999). A layout of narrow, medieval streets (as in parts of Ciutat Vella) has rendered vehicular access tortuous, if not impossible. Long a receptacle of waves of immigration, densities are still high: indeed, into the 1980s, ratios in one of its three districts (*sestieri*), Maddelena, were over ten times the city average. Again this was due to the preponderance of small or single households both among the elderly and young adults (Canepa, 1985), something that has endured.

Portrayed as the classic 'divided city' the Genovese Centro Storico has long been regarded as spatially and socially detached (Arvati, 1988; Petsimeris, 1998). Historically performing the function of a ghetto, it continues to enjoy a dubious reputation as the centre of crime, prostitution, drugs and illegal immigration – in some eyes, all interlinked, the rate of deterioration accelerating according to several respondents from the mid-1970s. Nonetheless, surveys have indicated that many residents feel a considerable attachment to their district and despite high prices a large proportion, especially those without cars, have continued to shop locally, in part of course *faute de mieux* (Gazzola & Seassaro, 1988). However, for many non-residents the area is to be avoided, particularly after dark, a reputation that has prompted out-migration of traditional families, public-rehabilitated housing in some of its 'riskier' parts failing to persuade them to remain (Russo, 1993). Prè, the westernmost *sestiere*, is the most marginalised and the most derelict. In part, it has long served as a fiefdom of the Neapolitan *Camorra*. That part of its housing stock which is barely habitable has become the preserve of African immigrants, often accommodated on a 'rotating beds' principle, and paying exorbitant rents to the mafia for the privilege (Canepa, 1985; Basile, 1999). Generally, as one moves east through the Centro Storico, retrievability prospects improve, with lower densities and more light, although the multivariate analysis of Piaggio (1997) produced a scattering of 'islands of deprivation' throughout the whole locality.

Innenstadt, Hamburg

Both Hamburg (and Liverpool) record a growing concentration of single-person and lone-parent households in their central neighbourhoods, although under-occupation rather than high densities is more of a feature (Friedrichs, 1985; BAGS, 1993a; Parkinson, 1998b).

The study area comprises 12 neighbourhoods in the *Kerngebiet* (city core) and adjacent locations to the west and contains mixed residential, industrial and commercial uses. Some tracts are blighted by a negative image as a red light district or open drug-trading areas (e.g. Hansaplatz area of St Georg); and the Reeperbahn area of St Pauli has long enjoyed a lubricious reputation, on which it has increasingly capitalised (see, for example, Zint, 1984). On the other hand, localities such as Karolinenviertel and other parts of St Pauli have progressively attracted 'gentrifiers' and new media industries. St Georg, adjacent to the main rail station, was among the first areas to be rehabilitated. It attracted early gentrification, as well as colonisation by offices housing public authorities. On the other hand, it has also retained a large proportion of long-standing residents (Casier *et al.*, 1991). Similarly Neustadt, adjacent to the Elbe, is a more-or-less completed renewal area with large amounts of new social housing. It contains many of the limited historic buildings remaining in the city, their restoration aiming to contribute to tourist potential and the growing night-time economy (Dangschat, 1991a). This area forms part of the 'Chain of Pearls' long-term renewal programme for the north bank of the Elbe and is adjacent to the major *Hafencity* regeneration of the dockside warehouses, both of which are discussed in the following chapter.

Inner city Liverpool

The inner city of Liverpool is characterised by large proportions of social housing and privately rented terraced property. Some of the better Georgian properties in the most central ward, Abercromby – particularly those near to the two cathedrals – have been impressively restored and are sought after, despite the surrounding blight of street prostitution. Others sadly have ichabod written all over them, or else they have been the victims of rehabilitation on the cheap, the frequent culprits being housing associations. Areas like Everton and Vauxhall, to the north of the city centre, have been subject to large-scale demolition. Unlike the other sampled cities, in many parts what was left behind was a superfluity of 'brownfield' sites awaiting uncertain redevelopment (Cooperative Development Services, undated; Liverpool FHSA, 1991). Nearby Kensington is judged to be in serious decline with an implosion of real housing values (see below). Granby Toxteth to the south of the City Centre has retained its dubious reputation as a locus of past riots and drug dealing, leading to chronic 'postcode' discrimination, a surfeit of hard-to-let housing and boarded-up commercial properties. Adjacent is Dingle, characterised by terraced housing leading down to the banks of the Mersey. On the other hand, there have been prestige residential and commercial re-developments in Albert Dock, adjacent to Liverpool's famous skyline of Pier Head, and latterly conversion in some prized central localities of former business or public establishments for luxury 'loft-style' flats, as well as growingly fashionable islets on the fringe of the inner core (Nevin & Lee, 2000).

Centre-Ville: Arrondissements 1, 2, 3, Marseilles

Among the northern and southern sampled cities, population densities in inner Marseilles are interstitial, in part due to opening up of central areas in the 19th century and considerable demolition in the second half of the last century. Demographic skewing has also been less marked. Although the three central arrondissements have recorded some of the highest levels of socio-economic deprivation in the city (e.g. Ville de Marseille, 1990a) there is by no means an exclusive homogeneity of the population, particularly in the first arrondissement. Here Body-Gendrot (2000b), for example, describes the location as one typified by affluent store owners, the Maghrebin who run smaller shops and Sephardic Jews in finance, though in different spatial segments. Equally, these arrondissements have distinct neighbourhoods, not least in terms of architecture. In this respect the northbound former main shopping street of the city, La Canebière, and the westbound 'Hausmannised' Boulevard de la République serve as both major axes and spatial delimiters. On the hill – detached and overlooking the Old Port – is the medieval centre of Marseilles, Le Panier, once serving the large number of Italian and Corsican immigrants. German bombing in 1943 destroyed part of the historic fabric releasing a prominent area for new development. A contained working-class area with a large proportion of elderly French residents and retaining a small-scale village atmosphere, it has suffered from deterioration of the housing stock and social deprivation. In the early 1980s over half of units had no bath or shower and 40 per cent had external lavatories (Ville de Marseille, 1985). Since then large parts have been gentrifying through private action and a lot of the rest both in the private-rented and owner-occupied sector has been the object of public-assisted rehabilitation (Ferracci, 1983; Ville de Marseille, 1995). Across the Blvd. de la République and on the 'wrong' side of Canebière is Belsunce, the major central neighbourhood of Marseilles' large Maghreb population and its commercial heart, the city centre having moved progressively eastwards (see SOMICA, 1985; Moore, 2001 and below). Despite a closure programme in the 1980s, 'irregular' cheap hotels for migrant workers and street prostitution have also characterised the area (Ville de Marseille, 1995). Nearby is Bellevue, long regarded as among the most deprived neighbourhoods in France (e.g. Ville de Marseille, 1990c), but now located at the centre of the ongoing major regeneration strategy for the central city, *Euroméditerannée*, which is discussed in Chapter 3.

Housing in the inner city

The principal and immediately visible physical characteristic of the inner core of the three southern cities is the amount of outstanding housing that is in a poor, sometimes dire state. In the northern city cores, standards are generally superior and there is a greater prominence of newer social housing. As a general rule, privately rented housing has offered the poorest quality, a fact exacerbated in many countries by lengthy imposition of tight rent controls. This being said, France and Germany have offered landlords a policy environment more conducive to better rates of return on investment (Emms, 1990; Kleinman, 1998). On the other hand, Maclennan and colleagues (1996) trace a cross-national process of residualisation of rented social housing, to the extent that it now represents a 'major contour of social exclusion'. In this regard the drift in the last 30 years towards deregulation and subsidies to people rather than bricks and mortar in an environment of growing restrictions on the public purse, as discussed by Boelhouwer and co-authors (1997), has depressed propensities to upgrade properties. The fortunes of the owner-occupied sector have in general been the most positive, despite cycles of boom and recession. National reviews of this sector by Ball (2002) indicate that in recent years new-build has performed better in terms of real increase in housing costs in France and Germany than the second-hand market typical of inner city areas. This contrasts with the situation in Italy and the larger Spanish cities. The prevailing boom in housing in the UK at the time of his report showed marked regional variations rendering generalisations unsafe.

Housing standards

Commenting on conditions at the beginning of the study period, Ferras (1977) reports that areas of Ciutat Vella, like Barri Xino, were at least as sordid as the shanty towns that still were a feature of the Barcelona townscape. As one would expect, a large proportion of the stock (two-thirds) is over 100 years old, and half of units are under 60 square metres, double the city average (Gomà & Rosetti, 1999). The task facing the post-Franco municipality was enormous, for attention to basic amenities had been seriously neglected. Thus, even by the late 1980s – at a time when public outlays for such projects amounted to a miniscule proportion of the municipal budget – about 60 per cent of the total stock required rehabilitation particularly with regard to the installation of bathrooms and toilets. Yet, only 10 per cent was still judged in an extreme state of deterioration and less than 2 per cent was in ruins (Serra, 1989; Taboada, 1991). In addition, there was much still to do to remedy defects in sub-standard, relatively new apartment blocks and makeshift housing, often added to existing buildings as extra storeys (Rodríguez, 1990). The outcome is that, in spite of the rehabilitation efforts in more than a quarter of a century since democratisation, many parts of the locality are still relatively run down. There are substantial numbers of old people trapped in upper storeys without access to lifts. Deficient sewerage and electricity supply, and humidity problems add to degradation. Actions aiming at infrastructural improvement were long depressed by inability to contribute to costs on the part of poor owner-occupiers or reluctance by landlords in receipt of extremely low rental returns. Nor did the high number of illegal tenancies help matters (e.g. García *et al.*, 1989; Nel.lo *et al.*, 1998; Barcelona Societat, 1999).

Serious wartime damage to one-third of Genoa's housing stock diverted attention to the urgency of reconstruction rather than rehabilitation of what remained. Consequently, in Centro Storico marked degradation, unoccupied and abandoned property, together with illegally over-occupied units, have been all too typical in the face of which – at least until the last decade – upgrading projects remained ineffectively small-scale (Seassaro & Pescaglia, 1993). In fact, housing conditions in this area, where many of the buildings date back at least to the 18th century, were among the worst of any large Italian city: over three-quarters of accommodation in the late 1970s was judged to be in poor state, of which half was barely habitable according to contemporary standards, conditions being best in Maddalena (Gazzola & Carminati, 1991; Comune di Genova, 1992a). As in Ciutat Vella there have been widespread problems of inadequate ingress of light and damp – much of which have proved difficult to eradicate – insecure foundations, sub-standard ceiling heights, lack of lifts, makeshift housing, poor sewerage and plagues of rats and so forth (Canepa *et al.*, 1985; Monteverde, 1989). Furthermore, apartments under 70 square metres predominated and in parts of the neighbourhood there were many less than 25 square metres, although elsewhere there was a relatively ample supply of large units (Seassaro & Pescaglia, 1993). Conditions by the late 1980s had deteriorated so much that only a modest proportion of the remaining housing stock in poor condition was judged readily modernisable in terms of the viability of its sale value (ILRES, 1988).

Central Hamburg, too, had been devastated in the Second World War, but unlike the case of Genoa, this provided an opportunity for large-scale housing renewal. Thus, only between one-third and half of housing in central areas pre-dates the War (Dangschat, 1991a). The 1987 census indicated that almost 70 per cent of housing in Mitte already offered sole access to baths and central heating, less than ten percentage points below the city average, although proportions were lower in neighbouring Altona. A mere 3 per cent of units in the whole city were judged to be in a very poor state, evidencing a marked reduction on previous surveys. But, there were areas such as St Pauli North where a minority of units were up to standard and much of the older housing there offered very cramped accommodation, prompting selective out-migration and accompanying marginalisation of the remaining population (GEWOS, 1982, 1989; Dohrendorf, 1990).

In comparison, despite the massive slum clearance programme, Liverpool still has one of the highest percentages of pre-1919 housing in Britain (Merseyside Improved Housing, Annual Report, 1995). The 2001 census records that the city is in the top quartile of English municipalities where standard housing amenities are the most deficient. Housing standards in the inner city have varied considerably: in 1991, access to all basic amenities was lowest in areas such as Kensington, something which almost 80 per cent of households in Everton already enjoyed. Everywhere quality was lowest in the private-rented sector and among a minority of owner-occupiers of unmodernised terraced housing (Liverpool City Council, 1995b). For a long period one of the greatest problems has been high vacancy rates and lack of repairs (Hatton, 1988). In the council sector, too, as late as 1999 over half of stock was regarded as sub-standard. Demand for public housing had fallen sharply and there was a surplus of hard-to-let units. As a very crude indication of housing state/market values the prevailing two lowest bands of the council tax in 2001 accounted for over 80 per cent of properties in the city – and 86 per cent in Abercromby in 2001 – compared with the English average of 45 per cent.

Marseilles entered the 1980s with housing standards in the central arrondissements the worst in the city by a significant margin. In these neighbourhoods, less than one-third of units offered access to basic amenities. At that time only about 10 per cent of units in arrondissement 2 post-dated the War. As with Liverpool, a chronic problem has been a high vacancy rate and by the end of the last century housing in one central regeneration area recorded outstanding problems of sole access to amenities amounting to almost one-quarter of the stock (AGAM, 1998).

Housing tenures

There has been a chronic complaint that new housing for sale in Barcelona, including that in the social sector, has been targeted too high up the income scale to address the issue of affordability (White, 1984). To this must be added the dire shortages of building land, the arrival on the market of the 'baby boomers' and economic growth triggers such as EU entry and the Olympics factor (Nel.lo, 1998). Latterly, as in Italy, inflationary pressures owed their origin to hidden stashes of income in pesetas, undeclared to tax authorities, which had to be disposed of due to the adoption of the euro (Ball, 2002). All these factors inevitably impacted cumulatively on the supply of cheaper, second-hand housing for sale or rent – stock typical in Ciutat Vella (Generalitat de Catalunya, 1987). At the end of the 1980s less than 40 per cent of housing there was owner-occupied (García *et al.*, 1989), but major changes in the more retrievable areas were already in train, only temporarily dented by the early 1990s recession. Much of the accommodation in these neighbourhoods, though small, was admirably suited to the growing numbers of affluent childless households attracted by the fact that costs were the lowest in the city. Prices were just over three-quarters of the mean level for the city, although they have been rising steeply – faster, in fact, than for Barcelona as a whole – particularly near increasingly fashionable squares, and in Barceloneta (Barcelona Economìa, 1993; Barcelona Societat, 1999). Accordingly, by the end of the 1990s, the study area had ceded its position at the bottom of the price league to the poor peripheral area of Nou Barris, by a considerable margin. These market trends had largely been aided by rising incomes disposed on the upgrading of existing housing attracting public subsidies (Generalitat de Catalunga, 2000a,b).

Though from a low initial base, the rate of owner-occupation in Centro Storico had also been rising above the Genoa average since the 1970s. Accordingly, by the early 1980s, the proportion of total stock in this sector, at 45 per cent, approached that of the city as a whole (Cassino *et al.*, 1983). In comparison with Barcelona, however, areas of easy retrievability have been less extensive, in part due to the more dense layouts impinging on light and space and the fact that perceptions of insecurity of specific localities are more pervasive, especially in Prè. On the other hand, the more desirable areas in Molo and Maddelena have long been targeted by private developers. To a lesser extent, the same factors leading to pressures on prices in Ciutat Vella are in evidence here, although data presented by Ball (2002) suggest that Genoa departs from the general tendency in other large Italian cities in the late 1990s of significantly higher increases in and around city centres than elsewhere.

Owner-occupied housing has been in relatively scarce supply in central Hamburg where general gentrification effects have been associated with better quality privately rented accommodation, although owner-occupiers, like private landlords, are offered tax incentives for investments in upgrading (Skifter Andersen, 1999). In the late 1980s, for example, only 2 per cent of the stock in Mitte was in this sector, although in adjacent Altona the proportion was already almost 10 per cent (Dangschat, 1991b). In comparison with Liverpool and Marseilles, owner-occupiers enjoy altogether more of an affluent status and there is little association in parts of the sector with poor and/or elderly households for whom rehabilitation costs, even with subsidies, may be beyond reach (for the situation in France, see Fribourg, 1999).

The pepper-pot effect of affluent housing in inner city Liverpool has already been mentioned and this has percolated to the more attractive sites on the central fringe primarily in terms of new construction (Nevin & Lee, 2000). Despite these developments and what at the time of writing is a period of rapid inflation of house prices in the more salubrious areas of the city, this has not filtered down into improving retrievability of some inner localities where there remains a serious problem of chronic real value depreciation (CURS, 1999). As one respondent in the 'New Deal' area of Kensington emphasised, in general housing in the city has been in surplus supply, so that prices in least desired localities are to quote him 'in free fall'. It follows that rehabilitation of standard, older terraced properties in the neighbourhood hardly posed a lucrative proposition.

New social housing for rent has all but disappeared in contemporary Spain; what is built in this sector is overwhelmingly for sale. Thus, in Barcelona, in the face of real need for affordable decent rented property, the efforts of the municipality since the transition to democracy is a mere drop in the ocean (Valls, 2001). As commented in the previous chapter, housing policy has been a bone of contention between the regional and city authorities. In fact, at a time of particular pressures on the housing market, Mayor Maragall openly criticised the Catalan government – which retains the major competence in the field – for opting for profit maximisation in authorising release of developable land for house-building (La Vanguardia, 1991). In turn, however, he was criticised by neighbourhood associations for being somewhat less than robust in the pursuit of the affordability agenda. Scarcity is similarly a feature of Genoa's social housing. Clientelistic practices in granting access to this stock have been commonly reported in Italy, a situation which in this city, as elsewhere, has been exacerbated in the opinion of several respondents by the heavy bureaucratic regulation.

On the other hand, as in Liverpool albeit there more chronically, there was a time in the early 1980s when there was surplus of social housing in Hamburg which in comparative terms has been one of the most generously endowed in Germany: as late as 1990, for example, accounting for not far from 40 per cent of total stock (Deutsche Städtetag, 1990). But as the 1980s evolved the situation was already changing rapidly. Demand was heightened by the fall of the Wall and the arrival of many new migrants from the former DDR and further east. Moreover, social housing had been enjoying mixed fortunes in Germany. The scandal of the bankruptcy of the large 'Neue Heimat' agency soured attitudes of Kohl's governments and financing for new construction was for a time withdrawn, followed by legislation to end the non-profit status of most of this housing (Emms, 1990; Ulbrich & Wullkopf, 1993). In fact, net new additions to the stock in Hamburg have been falling at a progressive rate since the 1970s. Supply has been further restricted by increasingly larger proportions of transfers of the better stock to the private sector at the end of the public loan period. A further factor has been that some of the social stock in prime sites continued to be occupied by affluent tenants willing to pay rental supplements, leaving the least desirable, particularly in peripheral estates, to those with little other choice (Dangschat, 1990; Müller, 1994).

The proportion of socially rented housing in Liverpool remains above the English average, with almost one-third of the stock under direct municipal ownership. Of all major cities the role of housing associations in provision has been prominent, both in terms of length of engagement and extent of supply, including that managed by cooperatives (Couch & Wynne, 1986). Following national policy, an increasing amount of council-owned property has been transferred to 'housing action trusts' under new landlords for the purposes of upgrading and improved management (Liverpool City Council, 1993b, 1999b). Apart from the quality of some of the accommodation offered it has been the low demand for it that has dogged the city administration. The general residualisation and surpluses of social housing has become an acute problem in the city. Stock built merely about 30 years ago in areas like Granby-Toxteth has been demolished as unlettable. Although the city has benefited from substantial central funding for rehabilitation of social housing for two decades, the persistent lack of sufficient applications for new tenancies produces high vacancy rates for upgraded accommodation in certain localities. This has posed particular management and budgetary problems for those social landlords whose properties are concentrated there (CURS, 1999; Liverpool Partnership Group, 2000).

Social housing for rent in Marseilles in the late 1990s amounted to not far off one-fifth of total stock, but half is concentrated in just three northern arrondissements, with less than 10 per cent being located in the study area. The major suppliers are joint ventures which manage the majority of property targeted in the series of physical and social regeneration projects (see Chapter 3). Although there have been some dedicated programmes improving access to better quality units for minority or deprived groups, these must be assessed against the general pressures housing agencies face from the need to balance their books (AGAM, 1998; Donzel, 1998; Peraldi, 2001). Since 1987 the social housing agencies in the city and elsewhere have been able to spend government allocations either on new construction or rehabilitation, including large-scale 'housing action areas' (Fribourg, 1999).

The role of privately rented housing varies considerably in the five cities, but is most prominent in their inner cores. In Ciutat Vella over half of properties were rented from a private landlord, the highest proportion in the city (Nel.lo, 1998). As in the owner-occupied sector, the improved economy of the city following EU entry and the Games effect put pressure on this local housing market and rents for many properties rose sharply: in the early 1990s by 200 per cent, albeit from a very low base (García, 1993). Although rents at this time were still among the very lowest in the city, as the decade progressed, in general, the differential between income take of rents and mortgages substantially declined (Ajuntament de Barcelona, 1991; Pareja & San Martín, 2002).

Access to this sector in Genoa, like social housing, has owed much to clientelism and patronage. By the early 1980s, almost two-thirds of accommodation in Centro Storico was under private landlord control, although trends already indicated a sharp contraction (ILRES, 1988). Several respondents complained of a continuing problem of access being denied to certain groups, particularly recent immigrants who congregate there. Whilst some landlords prefer to leave property empty, hoping for better returns for vacant sale later in the area's growing owner-occupied market, others have charged exorbitant rents for these clientele, forced into grossly overcrowded conditions.

A similar propensity to deny access to rented housing and a preference to leave properties empty in the belief that the land values would rise have also been recorded in Hamburg (Karolinen-Poker, 1984). Furthermore, the rediscovery of the attractions of living close to the centre has put pressures on the dwindling cheaper housing stock which was long the preserve of the poorest. Private landlords in Germany have been relatively well treated by the tax system, with concessions for upgrading and energy conservation, making investment in inner city property more lucrative (Tomann, 1990). Thus, many rehabilitation measures have only served to intensify competing demands, although, as stated in Chapter 1, there are some provisions in the legislation of 1971 to preserve the social composition of regenerated neighbourhoods. In an environment of sharp increases in general rent levels, market forces have often proved the more resilient. As survey evidence suggests, this has led to resistance towards agreeing to rehabilitation on the part of low-income tenants who fear higher rents or, else, enforced displacement (Coym & Schmid, 1985b; Dangschat & Ossenbrügge, 1990). Accordingly, at a time of growing shortages of housing in the late 1980s, there were attempts by the city to hold rent levels of upgraded private property below those of equivalent social housing (Freie und Hansestadt Hamburg, 1989a). However, whilst protecting tenants this had frequently led to unintended consequences. In order to avoid the regulation required by public subsidies, landlords have often preferred to fund rehabilitation privately. The attractiveness of this option arises from the fact that such works are still tax deductible and they are left a freer hand (Dohrendorf, 1991; Dangschat, 1993). Alternatively, they have tried to pass off routine maintenance measures – which do not permit rent increases – as 'modernisation', with the costs being partly offloaded onto tenants (Diesner *et al.*, 1994).

In Hamburg, as in other large German cities, affordability has therefore been an enduring concern, made worse by the fact that, at times, more than half of those who could be assisted by housing benefits did not apply for it (Ulbrich & Wullkopf, 1993). In the early 2000s the general level of increase of advertised rents in many central locations has continued to sharply outpace that prevailing in the suburbs, although there are still areas such as parts of St Pauli where this has not been the case (Hamburger Abendblatt, 2001b).

These pressures have not been present in Liverpool. Rather, private tenancies – of which the city still has an above average supply – remain the preserve of low-income groups and, later, attracted the student population. Yet, there is now evidence of this latter group leaving the most deprived areas for tailor-made student accommodation elsewhere. The general overcapacity of the housing market in the city critically impacts on this sector: Nevin and Lee (2000) report landlords complaining of increased costs due to anti-social tenants, high turnover and lengthy vacancy rates and other residualisation effects, all of which negate returns on their investments in upgrading. Large parts of inner city Marseilles share elements of the situation in Liverpool, though there are some fashionable squares in arrondissement 1. To stimulate the rate of rehabilitation, action was taken nationally in the late 1980s to reduce artificially low rents for properties being upgraded and this led to a substantial increase in levels demanded and, despite the stated intention, considerable displacement of original tenants (Blanc, 1990). Rents for improved housing may now be freely negotiated between landlord and tenant, although subsequent rents are regulated (Ball, 2002).

Social deprivation

This section selectively reviews some of the true location costs of living in deprived neighbourhoods like the inner city (although paucity of reasonably reliable data prevents inclusion of Genoa). For one, demand pressures on private housing and the nature of policy intervention can result in a higher proportion of income being allocated to accommodation among the poorest (e.g. Keller, 1999); this is particularly the case where the availability of socially subsided units is in short supply. For another, inner city populations are among those who are most reliant on discretionary social benefits exposing them to the vagaries of national and local welfare systems which, particularly in southern countries, are the most deficient and made worse by the relative sparseness of supportive in-kind services.

A composite deprivation index including such factors as unemployment, income and low educational attainment indicated that in the early 1980s the score for the Ciutat Vella was not far off double that of the city average (Soler *et al.*, 1987). Although income inequalities in Barcelona and other large cities declined after EU entry in 1986, tempering the rate of what Paugam (1991) has termed southern 'traditional poverty', pockets of poverty proved resistant. Thus, despite government attempts in the late 1980s to accelerate convergence of welfare budgets with the rest of the Union, in many cases 'disqualifying' exclusion actually intensified and one in four of the inner city population were judged to be in a state of precariousness (Ajuntament de Barcelona, 1989a). Furthermore, Nel.lo (1998) records that whilst poverty rates in Barcelona province have been lower than the national average, data presented by Gomà and Rosetti (1999) suggest that disposable incomes in the Ciutat Vella declined during the 1990s – as they did in certain peripheral estates – to amount to only 70 per cent of the city average.

Spatial attributes of social precariousness in Marseilles demonstrate differences by household type. Whilst in the northern social housing estates it is associated with families – many of them Maghrebin – in the three central districts single-person households are more typically enumerated. However, the number of 'at risk' families living centrally increased in the 1980s, in part due to the rise in single-parent families but also owing to the fact that in Belsunce, for example, almost four-fifths of the minority population earned incomes below the tax threshold (AGAM, 1990; Ville de Marseille, 1990a). Mid-1990s data on a range of targeted benefits for deprived groups indicate that rates peak in the north and in certain parts of the centre. Recipient rates for the inner area of Belsunce, for example, at almost half of all households was over three times the city average (INSEE, 1995; AGAM, 2000c). In the late 1990s rates of receipt of the *Revenu Minimum d'Insertion*, oriented to the long-term unemployed and other disadvantaged, were over double in the central areas (INSEE, 1999).

Relevant data for the two northern cities are the most extensive. Long among the richest city-regions in the EU, rates of receipt of assistential benefits in Hamburg sharply increased from the early 1980s. This occurred after a long period during which outlay burdens were favourable when compared to other large cities, with uptake largely confined to the elderly (Friedrichs, 1985; Coym & Schmid, 1985b). While the extent of relative poverty may have been less serious than in many other EU states, the expansion here mirrored that elsewhere, being largely due to those without entitlement to unemployment insurance benefits or those for whom they had expired, as well as growing expenditure on housing allowances and the homeless (Dangschat & Ossenbrügge, 1990). Economic oscillations merely tended to deepen income disparities. The city houses the greatest concentration of the very rich in Germany; but there have been very high rates of those dependent on means-tested allowances, even in the boom following Unification (Alisch & Dangschat, 1994). Predictably enough, all investigations reproduce similar spatial distributions with the inner city areas and certain adjacent areas like St Pauli being most affected (e.g. BAGS, 1993b). Data for 2000 indicate an almost 7 per cent receipt rate of social assistance in Hamburg. But, the proportion of claimants was almost double in St Pauli and high, too, in Altona's Altstadt. To the growing and disproportionate number of established minorities dependent on means-tested benefits has been added a large clientele among asylum seekers: already, by 1991, their receipt rate amounted to 90 per cent of their population (BAGS, 1991).

As in many large cities, several respondents identified the early 1990s as a phase of acute polarisation, a period when street begging mushroomed with a rise in those recorded as rough sleepers. More generally, trends in the rate of receipt of social assistance have impacted on households with children, where on average in the late 1990s one in four minors were wholly or partly dependent on this source, and in Mitte and Harburg the proportion was put at half (Schütte, 1994; Korte *et al.*, 1999). Despite the wide range of targeted social interventions, at the turn of the century, data suggest a below average decline in claimants when compared with other large cities. Significantly, there was a growing concentration among certain clientele: in Mitte in 1998 one in three were non-Germans and, of them, one-quarter were asylum seekers (BAGS, 2000, 2001b).

The wealth of relevant research is positively correlated with the severity of Liverpool's chronic deprivation. Hence, there is a need here to be very highly selective in this inner city review. In general, all investigations highlight such associated indices as high mortality, morbidity and disability rates, high receipt of free school meals, low educational achievement, low car-ownership, and high rates of child poverty though it should be stressed that many outer estates fare no better: frequently worse (e.g. Liverpool City Council, 1988a, 2000; CURS, 1999). Comparisons have consistently placed the city in the top rank of the most disadvantaged, either nationally or within the EU, with rates at least twice the prevailing average (e.g. Jack, 1987; Parkinson, 1988; Merrifield, 1995; Moore, 1997). The city has been conducting investigations of deprivation by locality since the late 1960s which strongly indicate that few neighbourhoods have escaped membership of the least fortunately placed. In the early 1990s, according to EU criteria, 46 per cent of minority households were 'poor' and almost one-fifth 'very poor' (Liverpool City Council, 1993a). Concentrated in several central wards of the city, these groups have endured 'postcode discrimination' in job search, with unemployment rates double and, at times, treble those of whites, the minority young in the most deprived neighbourhoods being particularly hard hit (Liverpool City Council, 1988a). One such locality,

Granby, was classified in an official report as effectively a 'no work' area (Gifford, 1989). Unemployment among ethnic minority youth has been particularly high, with over half of the relevant group in Abercromby and Granby being recorded in this category in the 1991 census. Based on receipt of a range of means-tested benefits, inner areas such as Everton, Granby and Vauxhall record rates up to double the city average, which in turn in the late 1990s was still over double the national average (Liverpool City Council, 1997, 1999a; Bailey *et al.*, 2002). In these three wards, over 70 per cent were claiming housing allowances or council tax reductions (Liverpool City Council, 1999a). Other deprivation indicators reveal a similar distribution (Liverpool City Council, 2000). Recent national indicators of multiple deprivation tell the same story with these and other inner wards (and also the outer estate of Speke) tending to be placed in the upper ranges of the top ten most deprived neighbourhoods in England (DETR, 2000).

The situation of ethnic minorities

Castles and Miller (1998) are among investigators attempting to classify countries along a 'citizenship orientation' continuum, from 'guest worker' exclusion, through assimilation to multi-culturalism. Yet, whatever the location of the present sample of countries, the brief reference to deprivation among ethnic minorities in the above section strongly supports the contention that in the EU one converging aspect of urban transformation is that, in a real sense, they form the core of what Rex (1984, p. 192) referred to 20 years ago, in relation to the UK, as the 'inner city's inner city'. Despite policy effort since then much of the evidence for five case cities scarcely makes encouraging reading.

Although the associated agenda has now achieved a higher political profile, not least as a result of the asylum issue, there are important outstanding statistical deficits which hinder the full monitoring of the predicaments of minority communities. In some cases – as in Italy and Spain – what is estimated to be a large presence of illegal immigrants, evading official surveying, adds to problems. In France, respecting republican traditions of citizenship, the ethnic origin of those with French nationality has been consciously excluded in many statistical series. Long-term residents and those born in Germany but lacking citizenship have routinely been officially recorded as 'foreigners'. British census authorities have made more progress in facilitating the recording of ethnic origin, irrespective of citizenship.

Statistical profile

Though everywhere figures vary enormously and few could be regarded as entirely reliable, all the cities, save Liverpool, report a rapid growth in illegal immigration. Even by the early 1990s guesstimates for Barcelona suggest that over 40 per cent of foreign residents were 'irregular' and were congregating in the Ciutat Vella, as well as in re-appearing shanty towns mostly in the periphery (El País, 1991). In the last two decades almost all immigrants have been under 40 and mostly from Africa.

Although less than 1 per cent of the Genoese population in the early 1980s was enumerated as foreign nationals, almost two-thirds were resident in Centro Storico, where they constituted between 7 and 10 per cent of the population (ILRES, 1991). Thereafter, disparate groups were increasingly attracted to the city and to Italy in general after the imposition of stricter laws in France, so that most current minorities have been resident from the mid-1980s onwards (Seassaro & Sola, 1992). Authorities agree that official statistics would at least double if illegal residents were included (ILRES, 1991; Somma, 1999). Centro Storico, and especially its worst areas in Prè, have been identified as a safety valve for the city. Here immigrants are tolerated, providing that they do not disperse elsewhere, strongly suggesting that the locality had increasingly shed its role as a zone of passage (e.g. Torti, 1992). In the past 20 years almost two-thirds of registered non-EC foreigners have been resident here, the majority being young African males, especially Moroccans and Senegalese (ISTAT, 1995).

The dozen years after 1970 witnessed a doubling of legal 'foreigners' in Hamburg to amount to 10 per cent of the population, a growth rate above the national average. On the other hand, as a proportion, this community remained inferior to that in other large German cities where, above all, a large Turkish community had been established from the 1960s to fuel Germany's economic miracle (Friedrichs, 1985). At the turn of this century 15 per cent of the population was non-German, with the proportion of those under 20 amounting to one-fifth of the cohort (BAGS, 2001b). By the late 1980s, Mitte housed over one-quarter of Turkish residents, with a further fifth primarily living in adjacent Altona. In certain of their neighbourhoods minority communities have been much more prevalent: in parts of St Georg, for example, they accounted for almost two-thirds of the population and in Karolinenviertel, Klostertor-Hammerbrook and parts of St Pauli around half or more.

Past under-reporting in official censuses has resulted in a chronic underestimation of the size of minority ethnic population of Liverpool, but by the 1980s it was assessed as constituting 8 per cent of the total, the largest number being born in city (Liverpool Black Caucus, 1986). Several respondents in the present study pointed out that, in some significant ways, spatial divisions by ethnicity have replaced those by denomination, although certain sectarian concentrations remain. Many of the highly diverse minority ethnic communities are at least fourth generation, some much longer. In general, they have congregated in three deprived inner wards: Abercromby, Dingle and especially Granby (Parkinson, 1994). Ben-Tovim (1988) has judged the situation of the largest group, people of Afro-Caribbean and mixed race origin, long established in the city from the time of its role as a major slave-trade metropolis, together with Somalis, as the most deprived. It is this community whose grievances have been the most articulated, assuming its most radical form in the series of riots in the city. The Somalis are also among the earliest settlers in significant numbers, from the First World War. But limited contact with the wider community and, spatially very concentrated in Granby, their lack of facility in English has contributed to the reported problems of 'capacity building'. Torkington (1991) confirms Ben-Tovim's assessment that they were among the most disadvantaged in terms of education, health and social outcomes, something which was still substantially observable a decade later (Foundation for Civil Society, 2000). In addition, the city houses the oldest large Chinese community in the UK, visible in its extensive China Town. Forming a self-contained labour market, more than 90 per cent of adults have been engaged in catering, contributing to low unemployment rates. Nonetheless, there have been criticisms over time of their having been poorly served by social facilities and housing (Loh Lynn, 1982), although subsequent voluntary sector provision has ameliorated this situation.

Finally, despite its reputation, successive official censuses have recorded a below average proportion of 'foreigners' in Marseilles. In 1990, for example, they amounted to just 7 per cent of the total, although this term excludes French-born minorities. In the city, as in the rest of France, the decline in Italian immigration during the 1960s was replaced by that from Maghreb. In fact, an established Maghrebin local community dates back to the First World War, with the central district of Belsunce and its famous bazaar as its initial base, and by 1975 they comprised 40 per cent of the population there, although there was increasing dispersal to the northern estates (Sanmarco & Morel, 1985; Donzel, 1988; Peraldi, 2001). More recent census data point to a growing salience of spatial distribution by ethnicity: there is a large concentration of North Africans in the centre but densities are even higher in the northern estates.

Evidence of discrimination

Pervasive discrimination has been recorded in many local sources. In Spain the large Romany population bore the original brunt of prejudice. In the past 30 years new groups have become its objects. Data from surveys in Barcelona in the 1980s indicated that over two-thirds of respondents were victims of racial insults and almost half claimed that they had been barred from local facilities such as bars; 40 per cent suspected denial of tenancies due to this motive (Carlota, 1987). In the same period Vintró i Castells (1991a) recorded the commonly expressed reservations of the host community to residing in close propinquity to immigrants. To tackle these problems the city council in the early 1990s established a commission for civil rights and in 1997 it convened a participatory advisory council on ethnic affairs incorporating the growing number of actors in the field (Morén-Alegret, 2001).

In a survey in the late 1980s a relatively low proportion of respondents in Genoa (one-third) reported having suffered victimisation (ILRES, 1991), although it predates the moral panic unleashed in the city by the growth in the numbers of asylum seekers and illegal immigrants. During the 1990s opinions seemed to have hardened here and in other Italian cities. Reacting to pressure from the host population, in 1993 the authorities sanctioned a crackdown on illegal immigrants in the Centro Storico, focussing on drugs, prostitution and illegal tenancies with an ultimate goal being deportation. It prompted riots among those who felt most victimised. Several respondents to the present study reported that policing particularly of the immigrant population in the historic core has remained intense, reaching something of a peak in the run-up to the G8 summit in the city in 2001. One respondent also recorded consistent harassment by street-level officers in their work with immigrants, even though their project had been cleared with middle management of the police authority. Finally, some investigations have centred on the role of the national and local press in fomenting prejudicial attitudes by equating the presence of immigrants with a 'crisis' of high crime rates (e.g. Torti, 1992; Somma, 1999).

Prejudice in Germany towards the large Turkish population is well documented and during the 1990s was extended to asylum seekers and, in particular, Romany and Sinti. According to respondents in this study, a link with a sharp rise in crime has been commonly made to residents of inner city areas of Hamburg, such as Karolinenviertel, and the increase in this population group. For much of the study period, German approaches to race relations have been typified as 'top-down', with limited engagement of the communities themselves, and primarily oriented to the assimilation of the second generation, albeit with poorly elaborated strategies (Hanhörster-Schiewer, 1999). The sponsoring of self-help has been prominent in Hamburg, including projects provoking opposition among the wider neighbourhood and some contentious coverage in local newspapers (see, for example, the case of the creation of the 'Roma Club' in STEG [1993] and Hamburger Abendblatt [2001a]). The city also instigated a special cultural budget for minorities from 1981 and convened a standing conference in 1990 to monitor their employment situation.

Racial discrimination contributed to a series of riots in both France and the UK. Liverpool's inner city was a principal location as early as 1972 and on several occasions throughout the 1980s, not least due to complaints about police harassment (University of Liverpool, 1991; Merrifield, 1995). Policy in the city is regulated by national race relations legislation which has been in place since 1965, with a dedicated equality commission established in 1976. However, the stance of the city council under Militant was indicted for raising the temperature, at a time when no councillor came from the ethnic minorities, where there was an official atmosphere hostile to effecting equal opportunities measures, particularly in municipal job recruitment, and resistance to subsidising dedicated housing associations. Some of these effects outlasted its political domination and delayed more positive policy responses, such as ethnic monitoring (see, for example, Ben-Tovim, 1983, 1988; Liverpool Black Caucus, 1986; PSS, 1994; Liverpool City Council, 1995b). New national measures in 2000 extended the monitoring of procedures which might be perpetuating institutional racism in services such as health and the police.

Violence against the growing Algerian population in Marseilles was unleashed as a result of the Algerian War of Independence and the pressures of receiving the repatriated *pieds noirs* (White, 1984). Resentment among the host population grew from the late 1960s, when the Maghrebin began entering the city in larger numbers, the suspicion being that such immigration was a deliberate tactic of the Deferre mayoralty to promote a low wage economy and to undermine the negotiating power of the white working class (see Pinson & Bekkar, 1999). From the mid-1980s, the *Front National* achieved considerable local success exploiting here (and elsewhere) the delicate issue of sanctioning the building of mosques. Their effective marshalling of opinion resulted in a drift to the party in the 1988 presidential elections among *pieds noirs* voters in the central districts (Mazauric, 1990). Thereafter, there has been the continuing shibboleth of the wearing of the *hijab* (Feldblum, 1993), initially in schools and re-emerging in 2003 in relation to identity card photographs. In the late 1980s, Mayor Vigouroux was attempting a wider policy networking of immigrant groups by establishing a special ethnic relations department (Mazauric, 1990). But, during the same period, there was also concern in city hall and among some economic actors such as the Chamber of Commerce, lest the large Maghreb presence in Belsunce might be constraining image reconstruction and limiting the commercial and tourist potential of the city (e.g. Obadia *et al.*, 1989). On the other hand, the mayor was keen to distance himself from the ongoing 're-conquest' discourse that had been entertained in some quarters (Sinounet, 1988). The strong spatial containment of the Maghreb community was identified as a factor in the relatively low rate of racial tension during the Gulf War of 1991, contrary to experiences of growing islamophobia elsewhere in France (Donzel, 1993). However, continuing prevarication on the part of the city council in the 1990s over the issue of mosque building did little to stimulate the compliance of aggrieved communities which the authorities wished to court in their plans for neighbourhood regeneration (Moore, 2001).

Together with access to employment and education, the prime constraint on the life chances of most minority ethnic communities arises from the operation of the housing market, with all available official statistics consistently highlighting an over-representation of these groups in the poorest accommodation. Waldorf (1990) singles out the lack of entry of more recent immigrants to social housing as critical, unleashing multiple spill-over effects relating to affordability and adequacy of accommodation on offer to them. On the other hand, Ratcliffe (1997), using small-area statistical analysis, cites British evidence of converging tenure patterns between young whites and minority households with UK-born heads.

Social housing policies can be discriminatory on several counts: either entry to that sector is rendered the more difficult by long residence requirements or minorities are allocated the worst properties. Respondents pointed to low aggregate access in Barcelona and Genoa. In Hamburg and Germany as a whole, the policy of imposing quotas, implemented to promote a greater social mix, in effect puts a limit on the access of the ethnic group to social housing in more desirable areas once that ceiling is reached, exacerbating their concentration in the least popular units (Bremer, 1999). Past allocation policies in Liverpool largely consigned ethnic minorities to certain inner city neighbourhoods, although in the early 1990s a system of 'ethnic coding' – albeit initially in these localities – has been employed with the aim of catering more effectively to their needs and has also resulted in greater customised targeting among housing associations (Liverpool City Council, 1992). In France, minority groups have been twice as dependent on social housing as the white population, but typically this has led to marked ethnic spatial concentration, as already reported in the case of Marseilles, although measures have been taken since the early 1990s to seek means of improving access for under-privileged groups by diversifying tenant composition (Pinson & Bekkar, 1999).

Nor have other municipal policies necessarily improved the lot of the minority community, particularly the new arrivals. Action in Barcelona, Marseilles and Genoa in the field of public health, for example, has led to the closure of illegal housing and hotels in the inner city, and without adequate guarantees of alternative accommodation has merely meant the displacement of their former residents to slum property. Crisis management by city authorities in respect of the inflow of new immigrants in the 1990s led, in Hamburg for example, to their offloading into cheap hotels of dubious quality and function, as well as the hasty conversion of containerships for emergency accommodation (SPD, 1992; BAGS, 1998).

Discriminatory allocation practices in the private-rented sector have been investigated in cities such as Hamburg. Several respondents to this study pointed out that certain groups such as the Romany were housed in seriously overcrowded accommodation in Karolinenviertel. A similar scenario has been reported in Centro Storico, some of the appalling lack of amenities in the worst rented property here barely deserving the nomination 'housing', for which exorbitant rents under mafia control have often been charged (ILRES, 1991; Campani, 1993). Even beneath this layer is the resort of those, like illegal immigrants without alternatives, to the remaining cheap hotel rooms in multiple occupation or, as in Barcelona from the mid-1990s, to the re-emerging shanty-town developments.

Finally, in some cities prejudicial attitudes have translated into growing support for frankly racist parties. Lower voting propensities in inner city areas and the fact that such support has tended to be more spatially diffuse must be taken into consideration in assessing underlying currents (for the example of Marseilles in the 1980s, see Donzel & Hayot, 1989). In addition, voting patterns may, in part, be contingent on the degree to which ethnic minorities themselves represent a strong concentrated electoral base, as in Liverpool, or whether, for the greatest part, they are deprived of voting rights, as in Genoa, Barcelona and Hamburg. The strength of the far right vote will also be contingent on the extent to which mainstream parties have resorted to 'robust' responses in rhetoric or action on race-related issues.

Voting behaviour in Ciutat Vella in municipal elections, 1995–2003, demonstrates continuing support for the socialists, albeit at declining strength, broadly in line with trends in Barcelona as a whole. New far right parties have not emerged. Since the late 1980s, reactions to the growing presence of immigrants in Italy have been reflected in the rise in electoral support for parties of the radical right (Campani, 1993). Municipal voting returns for Centro Storico during the period 1971–1990 indicate a consistent excess support over the city average for the far right MSI party, albeit within a declining overall trend (Comune di Genova, 2002). What has been noticeable since is the bifurcation of voting in the circumscription to which Centro Storico now belongs – and, to a lesser extent, in the city as a whole – with much of the vote in 2002 shared among the left and parties like *Forza Italia* and *Alleanza Nazionale*, owing much of their support to an anti-immigration ticket. During the early 1990s in Hamburg the right-wing Republican Party was gaining strength in deprived neighbourhoods, although there were exceptions such as St Pauli and Altona, in part a function of the weight of the student and gentrifier vote (Friedrichs, 1998). Thereafter, the Republicans have fared less well. For example, after peaking at over 6 per cent of the vote in Mitte in the 1993 city election (one of their best results among the boroughs) their share declined to 0.1 per cent in 2001. Racism has not been reflected in a strong vote for the far right either in Liverpool as a whole or in the inner city wards, where currently representation is broadly split between Liberal Democrats and Labour.

Support for the *Front National* has been more consistent in Marseilles – and in much of the rest of France, although the party suffered a setback in the parliamentary elections of 2002. From the early 1980s the *Front National* made the 'islamification' of large tracts of the centre of Marseilles a clarion call for 'reclamation', attracting by the late 1980s in various elections almost a quarter of the vote in the city. In the first round of the 2001 municipal election the *Front National* and the break away MNR party obtained about 15 per cent of the vote in the first electoral sector (which includes arrondissement 1) and failed to be elected there. On the other hand the vote for the extreme right was higher in the second sector (which includes arrondissements 2 and 3) and the MNR was elected. Miguet (2002) has analysed the results of the national elections of the following year. In the first round vote for the presidential candidates, support for these two parties nationally was stronger in the east and in regions of high unemployment and with a large minority population, being higher among males. Fear of crime was widely attributed to their success in attaining a combined vote of almost 20 per cent. Their vote in arrondissements 2 and 3 of Marseilles was even higher, at between 29 and 32 per cent, and higher still in the northern arrondissement 14. However, as stated, their electoral fortunes were reversed in the elections for the chamber of deputies.

The sum of evidence about the contemporary situation of ethnic minorities in Europe's inner cities challenges assumptions of a progressive escape from deprived 'back' to more affluent 'front' spaces (Dickens, 1990). Indeed, Musterd and de Winter (1998) argue that the contemporary urban concentration of minorities has all too often intensified, despite a general decentralisation of employment and housing systems, exacerbating what is already a problematic situation.

Issues of governance

A plurality of governing bodies at various tiers in the Greater Barcelona area – over 200 – has existed for much of the study period. As a remedy the city has taken the lead in coordinating a series of broadly based 'metropolitan plans' since the 1980s, embracing its hinterland. The current formulation, approved in 1998, outlines a horizon extending into the 2020s (Nel.lo, 1998). A similar scenario was reported in the Marseilles sub-region where several attempts since the 1960s to introduce 'metropolitanisation' failed to amount to much, until new measures were implemented in the closing years of the last century (see Chapter 1 and Donzel [2001]). Problems along these lines in Genoa were compounded by volatile political formations at both central and local level. These critically failed to provide firm legislative or funding bases to sustain policy direction, creating vacuums filled by a profusion of private actors, motivated more by profit than innovation (Jodogne, 1991; Seassaro, 1991). Efforts to remedy the state of local governance in the city and elsewhere in Italy has been a prolonged affair, extending throughout the 1990s. The period under review has also witnessed significant changes in local government in Liverpool. Merseyside County Council, created in 1974, was abolished by central government just over a decade later. Town Hall politics did not fill the gap: Parkinson (1988) judges the 10 years from 1974 under Liberal direction as a profoundly missed opportunity to push through a strategy of positive transformation, due, not least, to the lack of overall majority control. Thereafter, followed a period when the 'new urban left' Trotskyite Militant Tendency was in an increasingly provocative driving seat in the eyes of Westminster: something which is still vivid in both local and national memories (see below). The mushrooming of separate agencies, many non-governmental, on which the city has historically been dependent did not initially develop in the spirit of partnership (Robson *et al.*, 1994). Greater stability was experienced in Hamburg, which, among the sample, enjoyed the widest competences in this policy arena, being at once both a city and a federal state. However, constraints reported by respondents – at least until the 1990s – arose from the deep compartmentalisation of power bases within the city administration which hindered across-the-board strategic approaches. Accordingly, attempts at organisational innovation tended to supplement rather than replace pre-existing arrangements.

Vertical relations

As a policy agenda regeneration was a comparative newcomer at the beginning of the study period. Significantly, it coincided with the arrival of new political actors such as regional instances. Given the inchoate distributions of remits, it provided a ready battleground for disputes among the various tiers of government over competences. The possibility of obtaining increased funding or of attracting major investment projects only heightened the political stakes. In the present cities, relations during the 1980s were particularly problematic, even when those tiers were under the same political control, though they were most acute when they were not. In general, within the current sample, there has been a noticeable improvement in collaboration since then.

The state of relations between the Catalan government under Pujol of the nationalist *CiU* and the socialist city mayor, Maragall, is well documented. These partly centred on cultural competition between the two political entities, the Catalan parliament, a beneficiary of the rapid route to devolution in Spain, being particularly jealous to protect its alliance formations within its capital (Keating, 2001). Initially the mayor had opted for public-led regeneration in response to pressures from the neighbourhood association from whom he had derived considerable electoral support (Pol, 1989; Newman & Thornley, 1996). However, projects tended to be small-scale and ad hoc (Gausa, 1999). After 1985, when speculation was mounting about the success of the bid for the Olympic Games a more economically oriented, image-marketing strategy – with increased funding attached – was adopted. It was one which would court alliances among elites in the city and Catalonia, thereby encroaching on what the autonomous government saw as more within its remit. Matters were not improved when the region, against the wish of the city leadership, abolished the Barcelona metropolitan corporation in 1987 which, in terms of sub-regional strategic planning, was increasingly perceived as a competitor to Pujol's ambitions (e.g. Ajuntament de Barcelona, 1991; Pascual i Esteve, 1999). Once the Olympics were awarded to the city, there were growing tensions about the role of affordable housing in the overall planning of the project. Maragall (1986) had already openly complained of the subsidies the region, in the face of land shortages within the city, offered to the young to leave to seek accommodation elsewhere – exacerbating social imbalances – and later in an interview expressed his regret about the paucity of social housing in the Olympic village (La Vanguardia, 1991).

Similarly, at various points in the study period, Genoa city and its province were of a different political complexion than the Liguria region. Here, there has been a tendency for the region and sometimes the province to concern themselves with urban policies that would have been more appropriate at the municipal level (Seassaro, 1993; Governa & Salone, 2002). Mitterand's policies for decentralisation in the early 1980s fell within the ministerial portfolio of Deferre, who was at the same time the mayor of Marseilles. Paradoxically, despite the mayor's strong-hold on the city (see below), the effect of the innovation was to strengthen the negotiating power of the regions and départements with the state in comparison to that of the municipalities. The effect was to compromise the room for manoeuvre that his successor, Vigouroux, enjoyed in promoting a new strategic approach towards urban renewal (e.g. Fourest, 1989; Donzel, 1993).

However, tensions of these kinds pale into insignificance when compared to the situation in Liverpool between 1983 and 1987. As mentioned earlier, this was a period when the city council was under the domination of Militant whose principal spokesman was Hatton. Whilst Merseyside local authorities had often been motivated by rivalry, it was central government that was Militant's *bête noir*, something from which the rest of the municipalities in the county and the voluntary agencies within the city sought to distance themselves. The period was recorded by almost all respondents in the present study in what can only be termed as the frankest and strongest of terms, particularly with regard to the leading lights of Militant. In fact, it was inevitable that tensions would mount. Even before Militant took over, Thatcher's government had acted to break what it saw as a chronic mood of pessimism within the local political establishment by establishing a minister for Merseyside, initially in the person of a senior member of cabinet, Heseltine, and by creating regeneration agencies within the city which would answer directly to him (see next chapter). In this, municipal control was by-passed, something the incoming local leadership intensely resented and which led to, at best, cool and, more often, non-existent collaboration. Furthermore, Westminster had been tightening fiscal control over local government. These and other issues were to be a red rag to a bull for those in control of Militant within the city. For one, it chose to privilege a social housing-led regeneration strategy under its direct control, whilst the government was energetically pursuing a more economic and commercially led agenda and, more generally, downgrading the role of public housing. For another, it attempted to circumvent budgetary restrictions through a range of 'creative accountancy' measures and through the unsanctioned raising of loans from foreign banks. Critically at odds with Labour's national leadership, matters reached a head in 1987 when those councillors who had been party to these decisions were surcharged for expenditures and disqualified from office by the House of Lords (for different perceptions of events, see Crick, 1986; Hatton, 1988; Parkinson, 1988; Lawless, 1989). Subsequently, relations between the city and Westminster have been much more pacific with a substantial meeting of minds over regeneration priorities. Nonetheless, as stated earlier, these events inflicted damage to Liverpool's image that had long-term implications for its attractiveness to inward investors.

In comparison with these sorts of tensions, relations between the municipalities and lower-tier entities within their borders, for much of the period under review, have been typified more by the management of consultation. In Barcelona decentralised districts were implemented immediately after the first democratically elected municipality in 1979, deputy mayors being appointed by the mayor according to local electoral strengths and serving as a first port of call for involving community-based groups. More formal incorporation structures were introduced from the mid-1980s with the convening of neighbourhood participation commissions (Gomá & Brugue, 1994; Turró, 1998). Nonetheless, until recent years the sub-municipal level could draw on few effective powers (Morén-Alegret, 2001). Elections for councils at the level of circumscriptions in Genoa first took place in 1981, but they have largely been merely consultative, and cannot block decisions. Although the size of circumscriptions was enlarged in the 1990s and, as part of a package (discussed in the previous chapter), some extended remit was conferred, their effective powers remain relatively constrained. As several respondents emphasised, the frequent replacement of their aldermen, to reflect changing political strengths in the city, has done little to improve their influence over policy-making. At sub-city level, Hamburg has formally constituted and elected boroughs (*Bezirke*). Until the change of city council in 1997, however, the City State administration dominated the urban regeneration agenda although, thereafter, a greater range of competences has been devolved. Local administrations were established in 1982 for groupings of *arrondissements* in Marseilles. Again, their essential character is mostly advisory. Finally, formal decentralisation in Liverpool has largely taken the form of local area offices for municipal services, although in recent years area committees of city councillors have been formed, based on ward groupings with 'area assemblies' to enhance local participation pathways (Best Value, 2000), something harking back to experiments in the mid-1970s.

The impact of local political leadership

From the late 1980s there has been a growing focus in urban governance literature on the intervening impact of the nature of political leadership on regeneration prospects, particularly with regard to the quality of relations with economic elites: whether antagonistic, collaborative, monopolistic and so forth. Judd and Parkinson (1990), in their comparative examination of 12 case studies, nominate Hamburg as having the most unified coalition to respond to transformation pressures, whilst – at least until the late 1980s but for different reasons – deficits were particularly acute in the case of Liverpool and Marseilles. For Friedrichs (1993) this theoretical framework offers a more sophisticated analysis than simple models of urban trajectories. He contributes to theorising by speculating that the hold of economic elites on the traditional industrial base is a key factor. Where the latter has veered towards mono-functional dominance (as in the case of port cities) there is a higher propensity for such elites to respond in a reactionary manner, seeking to preserve their subsidised privileges and delaying the establishment of new key actors, thereby prolonging transformation adjustments.

In terms of specifying the agenda for the urban renewal of their cities the role of the elected mayors has been particularly prominent in Barcelona, Hamburg and Marseilles. Critically related was the opportunity afforded in the early 1980s to marshal elite coalitions to support long-term, overarching responses to remedy the mounting transformation pains affecting key sectors of the traditional local economies. This stands in contradistinction to what the overwhelming majority of commentators see as the destructive approach during that period adopted in Liverpool, or the substantial lack of solid action in Genoa.

The immediate feature of local leadership in Barcelona is its relative longevity under socialist-led administration. Since the first democratic elections in 1979 the mayors have enjoyed a high national (and international) profile. Serra, in office until 1982, went on to be a senior member of Gonzalez's cabinets. He was succeeded by Maragall, mayor until 1997. He was to oversee the crucial period of EU entry, preparation for the Olympics and exploitation of their aftermath and was a central figure in the relaunching of the city as a major Mediterranean metropolis. In turn, his successor Clos was the local mayor of the Ciutat Vella and a director of regeneration efforts there that contributed significantly to the reconstruction of the image of Barcelona. The award of the 1992 Olympics was an irresistible prize that brought into an engagement with Maragall major economic actors who had previously entertained their suspicions of the socialists. Anticipating the gains that could be derived, the mayor moved from a small-scale, largely socially-driven regeneration strategy to one that embraced robust entrepreneurial ambitions. There was criticism particularly within the neighbourhood movements of the downgrading of the previous social dimension in favour of explicit commercially-driven priorities. On the other hand, this networking, like the establishment of public–private joint enterprises, created an environment propitious to the mainstreaming of powerful cross-sectoral partnerships. These were to be supported by a wide gamut of new public management approaches advancing an agenda that was consciously pro-active and international in focus (Nel.lo, 1998; Pascual i Esteve, 1999; Raventós, 2000). Crucially, it laid the ground for policy lines that have been sustained during the mayoralty of Clos since 1997.

To a large extent this scenario is shared by Hamburg, long a stronghold of the Social Democratic Party (SPD), although during the 1980s and early 1990s it had to cede some ground to newer parties (Freie und Hansestadt Hamburg, 1993). In 2001 the party lost control of the city to a coalition led by the conservative CDU. The resignation of the SPD centrist mayor, Klose, in 1981 and his replacement by von Dohnanyi provided an import-ant opportunity for a change of direction in the management of economic policy in the city state. Dispensing with reliance on Keynesianism, the new mayor in 1983 presented to the principal local elites a new strategy for an entrepreneurial approach to economic regeneration. Encapsulated in the slogan '*Unternehmen Hamburg – Enterprise Hamburg*', it recognised the urgent need to diversify the economy, away from reliance on the port and argued the case for the rigorous pursuit of inward investment. In its pursuit, close alliance was forged with the powerful Chamber of Com-merce, an institution which had already specified its own plans for the commercial rejuvenation, advocating decentralised 'growth poles' around the periphery of the city centre, as well as some inner city and harbour reconstruction (*Das Hoch im Norden – the Highpoint in the North*). Thus, the scene was set for a strong partnership, at least among the most influential in Hamburg society, although there were also warnings that these blueprints paid scant regard to likely social impacts on those less well-placed (Dangschat, 1993). Incorporating other interests such as the major banks, one concrete result of this elite consensus was the creation of a development corporation in 1985, as the initiator of public–private joint responses to economic and infrastructural renewal (Dangschat & Ossen-brügge, 1990; Berger & Schmalfeld, 1999). Accordingly, a proactive policy was already in place before the windfall of Unification and EU expansion, discussed earlier.

In 1988 the mayoralty was assumed by Voscherau, who represented the younger generation on the right of the SPD. A few years into his office, the city government was made increasingly aware of mounting social polarisation. Growing wealth for a minority in the fashionable areas contrasted with deteriorating conditions in other localities. Fundamentally, there was a concern about the consequences for the political establishment of the steady attrition of electoral participation among the most deprived who had, hitherto, been SPD voters. Some obvious sign of action was clearly needed. Whilst retaining the broad economic strategy of his predecessor, the mayor supported proposals for socially motivated neighbourhood projects which, as already discussed, were among the most innovative in the country (Kürpick

& Weck, 1998). Nonetheless, Voscherau had also publicly committed himself to plans for major residential and commercial redevelopment (*Hafencity*) along the Elbe, adjacent to the city centre, by means of a project that was unambiguously targeting the top end of the market. The neglect of the housing affordability issue this implied was something tacitly acknowledged by Runde, his successor in 1997, who had made urban regeneration a leading issue in his campaign for the mayoralty (Stadtdialog, 2001). The evolving urban entrepreneurial policy line has been reinforced by the new leadership since 2001 under the CDU mayor, von Beust.

The long hegemony enjoyed by the socialist mayoralty of Deferre in Marseilles (1953–86) had in no small measure continued the clientelistic traditions of the city through his strong hold on local elites (Hoffmann-Martinot, 1992; Donzel, 1993). His death in office destabilised political arrangements at a time when the city was also suffering the effects of budgetary crisis. However, the hiatus it caused provided the opportunity for a reappraisal of the existing balance of power (Donzel & Guilhaumou, 2001). It was in this environment that new coalitions were to be formed by the new mayor, Vigouroux, also a socialist but a centrist, and influential actors, such as the Chamber of Commerce, anxious to prepare to exploit potentials of the European Single Market of 1992 (Redempteur, 1987). Vigouroux aimed to promote a regeneration strategy that would at least attempt some balance between economic and social objectives. His blueprint *Marseille Metropole, Ville Solidaire* was the result: a holistic strategy, targeting most deprived areas, but also set to upgrade what was – and still is – regarded as an unimpressive city centre for France's second metropolis (e.g. AGAM, 1993a). Incorporating policies towards the urban infrastructure, employment, education, health, social services and culture, its overall intention was to complement other interventions that had been specified in the urban contracts negotiated with the state and region, discussed in Chapter 1 (Donzel, 1990). This was subsequently followed by a 'grand project' targeting much of the central and port area for major commercial, cultural and residential investment (*Euroméditerranée* – see next chapter). Municipal elections, in 1995 in which investment in neighbourhood renewal had been a major issue, saw the election of a centre-right formation under the mayoralty of Gaudin, of the UDF. Gaudin, like Deferre in an earlier era, benefited from the possibility of simultaneously holding both national and local offices (*cumul des mandats*) in France. As urban affairs minister in the first government under Chirac's presidency, he anchored his local approach in the strongly entrepreneurial focus of his national 'Urban Relaunch Pact' (Donzel, 1998). He was comfortably re-elected in 2001.

Left-of-centre formations constituted the municipal leadership of Genoa from the mid-1970s to mid-1980s, during which a new governance and urban regeneration blueprint (*Progetto Genova*) was conceived (Comune di

Genova, 1979). It was also a time when social housing was afforded greater priority. However, with growing budgetary deficits and the volatility of subsequent multiparty *Pentopartito* coalitions, momentum for programmatic response was lost, displaced by a tactical reliance on a disparate series of over-varnished projects (discussed in Chapter 3) which, in the event, failed to deliver the expected outcomes in terms of a sustained re-launching of the city (Seassaro, 1991). Matters were not improved when the mayor and some of his colleagues were suspended from office and imprisoned briefly on suspicion of fraudulent disbursement of public funds. Nonetheless, the instigation of elected mayors in Italy from 1993 did in general provide a positive new departure point in providing the city with a catalyst to integrate the growing range of national regeneration policies with locally formulated designs. In Genoa, a leftist independent mayor, Sansa, was to launch this new approach. But the main actor has been Pericu, the incoming mayor, who owed his electoral success in 1997 to the left-leaning 'Olive Tree' alliance. He was re-elected in 2002. He and the team he appointed evidenced some degree of lesson-learning from the more successful competitor cities in the *Mediterranean Arc* and its hinterland in terms of the need for a more robust urban entrepreneurialism. Accordingly, under his instigation a long-term strategic plan was developed for the city (see next chapter).

In comparison to other large regional cities in the UK, Liverpool has never been a classic Labour fiefdom. In the period under review it has been under Liberal (now Liberal Democrat) and both hard-line and moderate Labour control. Given the tensions in Liverpool during the Militant era of the 1980s, important mediating leadership had to be forthcoming from outside the city council. Local economic representative elites were relatively weak: for example, in comparison to the other cities in the study, the role of the Chamber of Commerce, largely an organ of small and medium enterprises, had not been prominent. Thus, it was to be left to the good offices of the Anglican Bishop, Sheppard, and the Catholic Archbishop, Warlock, who in many ways represented agents of truce, to convey local interests to Westminster (Parkinson, 1990). After the demise of Militant a moderate labour formation took leadership in the Town Hall and initiated a more accommodating stance (Parkinson & Russell, 1994). The *rapprochement* between central and local government has survived party changes in municipal control (currently Liberal Democrat) and the city's approach to its regeneration has been very much along the lines of those of government, especially after New Labour assumed power in 1997 (Northern Housing, 2000). In fact, several respondents have judged the pervasive influence of Blairism as now more important in directing local policy than which party currently happens to be in power in the Town Hall. These improved relations proved vital in negotiating the successful outcome for Objective One status in two rounds of EU Structural Fund allocations from 1994 (Evans, 2002 – see also Chapters 3 and 6).

Conclusion

The present cities constitute a spectrum of success in economic regeneration. Yet, whatever their growth trajectory, evidence is abundant of the substantial ineffectiveness of filter processes in decanting benefits throughout all neighbourhoods. Thus, apart from ageing populations in many inner city localities, concerns have tended to revolve around urban deprivation with a twin-peaking in parts of the inner core and in the periphery. Increasingly – whether or not triggered by riots or the fear of them – this issue has crystallised around the situation of ethnic minorities and racism. Since the first Gulf War this has taken on more of an islamophobic dimension in cities where Moslem populations are prominent. To this must be added the contemporary moral panic about the 'flood' of asylum seekers. At times, in some of the cities, this has been reflected in the ballot box.

Issues of governance have been a prominent element in urban renewal. To varying degrees the cities, in facing up to the challenges of globalisation, have embraced lessons from 'new urban politics'. Thus, these and other cities are now presented as managed packages and marketed as commodities. One indispensable component is the stress on the 'image of place'. This is amply demonstrated in contemporary styles of municipal entrepreneurialism. Growing competition for inward public and private funding demands efficient institution-building through 'growth coalitions', broad partnership that can readily demonstrate the added value of 'associative capital'. These coalitions are also perceived as an essential aid to promoting internally sourced economic upswings, through the exploitation of the potential of niche markets. And, so it is argued, they are a vital prop in the reconstruction of the image of cities (see Boyle & Rogerson, 2001).

One product of these preoccupations has been the instigation of internal organisational modernisation, reflecting the importance attached to ever-wider cross-sectoral collaboration. Thus, the city fathers in Hamburg implemented reforms of first-rank bureaucracies, linking health with environment, and labour market with the economy; Liverpool introduced corporate management in which housing and consumer affairs are integrated. There is an insistence, too, that only a sub-regional dimension can deliver an effective integrated strategy across levels and sectors of intervention which, additionally, would facilitate the creation of more spatially equitable local fiscal systems. It is fair to say that developments in the study period have not been all one way. There has been a notable delay in establishing some form of 'metropolitanisation' and, in the case of Barcelona and Liverpool, existing sub-regional entities were, in fact, abolished. Similarly problematic has been the quality of relations between existing tiers of administration, where competition can be all the keener given the mounting political stakes of leadership in marketing location. It follows that politics still matters in the ability to engage – or provoke – the generality of actors, but its framework is now much broader than traditional party formations.

Certainly, pro-active networking in the early and mid-1980s provided a clear head start for Barcelona and Hamburg in negotiating their place in the emerging European urban hierarchy. Legal competences and sources of funding are critical here, too. Hamburg has been the most autonomous of the cities in regard to formulating regeneration strategies, whilst Marseilles, Genoa and Liverpool have been more dependent on programmes determined at higher political levels. How these kinds of factors have impacted on the rejuvenation of inner city neighbourhoods is taken up in the following chapters.

Current statistical and documentary material, with references to limited archival sources may be obtained from the following websites:

Barcelona

Policy documentation produced by the city	www.bcn.es./urbanisme www.bcn.es/infopime
Policy documents produced by the region	www.gencat.net
General site	www.bcn.es/estadistica

Genoa

Policy documentation produced by the city	www.comune.genova.it
Policy documents produced by the region	www.regione.liguria.it
Statistics	www.istat.it

Hamburg

Policy documentation	www.hamburg.de
Statistics	www.hamburg.de/Behoerden/stala

Liverpool

Policy documentation	www.liverpool.gov.uk
Statistics	www.statistics.gov.uk www.neighbourhood.statistics.gov.uk www.upmystreet.com (for local 'ACORN' profiles)

Marseilles

Policy documentation produced by the city	www.mairie-marseille.fr
Policy documentation produced by the département	www.cg.13.fr
Policy documentation produced by the region	www.cr-paca.fr
Statistics	www.insee.fr www.documentation-provence.org

Part II
Inner City Regeneration Strategies

3
Regenerating the Physical Structure

Issues relating to the infrastructural regeneration strategies pursued over the past three decades in the five inner city areas are addressed in this chapter. Examination of policy is broadly chronological, indicating which actor was the prime instigator, and is accompanied by brief evaluative comments, a topic taken up more substantively in Chapter 5. As should be apparent from the previous chapters, the degree of involvement of national government varies considerably, with the UK and French governments being the most *dirigiste*. In addition, in the three Mediterranean countries, regional instances have been significant players. At city level, as will be shown, authorities have entered into a variety of implicit or more formalised collaborations with voluntary associations, including those emanating directly from the targeted communities, and with commercial actors. In all cases, during the 1990s more explicit forms of horizontal and vertical partnership have been espoused. During that decade, too, EU institutions became more prominently engaged in the field, assessment of their substantive involvement being the subject of Chapter 6.

The sample spans a broad spectrum of physical problems in inner city Europe. In the north, housing quality has tended to be more varied, ranging from old stock lacking basic amenities to social housing in need of upgrading, and there is also the problem of the redevelopment of brownfield sites. On the other hand, the immediately visible physical characteristic of the inner core of the three southern cities has been the very poor state of old housing stock, mostly in the privately rented sector, cramped in medieval narrow street layouts, often incurring logistically difficult and expensive rehabilitation solutions. Furthermore, such areas have suffered from chronic lack of investment incentive for many landlords due to rent controls affording them very low returns. In Genoa and to a lesser extent Barcelona there has also been the dilemma of what to do about illegal landlords and tenants, and abandoned properties. In all of the cities, though less of a problem in Hamburg, the fact has been that many owners, whether occupiers or landlords, are elderly and/or poor and much of the stock is in multiple ownership, exacerbating the arrival at collective compliance.

Given the wide extent of potential coverage, investigation is necessarily selective: programmes largely restricted to slum clearance and funding schemes for the rehabilitation of individual properties have for the most part been excluded, although cumulatively they may have major impacts on areas. Included are policies for inner city rejuvenation which, whilst they may target relatively restricted areas, are intended to have a wider city or even sub-regional impact through upgrading the quality of infrastructure and enhancing collective image. Intervention schemas have ranged from the highly aggregate level, such as national plans in the French tradition; general town planning instruments and subsidiary neighbourhood land-use plans; large dedicated programmes for small-area regeneration funded by higher-tier authorities; municipal city-wide neighbourhood projects; through to those reserved for one or two localities.

Skifter Andersen (1999, 2003) has parsimoniously summarised the sorts of spheres of action which are to be addressed here. Among the different types of public regulation of tenure conditions he lists are rent control; tenancy protection; mortgage law; building and public health legislation; rehabilitation incentives provided by direct or fiscal subsidies; compulsory measures; and targeted or mainstream measures privileging preventive or curative interventions, clientele or property types. Each is subject to considerable cross-national variation, although he is among others identifying an emerging convergence of approach (see, for example, Maclennan *et al.*, 1996; Kleinman, 1998). Key elements of these trends include attempts to re-engage private landlords through rent deregulation, the search for reconciliation of housing affordability and access with wider concerns to do with social security, and sustainability. To these are added decentralisation of project implementation – either through local area management or 'contracting out' – and, above all, the abandoning of narrowly focussed bricks-and-mortar solutions in favour of across-the-board objectives.

Nonetheless, despite signs of convergence, policies concerning the physical fabric needs must address pressures specific to each inner city. Such pressures in cities like Barcelona and Hamburg have arisen from the encroachment of the central business district and other commercial interests. To these must be added the designs of private developers seeking readily 'retrievable' residential properties for upgrading and similar sites for new housing construction in a bid to exploit gentrification potentials. Closely associated, after the success of Baltimore, has been the rediscovery of dockland regeneration for commercial or high quality residential conversion (Jauhiainen, 1995). Among the cities under review, this has been typically assisted by the public purse but considerable social costs have been paid by others, primarily long-established communities or more recent ethnic minorities who find themselves squeezed out of the market or who suffer the effects of social peripheralisation 'in-proximity'.

Ciutat Vella

Barcelona historically has engaged in marked competition with Madrid as an Iberian metropolis of culture, particularly of the *avant-garde*. From the liberating effects of democratisation in 1977 a conscious policy of promoting the city and its ancient core, the Ciutat Vella, has been pursued, which has been central to these designs. However, it must be said that the Transition in Spain coincided with political recognition of mounting economic problems that had been repressed under Franco. The socialists formed a majority in the first democratically elected city council in 1979. Initially they entertained reservations about collaborating with the private sector, since many within the party were suspicious about accommodating the profit motive in urban renewal, which they regarded as an essentially social enterprise. This was soon to change and by the early 1980s there was growing official acknowledgement of the benefits that could accrue to the city by engaging commercial interests. These years proved crucial in terms of municipal alliance building, not least to alleviate the problems arising from tense relations with the nationalist-led Catalan government with which, after the acceleration of regional devolution in the late 1970s, policy competences were shared.

Wholesale regeneration of the city had been outlined in the 1976 metropolitan plan but, in the early years of democratic local government, small-scale disparate measures took primacy over programmatic responses (Granados-Cabezas, 1995). As discussed in the previous chapter, the party locally owed much of its success to the neighbourhood movement whose visions were firmly set on the rehabilitation of their own localities. The city fathers were minded to deliver. As Roca (1988) records, Barcelona was among the first Spanish cities to employ legislation of 1976 to engage in area regeneration, much of it concentrated in Ciutat Vella, which after revisions in 1981 extended subsidies for both public and private housing. In addition, to meet the demand for something immediately visible, the council bought up much available land and launched an investment programme to extend the range of public services.

Several commentators have pointed to the important regenerative platform created by the arrival of Bohigas as chief architect in 1980 and, 2 years later, the new mayor, Maragall (e.g. Esteban, 1999). Accordingly, in the early 1980s, specification of local area renewal within a broad city strategy was refined as an important re-packaging tactic to secure successful nomination as the site of the 1992 Olympic Games. Studies of the four *barris* of the inner city surveyed the distinct problems of each. They provided the basis for the formulation, in the first half of the decade, of neighbourhood-level projects (*PERIs*) according to the provisions of the 1976 plan. The *PERIs* detailed each intervention to be implemented, taking into account the wishes of the increasingly vocal communities concerned (Ajuntament de Barcelona, 1999; Gomà & Rosetti, 1999). Importantly, for its part the Catalan government also engaged in revitalisation of these and other neighbourhoods. Mindful of the fact that at that time one-fifth of all housing stock in the city had no hot water supply and that there was still a highly visible problem of shanty town developments, it pioneered measures to subsidise private rehabilitation (Direcció General d'Arquitectura i Habitatge, 1988; Valls, 2001). In sum, after decades of neglect under Franco, at the physical level alone, the outstanding task was enormous. The quality of much of the housing stock in degraded areas raised difficult questions about its viability and the profound lack of public open space in these neighbourhoods only made matters worse (Bohigas, 1986).

The award of the Olympic Games and EU entry, both achieved in 1986, became a focal point for a long planning phase, both preparatory and post-event, in order to fully exploit the city's ample metropolitan potential. These motives propelled the mayor, Maragall, into the centre-ground of important alliance building, although in this he had to contend with his competitor, Pujol, head of the Catalan government. To be the successful bidder, rapid and highly visible results were vital. It was clear that the narrow town planning ambitions of neighbourhood planning, contained in the 1976 plan, would simply not do; local economic development had to be added to the agenda (Gallén, 1999). Image reconstruction could not be delayed either. Among the actions stressed for their urgency were measures to assist the reconnection of the inner core to the sea. They were to be supplemented by the supply of more open space, particularly through the creation of new squares in the Ciutat Vella, as preliminary to the transfer of cultural and other 'monumental' facilities there. Work started in 1983 in the Mercè neighbourhood, adjacent to the main thoroughfare, Las Ramblas.

Prior to 1983 the neighbourhood plans had not been particularly strong on advocating engagement of private actors. That was swiftly to change. A decentralised office was opened in the heart of the locality to stimulate private rehabilitation. The later neighbourhood plans were more explicit in projecting private sector leverage. The new priorities were reinforced in 1986 by the introduction of 'integrated rehabilitation action areas' (*ARIs*). Whilst the pre-existing, somewhat disparate projects, were retained a more streamlined longer-term funding source was specified in which national, regional and municipal subsidies, and commercial loans were integrated. At the same time, in an attempt to accelerate regeneration outcome, the rate of compulsory purchases was expanded (Busquets, 1984; Abella, 1999). These reforms were presented within the envelope of a 15-year strategy. Initial prioritisation was to continue public-led interventions, but the aim was that these were to be rapidly followed by private actions, particularly as almost two-thirds of units requiring upgrading were in the private sector.

Guarantees were to be afforded to sitting tenants (Barcelona Societat, 1999). The rehabilitation agenda was broadened, with a significant proportion of the public budget reserved for the creation of public open space. Measures on education, health and social services, and policing were also to be adopted (Ripol-Millet, 1994; Ajuntament de Barcelona, 1997a). As for urban governance, a model of plural partnership was set in train. The first stages of its formation were to concentrate efforts on improving vertical relations between public tiers, but enhanced pathways for community participation were also to be built, taking advantage of the decentralisation of municipal government that had been occurring. Finally, to achieve a greater balance in infrastructural investment across the city, regeneration of the central area was to be supplemented by new 'growth poles' in nearby locations which were to be developed in partnership with the commercial sector (Pascual i Esteve, 1999). As a demonstration of the change of regeneration tactic, the last neighbourhood plan to be announced in this period, that for the coastal locality of Barceloneta, adjacent to what would be part of the Olympic Games development site, provided a formula for public–private partnership (Held, 1992). All these processes were carried forward – and considerably advanced – in the project for the Games themselves which incorporated international, as well as national and local actors. Apart from construction of the stadium this *grand projet* involved the building of the Olympic villages and the reclamation of the *Front Maritim*.

In the space of 5 years, then, the ambitions and governance of regeneration within the city had been radically reformed. Experiences during this period instilled a long-term preoccupation with sustainable development and continued enhancement of the physical attractiveness of the city, in part demonstrated in the *Barcelona posa't guapa* programme and the closure of many decrepit illegal bars and hotels. On the other hand, there were growing public suspicions – not least among residents of Ciutat Vella – that the social dimension of regeneration was being progressively sacrificed in favour of commercial motives. In their eyes, too many of the benefits derived from opening up the city to the sea and the embellishments associated with the Games were passing them by. They drew attention to the fact that most of the housing in the Olympic villages had been built for the open market, despite original plans for a greater supply of affordable units (Valls, 2001). For his part, the mayor sought to distance himself from these criticisms, pointing an accusing finger at the regional government which exercised the greater competence in housing matters (La Vanguardia, 1991).

Apart from being the largest project undertaken in Barcelona in the last century, the Games were important in other respects. Anticipatory planning in the form of a series of strategic blueprints for modernisation, initiated in 1988, aimed to sustain the impetus for growth the Olympics and the imminent Single European Market represented (Serra & Maragall, 1990). Crucially, as Marshall (1996) notes, the infrastructural project was essentially one in which the municipal authorities were in the driving seat, with the Catalan government primarily being concerned with the housing dimension. Significantly, too, public–private partnership became the principal mechanism for delivering the success of the project, albeit with the effect of reinforcing the more strictly entrepreneurial bias with a marginalisation of the social dimension. These partnerships, in which public funding was also more explicitly allocated to promoting entrepreneurial ambitions, would henceforth be conventionally applied to general planning practice, as initially demonstrated in the redevelopment for leisure and cultural use of the Old Port (Jauhiainen, 1995; Pascual i Esteve, 1999).

Yet, the first of the strategic plans – *Barcelona 2000* – pointedly bore the hallmarks of the city administration's desire to court wider public support by pointing to a need for an increased role of social housing for rent and purchase. In addition, it made reference to targeted interventions for clientele such as the elderly and to measures to tackle 'pockets of poverty'. All of this would be pursued within a wider approach stressing entrepreneurialism and the need for increased inward investment (Ajuntament de Barcelona, 1990). According to Newman and Thornley (1996), the planning style consolidated the mayor's position at the helm of traditional coalition formation for growth, incorporating the Chamber of Commerce, the unions, higher education and business into a broad consensus.

To advance the specific agenda of inner city rejuvenation a special joint venture, *Promoció Ciutat Vella*, was established in 1990. It was given the explicit remit of securing the retrievability of that part of the private housing stock that was still in a very poor state and subject to rental contracts, some of which were over 100 years old. Most of its activity was reserved for rehabilitation for rent with the aim of diversifying the social composition of the neighbourhoods, particularly for young families and the growing student population (Barcelona Societat, 1999).

The early 1990s were a time of preparation for the Games and for ensuring that planning gains would continue in their aftermath. For this purpose, an unambiguous socio-economic developmental strategy was embraced and was reflected in area actions associated with the ADES programme of 1990. Social pressures prompted something of a stronger stance on the part of the city administration in that the issue of affordable housing began to assume a greater prominence. Since EU entry, house prices had risen very sharply in the city and many of its young were quitting it, a cause for concern on the part of the mayor. Thus, in the new Housing Plan for 1992–95 produced by the regional government, the city had been able to secure that access for the young and the less prosperous would be addressed through diversification of subsidy regimes. The major scheme of this era – the long-awaited prolongation of the major arterial route, the *Diagonal*, southeastwards to the coast, together with the extension of the development of *Front Maritim*, increased the proportion of new housing to meet prevailing criteria of affordability (Valls, 2001). On the other hand, for Marshall (1996), whilst the second strategic plan for the city, produced in 1993, was more explicitly developmental, it bore all the hallmarks of privileging the economic agenda. Its reliance on neo-liberal solutions reinforced the role of public–private partnership. For the rest, it promoted the furthering of a 'festivalisation' of regeneration: within the Ciutat Vella, the upgrading of those squares and streets with any architectural interest continued at a pace. Areas within Raval, long regarded as irretrievable principally due to common fears about urban insecurity, were opened up. The major fire in 1994 at the Liceu Opera House, on the edge of this area, and its subsequent restoration furthered this approach and was accompanied by new museums, open spaces and yet more reclaimed enclaves (Subirós, 1999).

The upgrading of these previously hard-core areas of degradation rendered them suitable for gentrification, a process which continues to the present time. It has been attained by some displacement of the population, including anti-social or criminal elements, and by an intensification of patch policing. The result is that streets that had long enjoyed the reputation of no-go 'heroine alleys' were suddenly available for more general use. All these measures played a part in contributing to the heightened fashionable image of Barcelona, something which the present strategic plan devised in 1999 aims to perpetuate. A clear product of its times, it is strong on advocating economic sustainability, prescriptions for modernised urban governance, employment generation, improved education, greater social cohesion and so on.

No one who has visited the Ciutat Vella at various points over the past 15 years can fail to be impressed by the scale of regeneration there, and in adjacent areas. In many ways Barcelona is *par excellence* the European success story of the entrepreneurial city. However, that this has not been achieved without some social cost to elements of the population is a point taken up later in this chapter.

Centro Storico

The advanced stage of degradation of much of the Centro Storico has long dogged the image of Genoa as an entrepreneurial city, contributing to its reputation as the poor cousin of the three large north-western Italian cities. Although a dedicated planning office for the neighbourhood was created in the 1960s and within the *Projetto Genova* programme of the 1970s the area was nominated for major upgrading, it was not until the 1980s that the first substantive evidence of rehabilitation was discernible.

For much of the period under review an unambiguous strategy primarily conducted in the interests of architectural conservation has been dominant. It was not until the 1990s that more socially oriented elements began to gain greater political currency. Seassaro (2000) identifies four main types of interventions undertaken during the study period. There are 'grand isolated projects' centred on areas of great historical interest, such as the Piazza Caricamento adjacent to the old port. 'Complex programmes' are promoted by the state and the region, mostly in the same ambit as the grand projects. These are complemented by large works targeting single buildings, such as the reconstruction of the Opera House and the restoration of the Ducal Palace. And finally there is a profusion of small-area housing rehabilitation undertaken by the public hand and by a myriad of private and voluntary sector operators.

National legislation in 1978 regulating rehabilitation measures, followed in the early 1980s by the concession of experimental 'seedbed' funds and the revision of the basic urban plan for the city, approved in 1980, together amounted to the first important instruments to specify action for neighbourhood renewal in Centro Storico. Although criticised for its rigidity and for failing to be adequately proactive in stimulating urban transformation, the basic plan aimed at producing greater social diversity and mixed spatial uses (Segnalini, 1997). It would build on initiatives in the late 1970s to open up those parts of the area nearest to the main street of the city, the Via XX Settembre. One of the first outcomes was the approval, in the early 1980s, of a project for the public-sector rehabilitation of one of the more derelict localities in the area, Prè, profiting from national 'seedbed' and municipal funding. Implementing the programme was rendered problematic by the high-density environment into which a superabundance of very small housing units was crammed. This neighbourhood contained a large amount of semi-derelict housing under the control of 'irregular' landlords. There was also a widespread problem of abandoned ownership. Increasingly, it played host to a growing number of largely illegal immigrants. Above all it was an area associated in the popular mind with the greatest urban insecurity. This admixture scarcely made it attractive to private redevelopers and, consequently, it was largely left to public initiative. At least, by this means, large-scale demolition was to be avoided. Furthermore, most of properties to be upgraded were transferred to the public sector through compulsory purchase or were retained under private tenure but with rents subject to legislative control. In all, the original programme comprised eight sub-projects covering almost 500 housing units and necessitated the temporary or permanent relocation of over 1000 people. Other actions included the creation of public open space in an area where it was markedly scarce and modest improvement of social facilities (Comune di Genova, 1991; Cifatte, 1993).

Although relatively small-scale in comparison to major programmes launched at the same time in other EU states, Prè was an important milestone in urban regeneration in Genoa, several respondents emphasising that it represented a steep learning curve for the city. Central funding allocations proved far too small to cope with the ambitions of municipal designs which, in turn, being exclusively 'top-down', took little account of the wishes of the established community. Problems were encountered with private and cooperative joint consortia chosen to undertake the work since the level of reimbursement set nationally proved too low to ensure an acceptable return and the city had no competence to revise the amount. The result was a long delay in initiating the project and a highly protracted completion. Despite the attractions of a modernised flat, there was considerable hesitation by some potential residents to move into the area, given the entrenched views about high crime levels. One tactic the city adopted to fill vacancies was to allocate tenancies to security forces and other public functionaries. In the event the planned rehabilitation extended until the end of the century and even the briefest of expeditions into the area would convince any observer that its final upgrading has still a long way to go. Seassaro (2000) summarises the ongoing regeneration plans for the neighbourhood. The overarching goal is to improve the social mix by attracting a more stable community. However, she speculates that this will inevitably entail further marginalisation of the transient population of illegal immigrants. Part of this agenda involves opening up the area still further to encourage its frequenting by the general population who remain hesitant about entry, particularly in the evening.

The launching of the Prè projects did at least demonstrate obvious municipal will to engage in areas that had long been socially and politically abandoned. As the 1980s evolved, Centro Storico assumed increasing importance in relaunching the image of Genoa ahead of both the 1990 World Cup, partly to take place in the city, and the quincentenary Columbus exposition in 1992. Cosmetic action was urgently undertaken to embellish the historic *piazze* adjacent to the old port that was to be redeveloped as the centre of the Expo. This followed what by then had become a rather formulaic mixture for waterfront development of leisure, hotel, office and housing uses. But, to maximise the tourist potential of these events, it was officially acknowledged that regenerative efforts in the historic core would have to be spatially more diffuse. In turn, this led to a re-evaluation of nearby locations that were previously regarded as low in retrievable value. Accordingly, there was a flurry of activity to prepare the city for these big events, although in the assessment of Seassaro (1991), consequences were not always as intended. For instance, projects were not sufficiently prioritised in terms of either their impact potential or level of urgent social need. Moreover, implementation generated more one-off legal instruments on the part of central government, putting off the required formulation of an overall new strategic plan for the city.

As for the old port, a joint regional and municipal redevelopment plan was agreed in 1988 with the influential Port Authority for the creation of a regeneration public–private partnership involving the Chamber of Commerce and other key economic actors. Given that the Columbus event was only 4 years away, immediate plans took precedence over efforts to specify subsequent deployment of the site. What had to suffice were rather vague aspirations for conference and university facilities, drawing on the establishment of the Faculty of Architecture in a restored monastery in the heart of Centro Storico.

The flagship projects associated with the Expo event reinforced the primacy of the architectural agenda in Centro Storico. Moreover, it revived the hopes of local politicians that Genoa would regain its reputation as a city of culture. Indeed, critical funding outlays were dictated by this concern, as discussed later (Arvati, 1988). On the other hand, in the late 1980s some significant measures were implemented to set in train the longer-term process of housing rehabilitation. Important regional legislation in 1987, consolidating measures implemented 3 years earlier, offered the possibility of 100 per cent subsidy of costs, providing that property remained in – or was transferred to – the public sector. For the private sector, housing subsidies of up to 30 per cent of outlays were made available. These measures attempted something of a more integrated intervention, by infusing a social dimension with some guarantees to tenants and also by complementing the curative approach with one that was preventive (Seassaro & Sola, 1992).

Among the first beneficiaries of the legislation was the Porta Sorprana area in the south of Centro Storico, one of the less densely-built neighbourhoods that was most viably retrievable and, hence, of greater interest to the private investor. As an innovation, the city authorities established a joint enterprise, in which the municipality assumed the role of both promoter and regulator. Implementation of the project relied on stepwise regeneration. In the initial phases, the intention was to achieve a public–private funding leverage ratio of 1:1.4. Later stages were to attract more substantial regional and municipal outlays (Comune di Genova, 1991). The fact that the neighbourhood is dotted with attractive little *piazze* also increased its gentrification prospects, something that the planned creation of additional public open space and considerable new underground parking facilities could only enhance (ILRES, 1988).

The early 1990s were marked by the increasing political turmoil to which the country as a whole was subject. The collapse of the city council impeded the regenerative momentum in Centro Storico, which was further exacerbated by economic recession. To make matters worse, the Expo seriously under-delivered on planned tourist volume. Because of this – and fraudulent disbursement of funding – the city was left with a considerable budgetary deficit. There also remained the problem of disposal of much of the site (Jauhiainen, 1995). Faced with a potential white elephant and resistant outposts of urban insecurity, Genoa adopted a solution common among cities, as fieldwork evidenced. It entailed the relocation of university facilities and student residences to fill the vacuum. State funding after the Expo was made available for the purpose. This being said, another development on the site, the Aquarium, has proved successful.

As discussed in Chapter 1, despite the growing political difficulties, the early 1990s were also a period of innovation in the national regulation of regeneration and urban governance, with efforts to overcome the bureaucratic constraints impeding speedy action through integrated programmes. In 1993, national funds were made available for the rehabilitation of social housing via the PRU programme which extended the ongoing upgrading of the Porta Sorprana area, as well as other disparate sites in the Centro Storico, resorting to a variation of public–private partnership (Latini, 1997). Because of a decelerating rate of actions in the private sector, relaxation of regional legislation was conceded in the same year. This was a device to motivate small-scale actors in the hope of stimulating cumulative visual impact, albeit largely in the more easily retrievable areas.

Although not without its critics, one of the more innovative projects undertaken in Centro Storico in the study period arose during these years. This comprised the restoration of the basilica and the surrounding neighbourhood of Santa Maria delle Vigne. A key instigator was the parish priest who encouraged many of the local residents to become engaged in the project. Their collaboration was motivated by frustration with the deteriorating physical and social condition of the locality which, in their minds, arose from a link between increased drug-trading, prostitution and a large presence of illegal immigrants. The immediate outcome of mobilisation was the formation of a neighbourhood association to press for housing upgrading and better public facilities (Associazione 'Piazza delle Vigne', 1994). As a result, public outlays were allocated for salient environmental enhancement. Besio (1999) emphasises that, apart from the attempt to formalise participation, the project employed the 1987 regional legislation on rehabilitation innovatively in that, in the absence of interest from private developers, it permitted owner-occupiers – many on low incomes – to pay back public subsidies over a lengthy period.

From the mid-1990s the output of national regulation of urban regeneration intensified. For example, in 1995, 70 per cent of central government allocations were reserved for larger cities. Genoa was a major beneficiary, with activity on the reclamation of industrial land, including old dockyards, and further neighbourhood regeneration in Centro Storico, the aim being that between 70 and 80 per cent of outlays would come from private sources (Segnalini, 1997). In 1997, 'neighbourhood contracts' were introduced in respect of relatively small localities to oversee wholesale housing rehabilitation and a stronger social rehabilitation dimension. In Centro Storico, the area selected was Giustaniani. Municipal efforts were also redoubled in the late 1990s, after the arrival of Pericu as mayor in 1997. Further triggers, too, were provided by the preparations for the G8 summit in the city and by its nomination as the 2004 EU City of Culture. A new city plan was prepared which, whilst retaining a strong regulatory function, aimed to prioritise flexibility over rigid application and to stimulate neighbourhood economic development. In an attempt to integrate physical, social and economic regeneration of Centro Storico a reformed, decentralised, dedicated planning office was created (Avarello & Ricci, 2000; Seassaro, 2000).

By the late 1990s, therefore, there was a surfeit of planning instruments in operation in Centro Storico, a relatively small area of the city, not to mention projects financed by EU Community Initiatives and Objective Two of the Structural Funds. Hence, the adoption in 1998 of national projects for sustainable development at a sub-regional level (PRUSST) was an attempt to integrate all actions in the centre of Genoa and elsewhere. One of the largest of these projects in the country, the PRUSST was an attempt to reinvigorate urban governance and regenerative efforts in anticipation of a global long-term strategic plan for the city (PRUSST, 1999; Vinci, 2002). That plan was produced after negotiation with a wide range of key actors convened by Mayor Pericu in 2002 and specifies action on five broad fronts concerning such matters as the economy, community and governance for the period up to 2010.

There is no doubt that the regulation of urban regeneration in Centro Storico over the study period has been markedly improved. Modernisation of governance continues, with increased regional devolution in planning and housing matters and the city council has become noticeably more pro-actively entrepreneurial. Much of the physical infrastructure in this locality has been improved, most noticeably around the more attractive squares and action is now continuing to upgrade public facilities and policing measures (Comune di Genova, 2000). Yet, anyone today retracing the steps of Henry James in his progress through the locality – although they might not sympathise with his anti-modernising sentiments – would leave with the impression that much of what has been achieved is too disparate to have an immediately visible cumulative impact.

Innenstadt

Hamburg – a city-state – has enjoyed primacy in terms of the formulation and funding of urban regeneration. Moreover, as a relatively small political entity, the network of key political, economic and implementation actors has been particularly close-knit, though not necessarily always harmonious. Major agencies such as SAGA have long dominated the supply of social housing (Stegmann, 1976). They have been critically involved in its subsequent rehabilitation. A large part of the regeneration of the housing system in general has been entrusted to comparatively few specialist agencies in close collaboration with the city authorities (see below).

Although some federal funding was released in legislation of 1971 to stimulate rehabilitation and the maintenance of a degree of social mix, in the early phase of the study period the primary source for rejuvenation came from the city's own coffers. Following mass demolition programmes of the 1960s (extending into the 1970s), the city revised priorities in favour of area-based measures. Such a policy change was supported by a prevailing environment during which conservation and the modernisation of inner city housing gained more political importance (Dangschat, 1993). In 1973 a new structure plan was introduced. It specified a hierarchy of objectives, among them rehabilitation. An associated programme was announced immediately in areas like Neustadt, adjacent to the Elbe, where the primary aim was to reinvigorate leisure trade and the evening economy, as well as to increase the supply of social housing (Kreibaum & Mutschler, 1990).

The emphasis on area regeneration was further formalised by Mayor Klose in 1976, with the identification of deprived priority areas throughout the city, many of them in the study area. As a response to widespread criticism of mass demolition, which had provoked the house occupation protest movement, the city fathers were at pains to stress that, henceforth, revitalisation of the housing supply would proceed by means of 'small steps' – the so-called 'SiKS' programme. Through it, emphasis was afforded to protection and preservation of the existing stock. The new policy benefited from federal measures shortly afterwards encouraging energy conservation (see Chapter 1). However, the change in direction also set in train what has been, for much of the study period, a major problem in Hamburg. This derived from the fact that housing modernisation, of necessity, required the sustained engagement of private landlords who controlled much of the stock. The result of their compliance was felt in pressures on rent increases, in areas such as St Georg, Ottensen and St Pauli. This arose notwithstanding regulation, since stipulations were subsequently relaxed (Ambulante Hilfe, 1989; Wohlfahrt, 1990).

Outside Neustadt, one of the earlier regeneration localities was St Georg. The first plans for the area were announced in 1973 (Diesner *et al.*, 1994). The neighbourhood had the attraction of being a relatively self-contained area with an articulate community which, moreover, was pressing for action on degradation and associated social problems. A further trigger for their engagement arose from a desire to resist further incursion by the central business district, plans for which had been in the pipeline since the late 1960s. A definitive housing action area was produced in 1977 which assumed that much rehabilitation would be self-generated (Pfadt, 2000). Community participation and milieu protection have remained consistent considerations in what has been an ongoing project, much of it entrusted to the ASK regeneration agency (Freie und Hansestadt Hamburg, 1992; Pfadt, 1996).

The mid- to late 1970s witnessed a major construction boom in the city, in no small part due to wider regeneration plans for the central business and shopping districts, with spill-over effects in respect of housing in the inner core. During this time, there began to emerge among key commercial actors a view that these neighbourhoods were too valuable to be the reserve of cheap housing, not least because the city needed to stem the outflow of the affluent – and, with them, local tax contributions (Dangschat & Ossenbrügge, 1990). Accordingly, this decade typified many of the conflicting pressures on social and economic uses of the inner city area which remain to this day.

Federal partial funding for 'model' rejuvenation projects became available in 1983 and, through it, 22 housing improvement areas were nominated in the city. Their announcement came at a time of growing concern about the irreversible decline of much of the traditional economic base on which Hamburg had owed its prosperity. Faced with this crisis, the mayor, Dohnanyi, urged on by the Chamber of Commerce, adopted a more robust entrepreneurial policy platform, an immediate product being the creation of an economic regeneration agency, as discussed in Chapter 2. The pressure was on, then, to go for growth. The accompanying agenda with a push for redevelopment of inner areas rapidly led to conflict with local residents. As a concession the city authorities launched a programme in the mid-1980s to subsidise the activities of 'alternative' regeneration agencies. As discussed below, they were required to work closely with the self-help and cooperative movement. More central to concerns of officialdom, however, was the economic re-launching of the city, an important element of which was seen as the reclamation of the riverside.

Notwithstanding neighbourhood protests, it was at this time that the 'pearl necklace' (*Perlenkette*) concept gained political currency. This implied stepwise regeneration of the Elbe's northern bank, conforming to the SiKS approach of a decade earlier, but with an important additional objective of effecting major impact on the cultural image of the city (STEB, 2000a). As in the fashion for waterfront re-development elsewhere, where aesthetics have often crowded out social considerations, the driving force was expectation of infusion of inward investment, together with an increased supply of upmarket housing. These plans could not fail to threaten the interests of the long-established population, as well as asylum seekers housed in container ships docked in a prominent position along the river (Schubert, 1998b; Berger & Schmalfeld, 1999).

In the late 1980s an expanded estates action programme was launched, building on experiences of a few years earlier in the peripheral estates. Attention also turned to Karolinen neighbourhood in the north of St Pauli, an increasingly fashionable mixed-use, bohemian area with more than its fair share of social problems (Quartiersnachrichten, 2001). Here a strengthening of interactive physical and social regeneration was all the more necessary, since industry and housing competed for space. Thus, a long-term regeneration plan was announced, to be implemented by the STEG joint venture rehabilitation agency created by the city in 1989, with a remit to carry forward 'protective' reclamation of the western localities of the inner city for affordable housing, industrial and commercial use, details of which were to be agreed in close partnership with the communities concerned (ASJ-Foren, 1990; Lang, 1994).

By the end of the 1980s half of all public expenditure on housing was reserved for maintenance and modernisation. In the space of two decades the city had renovated around 150,000 units, although this had led to inflated rents (Alisch & zum Felde, 1991). These generally positive outcomes, however, were in for something of a setback in the immediate post-Unification period. Federal subsidies of all kinds were swiftly transferred eastwards and the city had to resort to its own resources to carry forward the regeneration programme. The 1991 election results provided a significant trigger for revision of established policy lines. Growing attrition of the voting base in many of the SPD's traditional heartlands in the city, together with the improving fortunes of the far right, prompted the party elite to ponder the effects of the polarising 'two-thirds society'. It was feared that excluded social 'power-kegs' (*soziale Brennpunkte*) were being created which, if left unchecked, would sooner or later explode (Schubert, 1998a). In fact, recognition of this neglected agenda was assisted by concession of the need for modernisation of governance, incurring further decentralisation of decision-making to borough level, and effecting within the City Hall moves towards a more streamlined corporate administration (Schubert & Harms, 1993a). The outcome was the announcement in 1992 of a 'social metropolis' strategy (*soziale Grossstadt*) which, whilst retaining a concern for wider measures such as the economic standing of the city and environmental conditions, focussed infrastructural and social regeneration efforts in inner city areas and peripheral estates. All of the city's seven boroughs nominated a neighbourhood – three in the case of Mitte – with projects entrusted to regeneration agencies such as STEG (Jorzich, 1993; Schubert, 1994; Schütte, 1994). The judgement of Alisch and Dangschat (1994) could be applied to many regeneration interventions in the EU in this period: worthy, trying harder on the community participation front, but with hopelessly short planning horizons.

In fact, following the results of an official report on poverty in the city in 1993, the policy line rapidly expanded, being transmuted into a 3-year 'poverty programme' (*Armutsbekämpfung*) to be fully operational from 1995 under the overall supervision of a new municipal department for city development (STEB). Within its ambit was the rationalisation of decision-making between the city and its constituent boroughs, wider and more formalised participation, and expansion of intervention to include education, health and social services, although – significantly – excluding policing. An ambitious enterprise, it sought to deliver an operational plan for sustainable development – now an official policy at federal and EU level. The new programme aimed to address the criticisms of its predecessor about lack of real evaluation by incorporating ongoing monitoring. Instigated in eight areas in all boroughs, including the St Georg and St Pauli neighbourhoods, it actively embraced the principles of new public management. This was to be achieved through strong local area management to further an agenda of neighbourhood economic and labour market development (Schmitz, 2001). The renewed effort in networking and in horizontal and vertical partnership, of necessity, entailed new collaborative styles with the boroughs, allocated primary responsibility for routine policy. It also required effective engagement of regeneration agencies like STEG and ASK which were responsible for implementation (Podzuweit, 1994). Predictably enough, realities fell short of expectations. Vertical partnership proved problematic, since too optimistic an assumption had been made on the jobs front. Community participation was very variable (Berger & Schmalfeld, 1999).

After 1997 there was clearly a new phase of policy evolution in Hamburg: a new mayor – the last in a long line of social democrats – assumed office. The end of the poverty programme was in sight and in 1998 a social democratic federal chancellor was elected. The city's approach to local regeneration was re-conceptualised by means of bifurcation of intervention routes. One 'pillar' mainly addressing the physical fabric, mostly in the inner city, whilst the other was concerned largely with socio-economic development, often but by no means exclusively in peripheral estates. The overall ambition was to achieve a multi-faceted, 'joined up' and partnership-led approach, underpinned by local area management. Stronger private funding leverage was also sought. In all, the reformed programme covered almost 15 per cent of the city's population and, in order not to dissipate policy input, new areas could not be added until existing projects ended (Nahr, 1999; STEB, 1999). Pepper-pot monies were available for bottom-up small-scale projects that could produce outcomes in the short term. Learning lessons from its predecessor, ambitions for job creation were deliberately modest, but 35 per cent of publicly subsidised posts in the city's labour market programme were to be reserved for the development areas (Kuhlmann, 2001).

However, at the same time that these reforms were being formalised, a plan for an unambiguously elitist flagship development was put forward. Baptised *HafenCity*, and located in an old warehouses area of the harbour adjacent to the Innenstadt, it is the largest single regeneration project in Hamburg and was originally sponsored by the outgoing mayor, Voscherau. Aiming to complement what had already been achieved in the contiguous 'pearl necklace' area it was hailed as the premier waterfront development in Europe. Over a 25-year period the plan is to create more than 5000 housing units. There will be new leisure and office space intended to achieve the target of over 20,000 new jobs. Management of this mega-project is entrusted to a public–private partnership in which the city and the port area development corporation have been the major instigators (HafenCity, 2000).

It was not long before complaints were circulating that this *grand projet* had been propelled onto the city without adequate public consultation and that it carried great environmental risks and would exacerbate social polarisation, since it was adjacent to some of the poorest neighbourhoods in Hamburg (Schubert, 1998b). As stated in Chapter 2, such accusations posed a sensitive issue for the new mayor, Runde. He was at pains to stress that the project by no means represented a privatisation of central urban spaces; that it would not be 'gated' and, moreover, that it would ensure that adjacent social facilities would remain viable. As for the forcing out of many smaller enterprises currently located there, he rejoined by arguing that the profits from the development, which would accrue to the city, would be used to construct new port facilities, thus protecting jobs. Furthermore, although housing might be expensive, he expressed the timid hope that average earners would share flats (Stadtdialog, 2001).

Meanwhile, at federal level, the new chancellor, Schröder, impressed by the Blairite 'new deal' package, announced a 5-year 'social city' programme for multi-dimensional urban revitalisation on the basis of matched funding from lower-tier authorities. In effect, this federal programme meant less to Hamburg, which had long been a pioneer in regeneration. Certainly, a relatively small amount of central funding was allocated to the city, when compared to other large conurbations. By 2001 – and building on existing interventions – there were seven projects in the city, including a 'model programme' in the peripheral social housing area of Lurup (STEB, 1999; Kuhlmann, 2001). Although networking and dissemination of best practice were the intention, several respondents to the present study, coming from the smaller agencies, asserted that the choice of projects had been more political than needs-driven. They complained that agencies like theirs were squeezed out in favour of the mainstream regenerators.

Among Germany's larger cities, Hamburg stands out as one of the few innovators in this field in the past three decades. Breckner and his colleagues (2002) review the wide range of interventions in train in 2000, ranging from local development, physical renewal 'in small steps', through to the Hafen-City. Yet, the new city development plan, issued in 1999 – after nearly a 20-year gap – sums up outstanding problems: whilst very strong at the level of physical infrastructure, the combating of socio-economic dimensions of urban deprivation has been less reassuring. In particular, its authors note the mixed fortunes over 20 years in terms of reductions of unemployment by locality and clientele and the continuing high rate of those dependent on social assistance (Freie und Hansestadt Hamburg, 1999). Others have highlighted intransigent problems such as the urban blight, intensive in some localities, caused by crime, drugs trading and unregulated street prostitution (Quartiersnachrichten, 2001).

Inner city Liverpool

The scale and chronicity of urban problems in Liverpool, as in Marseilles, have resulted in a longer-term critical engagement of central government in local regeneration than in the other three cities. One direct product, is that both these cities have been more dependent on central allocations and nationally determined prescriptions. Relatively early in the post-war period, Liverpool began one of the largest slum clearance programmes in the UK (University of Liverpool, 1991). In 1970 the city was among the few authorities chosen to take part in the government's Community Development Programme and was one of the three pilot projects chosen for the Inner Area studies undertaken in 1972 which would influence the Labour Party's formulations contained in the 1977 White Paper. It was also among the pioneers of general improvement areas in the late 1960s, followed by the largest programme of improvement implemented as a result of the 1974 legislation creating housing action areas (Pullen *et al.*, 1975; CDS, 1985). The combined effect was that, at this time, Liverpool was among the top performers in terms of total housing renewal effort (Marks & Couch, 1991).

The city council in the mid-1970s launched an experiment in local area management to tackle inner city deprivation through the engagement of local councillors in plans for decentralised delivery of services. Whilst this was something of an innovation in its day, in practice, the project was held to be rather top-down and lacking in effective coordination and community participation. In the event, it did not survive (Punter, 1981). The city was one of few selected for operationalisation of the inner city partnerships between the public and private sector in the revised Urban Programme of the late 1970s (see Chapter 1). However, it was the arrival of Mrs Thatcher to the premiership that was so radically to alter the urban regeneration scenario in the city and, as we have already seen, relations with Westminster. The incoming New Right government was already convinced that local authorities were not effective vehicles for delivering the required economic transformation that it prescribed. The outbreak of rioting in major cities, including Liverpool, in the early years of her first government only served to reinforce the prime minister's view that local government had to be sidelined, if her radicalised agenda had any chance of success. Chapter 1 has already outlined the series of measures she rapidly adopted, in respect of which – and more – Liverpool was a major recipient: development corporations, enterprise zones such as the one designated in 1980 for Speke on the city's periphery, task forces and city action teams.

Key policy evolution in the early 1980s followed the creation of a Minister of Merseyside, a post initially held by a senior cabinet member, Heseltine. One of his first tasks was to co-opt a Merseyside Task Force from among Whitehall civil servants as well as a Financial Institutions Group of seconded entrepreneurs who were given the remit of devising means of attracting inward investment into the region. Whilst, as Lawless (1989) recounts, the minister was defeated in cabinet on the issue of a major increase in public-sector investment, a special allocation for housing was forthcoming which supported projects in deprived areas like Vauxhall and

Toxteth (Department of the Environment, 1994b). However, this was no match for the deepening crisis in housing revenue accounts or the general coffers of the city, particularly as Urban Programme allocations in real terms were in decline throughout this period (Couch & Wynne, 1986; Liverpool City Council, 1987b). Instead of public subsidy, a more pro-active entrepreneurialism was favoured by the government. Thus, although not benefiting from any significant budget of its own, the Task Force was given responsibility for planning Britain's first national garden festival held in 1984, on reclaimed derelict dockland not far from the city centre. Another of its task was to oversee the establishment of a technological park. The preference for highly salient projects, in the judgement of Lawless (1989), distracted the Task Force from a more long-term strategic engagement, something which Heseltine's departure from the portfolio in 1983 only served to diminish. In comparison, others identify positive impacts emanating from the easy access to central government it afforded local actors (North West Network, 1994).

Even before the change of minister, policy was continuing apace. One significant departure was the creation, in 1981, of a development corporation to supervise regeneration of a relatively confined area of dockland around Pier Head. Significantly – as with other innovations of this era – it answered directly to the minister. Its flagship project would be the re-development, for leisure and office use, of old warehouses encompassing Albert Dock, the largest 'Grade One' architectural preservation site in England. Further flagship developments followed by means of the Urban Programme, among them renovation of the Philharmonic and St George's Halls, both in the city centre.

Both the new labour council under the Militant faction, taking control in 1983, and the deteriorating municipal budget served to radicalise the locally formulated agenda. This occurred at a time when, in any case, the more consensually based 'inner city partnership' was coming to an end. Not, in the view of a parliamentary committee, that this partnership had latterly been especially productive; albeit for different reasons, the various tiers of government had already taken anticipatory distancing action (Lawless, 1989). The prime concern of Militant was to defend and expand its control over funding to prosecute its ideas about regeneration. To advance its agenda, the faction blatantly resorted to a variety of money-raising tactics provoking further conflict with government. Militant's central platform for revitalising the city, specifying funding via the housing investment programme, was embodied in the 1983 Urban Regeneration Strategy, prescribing major social house-building and an associated improvement programme, designed to accentuate multiplier effects. For these – and projected secondary economic impacts – the council leadership obtained consent for significant outlays (Liverpool City Council,1985; Moore, 1994). Several authors have pointed out that there was little that was inherently objectionable in the strategy's targets; it was just that they were out of kilter with government preferences. On the other hand, more substantial criticism focussed on means. Respondents in the present study complained that the plan was largely designed by a caucus of councillors who neglected to consult tenant or community groups. This was a particularly sensitive issue, given the leadership's problematic relations with spokespersons for ethnic minorities. Neither had there been any serious attempt to involve housing associations which were major suppliers of accommodation in the city. On the contrary, they accused Militant of demonstrating its distaste of the voluntary movement by failing to allocate to them dedicated central funding which, unused, was eventually returned to Whitehall (Crick, 1986). More positively, under Militant, the declaration of housing action areas had continued at a pace (CDS, 1985).

Meanwhile, central government was making further intrusions into the local government arena, in part as a result of a further bout of civil unrest. To improve the coordination of its policies for major conurbations 'city action teams', including one for Liverpool, were created in 1985 within the Whitehall ministries, with a primary economic development remit. They were followed a year later by a small number of local area 'task forces' comprised of civil servants, but based locally and aiming for partnership with the private and voluntary sectors as well as the target community (Action for Cities, 1991). The city's team was located in the deprived inner neighbourhood of Granby-Toxteth, with a protocol of stimulating local economic development through targeting 'seedbed' help on small enterprises, assisting in skills audits, and so on. These small teams were deliberately time-limited and expected to formulate strong exit strategies; in the event, the life of the Granby Task Force extended into the mid-1990s.

The Strategy of 1983 did not survive the downfall of Militant in 1987 and the new council, still under Labour control, revised its priorities within the Urban Programme to conform more to the government's policy, by increasing allocations to economic projects, a trend which grew in the last years of the 1980s (Liverpool City Council, 1991). This more collaborative stance with central administration extended into general relations between the city and Whitehall, both sharing a desire to repair the damage to Liverpool's image, which had been perpetrated during the Militant era, in order to improve the prospects for inward investment. This period also coincided with the third Thatcher term and its declared intention to commit to serious action on 'those inner cities'.

Within the 1988 'action for cities' policy review, the area within the Merseyside Development Corporation was extended, to encompass neighbourhoods on both sides of the river. There had, in fact, been critical assessments of operation during the Corporation's first phase. The Albert Dock redevelopment had enjoyed considerable success on a number of fronts – it had, for example, increasingly drawn tourists, albeit largely day trippers, and was becoming one of the country's premier attractions (Dalby, 1990). Yet, it was criticised by the National Audit Office for its operational tendency to be reactive and for failing to deliver the hoped-for strategy, something that for Dawson and Parkinson (1991) owed more to the local economic climate. When the size of this scheme was taken into account and added to what was expected of the nearby Garden Festival, job creation trade-offs were disappointing, although steady growth was recorded in later years. Private-sector leverage was initially slower than anticipated, holding back further site reclamations. Housing development, too, had been sluggish. For Lawless (1989), there was simply too much local competition among the plethora of subsidised developments for each to pay immediate dividends. All of these factors led to a revision of the original agenda, prompting action more closely to follow prevailing market preferences, particularly in accelerating investment in tourism (Thornley, 1991).

The expansion of the corporation's boundaries, of necessity, extended its remit into social and wider economic, as opposed to narrowly commercial, preoccupations. It also brought it into a more intimate relationship with the local community, not least the prominent Eldonian cooperative that was then enclosed within its territory (see Chapter 5). By the early 1990s private investment was exceeding forecasts (Merseyside Development Corporation, 1993), with the housing element assuming a stronger profile than commercial development. However, the city council insisted that, along with many other national regeneration projects, interventions were largely tinkering around the edge of economic problems (Liverpool City Council, 1992). For their part, the Audit Commissioners indicted a lack of strategic coordination as making matters worse (Parkinson, 1998b). In the event, the corporation continued in operation until the late 1990s.

Central government – and increasingly EU – actions were steadily to dominate Liverpool's urban revitalisation agenda throughout the 1990s. An important central innovation, reinforcing its commitment to promoting the entrepreneurial city, was the introduction, in a climate of national economic recession, of City Challenge through competitive bidding among local authorities. The city made a successful bid in the first round of 5-year funding, identifying the degraded area of the eastern city centre as the site for intervention, but also being allowed to include adjacent areas such as West Everton and Granby. A strongly capital-led project approach was the order of the day, as too was reliance on partnership, initially between tiers of government, coordinated by the Merseyside Task Force, but soon expanded to incorporation largely of private actors (Parkinson & Russell, 1994). Within the general objective of resource concentration to effect maximum gain, the plan disaggregated global objectives in areas such as the environment, transport, housing and employment in an itemised list of specific targets, in order to refine operational evaluation. Significant advances were made towards fulfilling the city's ambitions to compete internationally in the field of culture with, for example, the creation of the Liverpool Institute for Performing Arts, in which Paul MacCartney played a central role. Properties were also rehabilitated for higher education and student accommodation. Local labour contracts were employed to increase employment potentials – and the rather modest targets set were more than matched. On the other hand, general unemployment in the city remained high. Critically, private funding leverages far outpaced initial targets. Less positive was action on the housing front. Overall, the funding period was judged too brief to deliver the full plan, particularly in terms of capacity-building (Russell, 1997). There were also concerns that heavy focus on capital projects would reduce community engagement and the involvement of voluntary agencies, which were, in addition, feeling the effects of retrechment (Merseyside Improved Housing, 1992).

The city was unsuccessful in the second round of bidding for City Challenge in 1992. But a major funding change was already on the horizon, in the form of the 'single regeneration budget' (SRB), introduced in 1995, which aimed to integrate disparate but associated central allocations into one pot, to be awarded annually. At the same time it was announced that the Urban Programme would be discontinued. Although put forward in the most positive of terms, in fact, the inflow of funding into the city – admittedly substantial – was, nevertheless, less than the old Urban Programme. Moreover, much of it was ring-fenced (Liverpool City Council, 1994a). Objective specifications followed the sort of refined strategic catalogue initiated by City Challenge, but this time the target areas were Speke-Garston, a peripheral social housing area, although the project extended into the inner city neighbourhood of Dingle. Other localities would benefit only from general funding. The annual rounds of SRB (now 'single programme budget') have continued to the present time, although with revised objectives, particularly with regard to permitting the newly established regional development agencies greater discretion over disbursements (see Chapter 1).

The importance of SRB to the city must be interpreted in the light of the nomination, during the same period, of the Merseyside sub-region as an EU Objective One area. Together, they represented a critical milestone in urban governance locally, underlining the importance of collaboration between the municipality, Whitehall and the (then) Government Office for Merseyside. Crucially, they continued the moves away from pepper-pot initiatives towards much longer-term programmatic responses (Government Office for Merseyside, 1994). When matched funding was added, Objective One represented a vital infusion of new money into the region that would eventually amount to about one and a half billion pounds at the end of the 6-year funding period, with almost two-thirds of outlays deriving from the Regional Fund element. The planning document, 'Merseyside 2000', specified strategic action across five 'drivers for change' relating to a broad socio-economic arena, subdivided into specific implementation measures. Regarded as the most innovative driver was that prescribing 'action for people', comprising spatially targeted interventions in 38 deprived 'pathway to integration' areas across the sub-region. Within Liverpool over one-third of the population lived in the nominated locations, such as Dingle and Granby-Toxteth and in outlying housing estates. Forty per cent of total expenditure was directed to this 'driver', to improve the prospects that the pathways would create robust partnerships – ideally embracing the private sector, as well as public and community actors – and to ensure greater social cohesion between these localities and the wider area (Evans, 2000). Chapter 6 contains further discussion.

Even before the demise of Conservative government in 1997, a new phase of the policy cycle was clearly in evidence in the city. The termination of the Urban Programme and City Challenge, the introduction of the SRB and Objective One, and the winding up of the Granby-Toxteth Task Force and the Merseyside Development Corporation each contributed to changing policy parameters. The city council assumed responsibility for remaining actions in Granby-Toxteth and committed itself to increasing the rate of housing rehabilitation in the area, although the low value of properties limited responses on the part of owners who also resisted the alternative of compulsory purchase orders (Merrifield, 1995). National legislation, in 1996, aimed to provide a new impetus for sustainable, area-based physical rehabilitation which also featured prominently in the city's unitary development plan of that year (Couch & Dennemann, 2000). Accordingly, Liverpool's housing strategy for 1999–2002 amounted to a major return to an approach characteristic of earlier decades. Three-quarters of the available discretionary grants were awarded to nominated priority areas (Liverpool City Council, 1999b).

In 1997, Britain returned its first centre-left government in 18 years under the premiership of Blair. Espousing the idea of a stakeholding 'middle way', the new regime wasted little time in implementing a series of 'new deal' programmes (discussed in Chapter 1). Again, Liverpool was to be a major focus of government attention. In response to its nomination in the first round of the 'New Deal for Communities' national programme, announced in 1998 (discussed in Chapter 1), a 'pathfinder delivery plan' for Kensington – an area adjacent to the city centre – specified a catalogue of actions to be sustained throughout the current decade, to be delivered by a new regeneration agency. The area is emblematic of the outstanding tasks in regenerating inner city Liverpool. It ranks second as the most deprived neighbourhood in the city. There is an imploding housing market in terms of real market values. Supplementing these problems are poor mortality and morbidity rates, a low skills base, a male unemployment rate of almost 20 per cent – with many of the jobs on offer low-paid and part-time, and providing little incentive to quit the welfare system – and a high level of crime, and fear of crime (Liverpool New Deal for Communities, 2000). Included among many targets are the tackling of crime and associated issues of drugs and prostitution, and action on improving education facilities. One of the most urgent items on the agenda is how to resolve housing problems, in particular the management of the large stock in the social sector. An avenue being explored is the possibility of establishing a single social landlord. Significantly, the funding stakes are raised, with an ambitious aim of private-sector leverage at a ratio of 3:1 (Northern Housing, 2000). In a second round of this 'new deal' in 2000, North Huyton in the neighbouring borough of Knowsley was the successful bid.

Liverpool was also selected as yet another 'pathfinder', this time in the strategy developed by the Local Government Association, the 1999 'New Commitment to Regeneration', whose ambitions were discussed in Chapter 1. Accordingly, a 10-year strategic plan, 'Liverpool First', was formulated to secure broad and long-term local partnership on a broad action front, aiming to achieve closer harmonisation of mainstream and earmarked budgets. Building on the report of the government's Urban Task Force, three key 'drivers' were specified – social cohesion, economic competitiveness and sustainability of outcomes – the ambition, as ever, being to restore the city to premier European ranking. For this an inflow of funding from all sources of more than 1.5 billion pounds – much of it from inward private investment – was required (Liverpool First, 2000).

The hyperactivity in policy output in this period continued with the government's nomination of the city as a site of one of the first three urban regeneration companies. 'Liverpool Vision' has the task of seeking means to revitalise the city centre to promote employment, tourist potential and so forth. Strong partnership, as ever, is the order of the day, an important contributor being the new regional development agency as well as the established local strategic partnerships. Similarly, its list of aspirations includes very ambitious private funding leverage, one initial proposal being the creation of a 'one-stop funding shop' to facilitate private sector access to the public purse (Liverpool Vision, 2000).

By 1998, per capita expenditure on public services in Liverpool was almost one-third above the national average, even before the effects of New Labour's urban agenda had filtered through. The sixth round of the SRB announced for 2000 attempted an integration of the hyper-output of new policies. According to Hutchinson (2000) the city had at its disposal a total government-funded regeneration package of about 1.7 billion pounds by 2001. However, as he admits, his estimates of inflows must be judged in the context of comparative need. To this source must be added the successful second nomination of Merseyside for EU Objective One status. In the funding period 2000–2006, a total of more than 800 million pounds has been allocated to the sub-region, excluding matched funding and private leverage. The supporting single planning document in many ways summarises the evolution of regeneration in the city by providing a conscious balance of remaining weakness in the context of strong opportunities. Thus, it reports that Merseyside remains one of the poorest areas of the UK, with high unemployment, low competitiveness and a declining population. But, equally, it highlights some of the positive outcomes from the first round of EU funding, not least in inward investment and the harnessing of social capital. Accordingly, consolidation of effort rather than a major new departure was prescribed (see Chapter 6).

Of all British cities, Liverpool has been a primary object of a myriad of regeneration schemes, many targeting its inner neighbourhoods: some the initiative of the city, many more of national government. An underlying motive behind much of this effort has been concerned with its long-standing reputation as a conflict-ridden and degraded 'welfare city'. Alongside what could be termed routine infrastructural regeneration, the objective of radical image enhancement has been pursued through the rehabilitation of building stock of historic value. There has, for example, been considerable reclamation of the city's large Georgian architectural heritage. Additionally a panoply of flagship projects furthering the exploitation of tourism and cultural potentials have been executed. These include restoration of Albert Dock and St George's Hall, and the upgrading of the immediate area around Pier Head which will be continued with the construction of a major new prestige building, the so-called 'Fourth Grace'. There have been bids to be the EU 'city of architecture' and the successful nomination as the 2008 European 'city of culture'. Other areas of attention include expansion of higher educational facilities and development of the night-time economy – and much more. Yet, as discussed in the next chapter, of outstanding problems, the poor local skillsbase and the consequent chronic failure to generate adequate employment are among the most pressing. Equally problematic has been the weak demand for housing, as is conceded by central government when, in 2003, the city and adjacent municipalities were nominated as one of its new 'housing market renewal pathfinders'.

Centre-Ville

Marseilles, like Liverpool, has been the object of strong higher-tier intervention in urban policy, in particular by central government and the region (Provence Alpes Côte d'Azur). Similarly, there has been a long-term concern about its reputation, notably its failure to effect economic recovery and its chronic image as prime crime-ridden city of France. Above all, there has been preoccupation among local elites with the relative shabbiness of the centre which sustains its dubious status as a 'peddler city', unworthy of its status as the second metropolis of France (SOMICA, 1985). Over the study period much of the regeneration effort in the inner city has been principally directed to addressing these issues.

In fact, the deteriorating state of the centre of the city either side of La Canebière, characterised by decaying and empty property away from its more munificent southernmost part, prompted early intervention within the city plan of the late 1960s and its revision in the mid-1970s. This was consolidated in the late 1970s through a series of area improvement schemes (*OPAHs*), largely state-funded, in the vicinity – the first city in France where they were adopted (AGAM, 1993a). At the same time direct national effort in neighbourhood regeneration, in the form of the *Habitat et Vie Sociale* project, was initially focussed on restricted areas in the northern social housing estates (Donzel, 1998). The municipality's plans for revitalisation of the Canebière zone incurred intrusion into the adjacent mixed use area of Belsunce, where large-scale demolition of part of the neighbourhood was required for the new shopping and commercial complex of *Centre Bourse* (Streff, 1989).

The city also initiated what was to be a continuous series of area improvement schemes in the rest of these neighbourhoods and in Le Panier, whose characteristics were described in the previous chapter. Le Panier, as the medieval core, has been an important location of policies to improve the city's architectural and cultural assets. This has been no mean task since the neighbourhood contained a lot of deteriorating property increasingly accommodating an ethnically mixed population. Here, modernisation programmes have been undertaken which have prioritised the protection of the existing community, comprising mostly private tenants or owner-occupiers of poor-quality housing (Marseille Habitat, 1992). On the other hand, Ferracci (1983) also detects a secondary agenda in a political motivation to retain the strong local vote for the socialists, given that the majority of beneficiaries of public subsidy had been native French. In comparison, the rehabilitation of Belsunce was – and remains – more socially sensitive. Its large community of Maghreb small traders had earned it the reputation as the 'cashbar' of France. For the city fathers and the local economic elite, anxious about the image of the city as a whole, this central neighbourhood – hard on the city centre – urgently required comprehensive transformation (Benyoussef & Hayot, 1987). What the municipality had in mind was a major long-term reclamation around a principal axis of the city, from the centre to Porte d'Aix. To achieve its overall aims, there was substantial investment to improve public services together with new styles of delivery in the form of decentralisation. Additionally, certain high-profile public and cultural establishments were relocated there, in the hope that a more diverse population would be attracted to the neighbourhood (Ville de Marseille, 1990a). What was in the minds of many Marseillais was the idea of 'recapture'; in the minds of the local Maghreb community was the threat of eviction (Pinson & Bekkar, 1999). In many ways, the tensions arising from the desire to achieve retrieval of the area and improve social mix whilst reassuring the local community that they were not at risk of mass displacement has remained an important dynamic in the political management of the neighbourhood.

The arrival of Mitterand to the presidency in 1981 was a key event in the city, not least because its mayor, Deferre, was appointed interior minister with the remit of marshalling through the decentralisation programme (Donzel, 1993). The ensuing Eighth National Plan re-emphasised local-area rehabilitation, which would henceforth be prosecuted through a series of more formal contractual engagements requiring tighter vertical partnership, reflecting the new enthusiasms for devolution. In the city, a new land-use plan was published to provide overall policy direction (Tulasne, 1994). State-centred intervention for neighbourhood-level development was intensified by the announcement of the national programme of DSQs (see Chapter 1). The city benefited from the first pilot projects, initially targeting the Le Panier and Belsunce-Ste Barbe areas and the northern arrondissements (SOMICA, 1985). Local improvement also continued through the OPAH schemes, extending action to embrace increasing numbers of inner city owner-occupiers and, mindful of local sensitivities, with more effort in the direction of community participation (Nelson, 1985). These areas, too, were beneficiaries of larger allocations of EU Objective Two funding.

Mitterand's first full-length national plan (the ninth) provided for 'city–state–region' urban contracts to prescribe an extensive agenda of continuing rehabilitation. There was to be a greater focus on social housing estates but *grands projets* would not be neglected (Fribourg, 1999). The contract for the city released an important funding stream which, apart from the northern estates, was significantly allocated to the inner core. Thus, Belsunce was identified for further amelioration where the DSQ programme was already funding increased public investment in social facilities such as sports and the *Cité de la Musique*. There was attention, too, towards the wider inner core, which, despite a decade or so of attempts at revitalisation, was still encountering difficulties in attracting investment and, moreover, suffering from continuing population loss (Ville de Marseille, 1990a). Accordingly, in 1985 a special decentralised facility was established, the *Mission Centre Ville*, to oversee regeneration and crime prevention policy within the three arrondissements and adjacent areas.

In line with the broad remit of the *Contrat*, the resulting *Plan Canibière*, announced in 1986, gave the Mission the task of capacity-building among local commercial actors and the community, again with an emphasis on minimising displacement effects of the population, although plans in train meant that the guarantee could not be extended to all. The formulation was firmly rooted in the growing planning fashion for attention to the quality of everyday life. Bearing in mind that the city had been a low spender on such items, the Plan foresaw a growing role for leisure and culture, building on previous flagship projects, in order to strengthen the evening economy. The developing function as a locus for higher education and public administration was to be further stimulated (Ville de Marseille, 1990b). To attain this goal would require action to reduce a pervasive feeling of urban insecurity associated with these neighbourhoods. Thus, patch policing, control of the street use of drugs, vagrancy and improved refuse collection were identified as priorities (Mission Centre Ville, 1990).

The year 1986 was a key year in the evolution of city politics. It saw the death of the long-serving mayor, Deferre, the change of political composition of the regional authority and the first 'cohabiting' conservative government in Paris. Within the DSQ programme there was more attention to the older neighbourhoods. Inside the city the impact of a centre-right regional administration served to isolate the new socialist mayor, Vigouroux. The result was that he went out alone in embarking on his vision in the *Marseille Metropole, Ville Solidaire* blueprint. Mindful that the city was not enjoying the level of prosperity elsewhere in France, the mayor launched an across-the-board programme identifying 50 key elements for attention, including job creation, social deprivation, education and health within an overall re-launching of the city economy (Donzel, 1990).

The return of Mitterand for a second septennate – on a manifesto where urban social exclusion had been central – led to a flurry of new policy which, in many ways, complemented Vigouroux's local efforts to marry entrepreneurialism to promote Marseilles' metropolitan ambitions with a welfarist agenda. Important evolutions unfolded during the tenth national plan (1988–93). Supporting the revised policy-line were new urban contracts to prepare French cities effectively to engage in the opportunities provided by the Single European Market project. The new contracts involved items negotiated between municipalities, regions and the state, and elements such as earmarking neighbourhoods for more intense investment (*GPUs*, see Chapter 1) for which essentially the two latter actors were signatories (Tulasne, 1994). Once again, the city was chosen as one of 13 pilot projects for the contracts and received almost one-sixth of initial total state allocations, funding being matched by the region and municipality (Ville de Marseille, 1989). Two-thirds of investment was for housing and infrastructure, to balance social and economic regeneration ambitions (PACT, 1990; Ville de Marseille, 1990b). The neighbourhoods targeted were, by now, predictable enough: a mixture of the deprived core and periphery, termed *quartiers sensibles* (AGAM, 1989), although several respondents judged that the projects amounted to more of a disparate set of measures than a programmatic response. On the other hand, apart from these routine area rehabilitation schemes, the national neighbourhood projects (*DSQs*) were reformed, with a more strongly developmental focus integrated in a wider framework of urban regeneration: the so-called *DSUs* (see Chapter 1). Several of the 11 sites within the city were located in the centre: one was Bellevue, regarded as one of the worst estates in the country, with poor quality stock, high vacancy rates, population decline and rapidly mounting social deprivation

(PACA, 1992). In all, these projects enveloped one-quarter of the city's population, over half of its social housing and almost 40 per cent of its unemployed (Donzel, 1998).

In 1990 one of the city's parliamentary deputies, Tapie, was named the founding minister for urban regeneration. This was followed by the nomination of 'sub-prefects' to coordinate policy for the more deprived sub-regions, including Bouches-du-Rhone *département* in which Marseilles is situated. One element of his task involved the concluding of 'city charters', although problems with funding allocation led to abandonment locally (Sallez, 1998). The portfolio of measures was supplemented in 1991 by the announcement of *Grands Projets Urbains* for larger-scale, longer-term regeneration (see Chapter 1). Finally implemented in 1994, they were concentrated in a dozen localities, mostly in Greater Paris, but with one in the estates of the northern Marseilles. It was during this period that a city land-use plan was produced that re-specified the existing primary aims of social and economic revitalisation. One of its offshoots was an earmarked policy of housing rehabilitation tailored to the young and the growing student population to encourage residence in the central neighbourhoods. More significantly, it prepared the ground for what has been the most important regeneration programme for the central districts. *Euroméditerranée*, a 15-year programme, has grandiose ambitions, as its name suggests. Conceived in 1992 and launched in 1995, it envisages the extensive reclamation of old dockland, something which had long been on the active agenda, albeit having produced limited outcomes (Sinounet, 1988). A catalogue of ongoing measures in the wider central area of the city is supplementing these actions, with re-investment in the harbour, improvement of transport infrastructure and the creation of new leisure, cultural and housing developments. Twenty thousand new jobs are planned, most of them in the tertiary sector, although how many of them would be suitable for the current skills base among the inner city population is not addressed in the documentation (AGAM, 1993b; Bertoncello & Rodrigues Malta, 2001). A public regeneration company is steering the public–private partnership (Sallez, 1998).

The urban contract for the period 1994–98 was to straddle two presidencies, changes of government and, within Marseilles, the election of a new centre-right mayor. Overall, it carried forward much of the previous agenda. In terms of operational style, the scope of this round of contracts was expanded, but with fewer individual projects and greater effort at more precise targeting. Several respondents to this study remarked on the change of focus, with stronger attention to sustainable local development and renewed efforts to forge effective horizontal collaboration with welfare and labour market agencies. On the other hand, despite increased central outlays, respondents also complained of the constraints imposed on a comparatively poor city like Marseilles arising from the contract's stipulations about matched funding. Moreover, they detected a resultant greater dirigisme on the part of government, reinforcing what, in any case, had been an ongoing re-centralisation of the policy agenda.

In one way or another the area focus within the contract included about a quarter of the city's population. An innovation of this programme was the implementation of the *Grand Projet Urbain* (*GPU*) in two northern arrondissements, a location of high unemployment containing a population of about 70,000, the most extensive of the schemes in the country. The existing area rejuvenation *DSU* policy was revised to improve targeting and administration, with each of the three sites in the city benefiting from a dedicated development team and a more formalised partnership commission. That for the centre of Marseilles also covered the area included in *Euroméditerranée*. Again, there was a goal of introducing a new population and new commercial, educational and cultural economic functions to locations that still bore all the hallmarks of social precariousness (Ville de Marseille, 1996).

The contract also specified further general housing rehabilitation in areas such as Le Panier, with still greater efforts to stimulate private investment (AGAM, 2000b). However, improvement schemes such as the *PRI* (for internal and external works, as well as general environmental upgrading) were to make relatively slow progress. In part, this was due to problems of extensive multiple ownership of buildings which dogged collective decision-making. By the end of the decade only one-fifth of the envisaged programme in that neighbourhood had been completed (Marseille Aménagement , 2000). Accordingly, a tougher line has been subsequently adopted in terms of greater resort to compulsory purchase.

It was during the period of this contract that Chirac arrived at the presidency. A measure of policy reformulation was inevitable since his assumption of office was accompanied by a change of government to the right. Gaudin, a minister in the new administration – and simultaneously the new mayor of Marseilles – was given the task of formulating a 're-launch of urban policy' in 1996, described in Chapter 1. Addressing criticism of comparatively modest outcomes, the government was seeking greater private-sector leverage in a range of policies that variously subsidised employment promotion schemes, including the controversial tax-free areas (*zones franches*), one of which was situated in the city.

The strengths and weaknesses of the urban contract were summarised in the new version specifying action for the period 2000–2006. It cited the strengthening of the developmental focus which had stimulated new spaces for professional role-playing and collaboration. Both vertical and horizontal partnerships had progressed and there was more genuine community engagement, all of which it claimed to some extent had unblocked what had been counterproductive administrative complexities. Yet, the document expresses disappointment that decision-making was still someway off the close integration that would permit a fully coordinated total service delivery. Part of the problem lies in the fact that principal actors were trying to do too much with limited resources (Ville de Marseille, 2000).

For these reasons, the current urban contract prioritises 'added value' to be achieved through a cross-sectoral, programmatic approach, earmarking additional funding for capacity-building within partnerships. In comparison to its predecessor, the present programme for Marseilles presents a more refined agenda of thematic and area-based actions identified through a more sophisticated employment of socio-economic indicators. There is to be tighter monitoring of implementation and outcome performance. Taking into account matched funding from all tiers of government and other public agencies, the budget in real terms is some 40 per cent higher, with increased built-in private leverage expectations.

The principal themes are obvious enough. Among the eight sub-projects, economic development takes pride of place, through further expansion of *Euroméditerranée* and associated cultural and tourism facilities and through increased investment in new technology. The tackling of unemployment is also high on the agenda, since areas within that project's purview still recorded rates in excess of one-third of the potentially economically active male population. Broader issues of social exclusion are predictably prominent, particularly as, on a number of counts, the situation in city appeared to be deteriorating. The number of recipients of the assistential *RMI* benefit, for example, had increased by 10 per cent during the course of the last contract. It acknowledged that the 'colour blind' approach in which possession of French citizenship was sufficient to guarantee equality had patently not worked, and it specified action by the local 'commission of access to citizenship' to improve the reach of basic frontline services, especially in job promotion. For everyone, access to public facilities was to be improved by means of greater decentralisation of delivery, with innovations in health and educational priority areas. The housing rehabilitation agenda was, of necessity, still expansive: despite over three decades of consistent action, institutional and legal constraints continued to hinder progress. Thus, whilst sanctioning the creation of further housing improvement areas – in neighbourhoods that had been a constant target over the years – the contract repeated the government's intention of resolving the problem of multiple ownership (*co-proprieté*). In the event, national legislation on this outstanding problem was introduced in 2003. Finally, new measures relating to the growing concern about urban security included improved patch policing, better quality victim support and a wider intervention in the field of drugs.

In terms of the spatial dimension, the contract concentrates its efforts on three projects: the *Euroméditerranée*, the *DSU* national programme, including the project in operation in the central neighbourhoods such as Belsunce, and the larger-scale *GPU* intervention in the northern districts. This latter programme was revised to provide a more genuinely comprehensive framework for regeneration in 50 locations within France. Renamed the *Grands Projets de Ville* (*GPV*) its area of operation in Marseilles was expanded to include some more centrally positioned neighbourhoods, with the possibility of later inclusion of localities such as Le Panier (AGAM, 2000b). As an indicator of the spread of policy input, there were 12 *zones urbaines sensibles* operating in 2003 in all but four of the city's 16 arrondissments.

Marseilles, as Liverpool, has been the object of the greatest rehabilitation effort among the present case studies. Yet, policy accumulation has advanced rapidly, with insufficient attention to evaluation, something the present urban contract seeks to remedy. Although changing over the past 10 years, with the exception of Genoa, there has been comparatively little regard in the evolving funding culture to private-sector leverage (see Bertoncello & Rodrigues Malta, 2001). The sphere of action of the urban contracts in significant ways has required a more sub-regional dimension than was feasible over much of the study period, although as recorded in Chapter 1, here again, there has been more recent policy innovation (Donzel, 2001). The combined effect of these sorts of factors has been to produce a vacuum, which has largely been filled by central government, sitting somewhat awkwardly with the decentralisation agenda espoused since the early 1980s. On the other hand, what has increasingly been appreciated at all levels of urban governance is the need for a variable geometry of public sector engagement in the regeneration task.

Inner city rehabilitation: towards a chiming of policy?

A handful of critical factors encapsulate much of the history of the rehabilitation of the fabric of the inner cities under review, although inevitably they vary in prominence. First, policy departed from the ad hoc and small-scale towards more enduring strategic interventions, with social and then economic dimensions being added to the agenda. A widening of competence is also prominent, initially settling what had often been problematic vertical relations. In many cases this has created avenues for a progressive *dirigisme* on the part of central government, particularly with regard to funding sources. Then followed greater attention to styles of decision-making, especially in terms of opportunities for more 'joined up' approaches that might be obtained from embracing broader horizontal partnership. Fostering the 'entrepreneurial city', with a dominant concern about the competitive edge offered by enhancement of image, has been viewed as quintessential in assisting cities to compete in the new European urban order. Here, inner city neighbourhoods have been rediscovered in terms of asset-building potentials, not least through their location for prime flagship infrastructural projects.

Depending on conjunctural trends, some of the areas that were once seen as dilapidated central locations offering little or no commercial returns on rejuvenation have been reassessed in terms of retrievability – some might say recapture. Such revisions of views about investment risk can occur over a comparatively short space of time, particularly when the public purse has been used to underpin general environmental enhancement. For other neighbourhoods, rehabilitation has required a heavier, even exclusive contribution from the public purse and has been justified in terms of greater social equity – of retrieving elements of social citizenship, if you will. Whatever the specificities of local prospects, the notion that physical revitalisation requires merely one-off, time-limited public and private investment has been discarded in favour of the view that the task, in many ways, mirrors the labours of Sisyphus. Within this perspective what, during the 1990s, became widely held as most important was sustainability. The consequences for policy pathways are still being negotiated, not least in terms of evolving funding cultures and styles of governance.

4
Extending the Policy Remit: Socio-Economic Interventions

Some of the multifarious factors impinging on socio-economic regeneration are examined in this chapter, the prime object of attention being area-targeted interventions in the labour market and in public services such as health and social services, education and policing. Each policy arena has its own provenance and innovation pathways. Each originally operated as an independent sphere but, in several of the countries under review, progressively they have become regarded as all of a piece in the common task of urban renewal. Nevertheless, the practical application of this reality still varies cross-nationally. Interventions range from those without a specific area target, those which are focussed on areas but in an ad hoc or short-term un-integrated way, through to integrated and mainstreamed cross-sectoral targeting. Relatively few generalised programmes are reviewed here, although they may achieve greater local impact overall, despite the common observation that they have too often been insufficiently interactive with the neighbourhood focus.

Labour markets and the inner city

Despite an emerging policy preference for neighbourhood economic development, there is strictly speaking no such thing as a distinct inner city labour market. Although certain sectors may serve particular clientele who may be significantly restricted in terms of spatial mobility due to the operation of housing markets and transport systems, most employment opportunities are embedded in the sub-regional economic system. These observations do not in any sense negate the fact that inner city and other deprived populations have had to negotiate an increasingly dual labour market, where segregation and segmentation is a critical element of 'insider–outsider' effects of work-related social citizenship (van Parijs, 1986; Lindbeck & Snower, 1989). The dual nature of labour markets has become increasingly differentiated in the last two decades, but the points made in the mid-1980s about its manifestations in Britain by Atkinson and Gregory

(1986) hold elsewhere. The quest in late capitalism for greater 'flexibility' has produced a range of statuses outside 'core' employment from short-term and part-time, but protected, work through to the precariousness of the submerged economy. One element in this widening diversity is the growing policy reliance on stimulating jobs in small and medium enterprises, many of which are exposed to a limited longevity and offer poorer quality benefits to workers among whose ranks women are disproportionately found (Sarfati, 2002). Another is the profusion of opportunities offered within the submerged economy involving legal but unregulated tasks, though others are frankly criminal. Although some British investigations have indicated that a lot of work in this economy is performed by those in formal employment (e.g. Williams & Windebank, 2001), much is also a cultural by-product of chronic unemployment. Moreover, the scale of immigration flows from the last decade onwards have increasingly undermined the effective regulation of the 'first' labour market – which was always weakly policed in the south. The result is a flourishing submerged economy, providing opportunities for employment – and exploitation – of minority groups. For those without any work, joblessness is now characterised as much by sequential as by chronic exclusion from labour markets; it retains marked regional and local variations throughout Europe, as well as remaining prominent among certain kinds of job seekers. The positive impact of education on their employability is by no means everywhere being guaranteed (Bonoli & Sarfati, 2002; Goul Andersen & Bendix Jensen, 2002).

In order to provide a contextualised discussion of the labour markets in the five cities, I start with some brief comments on the national employment regimes. At the risk of collapsing classifications and creating a league table, there appears to be a general consensus that three regimes apply: a 'liberal market' regime of 'balkanised' 'competitive capitalism', most typical of the Thatcher–Major era in the UK; a neo-corporatist 'state market economy' regime of 'coordinated capitalism' in operation in France and, to varying extents, in other southern countries; and a corporatist 'social market economy regime' of 'welfare capitalism' typical of Germany (see Schmid & Roth, 2000; Detzel & Rubery, 2002; Schmid, 2002). It is important to note that these categories are not mutually exclusive. On the one hand, countries such as Germany stand out as models of vocational training producing relatively low youth unemployment (e.g. Albert *et al.*, 2002); on the other hand, adding tertiary education to the nomination of 'training' results in some international re-ordering of assessments (see, for example, Schömann, 2002). Furthermore, the dynamic nature of policy evolution has ensured that there are elements of convergence. Among them can be counted certain 'flexicurity' guarantees and greater attention to background factors in employability, such as the provision of childcare and parental leave – an agenda advanced at EU level (e.g. de Koning & Mosley, 2002). Finally, Giraud (2002) observes in relation to France and Germany that firms competing in the same sector of the globalising economy are tending to adopt similar employment strategies, irrespective of country.

In the past 20 years, Catalonia and its capital Barcelona have been increasingly dependent on international capital. But small and medium local enterprises have also played a vital role (Keating, 2001). Smaller companies, in particular, were prominent in economic developments in many areas of *Ciutat Vella* which, together with massive construction projects in the city pre- and post-Olympic Games, contributed to the decline in unemployment in the study area – although rates there were still well above the city average and reductions were often achieved at the cost of an increase in precarious work engagement (e.g. PROCIVESA, 1989; Held, 1992). A key feature of employment in the study area has been its essentially local nature. In the mid-1990s almost one-third lived and worked in the neighbourhood (Ripol-Millet, 1994), although this had the effect of entrenching employment in low-paid occupations (PROCIVESA, 1991). Equally prominent has been the pervasiveness of the submerged economy. Surveys as early as the 1980s indicated that it might envelop as many as half of those under 25 (Soler *et al.*, 1987) – something which the greater deregulation of labour markets in the 1990s only served to reinforce. A growing clientele has been the newer waves of immigrants who find unregulated work in agriculture in the hinterland, and in domestic work and construction in the city (Sole, 1987; Martínez Veiga, 1997). In short, the effect of Barcelona's prosperity has not equally trickled down to the *Ciutat Vella*, where the low skills and education base is identified as a continuing constraint. This accounts for labour market segmentation effects to which many of its population are exposed and for the fact that what was a low-incomes base in relation to the city average declined still further in the last decade (Barcelona Societat, 1999; Gomà & Rosetti, 1999).

There are clear similarities between the experience of *Ciutat Vella* and *Centro Storico*, not least in terms of the chronically low economic activity. Surveys in the mid-1980s revealed that unemployment was at least double the city average and local job opportunities were disappearing rapidly for those with low education and skills acquisition. One salient outcome was that 40 per cent of households were without a gainfully employed member (Canepa, 1985; Canepa *et al.*, 1985). Since then, as several respondents to the study noted impressionistically (in the absence of adequate micro data), there have been 'islets' of tertiary sector enterprise – artisan workshops and small shops, each employing a handful of people – something which the emphasis on neighbourhood economic development in the 1990s, discussed later, has stimulated. However, respondents also stressed that without the operation of an extensive submerged economy and the informal welfare support of the family the level of precariousness would be much higher. Again, it is in this economy that immigrant workers find the easiest access. In Genoa, many are engaged in illegal work such as unlicensed ambulatory street trading or in the case of females – and particularly Filipinos – in domestic service. For those even less fortunate, one alternative is prostitution, a trade exploiting growing number of telephone call shops in the Ciutat Vella (e.g. Arcuri, 1987; Gazzola & Carminati, 1991). For others, precariousness has meant, at best, sporadic opportunities to work, too often the alternative being the resort to drug dealing (Seassaro & Sola, 1992).

Dualistic tendencies were also deepening in the local Hamburg labour market from the 1980s, sharpening the divide between those with skills and those without (ASJ-Foren, 1990). The operation of the dual system of vocational training has tempered the effects of unemployment for those without academic qualifications. Nonetheless, rates have in the city been highest in central boroughs like Mitte and Altona and particularly high among 'foreign' residents there. Despite a comparatively heavy policing by the labour inspectorate, this has led to a flourishing submerged economy (e.g. BfA, 1995). This being said, Hamburg outperforms the rest of the sample in reporting broadly the same trajectory within the study area as within the wider city in the 1990s, particularly with regard to growth in overall activity levels and trends in unemployment (BfA, 1996, 2000; Breckner & Hermann, 2003). Läpple (2000) reviews evidence suggesting the importance of neighbourhood economies in the city, indicating that, even by the early 1990s, local jobs contributed 16 per cent of Hamburg's total employment base.

Of the five cities, small-area labour market statistics are the most extensive in the case of Liverpool. From them a general conclusion is of limited spill-over and trickle-down effects of what in any case has been comparatively sluggish commercial and wider tertiary sector expansion (for a early discussion, see Liverpool City Council, 1986a). Many of the flagship projects in the 1980s and 1990s, promoting substantial investment in culture and tourism, have had a limited impact in terms of quality and range of jobs, given the predominance of the day-tripper trade. One particular problem of the local labour market, which was discussed in Chapter 2, has been what is claimed to be 'postcode' determined prejudice which has particularly limited access to work of many among the young ethnic minority population. Large private enterprises and the public sector were both indicted during the 1980s for engaging in these practices (e.g. Cousins, 1980; Ben-Tovim, 1983). Sharply declining dock-related occupation and cutbacks in the car industry – fiefdoms of white employment – meant that many displaced workers were having to compete with minority groups for the remaining jobs on offer, thus exacerbating what were already poorer chances of recruitment (University of Liverpool, 1991). Towards the beginning of the study period unemployment in areas such as Everton, Vauxhall and Granby topped the English league: they remained among the most affected neighbourhoods at the end of it, albeit with a greater diffusion among categories of 'non-employed' (Robson, 1988; DETR, 2000).

As with Liverpool, the public sector has formed a large part of employment opportunities in Marseilles. At its peak in the 1950s it enveloped a quarter of the workforce. By the early 1990s the health service was the largest employer in the city and a prime source of work for the study area population (Apotheloz & Lambert, 1994). Another similarity with Liverpool – at least its large Chinese community – is the dependence for work of Maghreb residents in the study area on their own generated economy in the commercial sector. This helps to explain the above-average activity rates in the central arrondissements when compared to the city average (e.g. SOMICA, 1985), although that population suffers from high unemployment rates in the other areas of the city where it is concentrated: the northern estates (Peraldi, 2001).

Intervening in labour markets

From the mid-1980s the logic of intervening in labour markets has been progressively informed by lessons of 'new economic geography', and the associated 'new urban politics', briefly discussed in Chapter 2. To create the 'leading edge' labour force consonant with the competitive 'entrepreneurial city', emphasis is afforded to process investment. Accordingly, a panoply of 'new public management' techniques has been embraced to enhance the quality of governance, in part through stimulating 'institutional thickness'. These factors are evidenced in expansions of territorial networking and in a broad range of partnerships where 'top-down' seeks common ground with 'bottom-up', so that 'growth coalitions', whose overarching concern is with the marketing of place, can be forged. The pursuit of 'niche markets' challenges traditional assumptions of core–peripheral effects and reflects the contemporary change in dynamic balance between positive effects of 'agglomeration' and 'dispersion' forces. Within the 'post-modernist' hypothesis, the quality of social capital and flexible, but specialised, individual human capital are privileged as essential ingredients of sustainable development, displacing the value of theories predicated on the 'traditional industrial district' (for further discussion, see Cappellin & Orsenigo, 2000; Boyle & Rogerson, 2001; Garofoli, 2002).

To be sure, there are critics who have questioned the cogency of these arguments, particularly their heavy dependence on a few select examples. For them 'growth coalitions', for example, run the risk of being subverted by reactionary interest groups anxious to preserve the status quo, as discussed in relation to port-related industrial actors in Chapter 2. Or such alliances may advance a developmental agenda which intensifies exclusionary pressures on elements of the population. Rational investors may simply tactically follow the subsidies, moving from place to place rather than settling in a spatial 'niche' (see Rodgers, 1995; Keating, 2001). It is surely true, as Parkinson and Harding (1993) assert, that the 'entrepreneurial city' is an evolving elaboration rather than an end condition. Accordingly, even the more successful among its ranks may simultaneously retain elements of the 'welfare city', principally managing need among a segregated population. Their fate is one of precariousness, owing to what MacGregor (1992: 5) calls the 'mismatch of opportunities, talents and ambitions geographically'. In this segmented economy there can be high dependence on public subsidy, which provides a vital lifeline for some of the suppliers and many of those seeking employment (Lehto, 2000; Oberti, 2000). Furthermore, one lesson of 'new economic geography', at least in the UK, has been a preference among many location investors for greenfield development. Opportunities are more abundant in smaller towns than in large cities and, certainly, recent empirical evidence strongly indicates that it is in the former where the highest aggregate demand for labour is over-proportionally concentrated (Turok & Edge, 1999).

The trajectory of interventions shows an early preference for heavy subsidisation of ailing industries to protect jobs – particularly common in southern Europe – accompanied by often small-scale and short-term job creation or training schemes for the unemployed. This was followed by more systemic reform of labour markets to engender greater flexibility of contractual engagement and to improve competitiveness by tempering non-wage costs. Latterly, all countries have been active in reforming social security to harness benefits to improving employability. Initially, the arena of action was largely motivated by a politically and socially driven tactic of alleviating the situation of the unskilled (e.g. Cheshire & Hay, 1989; Born, 2001). However, for the past two decades there has been a salient move towards neo-liberal strategic supply-side measures. Here investment in human capital is centred within wider economic and urban regeneration prioritising anticipatory and sustainable measures, more in tune with exploiting opportunities arising from globalisation, over ad hoc, reactive policies. Much of this agenda within the EU has been stimulated by the European Commission, particularly after the issuing of Delors' Competition and Growth White Paper in 1993.

This is not to deny the considerable variation in policy directions still in force among the member states, as demonstrated by national differences in funding preferences among the four pillars of the European Employment Strategy (see Chapter 6). Clasen (1999), however, is critical of crude categorical divisions between active and passive measures. He argues that the so-called 'active measures' can be at the expense of benefits and by offering only poor quality skills acquisition may be essentially passive in effect. For him, it is the scope and direction of policy effort that is critical. *Pace* Clasen, statistics based on the conventional distinction provided by Eurostat (2002), reveal marked divergence among EU states in public outlays on 'active' measures as a percentage of GDP, with the Scandinavians predictably investing most heavily, in comparison to southern Europe and the UK. These investments relate, of course, to the attributes of 'employment regimes' discussed above. They must also be interpreted in association with the quality of the unemployment compensation regimes which Gallie and Paugam (2000) characterise as a triad of 'sub-protective' systems typical of southern Europe: 'liberal–minimal' in the UK; 'employment-centred' such as in Germany and France; and the 'universalistic', albeit heavily conditional regulations of Scandinavia.

National actions in labour markets, whether of subsidisation of industry or jobs or training remain paramount. In the case of the latter, as MacGregor (2001) argues, there is now a growing contemporary preference to devolve responsibilities to quangos or various forms of partnerships. In terms of training programmes, Hantrais (2000) outlines differences among member states relating to long-term versus short-term perspectives, the degree of penetration and institutional integration. There are also, as Sparkes (1999) discerns, important divergences in the significance attached to balance of acquisition of 'hard' as opposed to 'soft' skills. The UK and Italy have been more market-led and industry-based, whilst France, the Netherlands and Sweden are training-led and school-based. In Germany the system is largely training-led and industry-based. Broadly speaking, in the UK, employers have tended to view provision as a costly short-term measure, whilst in Germany employers regard it as a long-term investment. There are also variations in priorities attached by employers to continuous/further training and the role afforded to trade unions in designing policy. The outcome is that vocational qualifications in many countries are less centrally regulated, less universally recognised and more often regarded as inferior to academic qualifications, which has an obvious impact on the human capital investment decisions of individuals (Cruz-Castro & Conlon, 2001).

In general, it is the municipal level that has been the last tier of government to be engaged in any significant way in economic development, due to earlier legislative restrictions on their competences. Initial actions were largely limited to local contracting stipulations or expansions of their own employment base. Their mainstreaming of labour market policies has come through the evolution of urban regeneration approaches. One focus which has steadily grown in salience is the espousal of local economic development, although, in turn, there is now more attention in designing associated policies to ensure a greater level of integration into sub-regional blueprints. In general, inner city areas have offered more opportunity for neighbourhood economic development because of their mixed use, in comparison to single-purpose estates on the periphery. Nevertheless, opportunities must be balanced against threats. As González and Hermann (2001) assert, project design needs careful planning, particularly in terms of flexible boundary setting, so as not to penalise adjacent firms outside narrowly defined areas. Furthermore, differences in political perspectives need to be borne in mind: for example, city-level or regional instances may be more oriented to larger companies and, accordingly, downplay the cumulative impact of small, local enterprise.

Ciutat Vella

Labour market programmes in the neighbourhood and in the city have evolved within the general national context of chronically high unemployment, affecting the young and the long-term excluded particularly hard. One solution pursued in Spain from the 1980s was to rely heavily on short-term contracts. However, by the early 1990s their rapid proliferation was causing concern that expansion had advanced far into occupational contexts that were in no way temporary in character. Successive governments have attempted to address the problem by seeking means of subsidising permanent contracts. These policies have been prosecuted within a general framework of advancing deregulation of labour markets. Regional government has been a principal actor: Catalonia was one of the first parts of Spain to adopt a version of the French *revenu minimum d'insertion*. Moreover, in the 1990s most of the competences for employment policy and planning were devolved by Madrid.

Although municipalities do not have specifically reserved competences, the city council has become increasingly engaged in labour market affairs, particularly with the change of policy towards a more pro-active economic agenda, adopted by Mayor Maragall in the mid-1980s, ahead of the Olympic Games. Beforehand, subsidised labour market projects were largely small-scale and endorsed for largely social reasons. Some were under the direct remit of the city, but many others were managed by the trade unions, cooperatives and charities such as Caritas and targeted youth, the long-term unemployed or recent immigrants. Social rehabilitation was as strong an objective as employability. This scale of intervention has continued as an important feature of local policy, frequently supported by EU funding (e.g. Masllorens, 1992; Càritas, 1993; Estivill & de la Hoz, 1993). Relatively few projects have been specifically area-based, although one notable early exception concerned the retraining of male and female prostitutes operating in Ciutat Vella, as part of the EU Second Poverty Programme (Ajuntament de Barcelona, 1988). The declaration of the city as a 'zone of urgent re-industrialisation' in 1986 with action on economic, social and technological development helped trigger a change of policy line towards a more strategic perspective, leading to the preparation of the 'Barcelona 2000' plan discussed in the last chapter (García, 1991). To assist the transformation a local development agency, *Barcelona Activa*, was created with a joint enterprise, *Barcelona Impuls*, acting as an investment bank. As a result, municipal spending on local economic development increased from less than 2 per cent in 1988 to 5 per cent of the council budget by 1990.

Barcelona Activa was intended to forge vertical and horizontal collaboration, a particular goal being the stimulation of small and medium enterprises. Also within its remit was promotion of new technology skills acquisition among trainees, as well as the administration of funding from EU, regional, municipal and private sources. It operates a network of decentralised offices throughout the city. Its annual reports indicate a steady growth in the 1990s in number of clients serviced to total over 70,000 by the end of the decade, with a sharp growth among females. In the first 10 years of operation it assisted in the creation of over 2000 new businesses (some very small) which in one way or another generated more than 5000 new jobs (Barcelona Activa, 1997, 1999). On the other hand, only a small minority of clients at its local office in Ciutat Vella lived in the neighbourhood, indicating that it retains a continuing problem of outreach (Centre de Serveis, 2000).

Centro Storico

National labour market actions in Italy bear some comparison with those in Spain, with urgent 're-conversion' measures and special youth employment plans, and so forth. Similarly, major competence for policy and planning lies at the regional level (Palumbo, 1997). From the late 1980s Liguria has implemented a range of incentives for employers, as well as training schemes and counselling and job creation for the unemployed. The regional economic development agency, FILSE, provides sponsorship, particularly with regard to credit for the creation of SMEs. The regional authorities have also relaxed planning regulations to speed up change of property use. There has also been assistance for the setting up of artisan cooperatives, although respondents to this study maintained these were relatively restricted in scope and effect. The regional authorities attempted to fill the political vacuum created by the crisis in the Genoa city council in the early 1990s by adopting a more strategic approach to economic development. Refined labour market targeting also paid greater attention to contextual social problems diminishing employability prospects. In the late 1990s the Ligurian administration convened a 'pact for labour market inclusion' to secure a broad partnership approach to resolving problems. One of its motives was to circumvent the involvement of a national government embroiled in prolonged problems of initiating the partnerships required for EU funding of 'territorial employment pacts'.

In comparison with the evolving agenda of the region, the municipality was slow to develop a response to the rapid evaporation of much of its port- and steel-related industrial base (Seassaro, 1991). There were some faltering early steps towards a neighbourhood development approach in the Centro Storico, which did not amount to much (e.g. Comune di Genova, 1983). Rather than a conscious area-based approach, many projects were by default focussed on this zone, given the concentration of deprivation there. As with

Barcelona, most were small-scale actions, many primarily of a social ambition, undertaken by voluntary associations such as the FRSL (founded in 1986 with municipal, regional, trade union and private support) or by Caritas, to create artisan cooperatives and to work more generally with clientele such as youths and immigrants (e.g. Priore & Marcaccini, 1989; FRSL, 1994). Beyond that, there were some spin-offs from physical rehabilitation projects, such as those centred on Porta Sorprana which were described in the last chapter (Comune di Genova, 1994a). In 1993 the city instituted a special office to coordinate policy and, thereafter, expanded the range of beneficiaries of its projects, although the scope of action remained modest in comparison to real demand (Palumbo, 1997). Several respondents in the final stage of interviews conceded that there was now a nascent strategic approach towards resolving unemployment which was embracing a multidimensional approach; on the other hand, labour market measures were still inadequately integrated with the wider task of urban regeneration. It remains to be seen how much, in reality, Mayor Pericu's strategic plan for Genoa, produced in 2002, will remedy these deficiencies (see Chapter 3).

Innenstadt

In comparison with its responsibilities for physical regeneration, the federal level enjoys major competence in employment policy and in overseeing the social insurance system. Landmark legislation which has been something of an international reference point for labour market promotion was passed in 1969. In the early 1980s the Bonn government initiated a stable of policies addressing what it termed the 'second labour market' – offering training and time-limited job creation, largely in social services and the ecological field. For the most part, implementation was entrusted to a range of NGOs receiving federal-state financing and oriented towards areas of high unemployment. An element of funding earmarked acquiring further qualifications. During this period there were also measures specifically for social assistance recipients, followed by a series of 'seedbed' programmes aimed at various targets such as underwriting the cost of employing the long-term jobless. Policy accumulation in that decade culminated in the 1989 pilot programme for economic regeneration in 30 'crisis-hit' cities, which was adopted in cooperation with local chambers of commerce. The job creation programme peaked in the late 1980s and, as for all policy areas, Unification was to effect a profound change in funding priorities, with a substantial budgetary diversion eastwards (BAGS, 1994). Thus, the labour market scenario since the early 1990s has been one of volatility of policy-input, with low jobs growth, comparatively sluggish transformation towards a stronger tertiary base and the evaporation of opportunities for the low skilled (Detzel & Rubery, 2002). It was largely left to the western Länder to make good the federal withdrawal as best they could. Reforms of the federal job creation programme were enacted in 1993. These led to the implementation of wage subsidies in the private and voluntary sector nationwide, but also a retrenchment of budgets for discretionary actions. Respondents to the study pointed out that they came after even more extensive cuts by Bonn in outlays for physical regeneration. This, at least, reinforced a jobs-based element to urban rejuvenation actions on the part of the states: many employment measures were statutory and, hence, the federal share of funding was guaranteed.

Further reforms, in one way or another, served to restrict welfare entitlements. In 1996 social assistance legislation was revised to reinforce the link with labour market integration. Measures were also adopted to improve school–work transitions. However, the principal catalyst for change was the return of the SPD to government in 1998. Inspired by the Blairite 'new deals', the German Chancellor launched a multi-faceted employment programme. The 'Social City' regeneration programme was also announced, with a strong employment element. All, in one way or another, paved the way for his 'Alliance for Jobs', launched as a major neo-corporatist job creation platform. Since then, reforms have concentrated on service delivery aspects. These include the improvement in cooperation between social assistance and employment offices to promote job placement (BAGS, 2001a). And, in 2002, recommendations were made for a more tailor-made job search assistance for clients, including more generous measures to assist self-employment.

As an industrial Land, Hamburg had been exposed to the economic transformation early and was among the pioneers in devising a wide range of area-based and client-targeted job creation policies, in part employing federal funds through the 'second labour market' allocations (Lang, 1994). As the city funded the social assistance programme, one of its earliest targets, in 1983, was the growing number of the unemployed dependent on it, after expiry of insurance-based entitlements (BAGS, 1990). The outcome was that during the first half of the 1980s the city's budget was seriously overstretched by its growing, largely reactive policy remit (Dangschat, 1992). The local fiscal crisis triggered a revision of policy towards a more proactive strategy, led by the Mayor Dohnanyi and assisted by the Chamber of Commerce, as discussed in Chapter 2. It marked the re-affirmation of Hamburg as a prime 'entrepreneurial city', one product being a more structured approach to labour market transformation with the setting of overarching goals. To assist in this enterprise a strong pro-development agency, the *Hamburgische Gesellschaft für Wirtschaftsförderung (HWF)*, was created as a joint venture owned by the city, chambers of commerce and local banks (Newman and Thornley, 1996).

Thereafter, employment creation entered a new phase. For one, there was a general decline in unemployment, although the prime beneficiaries tended to be new entrants to the local labour market, rather than the existing unemployed (Freie und Hansestadt Hamburg, 1989b). As discussed above, federal funding retrenchment followed swiftly on Unification. It was clear that, with ever-tighter budgets, more effective supply-side measures were urgently necessary. One example of a re-orientation was a trade union project initiated in 1988 to pay greater attention to social rehabilitation, as preparatory to labour re-entry by targeting the young unemployed who had broken off their vocational training. Action on motivation and 'after care' facilities were offered (Niemeyer, 1990). The early 1990s saw a proliferation of locally-funded projects of various scopes and timescales, with a strong self-help and cooperative strand and with outreach efforts to clients with additional problems, such as addiction and homelessness (e.g. Lawaetz Stiftung, 1991; BAGS, 1994). The housing rehabilitation agencies also extended their remits, in part by collaboration with training agencies, in areas thought likely to be urban 'hotspots'. To promote this move towards local economic development, a pilot public–private partnership was established in St Georg to test the waters for later city-wide adoption (discussed in Chapter 2) (SPD, 1992; Pomrehn, 1998). As Benfer (1996) recounts, this helped to create a policy environment more disposed to neighbourhood employment markets, particularly as surveys found that smaller enterprises were heavily dependent on local social networks for recruitment (STEB, 2000b).

The city's anti-poverty programme between 1994–98 targeted eight neighbourhoods and included a strong employment element (BAGS, 1997). Its successor, wider regeneration project, reinforced the emphasis by means of implementing a stronger skills acquisition strand and reserving over one-third of job creation posts for participating neighbourhoods (see Chapter 3). By 2000, this programme was consuming over 40 per cent of the total labour market budget for the city (Breckner *et al.*, 2002). In the late 1990s the new mayor, Runde, convened a new coalition with the social partners and the Chamber of Commerce to advance a more robust growth-led agenda. A major motivation was to create an avenue for reasserting Hamburg's competitive edge by regaining some of the services and media functions lost by the city as a result of the resumption of Berlin as the capital (BAGS, 2001a). Labour market planning was also reinvigorated, aligning it more closely to the goals of the European Employment Strategy and the reformed Structural Fund objectives (see Chapter 6).

From the early 1990s, labour market policy has been more intimately associated with platforms for urban renewal, in terms of policy, funding and institutional arrangements. The federal regeneration programme announced in 1998 and subsequent labour market strategies have reinforced the action arena. There is a panoply of client and area-targeted measures, and inner city Hamburg is well represented (BfA, 2000). Yet, there are those who question whether the policy effort expended on interventions, primarily in the second labour market, function as an effective bridge to the first (e.g. Schwarz, 1999).

Inner city Liverpool

After 1994, when its sub-region achieved Objective One status, EU-funded actions in Liverpool's labour market have been the most critical in the sample. As discussed in the preceding chapter, the initial funding programme, which extended until 1999, specified five 'drivers' for change, all of which in one way or another impacted on the labour market. The Chamber of Commerce was an important partner in devising the 32 sub-areas for specific interventions into which the 'drivers' were divided, with the Merseyside Special Investment Fund being used to access loan capital for small and medium enterprises (Liverpool City Council, 1994d). Merseyside retained its Objective One status in the present round of funding which was announced in 2000 (for further discussion, see Chapter 6).

National interventions impacting on the city's labour market are too numerous to detail and discussion here is limited to the briefest selection. Legislation, in 1972, set limits to how much local taxation could be dedicated to fostering economic development. This was followed by reform of the Urban Programme in the late 1970s which conferred on local authorities greater scope to engage in economic regeneration. On the other hand, restrictions on their budgetary freedoms imposed by the incoming Conservative government rendered these more apparent than real for many municipalities (Fox-Przeworski, 1991). Around the turn of the decade new actors were being created which would later be significant players in local partnerships. Thus, for example, Business in the Community was founded under government auspices in 1981, with private and voluntary sector engagement, as well as that of the trades unions. Its ambition was to encourage inner city investment through a variety of actions including mentoring, help with infrastructural design, and so forth (Crowther Hunt & Billinghurst, 1990). On the other hand, the government was also acting in this period to restrict the freedoms of local authorities – and not only on the income generating front. The urban development corporations, such as that for Merseyside, and the inner city task forces, one located in Granby-Toxteth, effectively by-passed municipal control. In different ways, they were significant players in their day in economic and labour market interventions, in terms of capacity building and subsidies for development (Merseyside Development Corporation, 1981; Granby-Toxteth Task Force, 1993).

During this period there was a myriad of nationally-determined interventions such as the YTS for the young unemployed, Business Start-Up and Jobclubs. At the end of the decade, local authorities were granted more powers in the field of economic regeneration. The instigation of City Challenge, in 1991, was strong on job promotion, with a dedicated local purchasing and construction charter built into the plan and a firm emphasis on higher education pathways (Liverpool City Council, 1994b).

It afforded a significant role for the new training and enterprise councils (TECs) to work in partnership with the private sector, although Evans (1990) questioned the limited funding of the TECs and over-optimistic expectations of commercial involvement. The prominence of labour market actions was also retained in the SRB, first adopted in 1994.

Policy under New Labour from 1997 has followed thick and fast. Its 'new deal' targeted the under 25s, the long-term unemployed and a selection of other clientele. Employment zones and the establishment of the national minimum wage were also intended to reinforce labour market integration (Hart & Johnston, 2000). These were followed by a welter of projects such as plans to reduce business taxes for small businesses and 'Inner City 25', as a showcase for the fastest growing unquoted companies in deprived areas. Regional development agencies and urban regeneration companies consolidated this agenda as, too, the unification of the budgets of three key ministries central to employment policy (DETR, 2000). It was also announced that, from 2004, there would be more intense support for unemployment black spots and an extension of the employment zones.

In relation to policy with specific implications within the city, Lawless (1989) records that, contrary to national trends, less than one-fifth of the Urban Programme in the early 1980s was being allocated to economic projects. And, though the Merseyside Enterprise Board was providing some equity to local companies, and EU funds were helping to establish facilities such as the Wavertree Technological Park by means of through public–private partnerships, it was all small beer in the face of the size of the unemployment problem. Whilst the city council's Urban Regeneration Strategy of 1983 was intended to stimulate jobs through public sector house-building, it flew in the face of government priorities and was compromised by their insistence of compulsory competitive tendering. The change of council in 1987 led to a revision of the city's economic development strategy and created a single local budget with the Merseyside Training Partnership and, later, with the TEC awarded coordinating roles (Liverpool City Council, 1987a).

From the late 1980s, too, the range and style of job creation projects expanded rapidly, a tendency that has intensified since. To provide some impression of these developments in the inner city, the following are the barest selection. There were top-down facilities such as those provided by the Merseyside Education, Training and Enterprise Ltd (METEL); bottom-up development projects such as the (ill-fated) market garden project devised by the Eldonian self-help community (Bailey, 1991); and client-targeted projects for women (Liverpool City Council, 1990). Those specifically dedicated to advancing the interests of ethnic minorities included the 'Black Sisters' (Liverpool City Council, 1989) and the Black Business Association (Granby-Toxteth Task Force, 1991). Among area-based innovations was 'Project Rosemary' in Abercromby, the brainchild of the late Dean of Liverpool (Hetherington, 1996), and development projects in West Everton (West

Everton Community Council, 1991). As in Hamburg, housing agencies also broadened their field of action. With the adoption of the 1990 training and economic development strategy by the city, more stress was placed on customised training. There was also greater concern with preparatory measures for elements among the unemployed regarded as a 'hard core'. For example, the 'Compact Plus' pilot project aimed to provide tailored assistance to improve motivation and prospects among the young who were chronically out of work (Merseyside Task Force, 1991). Finally, since the early 1990s partnership has become an indispensable means of obtaining funding in such programmes as City Challenge, the SRB and Objective One, one important element being the investment body, the 'Merseyside Partnership' (Evans, 2002).

Centre-Ville

Despite moves in the 1980s towards greater decentralisation and in the 1990s towards greater deregulation, the French central government reserves extensive competences for the regulation of labour markets (Detzel & Rubery, 2002). Training and job creation are closely integrated in the series of national plans referred to in earlier chapters and have also featured prominently in the urban contracts from the mid-1980s. The establishment of the *revenu minimum d'insertion* in 1988 explicitly linked benefits derived from social citizenship to a contractual obligation to social and labour market integration. In the same period a national initiative (*ADIE*) was launched to offer credit to the long-term unemployed to set up their own businesses (Pomrehn, 1998). National client-oriented schemes for adults have included the *Contrat de Retour a l'Emploi* and *Contrat Emploi-Solidarité*, the latter being the main instrument for adults since 1992 (OECD, 1998). Among the myriad of schemes largely or solely for youth is the *Emploi-Ville* mostly offering work in welfare and personal services.

In terms of international lesson-learning, a significant innovation in area-based economic development was initiated in the early 1980s in the form of the *régies des quartiers*. These are local enterprises mainly situated in the large social housing estates which have been targeted by the DSQ/DSU neighbourhood regeneration programme discussed in Chapter 1, although operating independently. In the late 1990s there were about a hundred *régies* offering about 3000 workplaces nationally. Marseilles was among the early pioneers with one in the city being located in the central neighbourhood of Bellevue (Ville de Marseille, 1990b). They offer employment to those who otherwise face long-term exclusion from the world of work. Located in the same type of milieu, but with a strong secondary crime prevention agenda , the *missions locales* are youth centres offering training and assistance for self-help projects (Graham & Bennett, 1995). Finally, there is a range of joint enterprise 'intermediate' agencies and *entreprises d'insertion* for candidates who are hard to place. The combined effect of these interventions cannot be depicted as an unalloyed success – the *Contrat Emploi-Solidarité*, for example, has been criticised for too often offering 'time-filler' work with poor skills acquisition that is of little interest to the open market. But, Jessen and Neumann (1999) assess that the benefits of the *régies* accrue from the regard in which they are held by many municipalities and the fact that other firms have been willing to accept their graduates. The effect has been that they have been able to secure a reasonably high level of transfer from the 'second' to the 'first' labour market. The association of *missions locales* with reduced crime rates is taken up later in the chapter.

Further enmeshing of urban and labour market policies occurred with the 1996 'relaunch' of urban policy which specified a tiered range of large-scale, subsidised, and short- and long-term job creation measures in nominated areas, the most generously endowed being the *zones franches*, one of which has operated in the north of Marseilles. A left government was re-elected in 1997 under Jospin, who promised the creation of almost three-quarters of a million new jobs. In addition, he committed his government to cutting the comparatively high rate of youth unemployment by half through a recruitment strategy paying the junior national minimum wage. His initial vociferous rejection of the anglo-saxon means of creating them was relatively short-lived and, in any case, a cross-Channel *rapprochement* was demonstrated in the European Employment Strategy that all sides were able to agree. Thus, the *exception française* regarding labour market policy has been giving way to tighter criteria for 'welfare to work'. The urban contracts for the period 2000–2006 continue with a stronger entrepreneurial focus, with improved funding for the creation of small and medium enterprises, and more personalised job search assistance. This agenda was carried forward in 2003 by means of a range of job creation proposals which included the extension of the *zones franches* to new areas.

The regional authorities, as signatories to the urban contracts, have considerable powers in economic development policy (Corolleur & Pecqueur, 1996). In Provence-Alpes-Côte d'Azur, the regional development agency, *Proxipaca*, advances credits to joint venture projects, many of which co-exist with other neighbourhood developments funded through the contracts. There have also been a large range of small-scale socially-oriented job creation projects in Marseilles, many operating as cooperatives (e.g. Ville de Marseille, 1990b; Centre Social Belsunce, 1991). In general, the larger youth-oriented programmes have been located in the northern arrondissements (Donzel, 1993; Roulleau-Berger, 1997). Housing rehabilitation agencies have also been extending their remits to embrace local economic development (Sinounet, 1988; Anderson & Vieillard-Baron, 2000). As discussed in Chapter 2, under the mayoralty of Vigouroux a more entrepreneurial exploitation of the urban contracts was prosecuted. This included the development of a Mediterranean 'technopole' (Ville de Marseille, 1990c). Thereafter, followed the creation of the contracts of *PACT Urbaines* for employment and related development (Ville de Marseille, 1993) and the ongoing range of measures specified in the 1996 'relaunch' of policy, from all of which areas of the city have benefited.

Social services

As with all the sectors being reviewed in this chapter, the five countries vary substantially in terms of the degree to which an area-based approach has been embraced in social service delivery, and even more so in terms of the extent to which the policy has been integrated within the urban regeneration agenda. The UK has been an early instigator, with France and Germany in the middle-range, whilst Spain – and particularly Italy – are comparative latecomers. These differences stem in part from important cleavages in political and administrative competences. But they are also a product of distinct professional structures and cultures which have privileged autonomous role-playing, as well as suspicions of potentially stigmatising effects of spatial targeting; accordingly 'de-specified' delivery styles have been preferred. This being said, owing to the spatial concentration of welfare-related problems in such areas as child and old-age poverty and chronic disability (e.g. Robson *et al.*, 2000), interventions by default do tend to demonstrate distinct locational distributions.

Despite pioneering 'one-stop' facilities, the increasing diversity of the service 'complex' – now meretriciously termed the 'welfare mix' – means that local knowledge and social networks can be critical in determining the quality of access that deprived communities have to welfare assistance, particularly 'in-kind' provisions. Access has also been shaped by factors outside the control of local populations. It has long been recognised that inner areas suffer from an 'inverse care law', a term first applied to the mismatch of need and supply of primary health care (Tudor Hart, 1971). As the extensive literature indicates, the law is equally applicable over the range of socio-health services, although the contemporary phrase in the vocabulary in Britain coins the idea of 'postcode lotteries'. Spatial problems are not improved by the fact that more specialist facilities, such as hospitals, are increasingly being displaced to greenfield peripheral sites. Finally, the chronic fiscal strictures of the central and local state impose substantial spill-over effects on overall welfare access. Retrenchment in nationally determined cash benefits can produce increased demand for in-kind services within the remit of overstretched and poor lower-tier authorities which may, in turn, seek to offload responsibilities onto the private and voluntary sectors.

The first democratically elected councils in Barcelona acted swiftly to remedy the under-investment in public social services under Franco with his heavy reliance on church-led charities perpetuating an assistential ethos. Planning systems were effectively in place by the early 1980s with the outcome that per capita funding was heavily targeted to the most needy areas such as Ciutat Vella, in order to increase supply in such sectors as child provision (Soler *et al.*, 1987). This input has been sustained (Gomà & Rosetti, 1999), although there have been allegations that the municipality was having to make good deficits in allocations by the regional authority to Barcelona. The city also instigated a decentralised delivery system which, from the mid-1980s in Ciutat Vella, has been associated with physical and social rehabilitation measures, progressively incorporated into overarching strategic plans for the city such as *Barcelona 2000* (Vintró i Castells, 1991b). Conversely, some respondents pointed out that the overall efficiency of sectorised and area-based municipal services has been compromised by reliance on a parallel extensive array of voluntary provisions not operating according to these principles. In the 1980s, both centrally and locally, the socialists were somewhat antagonistic to private welfare facilities (Mangen, 2001), although Turró (1998) records a subsequent accommodation, something which has been made explicit in planning projections. Caritas is a major player in the neighbourhood, particularly in providing for the growing ethnic minority population and also fulfilling a lobbying function (Càritas, 2000). Ciutat Vella, together with poor peripheral neighbourhoods like Nou Barris, remained a high-need location throughout the study period in terms of child poverty (Ajuntament de Barcelona, 1989a), elder care (Associació Centre Solidari, 1991) and minors on 'at risk' registers (Barcelona Societat, 1999).

A similar scenario was inherited by municipal authorities in Genoa in the 1970s in terms of a legacy of stigmatising assistentialism and a heavy focus on institutional solutions. As a response, a priority of 'de-specification' of provisions has strongly permeated Italian service delivery. The radical reform of Italian psychiatry and mental handicap services has been well documented (e.g. Mangen, 1989; Ramon & Giannichedda, 1991), but de-specification has extended to services for juvenile delinquents and into the education system. These trends have evolved in a policy arena which has been reliant on a highly plural system manifesting patchiness of supply, co-existing with duplication of effort and with much reliance placed on parish-based interventions (European Commission, 1992). Within Centro Storico, Caritas and the Red Cross have been important providers, especially for the immigrant population (ILRES, 1991). In the face of public sector deficits in facilities such as child and elder care, there has been considerable reliance on external facilities and, even more significantly, informal providers (Gazzola & Seassaro, 1988; ILRES, 1988; Malara, 1991).

The 'in-kind' welfare system in Germany depends on a plural mix of municipal and third-sector services, with many of the more innovative facilities arising from the mushrooming grass-roots neighbourhood movements of the 1970s. Respondents to this study referred to a relatively sluggish move towards decentralisation which only accelerated with the incorporation of the service arena within urban regeneration policy from the early 1990s. On the other hand, Hamburg was an early pioneer in developing child services for inner city clientele (Freie und Hansestadt Hamburg, 1990) and latterly, action has been taken to address the needs of immigrant children in over-crowded housing in areas such as Karolinenviertel through multi-sectoral approaches (Lang, 1994; STEG, 1994).

The authorities in Liverpool, more than other large cities in Britain, have long relied on a large voluntary sector and this is currently actively promoted by central government as the basis of ensuring 'best value'. In fact the welfare mix had been expanding during the 1990s when, as with all cities, the municipality received greater competences for community care, responsibilities being transferred from the health service, to be delivered through purchaser–provider partnership. Social services were decentralised and there were reports during the 1990s that the central area was deprived in terms of adequate provision on several counts: day nurseries and home helps being cases in point (PSS, 1995). On the other hand, localities such as Granby and Dingle have also demonstrated high levels of need based on indicators such as children receiving free school dinners or on 'at risk' registers (Princes Park Health Centre, 1991). There is also a large number of young male and female prostitutes, often addicts who trade locally, for whom outreach services have been designed (Woods, 1989). National policy to foster positive development in a child's early years has been particularly prominent in the 1990s with 'Fresh Start' and programmes under New Labour such as 'Sure Start', the national childcare strategy, the child care tax credit and new opportunities fund, all of which have been introduced in Liverpool (Scott *et al.*, 2002). As for the large deprived multi-ethnic population, voluntary agencies such as Age Concern and PSS have been progressively expanding dedicated services for each client group (Torkington, 1991; Age Concern, 2000). Of all the cities under review, social services priorities in Liverpool have been the most closely integrated in the urban revitalisation agenda, especially since the early 1990s.

As in Liverpool, the welfare services agenda has progressively formed a part of the regeneration of inner city Marseilles, outlined in the series of urban contracts (e.g. Streff, 1989). Once again, these areas have heightened levels of need (e.g. Ville de Marseille, 1990b, 2000) and there has been long-term reliance on a plurality of organisations, but with service deficiencies in the child and elderly care sectors (Prono, 1989; Ville de Marseille, 1989, 2000).

Health services

A converging agenda has been emerging in relation to spatial inequalities in health outcomes, one trigger having been provided by the multitargeted WHO 'Healthy Cities' programme initiated in 1981, which has been extended throughout Europe (e.g. Ashton, 1991). On most indicators, inner cities are among the worst areas: poorer housing, pollution, heavy smoking and drinking, and poor diets all being implicated, as well as their functions as a magnet for a drifting, indigent and recent immigrant population. The investigation by Rodríguez and Lemkow (1990) of Barcelona is typical of literally hundreds of studies reporting findings of a clear linear relation between income, location and selected morbidity and mortality rates. In this case, Ciutat Vella had the lowest life expectancy which, later in the 1990s, was exacerbated by the resurgence there of high rates of TB and the appearance of AIDS (Casas i Masjoan, 1994; Barcelona Societat, 1999); the locality also retained its prominent rank in terms of teenage primagravity (Nebot & Farré, 1991). These observations have been repeated in large measure in Centro Storico (e.g. Antica, 1985) and latterly neighbourhood health has been endangered by a plague of rats. Many also pertain to Mitte (e.g. Schmid-Hopfner, 1988; BAGS, 2001b). Liverpool's comparatively poor health standards on a wide range of counts have been extensively recorded (e.g. Liverpool City Council, 1988a; Merseyside's Health 2000, 2000). In particular, the inner city has suffered high rates of lung cancer and mental illness (e.g. Liverpool City Council, 1994c), and above-average 'Harman' scores used to target primary care funding to areas most in need (Parkinson, 1994).

Though by no means exclusively, inner cities are in the front rank of drug-related morbidity, something which, by its very salience, city authorities have regarded as blighting their urban regeneration efforts. In all the case-study areas there are reports of a deterioration from the late 1980s, associated in part with the replacement of heroine by crack cocaine as the most serious drug of preference, and multiple drug use (e.g. Manzanera *et al.*, 2000; BAGS, 2001b). New client groups emerged among recent immigrants (e.g. Ghirardelli *et al.*, 1991). Problems mounted with the growth in criminal activity and prostitution to feed the habit (e.g. Ruben, 1990). During the 1980s regional and municipal authorities formulated drug action plans, many of which have specific location targets and outreach goals (e.g. ILRES, 1989; Ville de Marseille, 1990c; Diesner *et al.*, 1994; Ajuntament de Barcelona, 2000). Liverpool was one of the frontline innovators in its approach to drug treatment through the promotion of a harm-reduction strategy, securing collaboration from police authorities to caution and refer rather than automatically to prosecute (Safer Merseyside Partnership, 1994). The inner city drug dependency clinic in Abercromby opened in 1985 and has implemented this partnership approach, offering methadone treatment and extensive outreach to specific categories of clients such as male and female prostitutes. One result has been that, although the city has a very high rate of addiction, the related HIV rate is comparatively low (Liverpool City Council, 1995a). The other cities have adopted many of these measures, including free needle exchange, mobile dispensaries, needle 'vending machines', and so on (e.g. Gallo & Scaltritti, 1994; Ajuntament de Barcelona, 2002); in Hamburg there is a drop-in centre for open drug consumption under supervision (BAGS, 2001b). There is ample literature about the consequences of this approach. Whilst it may serve hard-to-reach clients, there is a risk of perpetuating their inadequate supervision by health professionals. Furthermore, the service does little to assist rehabilitation. Machines can be prone to vandalism, and there has been opposition from some communities in which facilities are located, accompanied sometimes by ambivalent attitudes on the part of city authorities (ORS, 1998; Guelfi, 1999). Drugs policy has tended to be volatile and several respondents in cities like Hamburg and Genoa pointed to a current toughening of attitude, away from harm minimisation to criminalisation, with some downplaying of the earlier significance attached to target setting. Certainly, this has been the policy line adopted from the late 1990s in England (e.g. DETR, 2000).

The reappearance of TB as a major health risk – associated with AIDS, the recent inflow of international immigration and rough sleeping – has also impinged on inner city public health. For example, Ciutat Vella has been recording very high rates, including among children, although prevalence towards the end of the 1990s was in decline (Ajuntament de Barcelona, 1993, 2000). While rates are also highest in Hamburg's Mitte, particularly among immigrants, trends have been stabilising since the mid-1990s (BAGS, 2001b). A similar tendency has been observed in Liverpool (Merseyside's Health 2000, 2000). The spatial distribution of HIV/AIDS is a function of whether it is primarily associated with a homosexual or injecting population. Thus, the rate of AIDS (including related TB) has been up to five times as high in men in Ciutat Vella as the city average, due to the concentration of an addict population (Barcelona Societat, 1999) with respondents in Genoa recounting much the similar case for Centro Storico. However, in the northern cities there is only a weak spatial element, owing to its continuing predominance among homosexuals (BAGS, 2001b).

Area targeting

As with social services there was an urgent need to upgrade health facilities, particularly in the public sector, to reduce spatial inequalities and alleviate reliance on private services (Naylon, 1981). Health and local government reforms in the 1980s provided a catalyst for reform. Barcelona was one of the first Spanish cities to adopt a systematic planning approach, with the instigation of annual health surveys in 1983 and spatial analysis of particular problems to assist allocative decision-making (Costa, 1991). Decentralised delivery systems and a reform of area primary care have been fully implemented in Ciutat Vella since the early 1990s (Villalbi *et al.*, 1999). Problems of coordination with the hospital sector and between public and private services were still outstanding by the end of the decade and are partly demonstrated by the above-average resort to emergency services by the neighbourhood population (Ajuntament de Barcelona, 2000, 2002). Global health aims have been integrated in the series of strategic city plans, and local area regeneration programmes have also been developing along these lines (e.g. Pla Estratègic, 2000).

Despite the establishment of the Italian national health service in 1978, this area of provision has remained problematic. The legislation created sectorised health delivery which in Genoa was initially based on groups of neighbourhoods, although since the early 1990s the whole city has formed one sector. However, the European Commission (1992) has complained that the sector approach in Italy in reality has left little room for specific area-based action due to day-to-day pressures and funding limitations. There have been several national attempts at reform since then. A particular problem reported by respondents has been the access to health afforded to immigrants in Centro Storico (see also Il Laboratorio, 1991).

The German health system has been the object of ongoing reform since the late 1980s with the aim of reducing institutional cleavages between public and private services, and between hospital and extra-mural sectors. Independent office practitioners in this latter sector, for much of the study period, enjoyed a neo-monopoly of practice rights. Municipal health services in Hamburg operated on a decentralised principle and since the adoption of neighbourhood regeneration programmes health issues have featured prominently on the urban policy agenda (e.g. Trojan *et al.*, 1993; Breckner *et al.*, 2002).

Liverpool was a pioneer in public health, appointing Britain's first medical officer of health. City health planning employs a wide range of socio-economic indicators, most of which identify the inner city as among the neediest localities, attracting supplementary funding for primary care (Liverpool FHSA, 1991a; Princes Park Health Centre, 1991). Many client-targeted programmes for ethnic minorities by implication have a strong area focus (see, for example, Liverpool Central and Southern Community Health Council, 1990; Torkington, 1991). There have also been dedicated neighbourhood projects such as those in the peripheral estate at Croxteth, as well as several centred on the Princes Park Surgery in Granby-Toxteth, which was among the initiators of ethnic profiling (Public Health Sector, 2000). Current national spatial targeting takes the form of 'health action zones' in selected deprived localities and relies on partnership in service delivery and the establishment of public health targets, such as the reduction of suicides and childhood smoking. These have subsequently been specified in the NHS Plan of 2000 (DETR, 2000) and have also been assimilated into strategic planning of the city in terms of the SRB and Objective One programmes, among others.

Based on extent and longevity, the integration of health planning into the urban regeneration enterprise has been the most advanced in Liverpool and in Marseilles, where the series of urban contracts have progressively refined a health agenda. The current contract for 2000–2006 specifies a catalogue of targets, such as spatial inequalities of provisions and improvements in primary care, and establishes a network of *Ateliers Santé-Ville*, one of them in Marseilles, to advance them (Ville de Marseille, 2000).

Education

The judgement by Harrison (1983) that education, together with housing and the local economy, were the principal 'links in the chain binding the inner city and its children to their destiny' qualifies him for nomination as an unwitting Jeremiah. The welter of measures adopted in the intervening period have failed to overcome constraints on life chances imposed by impoverished and disruptive family backgrounds, poorly equipped, stigmatised schools and high staff turnovers. As the OECD (1998) demonstrates, these interventions represent a compromise between earmarked and mainstream prioritising. Some are pupil- and family-oriented; some support teachers and schools; some are internal to institutions, whilst others extend to outreach. Where it has been adopted, area-targeting, on the other hand, has been something of a movable feast, going in and out of fashion, but being most sustained in the case of France.

Again, the relative lack of access of inner city children to good quality local facilities is reported in many of the cities, particularly at the beginning of the study period (e.g. Naylon, 1981; White, 1984; Liverpool City Council, 1989; Cinieri, 1990). Since then, the contraction in the size of the school age cohort has provided an increased opportunity for their parents to shop around outside the immediate area, supplementing the practice in countries with extensive private facilities like Spain, France and more recently England, for the more affluent to avoid the state sector altogether (e.g. ILRES, 1988; Generalitat, 2000c). Among the reasons prompting flight to external facilities has been the reputation of local schools for behavioural problems and low academic attainment. In inner areas like Ciutat Vella and Centro Storico these and problems of high absenteeism – positively correlated with age of pupil – contributed to the perpetuation of above average rates of functional illiteracy in the adult population (e.g. Cassino *et al.*, 1983; Soler *et al.*, 1987) which, whilst now in decline among the native residents, has been replaced by the problem of children of recent immigrants who enter the education system semi-literate in their own tongue and lacking knowledge of the host language (Ajuntament de Barcelona, 1990; Gazzola & Carminati, 1991). The problem is compounded in the case of Barcelona by the official insistence on the primacy of the Catalan language in the school system (Bou & Pau, 1994).

The below-average academic attainment of inner city schoolchildren has been reported in all the cities (e.g. Canepa, 1985; Ville de Marseille, 1990c;

Ajuntament de Barcelona, 1991; Wohlert, 1991; Podzuweit *et al.*, 1992; Government Office for Merseyside, 1994; Ripol-Millet, 1994; Best Value, 2000). Increasingly, a stronger ethnic dimension to problems has emerged and, moreover, typically extending beyond recent immigrant populations. Thus, prior to the arrival of new immigrants in Ciutat Vella, educational failure was most acute among children of the long-settled Romany community, who also displayed higher propensities for truancy (Vintró i Castells, 1989). Similar observations were reported by respondents in the case of the same ethnic group in Hamburg's Karolinenviertel, the main area of their residence. Academic attainment in Liverpudlian neighbourhoods of high ethnic minority concentration, such as Granby-Toxteth, are amongst the lowest in the city, which in turn reports rates considerably below the national average (e.g. Granby-Toxteth Task Force, 1994). Absenteeism and linguistic problems leading to underachievement have been reported among certain pupil groups (Loh Lynn, 1982; Foundation for Civil Society, 2000). Similarly, neighbourhoods in Marseilles with a large minority ethnic population have recorded low educational attainment (Winchester, 1993). The consensus about contemporary outcomes in the most recent strategic plans for all these cities is scarcely encouraging.

Policy targets

Competence for public sector education in Barcelona is largely in the hands of Catalonia, one of the first 'autonomous communities' to receive devolved powers. Client-focussed targeting that, implicitly, has assumed a strong area dimension, commenced with the compensatory measure, *Marginats Socials*, in 1983, originally largely oriented to Romany pupils and involving the allocation of temporary or permanent additional teaching staff. Since then the arena of action has been expanded, particularly in Ciutat Vella, owing to the growing number of children of Maghreb origin, and programmes are currently investing resources in multi-cultural education, as well as a continuing emphasis on the teaching of Catalan (Generalitat, 1990, 1996a,b, 2000c). National legislation in 1996 has provided for specialist teaching centres for the most disadvantaged children – a high concentration of these facilities in Barcelona being situated in Ciutat Vella (Colmenares, 1999). In addition, the neighbourhood regeneration programmes from the mid-1980s earmarked resources for infrastructural investment in the school sector (PROCIVESA, 1989), and broad compensatory educational aims have been gradually refined within the overarching development plans for the city.

Targets adopted during the left municipal government of the mid-1970s in Genoa were discarded within 10 years, owing to recriminations that they resulted in perverse outcomes, including entrenched stigma of neighbourhoods. In their stead a policy of 'de-specified' delivery has been adopted, although some targeting for client groups such as disabled children was retained (European Commission, 1992). Respondents to this study maintained that the few local compensation measures in Ciutat Vella have, for the most part, been supplied by voluntary agencies such as Caritas or informal secular groups of volunteers and are not part of the formal curriculum.

For much of the study period area-targeting was not in force in Hamburg, although policies started to change with the adoption of neighbourhood development programmes from the early 1990s, with educational compensatory measures seeking broader collaboration with child and social services agencies. The joint enterprise rejuvenation agency, *STEG*, since then has been promoting more formalised horizontal partnership. This extends to local schools, where objectives include achieving more effective outreach and streamlined transition from school to the labour market for the older pupil, the latter having also been a national priority since the mid-1990s (Brinkmann, 2003). The federal government has also been perturbed by results of international surveys recording a comparatively weak performance of German children in mathematics and science, suggestive of institutional failings (Radtke, 2003). Accordingly, among other programmes, the federal model neighbourhood regeneration projects, one of which is situated in the peripheral Hamburg district of Lurup, has been concentrating effort on those among the most deprived of the pupil population (DIFU, 2003; Soziale Stadt, 2003).

Legislation in the mid-1960s in England and Wales provided earmarked funding to address the specific needs of ethnic minorities (the so-called 'Section 11' money), the overwhelming majority of which has been allocated to education. Education Priority Areas were instituted in 1968 in selected localities, among which many of Liverpool's neighbourhoods were the first beneficiaries (University of Liverpool, 1991). Much of the compensatory action originated in the Urban Programme and, to some extent, the Community Development Projects, discussed in Chapter 1. The election of a conservative government in 1979 heralded an era of repatriation of responsibilities for education to the national level, something that has continued under New Labour after 1997. Significantly, Mrs Thatcher's agenda in this policy sector formed part of her broader ambitions to redefine central–local relations and, as already discussed, incurred the creation of agencies that avoided local democratic control. As a relatively small-scale example of this departure, the government-nominated neighbourhood task force for Granby-Toxteth, among other equal opportunity actions, provided funding for outreach (Granby-Toxteth Task Force, 1991). Far more profound as an exemplar of central *dirigisme* was the legislation in 1988 abolishing education priority areas – which, in any case, had produced mixed outcomes – permitting schools to opt-out of local authority control and paving the way for a nationally-determined curriculum with targets and monitoring via performance indicators. Deprivation supplements to national educational allocations were severely cut back, with the corollary of curtailing the capacities of local authorities to engage in targeting. Moreover, the room for manoeuvre in

Liverpool was already being limited by the fact that the derivation of main-stream block grants paid insufficient regard to education indicators, despite the sector being the largest budgetary item (Couch and Wynne, 1986). In addition, the real value of 'Section 11' outlays was being pruned (Vize, 1994). Overall, while the subsequent creation of the SRB in 1994 and the successful nomination of Merseyside as a EU Objective One region did go some way to restoring the local scope for establishing broad priorities in education, there were complaints that, in real terms, nationally-derived funding was in decline. Accordingly, targeted measures implemented from the late 1980s to mid-1990s tended to be relatively small-scale. Among them were some local 'second chance' schemes funded through the Urban Programme and the European Social Fund (Granby-Toxteth Task Force, 1991) and school-based projects such as 'Children of Inner City Education – CHOICE' aiming through early mentoring to encourage young pupils to study and plan for the option of higher education (CDS, 1994).

The Conservative policy line has largely been perpetuated under Labour. Glennerster (2001) reviews the whole gamut of policy output which has continued at a hectic pace – 'Fresh Start', 'Sure Start', 'Beacon Schools' and 'Excellence in Cities' being the most significant. As Walton (2000) recounts, the nomination of 'Education Action Zones' consolidated the approach to compensating for educational disadvantage by aiming to reinforce multi-agency partnership whilst leaving scope for discretionary innovation on the part of local authorities. Among the principal aims are the tackling of school exclusions and the pervasive problem of truancy, some of it crime-related, with legislative provisions allowing for custodial sanctions against defaulting parents. Targeting of academic standards has been reinforced, among other things, by the creation of maintenance grants to enable children to under-take post-statutory education assisting the ultimate goal of attaining a 50 per cent cohort participation rate in higher education (DETR, 2000). How some of these measures have fared in practice is taken up in the follow-ing chapter.

Albeit within the context of a very different educational system, many of the priorities in England have also been prominent in France. Mitterand's first governments were concerned to press ahead with addressing the issue of educational failure which displayed marked social and spatial characteristics (Hugon, 1983). One of their early measures was the adoption of education priority zones (*ZEPs*) in 1981 the design of which, as Tizot (2001) describes, owed much to their equivalents in England and Wales. In the event, much of their funding has been derived from municipal sources, many parts of Marseilles being among the first to be nominated (Ville de Marseille, 1990c). In advance of subsequent policies in Britain, the French government in the mid-1980s announced a programme to increase radically the proportion of the relevant cohort gaining the matriculation qualification (*baccalauréat*) (Ambler, 2001). During this period, too, educational targeting was gradually being formulated within the remit of the national neighbourhood regeneration programmes (*DSQs* and latterly *DSUs*). Associated measures ranged from upgrading of infrastructure, improving outreach with a prime goal of tackling absenteeism, and broadening partnership. Nonetheless, it has to be said that for much of the period this agenda could count on only tepid engagement of the education ministry. A refinement of the catalogue of aims for education, within a more integrated policy network, has been progressively pursued in the series of urban contracts. Currently, the blueprint for Marseilles is prescribing action on improved investment in new construction, outreach, equal opportunities – in part through the further development of 'second chance' facilities – and the chronic problem of truancy (Ville de Marseille, 2000; AGAM, 2000a,b). With regard to persistent absenteeism, the government announced a reversal of its policy of suspending family allowances for offenders in favour of a graduated preventive approach of parental aid – whilst retaining the ultimate punitive sanction.

Deviant spaces

Of all the sectors being discussed in this chapter crime-related issues have rapidly soared to the top of the urban agenda, in some measure displacing local unemployment and physical degradation as the prime preoccupations in cities where these have become less pressing. Most surveys indicate that local populations have an acute sense of 'indicative mapping', identifying as high-risk locations what are often circumscribed areas (Foster, 1990; Bauman, 1998a), many of them being inner city neighbourhoods with a long-standing reputation of threat. Politically, perceptions in many ways are more important than realities. Empirically, rates of criminality in the inner city are not consistently greater than elsewhere, but crime there can be more visible, can effect retrieval investments and impinge on the potential of the night-time economy in rejuvenation efforts (Thomas & Bromley, 2000).

Mindful of the inadequacies of reported crime statistics, in the past two decades police authorities in several of the case-study cities have incorporated victimisation surveys into their policing strategies. These build on national and international surveys, and repeat their strengths and limitations (e.g. van Dijk *et al.*, 1990; Mayhew & van Dijk, 1997). Whilst they may reflect a deeper participatory approach and afford greater prominence to the victim's experience, there are serious report biases arising from the choice of sampling frame and whether they are based on telephone, questionnaire or interview research. Many have included only adult respondents and, therefore, underplay the prevalence of crime affecting juveniles. There can be under-reporting of sensitive crimes such as sex assaults or domestic violence. And, they may fail to reach those most exposed to crime or attract those who are more vocal on the subject. For these and other reasons, victimisation surveys can only be an aid to effective policing design. This being said, the consensus of results indicates that males are more exposed to violence in public spaces and females in private spaces (Mooney, 1997). Reported repeat victimisation in the relatively short term is on the increase, with much of it displaying marked spatial features (e.g. Mawby, 2001). Crime and victimisation has tended to be higher among minority ethnic populations and particularly the second generation, although intervening demographic risk factors have to be taken into account (Keim, 2000; McClain, 2001). Finally, Pain (2001) assesses how fear of crime is structured by gender, age and race and, as reported earlier, the role of the media plays an important role in shaping attitudes (see also Cottle, 1993). Many investigators are at one in arguing that fear of crime may be only weakly correlated with actual levels and, accordingly, the results of victimisation surveys can pervert effective policing by placing too great an emphasis on a 'uniformed' presence (Fitzpatrick, 2001; Johnson, 2001; Silverman & Della-Giustina, 2001).

Victimisation surveys in Barcelona began in 1983 and, at that time, Ciutat Vella returned the highest rates. As the 1980s progressed, the difference between neighbourhood and city recorded instances narrowed and by the end of the decade the inner core no longer reported the highest incidences (Torres i Carol, 1988; Barcelona Societat, 1999). A significant decline in local rates was elicited around the time of the Olympic Games and has been associated with more intense policing of central neighbourhoods. The availability of methadone treatment for addicts is also thought to have played a part. Conversely, there was some displacement to certain kinds of opportunistic crime such as car-related offences, owing to the comparative lack of secure parking in the vicinity (Sabaté & Aragay, 1995). The trends in Ciutat Vella continued until the late 1990s with the neighbourhood ranked second in terms of risk, although with a rise in repeat victimisation (Sabaté et al., 1999). However, thereafter there has been a significant reversal of trends both in the city and in the study area, where similar rates to the early 1980s have been recorded (Sabaté et al., 2001).

Respondents reported that there was no routine practice of victimisation surveys in Genoa, where official crime rates have been among the lowest of the larger Italian cities (Bramezza, 1998). Ad hoc surveys have all indicated a higher level of criminality and certainly a fear of victimisation in respect of Centro Storico (Gazzola, 1982; Arvati, 1988; Guelfi et al., 1990), with the growing presence of immigrants, and associated drug-trading and prostitution being identified as the main triggers (Canepa, 1985; Archivio de Studi Urbani e Regionali, 1993).

Whilst, empirically the total reported crime rate in Hamburg is broadly inversely related with the wealth of each locality, considerable diversity is recorded in deprived areas (Friedrichs, 1998). Data in the Appendix for reported offences in Innenstadt in 2001 suggest a rate almost five times the city average. By far the greatest concentration of this excess is recorded in just two locations: Altstadt and Klostertor-Hammerbrook. Of other inner neighbourhoods, St Pauli and St Georg have consistently been regarded in the popular mind as among the most high-risk areas for opportunistic offences. These perceptions are supported by survey evidence: Legge and Bathsteen (1996), in their investigation of four areas of high criminality, report a victimisation rate of 80 per cent in St Georg in the year previous to interview, with greatest risk related inversely to social status and age. On the other hand, it has tended to be the elderly who fear crime most, within a general context of growing insecurity and dissatisfaction with the quality of policing. It is also older respondents who most desired more obvious police presence and stricter enforcement (Legge *et al.*, 1994).

A national crime survey has been undertaken in Britain since 1981. Whilst there are discrepancies in recent findings between declining reported and increasing surveyed offences, there are clear indications that inner city dwellers experience and worry about crime most (DETR, 2000). The British Crime Survey of 2002 revealed a marked concentration of criminality in ten police authority areas in terms of robbery, and Merseyside was ranked sixth in terms of reported hotspots (Simmons & Dodd, 2003). Local victim surveys have been a legislative requirement since 1995 and consumer satisfaction surveys now form part of established 'best practice'. In fact such surveys on Merseyside date back to the early 1980s, with the first recording that its status as a hotspot has a relatively long pedigree (Kinsey, 1984). However, the 1985 survey also suggested that 'personal crimes' were only marginally higher than the national average (Merseyside Police, 1986). In the 1990s a cause of particular concern was the high rate of repeat victimisation in inner city areas (but also peripheral estates) which was closely associated with deteriorating perceptions of urban security among the older cohorts. At the same time, there were complaints – particularly among young and ethnic minority respondents to surveys – that the high rates in Granby had merely led to heavy-handed policing, with intensive resort to house search. In general, those surveyed there overwhelmingly pressed for more foot patrols based on greater community consultation (Merseyside Police, 1993; Safer Merseyside Partnership, 1994).

In the 1980s Marseilles enjoyed a dubious reputation as the crime capital of France, although, in reality, in terms of reported offences it was not ranked in the top three cities. Survey evidence of this period overwhelmingly associated crime in the city with the large Maghreb population and, at least, recorded petty street offences committed by the second generation did lend support to this view (Derogy & Pontant, 1984). In fact, the inner neighbourhood of Belsunce was the centre of organised crime and prostitution in the city long before the arrival of the Arab community. Nonetheless, the link between immigration and crime has persisted (Delgado, 1989). Ad hoc surveys indicate that Magrebin of the second generation have high propensities of offending, although this might merely reflect the arrest rate. Certainly the commissioner of police for the first arrondissement, participating in a study in the mid-1980s, opined that there was no more delinquency in the neighbourhood than elsewhere, something which is supported by crime data for the peripheral areas of the city (SOMICA, 1985; AGAM, 1987). Nonetheless, the issue of criminality in the central areas has remained a priority in regeneration planning (see, for example, AGAM 2000b,d).

The inner city and drug-related crime

The results of the study of seven areas of England by Wilson and colleagues (2002) hold for the present case studies. Despite harm reduction and crime detection strategies pursued since the late 1980s, local reports indicate a vigorous trade in heroin and crack in an increasingly competitive market of falling real prices. However, they also record that the local drug trade *per se* is not always a sufficiently robust predictor of overall neighbourhood decline, despite the raised violence that surrounds it.

One reason for this observation arises from a tendency for spatial displacement to certain areas where relative lack of policing may actually serve to allow deviant activities to proliferate. This eventuality is demonstrated in the case of Ciutat Vella where, due to police action in advance of the Olympic Games, there was progressive relocation of open drug-trading from the prestigious Plaça Reial, just off the main Ramblas thoroughfare, initially to confined areas in adjacent Raval, where it soon became associated with internecine crime. In turn, due to pressure from neighbourhood movements and the redevelopment of the narrow alleyways, where it had been rife, to create new and desirable residential squares, it moved on a little further southward to Montjuïc. On the other hand, Centro Storico has remained the prime locus of the drugs trade in Genoa and, within it, the circumscription of Prè, long a criminal patch controlled by a handful of *Camorra* families who extended their empire to the growing number of immigrant traders. From the late 1980s there were also signs that the hard drugs scene was expanding in Hamburg as the city gained a national reputation for cheap availability (Landeskriminalamt, 1991), with Hinrichs (1990) noting a generalised reluctance among residents in high-risk locations to alert the police, for fear of reprisals. Braver souls among the community have asserted that in areas like St Georg most drug pushers were second-generation Turks or immigrants from Gambia (e.g. Hohaus, 1992). Respondents to this study also supplied unpublished reports of the growing importance during the 1990s of Romany traders in the Karolinenviertel. Official statistics lend support to this spatial concentration of drug pushing, with almost half of drugs-related offences in the mid-1990s being recorded in St Georg and the main railway station area, although this was also, no doubt, due to the heavier police effort there (Legge & Bathsteen, 1996). As a result there has been a decentralisation of activity to areas such as Altona and local parkland where drugs are buried for subsequent trading (Landeskriminalamt, 2000;

Legge & Bathsteen, 2000). Despite the stronger national emphasis on penalisation rather than harm reduction, Merseyside Police continued their policy of collaboration with drug treatment agencies described above, although the force also redoubled its policy of targeting traffickers (Sharples, 1991; Merseyside Police, 2002). One of the first crack factories in Britain was uncovered in Granby in the late 1980s (Merrifield, 1995) and the neighbourhood remains a major centre of street and mobile-phone related trade. More recent reports confirm that Liverpool is a principal distribution centre for smuggled narcotics and, with it, associated gun-related crime has been on the increase (Neild & Elias, 2002). The same scene pertains in Marseilles, with drugs mainly being traded in specific central localities, as well as being rife in peripheral social housing estates (Ville de Marseille, 2000; AGAM, 2000b).

Urban blight and street prostitution

In all five cities the steady rise in incidence of street prostitution and problems of illegal drug consumption have become inextricably linked. To be sure, street trading in sex is nothing new to any of these port cities: in Ciutat Vella, for example, the Ramblas was long an area where open prostitution was tolerated, as too was the multitude of bars and hotels in Barri Xino (Ferras, 1977; Negre i Rigol, 1988); Hamburg's Reeperbahn is world famous for these personal services.

As part of a general clean-up of crime in preparation for the Olympic Games the Barcelona authorities took action to close establishments known to be a centre of trade, but the predictable effect was merely some displacement elsewhere (Ripol-Millet, 1994). The subsequent inflow of international immigrants has served to diversify practitioners, with some street surveys broadly indicating that the majority of female prostitutes are non-Spaniards (e.g. Carmona, 2000). Respondents to the study emphasised the distinct spatial distribution of different forms of prostitution with females, rent boys and transvestites plying in specific city locations. In general, the policing of female prostitution has been more manageable, since much of it still operates from establishments. In comparison, male prostitution is more street-based and its practitioners are deeply distrustful of the police. According to some surveys, the lack of willingness of these young men to make contact with official services arises from the fact that, apart from fear of stigma, over half are 'overstayers' – mostly from Maghreb (Romani i Alfonso, 1989). Despite general police action taken as a result of pressure from local residents and commercial interests, and targeted interventions to tackle child prostitution (Alabart *et al.*, 1990), in many parts of Ciutat Vella activity has gradually re-emerged. Genoa's Centro Storico presents a similar picture, with over 60 per cent of those convicted giving an address there (Gazzola, 1982). The survey undertaken by the Federazione Regionale Solidarietà Lavoro (2000), as part of their outreach work, suggested that the overwhelming majority of practitioners were immigrants who, after the police closure of bars and hotels associated with the trade, tended to operate from call centres that have sprouted up in the area. Ghirardelli and colleagues (1991) note a movement into the area of transvestites, the majority of whom were also drug-dependent. The opening of eastern Europe led rapidly to an increase in supply of prostitutes and a spatial diffusion in Hamburg. Beforehand, the growing problem of serious drug addiction had triggered a strong trend towards illegal street prostitution, involving even younger girls, under the control of pimps, although rent boys tended to operate from bars and within more confined spaces (Landeskriminalamt, 1989; Nixdorf, 1989). Police attempts to respond to neighbourhood demands to stem prostitution in St Georg, by negotiating its displacement to disused dockland and to St Pauli, met with limited success owing to safety concerns on the part of practitioners. Consequently, the neighbourhood continued to draw increasing numbers of teenagers engaged in the trade (Barth, 1989; Freie und Hansestadt Hamburg, 1991). In the 1990s, criminal surveys recorded the growing involvement of certain prostitute groups in the drugs trade (e.g. Landeskriminalamt, 1992). According to respondents to the present study, the more recent redesign of street layouts in St Georg, together with police follow-up of registration numbers of cars, have gone some way to mitigating the blight in the neighbourhood of kerb crawling, although this has produced displacement of activities elsewhere. This latter phenomenon has led to chronic neighbourhood complaints in gentrifying areas of Georgian Abercromby, in the area surrounding Liverpool Cathedral (e.g. Higgins, 1991). Despite a variety of policing tactics, it has proved resistant to eradication. In general in Liverpool, prostitution is overwhelmingly drugs-related and a street trade, although the mobile phone has been changing trading patterns (see also Merseyside Police, 1990; Neild, 1991). This latter practice of avoiding face-to-face negotiation has been longer established in Marseilles – with its centre of prostitution in the Belsunce area – through use of 'minitel'.

Police and policing

Policy objectives prosecuted in the past 25 years or so reveal a confusing set of priorities. The changing balances between suppression and 'social animation' to address causation, general urban security and targeted prevention, and varyingly heavy and 'soft' surveillance have constituted uncomfortable parameters for reconciliation (e.g. Gazzola & Seassaro, 1988; Pitts, 1998; McClain, 2001). The ambiguities of the agenda reinforce suspicions that the arena has been one of crisis management, with tactical attempts to assuage conflicts of interest between local and national accountability, elite and more democratic control (Dauge, 1991; Mawby, 1992).

Nor are matters improved in several of the countries by the continued institutional division between separate police forces, both in terms of national competence and local implementation. In France, Italy and Spain, elements of the police systems retain paramilitary attributes with the *Gendarmerie, Guardia Civil and Carabinieri* answering to the defence ministries, being recruited nationally and largely residing in barracks rather than in the wider community. On the other hand, with some exceptions (such as dedicated transport police services) the system in Britain is more unitary and decentralised; Germany occupies an interstitial position, with major competence being enjoyed by the Länder (see, for example, Mawby [2003]). Organisational structures and the professional cultures they foster have profound consequences for the styles of policing that are favoured or practicable. Thus, police respondents in Genoa and, to a lesser extent Barcelona, expressed reservations about the feasibility of widespread community policing since this would need to be underpinned by an integrated police service. Moreover, community policing also implies the street-level application of discretion and the powers of cautioning on the part of individual officers. Owing to the fact that, in several of the cities, 'legality' overrides the 'opportunity' principle in the exercise of policing roles, these possibilities are not routinely available (see, for example, the discussion in Silverman & Della-Giustina [2001]). Finally, the relative isolation of police forces from local communities, the preference for surveillance by car rather than by walking the beat and typically low clear-up rates have done little to improve public relations. Nor is this situation helped by the close association in the public memory, in some of the countries, of the police having enthusiastically served repressive fascist regimes (e.g. Heidensohn & Farrell, 1991).

In Spain the major policing preoccupations have been the combating of terrorism, the sharp rise of urban delinquency associated with drug addiction and, latterly, the illegal activities of 'non-regularised' immigrant groups. It has not been an agenda favourable to the pursuit of more socially oriented strategies, although some concessions to investing in crime prevention have been made (Recasens i Brunet A, 2001). There are three police forces: the *Guardia Civil* and the *Cuerpo Nacional* (formed in 1986 for urban policing) are within the state's competence; the less powerful municipal police answer to the mayor (Mawby, 1992). In addition, Catalonia has a special force (*Mossos d'Esquadra*) under the control of the regional government. Professional rivalries have been rife between the elements of the system and this has exacerbated arrival at coordinated operational approaches, a factor which has also contributed to low public satisfaction (Marti i Jusmet, 1990; Delgado, 1994). In Catalonia, a process was initiated in 1994 whereby the *Mossos* will become an integrated service, the state forces gradually ceding functions until full transfer of responsibilities is completed in 2008 (Recasens i Brunet, 2001). However, according to Coriminas (1994) there remained a large measure of demoralisation among the professions, particularly since suspicions were entertained that additional regional devolution, together with the steady accumulation of local powers by the mayors, were demoting the primacy of security over 'softer' targets. More positively, the measures have allowed more progress in establishing area-level coordination, building on the first experiments associated with rehabilitation programmes in Ciutat Vella.

Police respondents in Centro Storico stressed that, confronted by the scale of mafia-organised urban crime and drug-associated offences, proposals to move towards community policing would meet with considerable internal resistance. Besides, organisational divisions lessen its feasibility. Reforms in the early 1980s to reduce the militaristic character of the police, with the creation of the second 'state police' service, seem to have had little impact since its officers receive poorer training and enjoy lower status (see, for example, Carrer, 1988). In comparison, the police service in Germany has been embracing more area-focussed surveillance and prevention programmes, some linked with urban regeneration initiatives. A new type of community officer has been evolving, the employment of ethnic minorities having been eased from the late 1990s by the relaxation of nationality rules in recruitment (Aden, 2001).

Merseyside Police have, perforce, been among the most sensitive to the social and political relations. In the early 1980s, during a period of fractious dealings with the city council, there were accusations of democratic deficits, decision-making by 'quangos', problems over accountability and complaints of resistance in a post-riots era to expanding community policing (e.g. Simey, 1988). On the other hand, the riots and other tensions between police and public triggered greater national activity in designing a range of community programmes. As in the other countries, reforms met with a measure of resistance within the ranks, owing to suspicions that an alien 'social work' role was being foisted on the service, displacing what were regarded as higher-order tasks (Fyfe, 1995). By the end of the decade, Merseyside, as other English constabularies, had instigated a broad array of decentralised activities in the field of community and race relations, and liaison with schools. One result of greater consultation – which feeds into the 'command and control' system in force – was the increase in the number of officers on the beat (Merseyside Police, 1991). Strategies have since evolved along these lines, with the aim of fine-tuning resource deployment. The establishment of more devolved access points for local consultation has led to increased neighbourhood policing, in response to public demands. CCTV is now more intensively used in high crime spots. And there have been greater efforts in targeting: for example, drugs seizures, firearm offences and monitoring of pubs and clubs at closing time (Merseyside Police, 2002). Since 2002, central Liverpool has also been an object of the national 'street crime initiative' which has concentrated extra resources on a small number of localities in England exposed to very high incidence of opportunistic offences.

As part of his wider decentralisation agenda, in the early years of the Mitterand presidency a third force, the municipal police, was created under local control. However, in comparison to other elements of the police system, its officers still enjoy limited powers (Hebenton & Thomas, 1995). It was during this period that a broader prevention element was introduced to urban policy, discussed below, necessitating new collaborative forms of engagement. However, a relatively marginal contribution of the police to these efforts has been noted (e.g. Mawby, 1992; Body-Gendrot, 2000b). Proposals for targeted police deployment to high crime localities, which would have incurred the diversion of resources, met with professional opposition and also encountered the wrath of politicians in areas which would have been net losers (Body-Gendrot & Duprez, 2001). In general, Body-Gendrot (2001) assesses that there are serious outstanding problems in securing community participation in new policing styles, particularly in assisting detection outcomes. Within Marseilles, since the 1990s there have been schemes of decentralised policing, such as cadet training programmes located in deprived neighbourhoods. More general community projects have also targeted these areas, with an emphasis on police outreach to youth and the employment of local residents as mediators (e.g. the *Femmes Relais* scheme) to liaise with schools. However, there are accounts of problems of effecting policing innovation in the city due to inadequate dedicated resources, institutional compartmentalisation and ambivalence on the part of local political elites (e.g. Body-Gendrot, 2000b).

Area-based targeting

Area-based approaches, of course, are not limited to direct police actions. They run a whole gamut of allied interventions on the part of health, welfare and education agencies, bottom-up collaborative projects such as 'neighbourhood watch', and what Newburn (2001) terms the 'zones of private governance', including use of CCTV and the growing employment of private security services. For Johnson (2001) the rapid evolution of this arena demands sensitive and overarching management to avoid the pitfalls of inefficient over-policing, invasive security measures, inadequate account-ability and the mounting difficulties of disaggregating specific effectiveness.

Efforts to integrate issues of urban insecurity into the broader strategic planning of the city began in Barcelona in 1983 with the instigation of regular city victimisation surveys. These were followed soon after by the creation of corporate partnership to oversee crime and policing developments under the aegis of the mayor. Within this emerging focus the problem of high criminality in Ciutat Vella and its damaging effects on regeneration potential gained greater weight. Accordingly, to assist retrievability, measures attempted to combine heavier police surveillance with prevention and outreach work. As already discussed, the 'recapture' of Plaça Reial was emblematic of the desire to stimulate gentrification and the night-time economy. Supplementary action was taken to close nearby bars and hotels suspected of being dens of crime and prostitution. Prevention and outreach were fields new to Spanish policing in the democratic era. In Barcelona, the projects included liaison with the education authorities to tackle school absenteeism, monitoring the practice of street drinking – a growing problem among adolescents – and other actions targeting juveniles (Maragall, 1986; Prevenció, 1989). The preventive dimension was reinforced at the end of the decade through the convening of consultative partnership on social welfare by the mayor, together with a special council on crime prevention in Ciutat Vella (Clos, 1991). Nevertheless, policy effort was not all in one direction: Recasens i Brunet A (2001) records some dissipation of effort after the Olympic Games. Before leaving office the socialists responded to national concern over levels of urban crime by creating a national consultative council to advise on ways forward. However, at a time of growing threats of terrorism and drug-related serious crimes, the election of the right-of-centre government, in 1996, had a noticeable effect of downgrading the social dimension of the policy arena. But, one positive response was a move in the late 1990s to area policing responses by the *Cuerpo Nacional*. According to Recasens i Brunet A (2001), within Barcelona, although collaborative work between crime and social agencies continued, there was a change of emphasis on the part of the city council, incurring the downgrading of the partnership approach and a reinforcement of intensified security measures.

During the 1980s in Germany there were innovations in crime prevention on the part of certain left-led Länder which subsequently led to a mushrooming of partnerships. In the early 1990s in Hamburg, the issue of 'urban hotspots' gained prominence on the agenda and was rapidly integrated into the neighbourhood regeneration programme, assisted by a series of victimisation surveys. 'Recapture' strategies were also apparent, noticeably in St Georg and in the area of the main railway station (Berger & Schmalfeld, 1999). Nationwide, since 1997, there has been collaborative design of area prevention programmes. In comparison, the desires of the new chancellor, Schröder, to adopt the Blairite dual toughness on crime has been thwarted by the lack of support from his coalition partners and the fact that the policy area is largely within the remit of the Länder (Aden, 2001).

The most consistent intervention with regard to urban crime has been undertaken in Britain and France, albeit with diverging emphases. In the case of the former there has been a remarkable similarity of approaches, irrespective of the government in power; indeed, if anything, New Labour has pursued the tougher line (for further discussion, see Crawford, 2002). The idea of a partnership approach to crime prevention gained momentum in legislation of 1984 and was followed in the late 1980s by the 'Safer Cities' programme which, among other things, urged local authorities to engage with the police and others to devise, in partnership, means of 'designing out' crime in the policies under their control (Liverpool City Council, 1993c; Graham & Bennett, 1995). This was followed by earmarked funding to advance the agenda, through such measures as neighbourhood constables and 'neighbourhood watch' (Merseyside Police, 1993). Furthermore, a central plank of City Challenge and subsequent across-the-board regeneration programmes has been 'partnership' action to remedy Liverpool's negative image conveyed by its association with high crime levels (e.g. Safer Merseyside Partnership, 1994; Liverpool City Council, 1994b). The rapid output of policy under New Labour since 1997 and its prime objects of child and juvenile delinquency is discussed by Matthews (2001). The centrepiece of the government's approach was enshrined in 1998 legislation. It extended the sphere of action of partnerships, reinforced policing by objectives, instituted further performance targets, and expanded consultation processes – for example, by requiring the authorities to undertake household surveys. In addition, local government had to demonstrate that crime reduction objectives were being factored into mainstream policies. At the same time, a consciously tougher line was adopted through the mandating of curfews and electronic tagging of offenders (Taylor, 2000; Newburn, 2002; Mawby, 2003). High on the agenda has been the tackling of the 'broken windows' syndrome (Wilson & Kelling, 1982) through stricter responses to more effective and early bottom-up management of 'minor incivilities' which can speedily contribute to neighbourhood blight (Walklate, 2001). One local response was the creation of an 'anti-social behaviour unit' in Liverpool to ameliorate the reduction in the quality of urban life posed by such nuisances as unruly neighbours (Liverpool City Council, 1999b). As a further refinement of their approach, the government, in 2003, proposed the 'gating' of back alleyways between terraced housing, typical of inner city neighbourhoods.

The culture of partnership was institutionalised in France in 1983 with the establishment of a hierarchy of consultative crime prevention councils, organised from national down to local level. They arose as a result of the recommendations of the Bonnemaison Committee which provided the basis of the policy line pursued into the 1990s, reversing prior neglect of the neighbourhood focus in prevention (Dubouchet & Mekboul, 1992). For Crawford (2002) the explicit attempt to integrate strong community and preventive elements into crime control through a multidisciplinary approach bears favourable comparison to policies favoured by the British government at the time. Sustained local delivery and the long-view rather than the British search for the 'quick fix' was the anchor of the French system. Neighbourhood centres (*Missions Locales*) were vital to its operation, and policy innovation gave space to the creation of a new profession of youth community worker, as well as the recruitment of neighbourhood residents to act as mediators (*Femmes Relais*, see above) (Pitts, 1998). In the study area in Marseilles the *Mission Centre Ville* was entrusted with a broad remit (see Chapter 3), part of which was to encourage patch policing and community outreach (Ville de Marseille, 1995). The city's prevention council was one of the first to be established and, since 1989, has been closely involved in the formulation of the urban contracts; decentralised partnerships integrating police, social services and education agencies were created in the highest risk neighbourhoods to agree localised approaches (Ville de Marseille, 1990d; Donzel, 1991).

Body-Gendrot and Duprez (2001) detect in the return of a right government, in 1993, a demotion of the prevention focus with a tougher line on crime, this also being noted in the 'urban policy re-launch' package of 1996 which sought to redeploy police resources to the highest risk areas (see, Anderson & Vieillard Baron, 2000). In 1997, revised local security contracts aimed for greater harmonisation of prevention and criminal justice objectives in order to improve policing surveillance and security measures. In the reform, mayors and prefects were given wider powers. Nonetheless, Body-Gendrot (2000b) argues that implementation of the new contracts was compromised by resistance among key institutions, citing the education authorities and, critically, the police. In spite of the moves towards devolution and attempts in the late 1990s by the socialists to accelerate area-based strategies, in comparison to many other countries, she judges the French police forces as remaining highly centralised, with limited local accountability and begrudging engagement in local prevention schemes. For Crawford (2002), the creation of 'local crime prevention groups', led by public prosecutors, together with the creation of multi-agency *Maisons de la Justice*, has served to reinforce more of a security-led agenda, something also demonstrated in the reform of the local prevention councils in 1999. Whilst a new post of 'city warden' was developed – with recruitment among the young local unemployed to improve mediation – he maintains that, cumulatively, policies since the mid-1990s have substantially abandoned the progressive ambitions for the policy arena outlined by Bonnemaison. The repercussions for local strategies in Marseilles are manifest in the adoption of more intensive security measures in high-risk locations in the centre and in the northern estates, including the newly created *Grand Projet de Ville* (see Chapter 1). They are also in evidence in the formulation of goals to tackle crime – particularly juvenile and drug-related offences – contained in the urban contract for 2000–2006 (AGAM, 2000b; Ville de Marseille, 2000).

5
The Impacts of Regeneration

The principle vehicles for delivering regeneration are assessed in relation to key input, process and output factors. Discussion begins with selected comments on the source and style of funding inputs for housing rehabilitation in the inner city.

Funding

In the past three decades there have been cumulative reforms aiming to redress the ineffectiveness of handling budgets from increasingly diverse sources, including the growing importance of EU allocations. Progress in this direction is most advanced in the case of Britain and France and has been accompanied by moves away from ad hoc, short-term awards towards more reliable, longer-term dedicated or mainstream monies. However, evaluations of the significance of these innovations must be set in the context of the conditionality of these flows, as well as their additionality, since, as we have seen, 'new money' in one pot has often entailed cutbacks elsewhere.

Issues of multi-level governance and associated funding inputs received greater attention during the 1990s. In Barcelona, for example, a tiered formula was agreed between the three principal levels of administration in the early 1990s reinforcing the role of the city as the prime source of the public purse (Esteban, 1999; ARI, 2001). In the case of Genoa, until the 1990s, national allocations were ad hoc or 'experimental', respondents complaining that they all too often served to deflect a more pressing local agenda. Critically, they were also highly conditional and restricted to prestige projects or, when wider, imposing narrow definitions on what counted in eligibility for subsidised rehabilitation, particularly in mixed-use neighbourhoods (Besio, 1999). The case of Hamburg most clearly exemplifies the crucial interaction of public subsidies and conditionality, in stipulations concerning rent regulation and deregulation. It has also been the city subject to the most sustained and significant retrenchment of higher-tier allocations in the 1990s, as federal funding shifted eastwards (Alisch & Dangschat, 1991; STEB, 1999). In this environment the city had to fall back on its own already pressed budget with consequent cutbacks in subsidies to landlords, depressing the ability of the poorer among their rank to engage in rehabilitation (Keller, 1999). The short-term nature of federal funding, and its volatility, were among the factors cited for disjointed financial and planning horizons and for failing to underpin a context where collaborative partnership could mature (Schmitz, 2001; Breckner *et al.*, 2002). In terms of need–input ratios, in many ways, Liverpool and Marseilles were the cities most chronically deprived of adequate mainstream funding, as well as being the most dependent on public sources beyond their control. The increasing stipulations of matched funding has served to underline local fiscal incapacities to maximise revitalisation (see, for example, Liverpool City Council, 1986b; Berkouche *et al.*, 1988; Skifter Andersen, 2003).

Funding for private rehabilitation encompasses a more diverse arena, not least in the scale of investment and whether it draws on public subsidies. Until the mid-1980s, municipal engagement with the sector in the majority of these cities was largely restricted to subsidising works undertaken by owner-occupiers or small-scale landlords. Indeed, planning instruments of the time paid relatively little attention to the potential of wider private-sector involvement, its motives for action or its assessments of retrievability. This was a particular failure in climates of comparatively low overall demand for housing and in environments where the costs of works for cramped sites in historic areas were particularly elevated (Ambulante Hilfe, 1989; Gallén, 1999; Skifter Andersen, 1999). Arising from the slow advance of rehabilitation in some parts of the inner cities, came a gradual recognition of the need to engage the sector in a more formalised accommodation. This action was not only prompted by motives to harness the full potentials of private investment in a structured way; there was also concern to limit the negative consequences that were being observed in cities like Barcelona and Genoa arising from uncontrolled speculative investment in which further degradation of stock was tolerated, in the hope of greater future returns through land price rises or more generous public subsidies (e.g. Seassaro, 1991). In more buoyant central housing markets with a large rental sector, as in Hamburg for much of the study period, many private landlords were foregoing subsidies in order to let upgraded property free from contingent tenancy and rent controls, a practice resulting in significant reduction in the supply of protected accommodation (Dangschat, 1993). Correspondingly, less buoyant, low-rent markets, as in Marseilles, provided little incentive to landlords to invest in rehabilitation (Skifter Andersen, 1999). More generally, the overall effects of local urban renewal projects were being compromised by too narrow a focus on individual properties and by the large number of owners lacking the means to match what were inadequately targeted – and sometimes increasingly less generous – public grants (e.g. Bensasson & Teule, 2000; Valls, 2001).

The greater scale of regeneration, growing pressures on public budgets, and the expansion of strategies to compete in the new European urban order have encouraged cities to embrace new funding cultures. Hence, irre-spective of their relative ranking in deprivation, all of the case studies have factored ever-larger and more rapidly accumulating private-sector leverage assumptions into planning public allocations (e.g. Pfadt, 1996, 2000; POI, 1998; Barcelona Societat, 1999; Government Office for the North West, 1999; Ville de Marseille, 2000). At several points, we have noted the role of local political leaders in courting the sector, particularly from the mid-1980s. Accordingly, public actors have become more reliant on investment and profit horizons of their private partners, with resultant policies being more exposed to the vagaries of the market. The pursuit of greater leverage has not always proved unproblematic, and evidence suggests a considerable lead-in time is required to achieve desired levels. The experiences of Liverpool and Barcelona are two cases in point. As discussed in Chapter 3, initial leverage returns arising from the work of the Merseyside Development Corporation in the 1980s were disappointing. It was only after an expansion of its remit that there was a substantial upturn in private investment, which in fact out-paced expectations (Merseyside Development Corporation, 1993). In later years there were stronger signs of local 'learning by doing', with far better than predicted leverage being produced by the City Challenge programme, for example. However, even here less positive outcomes were noted in the case of housing investment (Russell, 1997). The growing privatisation of Barcelona's regeneration agenda were amply demonstrated by policies adopted to exploit the Games effect, demoting what had been public-led, socially motivated and, admittedly, rather un-programmatic rehabilitation responses of the early 1980s (Serra, 1989; ARI, 1999). And, to be sure – as already discussed – there were criticisms of the downgrading of the social dimension in the new policy line (e.g. Maragall, 1986). But the city fathers had not reckoned with the slump in the property market in the early 1990s which reduced demand for prestige private housing on the Olympics sites as well as producing a glut of office accommodation (Jauhiainen, 1995). Demand did recuperate later and Barcelona has deservedly taken its place among the top international regeneration success stories. However, private investment has been more conditional, being readily forthcoming for prime site developments such as *Front Maritim*. For less prestigious sites there has been a reduced factoring-in of social returns from 'planning gains', with the public purse increasingly funding wider environmental improvements. Fur-thermore, in many of these locations overall leverage projections were pruned back (Gomà & Rosetti, 1999; ARI, 2001).

Formulating and administering regeneration

The 'inward-looking'–'outward-looking' continuum of management styles, specified by Hall (1997), provides insights when attempting cross-national review of regeneration policy trajectories. Those turning inwards are typically narrow agency and management-led, whilst outward orientations are comparatively more cross-sectoral and strategic, and act to accumulate externality gains. If not always practised in reality, the outward policy style has become the orthodox rhetoric. With it has come greater reference to the quality of urban governance and improvements in 'institutional capacity'. As examined in Chapter 2, this has been interpreted as the formulation and administration of policy involving tighter vertical collaboration and wider horizontal partnership (for recent discussion, see Healey *et al.*, 2002).

A common trigger for moves in this direction has been the preoccupation with image reconstruction which interacts with the pursuit of the 'entrepreneurial city' (e.g. Seassaro & Sola, 1992). Strong civic leadership, broadly based partnership and differentiated delivery mechanisms are its currency. In some countries, a related concern has been the quality of legislation designed to underpin these evolutions. To take the worst case, it was a common complaint that the regeneration of Genoa has been hampered by reliance on poorly drafted laws that were rapidly supplemented by a profusion of special measures compromising original goals. This created serious policy vacuums, where private-sector interest could dominate (Pannella, 1980; Jodogne, 1991; Marcelloni, 1992). It was an environment in which much was promised through 'quick fix' salvation projects but little delivered, fuelling public scepticism (Bianchini *et al.*, 1990; Seassaro, 1991). Mindful of these limitations, public authorities involved in Genoa's regeneration have taken greater care from the 1990s onwards to legislate more synergistic and proactive blueprints (Seassaro, 2000). There is still someway to go in refining vertical collaboration in what, in any case, is an evolving environment of decentralisation. Even in relatively stable polities such as Hamburg's there have been reports of problems in negotiating the divide between the competences of the city state and its constituent boroughs (Lang, 1994; Forschung & Beratung, 1997; Schmitz, 2001). In both Liverpool and Marseilles there has been a relatively weaker action arena for regional instances and the corollary has been that policy priorities and their funding have been heavily dominated by the centre (e.g. AGAM, 2000c).

The following discussion on the evolution of partnership is largely confined to its role in physical regeneration; EBNSC (1997) provides a selective comparative review of approaches in relation to employment and social inclusion. The five countries have approached the development of new partnerships from different traditions with regard to urban provisions. In the UK, services historically were mainly supplied directly by public authorities. In continental countries, the 'subsidiarity principle' operates. Through it there has been extensive reliance, both on the voluntary sector and on contracting out to commercial firms or joint enterprises (Lorrain, 1992; 6 & Vidal, 1994). Common among all the countries is the fact that early engagement with the private sector, to stimulate rehabilitation, was generally confined to legal and financial instruments to modify behaviour through a range of tax incentives, direct subsidies and amendments to rent regulation. Later, more pro-active attempts at incorporation into policy-making and implementation, now associated with one aspect of horizontal partnership, began to emerge, albeit at differing speeds. At the same time there was much rhetoric about the benison of community participation to harness the resources of civic society, in recognition of the common ownership of social problems and their resolution. This contemporary view of the citizenry builds on earlier policies of engagement of grass-roots 'new social movements' and the espousal of self and mutual help.

It is no surprise that the stage of amalgamation of formal and informal actors into effective horizontal partnership varies among these EU states. The present sample may be very crudely divided into those countries which established strong partnership models earlier (the UK and France) and those that were relative laggards (Germany and Italy) (Stratmann, 1999; Froessler, 2000). Spain occupies something of a median position, although there are marked differences among Spanish municipalities (Raventós, 2000). However, most commentators on France judge the vertical dimension of collaboration stronger than the horizontal, particularly when compared to the contemporary British adoption of the 'private finance initiative' (e.g. Lovering, 1995; Le Galès & Harding, 1998; Vogt, 1998). Finally, an impulse for convergence, particularly for those countries with limited prior experience of partnership, has been provided by the instigation of the EU 'planning system' in 1988 for disbursement of the Structural Funds. Additionally, local partnership has been stimulated by Community programmes such as Poverty 3 and the Territorial Employment Pacts (Birkhölzer & Lorenz, 2001; Estivill, 2001) (see also Chapter 6). A further impulse – of varying degrees of operational importance among the countries – was also created by the UN-inspired local 'Agenda 21' for sustainable development (see, for example, von Petz & Schubert, 1998; Liverpool First, 2000; Blanco & Rebollo, 2003).

Ciutat Vella

Neighbourhood movements in Barcelona, in comparison with the rest of Spain, were already at a comparatively advanced stage before the death of Franco, having mobilised against his regime's structural plans for the city (Borja, 1977; Pindado Sánchez, 2000). In the Transition they were to play an important legitimising and mediating role, assisting the secularisation of the new Spanish democracy and actively courted by the new municipal authorities (Bier, 1980; Valls, 2001). A corollary has been that leaders of these informal associations were the most rapidly assimilated into formal political structures with the effect of taking the edge off their radical aspirations (Domingo & Bonet, 1998). The neutralising outcome of incorporation was institutionalised by local government legislation in the mid-1980s which formalised consultative pathways (Gomà & Brugue, 1994). It was during this period that new local community partnerships in alliance with private firms took a pro-active role in the implementation of *ARIs* through the conclusion of contracts with the council (*convenios*) (Held, 1994; Estivill, 2001) (see Chapter 3). This is not to say that community groupings were entirely compliant. There was, for example, growing suspicion about the lack of equity in the distribution of gains from the Games which provoked 'bottom-up' defensive reactions (Taboada, 1991; García, 1993; Esteban, 1999). This defensiveness was not inappropriate. Held (1992) detected a pronounced change in municipal priorities away from a prime focus on neighbourhood *convenios* towards wider incorporation of commercial actors in more formal and larger-scale public–private partnerships, something which has continued in the intervening period.

In fact, this embrace of commerce was not initially something that came naturally to the local socialist elite, which had long entertained reservations about the motives of the private sector. It was the nomination for the Olympics that encouraged Mayor Maragall fully to grasp the commercial nettle. But, his conversion to the cause of exploiting the projected multiplier dividends that could arise did not sit comfortably with the more socially inspired neighbourhood projects of his earlier period in office. In fact, Newman and Thornley (1996) argue that, in the mid-1980s, two regeneration approaches were simultaneously in operation: one retaining its community roots and prosecuting a social agenda; and the other in favour of pursuing windfall gains of bigger projects, a planning arena increasingly detached from wide democratic participation. But, by the late 1980s the policy climate was clearly privileging even more robust engagement with the private sector which, in turn, was responding enthusiastically, given that the more easily retrievable – and profitable – sites were being readily made available by the city (Ahtik & Sokoloff, 1990). Elsewhere, to encourage broader collaboration in less financially propitious locations in Ciutat Vella, in 1988 the city created a joint stock, limited-life company, *PROCIVESA*, to promote integrated responses within the context of more programmatic planning (Raventós, 2000). Developments on the formal partnership front were consolidated in the series of strategic plans for the city, already discussed. The Chamber of Commerce and associated organs were to take a prominent role in their formulation, although other actors – such as the trade unions – were also incorporated (e.g. CCOO, 1990; CITE, 1993; Pla Estratègic, 2000).

From the literature it is clear that in Barcelona there was a strong shift in favour of privatised forms of partnership, in order to advance modernisation of urban governance (see Held, 1994). Raventós (2000) notes that political issues about the balancing of public and private regeneration gains have become more acute, particularly as post-Games projects have often entailed higher risk and longer timescales for large private investors. As for community involvement, Font (2003), in reviewing recent evidence, discerns a marked clientelism in the political favouring of those in-groups that have been the most compliant in the process.

Centro Storico

Gabrielli (1989) repeats the already noted observation that early supine political inputs on the part of Genoese political elites, and the repeated fiscal crises besetting the city in the 1980s caused policy spaces filled by commercial actors and, to a lesser extent, cooperative movements. This created an environment in which much of the agenda could be dictated by private motives which privileged new construction over rehabilitation, minor works being largely the preserve of individual landlords and owner-occupiers (Seassaro, 1995). In this period there was a distinct spatial distribution of public–private investment in Centro Storico. In Prè, the northern cramped and deprived neighbourhood, upgrading was largely left to the public purse. The southern, somewhat more spacious and socially more mixed neigh-bourhoods, such as Porta Sorprana, attracted more private investment interest (see Chapter 3). Confronted by growing municipal budgetary retrenchment, faltering steps were taken during that decade to depart from this funding model, with the establishment of public–private ventures. Given that they were alien to Italian traditions, new legislation for their regulation was required. An initial consequence was to reinforce both the agenda and nego-tiating power of commercial agents. In comparison, in public-led projects, municipal actors were constrained by unrealistic nationally determined rehabilitation cost indices over which they exercised no control.

Measures to advance the regeneration of Centro Storico were adopted from the late 1980s, through the creation of *ARRED* and *FILSE*, joint venture enterprises. There was also more pro-active engagement on the part of the city council with the powerful port authority as regards the planned major redevelopment of the Porto Storico, the main site of the 1992 Colombus Exposition (Comune di Genova, 1991; Seassaro, 2000). On the other hand, apart from individual small-scale actions, reliance on larger commercial interests was effecting unplanned socio-spatial changes in the study area. Their decisions evidenced marked preferences for 'second home' development in the more prestigious *piazze*, and locations typified by advanced degradation and the presence of a large immigrant population were consistently shunned (Pescaglia & Seassaro, 1995).

The successful emergence of the left in municipal government in the mid-1970s, and increased engagement of the trade unions in community mobilisation, stimulated the development of neighbourhood movements in Italy, building on earlier experiences of job creation cooperatives, particularly in the north (MacFarlane & Laville, 1992; Somma, 1999). Community movements were stirred into action against a background of pronounced distrust of public institutions, something that the general inertia in delivering urban services only served to reinforce. The earliest and less problematic engagement of residents in rehabilitation in Centro Storico was located in its least degraded and more affluent area, Porta Sorprana. Long-standing inhabitants elsewhere in the neighbourhood were in far less of a favourable position. Colonisation of its better parts by gentrifiers had knock-on effects on rents and on risks of their deportation to social housing in the poorly served periphery. The arrival of growing numbers of immigrants exacerbated competition for declining supplies of cheaper housing – and for jobs. It was not surprising, therefore, that solidaristic mobilisation has been sorely challenged. In this atmosphere, some residents have perceived in rehabilitation projects a threat to their ability to remain, whilst much grassroots demand for neighbourhood enhancement has been stimulated by exclusionary motives to 'clear up' the commonly perceived blight of illegal immigration, and associated crime and prostitution (e.g. Colla & Germani, 1989). It has to be said that these concerns were among the main impulses prompting what has so far been the most explicitly community-led scheme in the Centro Storico. This was the project to reclaim the immediate neighbourhood around Vigne (discussed in Chapter 3), building on earlier actions by its central actors to survey the extent of urban degradation in the whole area, in order to build the case for urgent public subsidy. Besio (1999) recounts the legal and financial problems in implementing the project. These were not improved by what she regards as the lack of enthusiasm on the part of city authorities to assist in its success. For these, and other reasons, she is realistically circumspect in her assessments of the true extent of wider community participation achieved.

Nevertheless, bearing in mind the volatile political and funding climate of Italy in the 1990s, Seassaro (2000), in reviewing policy accumulation in that decade, remains relatively sanguine about prospects for building on what are, admittedly, limited achievements in establishing a more expansive collaborative model in the regeneration of Genoa.

Innenstadt

In comparison with many of its northern neighbours, German urban regeneration has remained more firmly within the hands of political and administrative actors (Weck, 2000), although in this regard Hamburg is, to some degree, an exception. As in other large German cities, community involvement originated in the protests against large-scale renewal projects and the displacement of residents to peripheral social housing. A broad alliance of neighbourhood and student groups was forged and, in turn, it helped stimulate a strong 'alternative self-help' movement (e.g. Stegmann, 1976; Dangschat, 1990; MacFarlane & Laville, 1992). Among the earliest initiatives in the city was the mobilisation of residents in St Georg in the early 1970s to resist mass demolition plans. This led to the creation of a representative committee to press the city to implement recent federal legislation providing for rehabilitation and to address the growing problems of blight associated with the sex industry (Soho, 1990). Growing speculative pressures within the city in the 1980s sparked further defence of local spaces, as the plans for the re-launching of the city inspired by the mayor's elite 'growth alliance' gathered pace. Emblematic of such defensive reaction was the conflict over the redevelopment of Hafenstrasse in St Pauli (e.g. Hermann *et al.*, 1987). The heated nature of these protests unsettled the city fathers, and some accommodation to their demands was made in the middle of the decade. Thus, the newly created 'alternative' rehabilitation and self-help agencies such as *Lawaetzstiftung* and *Stattbau* were progressively integrated into the planning system, although there were some who argued that they actually ran the risk of reinforcing marginalisation by targeting their projects only on the most needy (e.g. Schubert, 1990; Foelsch, 1994). There was also greater activity to engage the wider community in the consultative process (Rieper, 1992). By the early 1990s efforts to promote wider consultation had become routine, with decentralised planning offices aiming to assist the process. However, there was also a general worry about the degree to which different elements in the community were being effectively engaged. In this regard, low electoral turnouts in deprived areas was one of the factors leading to the approval of the city-wide neighbourhood regeneration programme of that period (Schubert, 1993). This new focus on revitalisation depended heavily upon the instigation of local area management prosecuted through more formalised partnership structures.

It was during this period that the explicit incorporation of public–private partnership into the urban strategy took root, an early and influential reference point being the success of the 'Media Park' in Cologne (Heinz, 1994). As stated in earlier chapters, private-sector interests have enjoyed strong representative input in the local polity, particularly through the Chamber of Commerce. From the mid-1980s, Mayor von Dohnanyi had been at pains to institutionalise their interests in his plans for area regeneration within the city. For this purpose, a joint enterprise, *STEG*, was created in 1989 to oversee the programme in a large part of Hamburg (Jorzich, 1993; Lang, 1994). In the post-Unification funding climate of the early 1990s, it was recognised that greater private engagement would be required, particularly as sparse federal funds were more forthcoming when private agencies had a greater input. The result was that, during that decade, public–private partnerships were in operation in several inner city localities, although so far they have tended towards small-scale projects (see Stratmann, 1999). The major exception is the development of *HafenCity*, discussed in the last chapter. It represents the strongest and largest privatised regeneration so far enacted in the city.

Partnerships in Hamburg, then, are in a comparatively developed state when compared to many other areas of Germany, although Chancellor Schröder from the late 1990s, on both the employment and urban regeneration front, has been stridently advocating such alliances (Birkhölzer & Lorenz, 2001). Yet, there are few who would argue that within the city they have attained an advanced state of maturity. Breckner and colleagues (2002), for example, have expressed concern that the development instruments and objectives are still too abstract to sustain involvement among the many actors whose agreement is required for the partnership to mature. Commenting on the ongoing city and federal programmes, some respondents from private agencies complained of a certain 'crowding out' by those closer to the city authorities, such as *STEG* and some of the 'alternative' actors. Community participation has, as everywhere, produced mixed results, with areas such as St Georg – with longer mobilisation experience – better organised to negotiate than the more socially heterogeneous St Pauli or working class Lurup, for example (Forschung & Beratung, 1997; Tengeler, 2001; Breckner & Herrmann, 2003). Rapidly rising property values in some neighbourhoods have also privileged the protection of private interests over community gain, particularly where greater social tolerance could undermine investment potential (Schütte, 1993): witness the resentment among some residents that an unwelcome manifestation of new forms of gentrification in St Georg was the increasing number of gay men buying into the area, rendering it *überschwult* (Burchard, 2000).

Inner city Liverpool

Although experiencing something of a lean time during the period of Militant domination of the city council in the 1980s, the city has long depended on an extensive partnership with the voluntary sector in the delivery of urban and welfare services (Nevin & Lee, 2000). Frontline suppliers include Merseyside Improved (now Riverside) Housing, engaged in rehabilitation and new-build cooperatives, as well as having expanded into labour market measures (Merseyside Improved Housing Annual Report, 1995; Riverside Housing, 1999). Cooperative Development Services (CDS, 1994, 2000) originated in local protests against mass slum clearance and was an early actor in 'housing action areas' stipulated in legislation in 1974. Apart from national players, other local agencies central to regeneration activities include Personal Social Services, the oldest such organisation in the country (PSS, 1995) and Liverpool Housing Trust (LHT, 2000). In comparison, until recent decades, more formalised private-sector integration into local political structures was the weakest in the five cities. Greater incorporation of commercial interests into a strategy for urban renewal was largely instigated by central government from the early 1980s and, as already discussed, several innovations signally by-passed municipal control. By the turn of the decade, some years after the change of council, the idea of broad-based partnership had already become an orthodoxy and several public–private ventures were strategically in place to assist the city's regeneration ambitions, one of them being the technology park at Wavertree (Economic Development Strategy Forum, 1991). Both City Challenge and the introduction of the SRB brought new regeneration partnerships into being, such as the Dingle and North Liverpool Partnerships.

Merseyside Partnership was central to the preparation of the Objective One bid and Liverpool Partnership Group for the 'Liverpool First' strategic plan (see Chapter 3). In short, formal alliances have become the central plank of local governance, incorporated into every EU, national and municipal blueprint for the city (Parkinson & Russell, 1994; Best Value, 2000). Critical to this enterprise has been the creation of decentralised government offices, as well as the establishment of the regional development agencies (e.g. Government Office for the North West, 1999).

Liverpool is also characterised by the strength of its community movements, often working in partnership with the voluntary sector (Meegan, 1994; Duffy & Breitenbach, 1995). Local housing cooperative movements spread from the early 1970s, being some of the first to be engaged in the new 'general improvement areas' that had been legislated (Pullen *et al.*, 1975). The Weller Street cooperative in Dingle was formed in 1977, the first of its kind in Britain, to resist the re-housing plans by the council and, instead, to implement a new-build cooperative on the site. It was to be a catalyst for the many other associations that have followed, although they were all out of favour during Militant's period in office (McDonald, 1986). Among them are the Eldonians, founded in the mid-1980s in Vauxhall among a tightly knit Catholic community of Irish origin. Working with Merseyside Improved Housing, they developed a new 'village' and later expanded their remit into local economic development, although with mixed results. An important component of their work was networking, media representation and collaboration with, for example, the Merseyside Development Corporation. They attracted endorsement by the Prince of Wales (Crowther Hunt & Billinghurst, 1990; Dawson, 1990; Bailey, 1991). Vauxhall Neighbourhood Council came into existence for motives similar to those of the Eldonians, although it had tended, in operation, to be more closely linked to the municipal authorities (Meegan & Mitchell, 2001). There have also been numerous associations among ethnic minorities. In all, as early as the mid-1980s, Cooperative Development Services was working with almost 40 housing co-ops (CDS, 1987). Other innovations of the time arose from engagement with the government's neighbourhood task force (e.g. Granby-Toxteth Task Force, 1991) or took root as a result of more elite engagement such as 'Project Rosemary' for the redevelopment of an area surrounding the Cathedral, initiated by the late Dean of Liverpool and which aimed at substantial private funding leverage (Hetherington, 1996).

These sorts of projects set in train what has been an ongoing assimilation of bottom-up and top-down approaches in the rejuvenation of inner city Liverpool and all bidding proposals from the early 1990s have been packaged in this way. The increasingly variegated system of partnership has accelerated since the arrival of New Labour in government with its espousal of 'stakeholding' (Geddes, 2001). A problem, however, has been that the very proliferation of partnerships has made for unwieldy local governance. There has also been a concern about effective representation, particularly in the more deprived multi-ethnic areas (e.g. Duffy & Breitenbach, 1995; Moore, 1997). However, following its experience in implementing New Commitment to Regeneration 'pathfinder partnerships', proposals by the council to radically rationalise their number, have met with resistance to mergers. This, for Meegan & Mitchell (2001), demonstrates the highly localised nature of solidarities on which such partnerships are constructed.

Centre-Ville

Mention has already been made of the crucial alliance negotiated in the mid-1980s between municipal authorities and the Chamber of Commerce to advance Marseilles' rejuvenation agenda (see also Redempteur, 1987; Donzel, 1990). By comparison, for much of the study period, other private actors in the central arrondissements have been less closely incorporated. Indeed, their competing interests have, at times, required sensitive management, as was the case during the first Gulf War. This situation was not improved by the fact that the influences that different interest formations can bring to bear vary substantially. According to several respondents, the wholesalers' association, dominated by *Pieds Noirs*, largely operated in the same locations as that of the small shop owners who are predominantly Maghrebin and comparatively less well mobilised (see also Mazzella, 1996). The organised interests of landlords and tenants associations have also clashed. The former, largely representing small owners, often resisted the demands for upgrading on the part of neighbourhood associations in the 1980s, particularly when they were accompanied by demands for tenancy and rent protection (Prono, 1989).

Until 1990 the main rehabilitation agent in Centre-Ville was the *PACT-ARIM* national agency, although subsequently there has been a municipal preference for rehabilitative activity through joint ventures such as *Marseille Habitat* and *Marseille Aménagement* (previously known as *SOMICA*) (Marseille Habitat, 1992; AGAM, 1993a; Marseille Aménagement, 2000).

From the 1970s onwards national programmes like *Habitat et Vie Sociale*, the *DSQ* neighbourhood projects and the crime prevention councils, together with the successive urban contracts, have prioritised further development of local and, later, city-wide partnerships (Geddes and Benington, 2001). Within Marseilles neighbourhood consultative committees have been established in all parts of the city (Mattina, 2001). Nevertheless, effective community mobilisation in the more socially heterogeneous inner city areas has not matched that of the northern estates, where community social workers have also been the most active (Anselme, 1990; Donzel, 1993; Donzel & Guilhaumou, 2001). These spatial features have been noted nationally, too (Maclennan *et al.*, 1996). Streff (1989), in her study of Belsunce, recorded the fears among the elderly population that collaboration in rehabilitation projects might lead to their displacement, views also expressed by Maghreb residents and shop owners. Similar concerns were also produced in surveys of Le Panier. From this time, the growth of the right-wing vote and wider islamophobia has made inroads into grass-roots solidaristic responses (Moore, 2001).

Public–private partnership in Marseilles, as in the rest of France, has diversified in line with the evolution of nationally directed urban regeneration policy and the general processes of decentralisation. Collaboration now ranges from relatively small-scale collaborations in housing action areas (*OPAHs*) to grander scale projects like *Euroméditerranée* (Ascher, 1994; Sallez, 1998). Yet, it remains the case that much of the collaborative investment has been expended in refining vertical relations. In fact, some authors indict the legal and organisational complexities of the urban contracts and more recent legislation such as the 2000 *Loi sur la Solidarité et le Renouvellement Urbain* for having exacerbated access for many actors to potential horizontal partnership (Bensasson & Teule, 2000; Le Galès & Loncle-Moriceau, 2001; Crawford, 2002).

Reviewing outcomes

The impact on housing

Statistics on the total effort in all aspects of housing rehabilitation do not exist since much has been undertaken entirely at private expense and is unmonitored, particularly when works involve upgrading of existing facilities that do not require planning or building permission. Furthermore, even those statistics detailing publicly subsidised work may omit accompanying, unsubsidised modernisation. For these reasons, there can be substantial bias in recorded data, especially by tenure, with the most reliable statistics being those for major rehabilitation of social housing. Aggregate statistics on access to basic amenities have also been subject to revision, reflecting changes in social values. Thus, in most countries central heating would now be regarded as an essential asset, whereas 30 years ago it would have been sole use of toilet, bath facilities and access to running hot water. Available data reveal a sharp decline in the number of units still lacking these latter facilities, although on certain counts the volume of deficient accommodation is highest in Barcelona and Genoa. Across the sample, the remaining stock with the minimal amenities now tends to be highly concentrated by location, accommodation type and household characteristics. Despite the universal achievement in inner city residential rehabilitation, what is now more pressing than basic amenities, in several countries, is the appearance or re-appearance of fresh problems. These include hard-to-let, unoccupied or abandoned property, poor sanitation and supply of basic services, resistant problems of damp, and the re-emergence of shanty town or makeshift urban developments.

Of the five cities, these last factors remain a feature in the study areas in Barcelona and Genoa. Some assessment of overall improvements in the urban fabric is provided by the municipal reports on publicly supported rehabilitation, in terms of the proportion of stock that has so far received funding, as well as recording wider infrastructural improvements (e.g. ARI, 2001). These are more detailed in the case of Ciutat Vella, and indicate that effort in upgrading gathered pace particularly from the mid-1990s (see Gomà & Rosetti, 1999). Supplementing these statistics with crude indicators of improvement such as census statistics on the rate of increase in owner-occupation suggests a rapid narrowing of the gap, reaching almost two-thirds of the city average by 1996, the latest data available. However, other indicators, such as supply of hot water, highlight the still considerable deficit in prevailing standards in the neighbourhood (see Appendix). Quality is most deficient for the growing immigrant population: some find shelter in what is little more than makeshift housing, others are accommodated in stock that reports label as 'internal shanties'. Of these two case studies, regenerative achievements are most apparent in Ciutat Vella, extending into what, until recently, had been the most degraded, 'no go' areas of Raval. Whilst, as statistics indicate, there is still outstanding work, the goals for the neighbourhood – stimulation of a broader social mix and reconnection with the littoral – are on the way to being met, although, as already discussed, at some social cost. In comparison, rehabilitation of Centro Storico appears more limited, failing to convey a major overall impact, being spatially concentrated in its southern part. Much of the north still depends on the public hand, including the growing relocation of public facilities there (see PRUSST, 1999; Comune di Genova, 2000). Several respondents emphasised that much work on improving housing stock has been of poor quality with serious problems of damp and subsidence quickly re-emerging. Despite its importance in the proclamation of Genoa as the European City of Culture, 2004, the blight of the neighbourhood continues to be highlighted by the raised urban motorway (*Sopraelevata*) – truly one of the great European eyesores – running the entire length of the frontage with the old port.

Of the cities, housing rehabilitation in Hamburg started from the most favourable baseline, though sharing of amenities was not uncommon (see Chapter 2). Commercial and residential property demand has, for much of the period, been extremely buoyant and much of the Innenstadt has been upgraded privately, often eschewing available public subsidy in order to avoid regulatory constraints. Whilst there remain some still highly concentrated areas of sub-standard accommodation, problems of housing are now largely those of shortage of supply. Similarly, inner city Liverpool can report much progress in reducing lack of access to basic amenities. Indeed, rates of this upgrading have outpaced the city average (see Appendix) and there have been 'prestige' residential conversions in several central locations, as well as major investment in developments in leisure and tourist facilities. On the other hand, it is the lack of demand in certain inner and peripheral neighbourhoods that is the more pressing (Nevin & Lee, 2000). Low demand extends into the commercial sector. One example is provided by the site of the 1984 Garden Festival, not far from the city centre and on the banks of the Mersey, which, in spite of several plans over the years for re-use, still awaits development. To a significant extent, Centre-Ville has shared the same experiences as inner city Liverpool. The area north of La Canebière, in spite of the series of rehabilitation projects, retains its image of degradation. Neighbourhoods like Belsunce still provide the poorest access to basic amenities according to 1999 census figures. They are included in the 'Centre' *DSU* programme area where, in the late 1990s, over 16 per cent of housing was vacant and almost a quarter assessed as *inconfortable* in terms of amenities, figures in excess for those of the inner city as a whole – and far higher than the city average. Predictably it was also the area with a high 'foreign' population, above average unemployment rates and a superior general 'index of precariousness' (see AGAM, 1998; Ville de Marseille, 2000). Despite being located in the city's major regeneration project, *Euroméditerranée*, it has been officially acknowledged that, in its initial phase, the scheme's achievements in housing have been unimpressive (AGAM, 2000a).

The social effects of physical rehabilitation

Demographic changes have been discussed in Chapter 2 and there are summary indicators in the Appendix. To repeat an observation already made at several points, speculative pressures have varied considerably among the case studies. This is most clearly reflected in the 'gentrifying' composition of parts of the inner city area. Where, as in the case of Liverpool and Marseilles, social housing has formed a more prominent part of the housing stock, these effects have been much less evident. Of all the cities, Barcelona has prosecuted the most explicit policy of gentrification for its inner core (Maragall, 1986; Nel.lo, 1998). City authorities in Hamburg, too, were motivated to pursue this route, mainly for reasons of greater fiscal solvency (Dangschat & Ossenbrügge, 1990; Casier *et al.*, 1991). The effect in Barcelona is amply demonstrated by the narrowing gap in property prices in Ciutat Vella, data for 2000 suggesting that, in terms of price per square metre, purchase prices have risen to over 80 per cent and rents 93 per cent of the city average (Ajuntament de Barcelona, 2003). Gentrification in Centro Storico has confined to what Russo (1993) terms 'happy islands', although internal conflict as a result of growing social polarisation during the 1990s may have dented the sense of contentment (e.g. Seassaro, 1995).

Social segmentation in Liverpool historically was characterised by denomination. In more recent decades, pronounced ethnic segregation has been to the fore (see Torkington, 1983, among many others). On the other hand, gentrification in the inner city has been relatively spatially confined. Apart from up-market loft conversions in restored dockland and in other prime 'niche' central sites – much by the 'Urban Splash' company – the other area targeted has been some of the Georgian terraces of Abercromby, notwithstanding the blight imposed by street prostitution. As a crude indicator, according to Land Registry and Census material, the average value of owner-occupied housing in the ward in 2001 was considerably above the city average and, in general, approached almost 90 per cent of that for England and Wales. However, these data take no account of differences in property size. In general, Nevin and Lee (2000) record the continuing preference for professional groups working in the city to reside outside its boundaries. In Marseilles the first inner neighbourhood of interest to gentrifiers was Le Panier, which was also among the first to benefit from subsidised rehabilitation. In Le Panier, residential upgrading was accompanied by dispatching of some ethnic minority residents, although elsewhere in the inner city this was limited by the practice of that population to sell on within its own community (Ferracci, 1983). The ongoing *Euroméditerranée* project has an agenda to increase the supply of housing in the upper-range (AGAM, 1993b), although, as discussed earlier, developments have proceeded at a slow pace, and contemporary data suggest that the same broad spatial distribution of social precariousness still persists (Ville de Marseille, 2000; AGAM, 2000c).

Of the five cities, gentrification effects have been most extensively investigated in Hamburg. Because of the preference to retain the more affluent, the city authorities were criticised for their lack of enthusiasm in applying federal laws guaranteeing the rights of existing tenants (e.g. Ambulante Hilfe, 1989; Dohrendorf, 1991). This limited application has continued (Pfadt, 1996; Pressestelle, 2000). Empirical studies point to intensive gentrification pressures near the Alster Lake and the riverside, but also in 'bohemian' areas elsewhere which, from the late 1970s, were the object of increasing interest to early 'pioneers' (Deutsche Städtetag, 1990; Dangschat, 1991b; Pfadt, 1996). The investigations also record gradual spatial diffusion of gentrification (e.g. Dangschat, 1993; Alisch & Dangschat, 1994). Reviewing trends in the 1980s, Busse (1991) judged outcomes as positive when contributory to the 'natural' community dynamic and improved local economic prospects, but unfavourable when they accelerated social displacement. Several authors have attempted to assess the more general effects of these pressures: in St Georg, for example, Pfadt (2000) argues that unintended consequences have included a diminution of neighbourhood employment, since local small firms have been squeezed out by growing pressure on rents.

Labour markets

Marseilles, Liverpool and Hamburg were the only cities in the sample where reasonably consistent and regularly produced data were discovered. Even so, trends in small-area activity and unemployment rates may reflect changing social compositions of neighbourhoods as much as the direct consequences of policy. It follows that, even when available at small-area level, they tell only part of the story. This being said, the unemployment gap in Hamburg between inner city residents and the city population as a whole in 2001 was the narrowest. However, whilst the indicators reveal considerable continuing divergences in Marseilles and Liverpool, the discrepancy in relation to long-term unemployment is much narrower and may be suggestive of the impact of targeted labour market measures. In comparison, recent data for youth unemployment are less assuring (see Appendix).

Recent research attempts to assess at what points interventions in the 'insertion pathway' reap the most dividends. With regard to populations chronically excluded from 'core' labour markets, a focus of research attention has been the issue of motivation and its long-term effect on socialisation of future generations. The negative effects of poorly designed training programmes, largely provided as time-fillers offering limited spin-offs, and the constraints on opportunities imposed by living in stigmatised spaces have also been well explored (e.g. MacGregor, 2001; Boddy, 2002; Detzel & Rubery, 2002; Sarfati, 2002). Politicians, such as British Chancellor Brown, have been prompted to complain of a 'culture of worklessness' that can mature even in fairly buoyant sub-regional labour markets. Rehabilitative measures have therefore invested more effort in a preparatory stage to reinforce positive attitudes, whilst also making some accommodation to the background social supports that might be required, such as the supply of child care. Another consideration in the construction of an effective pathway has been attention to the length of intervention and its consequences for the sustainability of successful outcomes of employability. In this regard, there has been a general criticism that labour measures connected with neighbourhood regeneration have typically been too marginal or short term, although they may represent 'added value' in terms of environmental upgrading (e.g. Forschung & Beratung, 1997; Schwarz, 1999).

There is also a research literature on differential outcomes arising from the selection of client targets in terms of their histories of engagement in the labour market (see, for example, Walton, 2000). One critical indicator has been the age of client and its interaction with welfare entitlements (e.g. Richardson & Hills, 2000). In the south, the young unemployed may have limited access to formal welfare and be dependent on their families, depressing their propensities to be mobile, when this entails loss of informal support merely to gain a low-paid and precarious situation (Mingione, 1995). Bison and Esping Andersen (2000) have examined the effects of replacement values of social security on applicants with children, some of whom may 'price themselves out' of the jobs available.

Issues relating to targeting location and sector have also been well-aired. Whilst, the notion that the inner city represents a discrete economy has been questioned (e.g. Deakin & Edwards, 1993), as reviewed in the last chapter, there is growing empirical evidence of the role of local economies in supplying employment. But there can be perverse consequences in prioritising location through mere displacement of opportunities from adjacent, non-subsidised areas. Furthermore, there is agreement that, mainly due to their skills base, inner city populations may not be the prime beneficiaries of spatial targeting: witness the 'windfall' of the Olympic Games on Ciutat Vella or the series of urban contracts on Centre-Ville (e.g. Ajuntament de Barcelona, 1997a; Donzel, 1998). Even when they do, this may not be reflected in local-area statistics, since securing good employment is also associated with spatial mobility. The seemingly positive results of intervention may also be due to 'deadweight loss' – improvements that would have occurred anyway – or 'crowding out' or substitution, whereby sub-optimal subsidised firms survive only at the cost of those unsubsidised. Government support for firms, too, may merely protect 'insider' workers at the cost of potential entrants to labour markets (for further discussion, see Barbierie, *et al.*, 2000; Bonoli & Sarfati, 2002). The issue of risk tolerance is also relevant. Favouring small or medium enterprise or promoting self-employment carries with it a higher failure profile, as discussed in the preceding chapter in relation to Liverpool. Small companies more typically shed staff faster and offer lower-quality employment conditions (see Gallie & Paugam, 2000). On the other hand, they may confer better prospects than courting large-scale inward investment. Lhermite (2000), for instance, found that half of the jobs created in Marseilles in the period scrutinised were in firms already established locally.

Balancing different objectives within the broad field of skills acquisition has also received increasing attention, particularly with regard to the pursuit of the academic or vocational route. Current evidence suggests that the acquisition of generalisable skills associated with the former may offer a more solid guarantee against unemployment, although these observations are tempered by strong gender and spatial considerations (e.g. Detzel & Rubery, 2002; Schömann, 2002; Schömann & Becker, 2002). Personal investment decisions are informed by the widely circulating evidence that many dedicated programmes for the unemployed primarily follow a 'welfarist' agenda. As such, they simply fail to guarantee a sufficient basis for sustainable employability, offering too limited a range of marketable experiences (e.g. Walton, 2000; Mosley & Schütz, 2001; Schmid *et al.*, 2001). In this they may entrench marginalisation, particularly when they interact with nationality regulations that restrict the employment of non-nationals in certain positions in the public sector, a case in point being Germany (Röseler & Vogel, 1993; Friedrichs, 1998; Bremer, 1999; Nispel, 2000). Finally, the growing consensus confirms the view that socially motivated training and job creation can make only modest inroads into alleviating unemployment over the long pull and remain insufficiently targeted (e.g. Riez, 2000; Davia *et al.*, 2001). Analysis of the Hamburg labour market, for example, indicates that transfers from the 'second labour market' to the open market is relatively modest.

Local data has suggested that only about one in six of the long-term unemployed effect a successful and sustained transition. Far weightier is the evidence of high rotation and substitution rates (Schwarz, 1999). British investigations have also uncovered a large failure rate, particularly for the least skilled and poorly motivated groups (Walton, 2000).

The case of Liverpool most clearly demonstrates the enormous scale of the task in labour market regeneration in some of Europe's most deprived local economies. During the second half of the 1990s, to reduce unemployment levels in the city to the national average would have required sustained economic growth rates in excess of national projections for the UK as a whole (Parkinson & Russell, 1994; European Commission, 1999a). Measures contained in the Objective One and SRB programmes did help to ensure a threefold increase in job creation, when compared with the preceding 5 years, but they could not keep pace with growing demand for employment. Consequently, unemployment rates actually deteriorated when compared with national trends (Boland, 2000; Evans, 2000). It is important, too, to differentiate impacts. Again, in Liverpool, the national programmes cited above proved more effective in safeguarding existing jobs than in directly creating new ones (Best Value, 2000). Targeting employment in the growing culture and tourism industries may merely entrench a low-income base (Bianchini, 1990; García *et al.*, 1992). Finally, sustainable job creation and placement have to be related to their cost-effectiveness, including duration of savings on unemployment budgets. British Enterprise Zones in the 1980s and the French *Zones Franches* in the late 1990s were judged as relatively expensive vehicles for delivering new sources of work (National Audit Office, 1990; OECD, 1998; Jessen & Neumann, 1999). On the other hand, based on net jobs created in the 1980s, Robson (1988) assesses that British local authority schemes offered the cheaper option. In similar vein, Pomrehn (1998) cites results which suggest that the cost of jobs created in France for the long-term unemployed through 'set-up' credit schemes for small firms and self-employment amounted to only half of the saved benefits outlays.

Other outcomes

The assessment of direct effects of area-targeted programmes in sectors such as education, health and policing are even more difficult to produce than the topics addressed so far, not least because they typically lack sufficient specificity of focus. Evaluations of what appear to be successful crime prevention or policing policies must take into account changes in reporting propensities, recording styles, demographic and conjunctural changes and the possibility of strong displacement factors (e.g. Graham & Bennett, 1995; Pitts, 1998; Landeskriminalamt, 2000; Johnson, 2001). There are process dimensions. These include considerations of how dominant professional cultures encourage or undermine innovative impulses. Available evidence suggests that this is most likely to occur where new action arena are, in some way, internally perceived as 'downgrading', exposing practitioners to the risks of fulfilling roles merely as 'catch-all' receptacles to contain social problems (Dauge, 1991).

Allied health programmes must be interpreted in the light of general environmental changes (positive and negative) and the emergence of new phenomena that seriously challenge prior policy lines. Respondents in Barcelona, for example, maintained that the sharp increase in prevalence of hard drug consumption and the appearance of HIV/AIDs had substantially reversed overall health gains during the 1990s. Although performance does vary according to the programme, and the local and national contexts in which they operate, at the risk of some over-generalisation, targeted measures in education have, at best, recorded mixed results. These tend to be strongest for 'softer' indicators, such as improvement in pupil behaviour, self-esteem and truancy rates. Less impressive are outcomes for 'harder' academic performance, mounting problems of social exclusion being typically implicated (e.g. Colmenares, 1999). This being said, area targeting in this sector has not always been particularly strong, well-funded or sustained. There was criticism, for example, of the former educational priority area policy in inner city Liverpool (e.g. University of Liverpool, 1991). Where implementation has been more effective – as in France – examination performance gaps, when compared to the national average, have been relatively small (OECD, 1998). British studies suggest that, despite the gamut of measures, the gap between the worst and best performing schools, depending on the sector, has been widening (e.g. Sparkes, 1999). In support of this observation, Glennerster (2001) identifies more favourable outcomes in primary, as opposed to secondary schools. In assessing any area outcomes, broader socio-demographic trends must be taken into account. Thus, in several of the case studies, a greater possibility has arisen for some inner city schoolchildren to gain admission to establishments with better reputations, owing to declining school rolls. The phenomenon of 'white flight' to the church schools or the private sector also represents significant 'creaming off' effects.

Conclusion

Evaluation of regeneration not only requires disaggregation by sector, the identification of effects along the input–output dimension, and direct as opposed to associational or 'autocorrelated' effects, but also demands that these be integrated into a plausible net sum equation. This is no small task, given the prevailing deficiencies in small-area and city-level statistics which remain acute in some of the cities, particularly when we move away from input data.[1] Contextualisation is a vital part of this enterprise. Here the differential ability to mitigate locational problems by, for example, external remedies (e.g. consumption of services elsewhere) is an obvious case in point. Whilst the blight of poor housing and crime may often be chronically fixed in space, local health care and education deficits might be speedily offset simply by uptake elsewhere. Thus, the balance of presenting problems will have an important impact on assessments of total regeneration achieved so far on and future potentials. This leads to the associated question of the selection of key criteria and their prioritisation. Moreover, there are rarely uniform impacts. Positive outcomes, for some elements of the population, may exacerbate the social situation of others, as was, for instance, argued in the case of gentrification and displacement. The problematic, too, is highly dynamic, with policy output indices rarely remaining fixed for long.

In a complex evaluative exercise such as urban rejuvenation, no single benchmark approaches adequacy. As for the 'regenerative effort' they confronted, the five cities started from different deficit baselines, and in the range of acute problems which emerged thereafter. Specific dividends also accrue – and are reversed – differentially over time. It could not be claimed that any of the cities has enjoyed unalloyed success in every aspect, and it would be invidious to make a case for an unproblematic 'league table', if only because different criteria would determine ordering. Certainly, if policy input and process (that is to say 'policy effort') were regarded as the more important, Liverpool and Marseilles might arguably head the rankings. In terms of net global socio-economic effects and the visibility of overall regeneration, Barcelona and Hamburg stand out. This being said, both enjoyed 'external' windfalls – EU entry, connecting the former to the continental heartland, and the 'fall of the Wall' in the case of the latter, once more restoring its wider economic hinterland.

Note

1. For this reason the establishment by the European Commission of an *Urban Audit*, creating a cross-national multivariable database for prime urban indicators, is to be particularly welcomed. Present data are available for 58 cities, including the five case studies, the latest material referring to 1996 (though not in the case of Marseilles and Liverpool). Data assimilation for an expanded sample of 180 cities is currently in progress.

Part III
Evolving Regeneration Regimes

6
Inner City Regeneration: Mainstreaming the EU's Urban Agenda

The extent to which EU-level interventions contribute to regeneration regimes and the appropriate new international and 'entrepreneurial' urban order is explored in the present chapter. Primarily drawing on material from the five case studies, the most relevant policies since the introduction of the 1988 'planning system' are examined, in terms of whether they constitute an important and effective action arena in urban rejuvenation, in collaboration with lower-tier authorities and horizontal actors. Although still lacking legal competence for the full range of actions conventionally understood as forming urban policy, in the past 15 years the relevant EU remit has expanded on a number of important fronts. Successive reforms of the Structural Funds have afforded ever-greater prominence to an urban dimension. Allied programmes designed to refine a 'developmental' approach have targeted infrastructural regeneration, economic redevelopment, employment creation and the combating of social exclusion. Yet, apart from supporting the legitimacy of the EU institutions, there remain doubts about the effectiveness and appropriateness of these interventions. Since cities are identified as the very engines of economic growth, with their local economies contributing to competitive advantage, attempts to formulate a reconcilable EU-wide spatial policy agenda that goes beyond mere symbolic compensation for the laggards have always been open to question (for an early discussion, see Cheshire & Hay, 1989).

The 'planning system'

In its earlier phases, EEC action was largely oriented to under-developed regions. The introduction of the new regional development fund (ERDF) in the mid-1970s, operating alongside the other main fund, the social fund (ESF), initially continued this practice. On the whole, since overall budgets were modest, there was only limited action to remedy the ingrained perception

177

that allocations represented 'side payments', ensuring continuing compliance of recipient areas in furthering the European project. Rapid economic decline in large parts of the Community's industrial heartland changed scenarios. Unavoidably the Structural Funds, and their past role as relatively non-programmatic small-scale subsidies to the periphery, became embroiled in the wider political concerns about industrial decline, with its sharper urban profile. The simultaneous ambitions of EC President, Delors, and his modernising agenda expounded in the mid-1980s to prepare for the Single Market, together with the pressures emanating from new southern members for increased funding, have been extensively discussed in the literature. Suffice it to say that one product was the negotiation of the 1988 'planning system' to establish new rules of the game, now made more lucrative by the doubling of allocations. To be sure, there were fears that the imposition on beneficiaries of the condition of matched funding would, perforce, penalise non-governmental actors. From other quarters came worries that the effect of improved outlays might simply reinforce 'welfare dependency' and extend dangers of clientelism in their receipt. In fact, total budgetary inputs remained relatively modest. In the first 5 years of implementation, according to calculations by Kleinman and Piachaud (1993), they amounted to less than 6 per cent of the projected gains that were expected to accrue from the completion of the Single Market. Equally, if not more, significant in establishing a long-term policy regime was the institutionalisation of a structured decision-making process in which funding decisions were determined by a hierarchy of aims. Whilst allocations were disbursed according to a code of implementation principles, there was substantial leeway for applicants in the drafting of specific policy content. The reform not only strengthened the supervisory role of the Commission as overseers of the process, it also substantially expanded its discretion in terms of finalising preferences within the competitive bidding environment.

For Keating (2001), the introduction of the 'planning system' rapidly resulted in a strong Europeanisation of regional development and allied policies, whilst retaining the rural bias. Thus, client and spatially oriented objectives still top-loaded the major volume of outlays (about two-thirds of the total) to 'lagging regions' – Objective One areas – defined in terms of their GDP being below 75 per cent of the EU average. Here, employment-related actions formed a major element. Of greater relevance to the present sample of cities was nomination for Objective Two. This was designed to tackle the problems of 'declining industrial areas', typically associated with heavy industry and port-related activities. By comparison, it received on average a modest 11 per cent of funding. Among the remaining Objectives were the young and long-term unemployed, and measures for preparing workers for the demands of accelerating economic transformation (Objectives Three and Four). In addition – and a sign of a nascent distinct sphere of EU action – just under 10 per cent of allocations were 'top-sliced' for special

'Community Initiatives' determined according to the Commission's own priorities. These were to mushroom over time. Early schemes included *RENAVAL*, targeting declining port economies; *RESIDER*, for the iron and steel industry; the human resources (*EMPLOYMENT*) initiatives – *NOW* for women, *HORIZON* for the disabled, *YOUTHSTART* and *INTEGRA* for 'vulnerable groups'; and, in the mid-1990s, *URBAN*, to provide seedbed money for projects associated with urban deprivation. In one way or another, all impacted on policy development in the case-study cities.

Complementing prioritisation by objective was the much more pro-active role of the Commission in the design and implementation of policies. This was prosecuted through instigation of a programmatic and evaluative response, based on a catalogue of guiding principles, each of more or less equal ranking. Among them were proof of *additionality* – EU monies were to represent 'added value', not merely substituting domestic funding; programming – *multi-annual, multi-dimensional policy packages* and block grants were to replace ad hoc projects; *concentration of effort* – through more effective targeting and concerted actions; *dissemination* of good practice, also serving legitimacy by fostering a higher profile for EU interventions; and *partnership* – national, regional and local actors were to be integrated in a sustained collaboration to negotiate planning goals and implementation.

As policy has evolved, these principles, supplemented by others, have been further elaborated. Among the relative newcomers were a mounting concern about sustainability, anticipatory prevention, benchmarking, area-based management and private funding leverage. These innovations reflected growing preferences for the embrace of 'new public management' and, as such, were relatively uncontroversial. In comparison, *subsidiarity* proved a thorny issue. Variously interpreted – depending on which actor's point of view was being advanced – this social catholic dictum specified that the lowest-tier formal or informal agency appropriate for effective implementation should assume competence. Yet, for certain member state governments, the argument began and ended with what they regarded as the appropriate division of national and EU responsibilities, even though in many states competences for urban policy had been significantly devolved to the regional tier. In the present context, contention arose because, as stated above, the EU does not *strictu sensu* enjoy direct competence for the broad area of urban affairs, particularly when it encroaches on housing matters or the funding of welfare benefits. The governments of Mrs Thatcher and, to a lesser extent, Chancellor Kohl were particularly exercised about the issue. In the event, the German government was successful in achieving the abandonment of a proposed fourth EU poverty programme in the mid-1990s. In general, Kellas (1991) detects, in the years immediately after the introduction of the 'planning system', a trend of increasing dominance of central governments as the principal partners in negotiating relations with the Commission. Furthermore, certain lobbies – such as the umbrella groups representing agriculture and the major industries – were able to crowd out regional and urban deprivation pressure groups in determining the formulation of overarching policy. The persistence of the 'skew' it represented in no small part shaped the motives of the Commission in acting to strengthen its coalition-building by successfully gaining approval for the creation of new players such as the Committee of the Regions (in the event, at least initially, something of a disappointment) and 'trans-European' networks in health, culture, education and so on. The management of subsidiarity has been, and will continue to be, an ongoing affair in combination with the elaboration of partnership models: for example, one consequence of 'Agenda 2000' (see below) has been the pronounced commitment to seeking means of integrating non-governmental actors more effectively.

Additionality has also been difficult to establish and exacerbated by different national accounting systems. One common problem reported by respondents to this study was the degree to which, in disbursement, EU funds tended to 'stand too much alone' in isolated one-off projects rather than being more effectively integrated to 'add value'. Or, since allocations outside Objective One regions have been modest in relation to the total budgets being managed by municipalities, there was a temptation in routine operation, merely to divert them to established national and local agenda, the use of the social fund being the most typically cited instance.

Of all the principles, it is partnership that has received the greatest attention in the literature. The sense of feeling 'cold shouldered' has already been alluded to. This was reported in the present study among informal agencies, certainly in recalling the initial period of the reform. Yet it could be argued that this is scarcely surprising, given that originally the EEC had relied on rather formal corporatist partnership embracing the social partners (Geddes & Benington, 2001). Kleinman (2002) has deliberated over whether the 'top-down functionalism' of the 'planning process' can, in reality, allocate sufficient space to these actors, beyond mere consultation. For him, the imposed style runs the risk of contravening the declared ambition of advancing participatory legitimacy and, unless checked, may simply entrenching clientelistic networking. For the past decade – aided by exhortations from the Parliament and consultative bodies like ECOSOC – the Commission has expended considerable effort in widening partnership, to support the institutionalisation of 'networked governance' (for further discussion, see Rhodes *et al.*, 1996; Mayo, 1997; Benington, 2001). Accordingly, both in its mainstream and earmarked programmes, funding is contingent upon establishing that a feasible model is in place locally, although, as later discussion suggests, realities have sometimes failed to deliver on prospects. Because many EU programmes are typically short term and require speedy operationalisation, defects in participation have been most acute in engaging wide elements of the community. In acknowledgment that communities vary in the degree to which they are effectively mobilised to contribute to successful bidding (e.g. European Commission, 1996; Institut für Landes- und Stadtentwicklungsforschung, 2000), the current ESF contains a specific programme for developing local social capital, building on experiences from such projects as the 'territorial employment pacts', discussed later (European Commission, 2000).

Inevitably, such funding is set to become a permanent feature, since the issue of differences in the implementation of effective and wide-ranging partnerships has profound consequences for how 'networked governance' will mature in the much expanded Union – among countries in which community participation, until very recent years, has been an alien phenomenon.

Urban regeneration and EU policy evolution

Developments in the first phase of the 'planning system'

The first steps towards creating what Levin (1997) has picturesquely called a distinct urban 'policy bridgehead' can be traced to the mid-1980s, in worthy innovations such as the nomination of a European 'city of culture', which barely concealed a strong regeneration subtext. There has also been a variety of city networks with lobbying functions to advance a specific urban strand in EU interventions: for example, in 1986 Mayor Vigouroux of Marseilles was one of the initiators of the second-city *Eurocities* (Donzel, 1990). The self-explanatory 'Euroports' has pursued a similar strategy in policy mediation with EU-level institutions, as too has *RECITE* (regions and cities cooperation network) and the European Anti-Poverty Network, established in 1990. By the early 1990s networking was intensifying, creating a policy momentum that would establish more formal incorporation of urban social exclusion into reforms of the Structural Funds agreed in 1993. This agenda was also supported by other developments such as the environment green paper, the innovations concluded in the 1991 Maastricht Treaty and the creation of the Committee of the Regions.

In the meantime, more concrete policy departures had been enacted. Testing the waters for subsequently greater substantive action, in the *URBAN* Community Initiative, in 1989 two pilot projects were approved to contribute to regeneration in certain deprived neighbourhoods of Marseilles and London. Funding was made possible through the stipulations concerning reserved finance (article 10) within the regional fund. In Marseille, these EC monies helped create the *Cité de la Musique* in Belsunce and refurbishment of parts of Le Panier to create artisan studios, matched funding coming from the national *DSU* programme. These two cities served as pilots for the Commission's 'Urban Social Programme' which in 1991 was consolidated into the *Quartiers en Crise* network of projects, at times encompassing 27 neighbourhoods in ten member states. Although amounting to 'seedbed funding', it focussed on training, economic goals, revitalisation of historic cores and technological innovation – all intended to produce strong 'demonstration effects' (European Commission, 1992; Drewe, 2000). Genoa's Centro Storico was one of the nominated *quartiers*. An 'archaeological park' was created along with a permanent urban observatory and restoration of certain medieval buildings for cultural and academic use. In addition, a stimulus was provided for the wider rehabilitation of the surrounding Porta Sorprana neighbourhood, in part through stimulating greater community involvement (Comune di Genova, 1994a, 1997).

The Third Poverty Programme (1989–94) also focussed attention on horizontal and vertical partnership and a multi-dimensional approach to urban social exclusion (Duffy, 1995). Among the case-study cities, there were projects in Eimsbüttel, a high-rise estate in Hamburg, with a strong emphasis on youth work, and in Granby-Toxteth in inner city Liverpool. While the evaluation of partnership in Poverty 3 records generally positive effects, the Granby project was to prove more controversial. It exemplified the dangers of *naïveté* in attempting speedily to implant what was, after all, a supranationally focussed intervention in a chronically troubled neighbourhood suffering high levels of deprivation, with strong racial overtones. From the start there were local – and national – reservations about the selection of this neighbourhood. There were concerns about what was regarded as a too narrowly drawn agenda, primarily limited to the issue of racism, as well as the real extent of participation. Whilst those central to its implementation stressed the positive 'process' outcomes in terms of a feeling of empowerment which, for them, firmly established the link between chronic prejudice and entrenched poverty (Young, 1995), others were not so convinced about successful execution of the intended agenda. Suspicions soon arose that the project had been hijacked by interests representing only certain elements of the community and that this had led to the early departure of key formal actors (Duffy, 1995; Duffy & Breitenbach, 1995; Moore, 1997).

In the first phase of the 'planning system', all five cities were beneficiaries of the spatially defined Objective Two, the client-oriented Objectives and many of the Community Initiatives. During this period, it must be admitted that total amounts allocated were relatively modest and many of the individual projects funded largely served to establish a 'presence': among examples are the partial funding through the ESF for local economic development in a peripheral estate in Barcelona (Poal, 1989); restoration of murals and limited upgrading works in Centro Storico (ILRES, 1994); the sponsoring of alternative rehabilitation schemes in parts of Hamburg such as Karolinenviertel (e.g. Lawaetz Stiftung, 1993); and help to restore Victorian parks and the Canning Street area of Liverpool (Government Office for Merseyside, 1994). To be sure, there were larger-scale interventions: for instance, RESIDER, RENAVAL and further Objective Two monies were allocated to assist the conversion of derelict industrial sites and dockland (e.g. Freie und Hansestadt Hamburg, 1991; Comune di Genova, 1992b;

Schubert & Harms, 1993b) and Objectives Three and Four funding made some inroads into local training needs (e.g. Economic Development Strategy Forum, 1991; BAGS, 1994; ILRES, 1994). More significantly, as a longer-term outcome, the reform of EU funding and planning styles, and implementation through 'integrated development operations' opened up new possibilities for the further elaboration of local urban policy-making regimes. It stimulated the first steps towards formalised horizontal partnership in cities where it had been absent and a catalyst was provided for expansion elsewhere. Significantly, the potential of leverage from other public purses and private sources was specifically taken into account in the planning funding (Robson *et al.*, 1994; Evans, 2002).

Finally, in this phase, the effect of the recession in the early 1990s was to raise the issue of European competitiveness high on the post-Maastricht agenda, culminating in the Delors 1993 *Growth, Competitiveness and Employment* White Paper. More attention was afforded to the role of cities in shaping the new economic order, as well as the potential returns of investment in local economic development, for which an action research programme was launched. Alongside competitiveness, growth and the preservation of the 'European Social Model', the question of sustainability was increasingly being aired in the international arena, stimulated by the 1992 UN Rio conference. In fact, a green paper on the urban environment had been issued in 1990 and was followed from 1992 by the EU fifth environment action programme (*Towards Sustainability*). The *dirigiste* ambitions of the Commission, in coordinating the spatial planning of the European urban system, demonstrated by 'Europe 2000', continued the growing concern with sustainable development, as did its successor, 'Europe 2000+', albeit in a context more respectful of subsidiarity and greater partnership with the member states (European Commission, 1991, 1994).

The 1993 reforms and their aftermath

The reform of the Structural Funds for the period 1994–99, in which allocations were again doubled, aimed to strengthen the concentration of effort, additionality and partnership principles. There were improvements in streamlining of the planning process, with the ability of member states to submit a 'single planning document'. Within the revised Objective Four, there were moves towards an anticipatory focus, for example through the specification of interventions for those at risk of unemployment owing to the vagaries of economic transformation. A reformed Objective Three contained stronger commitment to tackling social exclusion. Although, in the event, there was erosion of the concentration principle, the reform package did, at least, reinforce the urban focus and, due to their continuing declining fortunes, new urban areas, like those on Merseyside, achieved Objective One status. More generally, the sustainability agenda was also advanced in this period – under the aegis of EU and other international institutions. The Aalborg *Charter of European Cities and Towns Towards Sustainability* was signed in 1994, to accelerate implementation of the *Agenda 21* roadmap, prescribed at the UN Rio conference. This was followed by the 1996 EU Lisbon action plan. Among other policy outputs, was the 1998 communication *Sustainable Urban Development in the EU: A Framework for Action* (European Commission, 1998; von Petz & Schubert, 1998).

Barcelona not only benefited from revised Objective Two funding but also received monies from the Cohesion Funds agreed in the Maastricht Treaty, from which the upgrading of Casc Antic and the more problematic neighbourhood of Raval were to benefit (e.g. Gomà and Rosetti, 1999). Of the other cities under investigation, Marseilles became a major beneficiary of Objective Two. Here, allocations were amalgamated with those deriving from the national urban policy relaunch pact of 1996 and were targeted on northern and certain inner city localities (Donzel, 1998). However, as some respondents stressed, due to the reluctance to contribute the required matched funding, some of the city's allocation was returned to Brussels unused. Similar problems of disbursing Objective Two monies were recorded early in the new funding period in Genoa, due to the collapse of the regional government.

Among the five cities, this phase of EU funding was to have the greatest consequence for Liverpool when, for the first time, it was included in an Objective One region, a consequence of its continuing poor economic record (Government Office for Merseyside, 1994). The nomination has had an enduring effect on local urban governance, in no small part helping to overcome remaining reservations entertained by potential partners, after their experiences in the Militant years (Hackett, 1993). The accompanying single planning document, *Merseyside 2000*, outlined an ambitious programme aiming at 15 per cent overall growth and the creation of 25,000 jobs. The plan outlined seven 'strategic objectives', such as investment in industry, people and technology, and the development of culture, media and tourism potential – all selected to boost image and assist the sub-region's self-proclaimed destiny as a 'gateway between Europe and the rest of the world'. To achieve these goals five 'drivers for change' were specified – including action in the corporate sector, assistance to small and medium enterprises and knowledge-based industries. As discussed in Chapter 3, an important driver related to investment in the community. This was further refined in the specific measures to create 'pathways to integration' in neighbourhoods throughout Merseyside, including inner city Liverpool. In all, the catalogue of interventions was carefully itemised to permit effective monitoring and evaluation (Liverpool City Council, 1994a,d). To ensure the delivery of the plan, a strengthened urban governance was prescribed through a wider embrace of partnership in which the local universities would play a more prominent role, in line with the courting of inward investment for creative capital. By the end of the programme, together with matched funding, total outlays were estimated to have amounted to about 2 billion euros (Meegan & Mitchell, 2001; Evans, 2002). On the other hand, some respondents to this study, anxious to put the annual public sector commitments into context, stressed that these receipts accruing to the city were, in fact, less than the budget allocated to the secondary school sector.

From the outset, there were those who were less than sanguine about the prospects for the plan and, in fact, its first version had been rejected by the Commission, with the support of officials at the Government Office for Merseyside. Chief amongst critics, the local economist, Professor Minford, castigated the programme for its heavy structure and for lacking critical analysis of problems incurred in economic conversion. For him it represented a messy compromise that would be incapable of gearing the nominated drivers efficiently to transformation and, through unfocussed subsidisation and training, ran the risk of increased welfare dependency all round (Shennan, 1994). Subsequent evaluations have proved reasonably positive, when taking the broad sweep of factors into account. For Evans (2002) Objective One status provided the context for consensual coalition formation which was also facilitated by the change of government in 1997, alleviating outstanding tensions in central–local government relations. Hibbitt and colleagues (2001) also judge that, despite problems in execution, the maturation of the partnership model was among the most effective outcomes. Yet, on vital 'hard' outcomes of growth and employment, results were less reassuring. At the end of the programme, the sub-region still recorded the highest economic inactivity rate in the country, and unemployment actually deteriorated in relation to national trends, as did the GDP ratio – to 70 per cent of the UK average (Boland, 2000; Liverpool Vision, 2000).

URBAN1

The first Community Initiative expressly addressing problems of urban social exclusion, *URBAN*, was announced in 1994, intended to run in tandem with the general Structural Fund planning period. Pressures for a dedicated initiative came from the European Parliament as well as from city networks, previously cited. Albeit with a small total budget (eventually rising to nearly 900 million euros, excluding matched funding), it aimed to provide seedbed monies for innovative 'best practice' partnership for economic and social regeneration. A narrow 'bricks and mortar' solution – which, in any case, lay beyond EU competence was avoided. On the other hand, an agenda to stimulate private-sector leverage was strongly advanced. Otherwise, the explicit intention was to consolidate lessons from the Urban Priority Projects, as well as to mainstream positive aspects of the new programme in advance of the reform of the Structural Funds being planned for 2000. Specific actions were to include local economic development and training, and measures in flanking areas such as social services, health and safety, and crime prevention. In order to improve prospects for measurable returns, the Initiative specified that nominations would be chosen from among delineated 'crisis hit' districts marked by urban decay, poor housing, lack of infrastructural investment and high unemployment. Neighbourhoods in cities of over 100,000 population located in Objective One regions were given priority, with 57 per cent of funding, followed by Objective Two locations, with 27 per cent. Over two-fifths of allocations were directed to inner cities, one-fifth to historic cores and about one-third to peripheral estates. Ultimately, 118 projects were selected (European Commission, 2002a) – with the result of spreading available monies very thinly.

Barcelona and Hamburg were not participants, but a locality in Genoa was selected (the city was the only one of the five to be a beneficiary of the Urban Pilot Projects, *URBAN1* and its successor, *URBAN2*). The area selected for *URBAN1* lay outside the inner city, in Cornigliano-Sestri, a declining industrial area. Given the limited funding available, 'demonstration projects' were all that were feasible: for example, monies went towards the costs of establishing a documentation centre to promote employment and community participation, help towards creating an elderly day centre and for projects in sustainable traffic mobility (Comune di Genova, 1994b). Part of the initiative on Merseyside was located in four inner city wards. The objectives specified process factors, such as the improvement of neighbourhood participation capacities. Among the 'harder' aims were actions on training and employment, particularly for the lowest skilled. Here, existing policy frameworks were to be harnessed, including established partnerships such as those for North Liverpool, Granby-Toxteth and Dingle (Paulus, 2000). The programme in Marseilles took place in Le Panier, St Mauront and Belsunce in the central arrondissements, where it was integrated with ongoing projects relating to the urban contract and the development of *Euroméditerranée*. Funding was made available to contribute to other subsidies to small firms. Community development aspects included help towards creation of local child care support, cultural and sports facilities and the training of a small group of young people as community watch officers.

At the time of writing, the final official evaluation of *URBAN1* is still awaited. The European Court of Auditors (2001) has already raised doubts about the level of impact the Initiative can achieve, given the scale of presenting problems in the selected neighbourhoods. It also expressed concern about the quality of implementation styles, particularly the relative lack of scope for international exchange and dissemination. In response to the latter reproach, the Commission has sought approval to interpolate remedial action in the ongoing successor, *URBAN2*. This takes the form of *URBACT*, a network of over 200 cities that have benefited from funding from the Urban Pilot Projects or the two rounds of the Initiative. From 2003 this network has been charged with offering exchange, dissemination of information and monitoring, and giving technical support to the participants in the present schemes (Jacquier & Laino, 2002). In creating *URBACT* the Commission has anticipated some of the reservations about the first round of *URBAN* that are likely to be contained in the official evaluation. It is expected that the small scale of projects, the relatively modest and brief funding, the over-ambitious agenda, and the effects all these bring to bear on attempts to accommodate different partnerships and wider governance capacities in such a broad range of neighbourhoods will be among the limitations identified. For its part, in advance of the formal evaluation, the Commission has itself judged that partnership has been operating at an adequately effective level in over 80 per cent of cases (European Commission, 2002b). The kinds of implementation deficits expected to be specified problems have, in fact, already been aired in the academic literature. Set-up times and the resolution of other problems were affected by widely different local circumstances, such as political and funding stability (Stanghellini, 2000; Chorianopoulos, 2002). The markedly varying capacities to establish the required participation and multi-dimensional operational framework have also been reported (Paulus, 2000). Avarello and Ricci (2000) judge that the initiative in Italy was less successful in the larger cities, due to complex interaction of problems and the lack of visible results which provided a disincentive for community engagement. Tosi (2000) questions whether in Italy, where urban regeneration remains relatively an under-developed policy area, short-term actions on the margins, which are primarily 'socially driven', could expect to have much impact. On the other hand, other Italian researchers have argued that *URBAN*, along with other EU policies, informed national government in the formulation of its series of area-based planning reforms during the late 1990s (Campagna & Ricci, 2000; Palermo, 2000; Nuvolati, 2002).

Policy evolution after Amsterdam

The 1997 Amsterdam Treaty advanced the EU urban agenda on a number of related fronts. For one, there was a renewed legal commitment to tackling social exclusion and, for the first time, in Article 13, a strong legal basis was stipulated for action on many aspects of discrimination, including racial prejudice. In the same year the communication *Towards an Urban Agenda in the EU* was issued which repeated obligations to develop a reconcilable policy programme combining competition, growth, employment, sustainability and social inclusion. This was followed a year later by its stable-mate *Sustainable Urban Development in the EU; A Framework for Action*. Other consolidating measures, in different ways contributing to expanding the EU sphere of action, included the approval of the European Spatial Development Perspective and the convening of the first Urban Forum in 1998 (Atkinson, 2000b). The negotiation of the European Employment Strategy set in train what would be a wide institutionalisation of the 'open method of coordination' (OMC) in EU policy-making. Its operational basis comprises flexible reliance on networking, benchmarking, exchange of experience and a large measure of self-regulation on the part of member states. Governments are required to formulate regular national action plans detailing how they are addressing the four 'pillars' of the strategy – employability, adaptability, entrepreneurialism and equal opportunities – which then inform the EU Employment Guidelines. As discussed below, OMC – proclaimed a new phase in the resolution of multi-level governance – has subsequently had direct bearing on policy addressing urban deprivation.

The EES was agreed in the period following the announcement of Commission President Santer's *Confidence Pact on Employment*. This, in turn, built upon experiences in the operation of the 'soft' governance represented, among others, by a time-limited programme implemented in 1994 to establish *Territorial Employment Pacts* (TEPs), a device owing much to innovations in development in Latin America. In fact, all the measures adopted in the years since the 1993 Structural Fund reforms were in one way or another being used to direct further revisions due after 1999, at the end of the funding period. The hope was that good practice from the TEPs would be mainstreamed, to guarantee better deployment of the revised funds. Eighty-nine pacts were nominated throughout the Union. Very modestly financed by Brussels – a mere 43 euros per citizen, although public-matched funding and private leverage added more – they were designed to forge strong, local, cross-sectoral partnership for economic development. As a sign of the times, they were required to demonstrate a clear quantitative impact on jobs (European Commission, 1999b). The site chosen for the TEP in Greater Barcelona was in Vallès Occidental and on Merseyside in St Helens, both outside the study area. In Hamburg the Lawaetz Foundation, associated since the mid-1980s with the 'alternative' rehabilitation and job creation movement, was selected to manage the local pact. Predictably enough, evaluation of the TEPs reveals divergences. But, in general, it was judged that where the action area was too wide, the cost was the surrender of specificity of aims. In addition, local official enthusiasm for collaboration was a prime marker of cross-national difference, although for different reasons. Thus, Europe Innovation 2000 (2001) detected a minimal impact on Spanish public authorities. The agency observed that, in the UK, authorities attached greater significance to national schemes such as the Employment Zones. On the other hand, the projects in Italy created a virtuous circle, reinforcing the impact of other EU measures on attempts to modernise urban governance.

The future of the Structural Funds formed part of *AGENDA 2000* to address the modernisation of EU institutional arrangements in advance of expansion into central and eastern Europe. Reforms, implemented from 2000, offer a more explicit urban dimension, since it was recognised that, increasingly, it is fundamentally shaping new regional disparities. Action was principally to be taken via the new Objective 2, which includes an 'urban areas in difficulty' stream, based on a range of criteria such as unemployment, weak economy, housing conditions, educational attainment and crime. Following recommendations arising from *AGENDA 2000*, a renewed concentration of effort has been attempted by reducing the entitled population from just over half to about 35–40 per cent of the EU total, to temper the prevalence of funding spread too thinly. In the financial envelope extending to 2006, up to 95 per cent of monies will be allocated to a scaled-down categorisation of three objectives and disbursed through streamlined allocation and management principles. Two spatially defined objectives (Objective One for territorial development; Objective Two for areas in structural decline) – locations being selected by the Commission – are complemented by a thematic human resources dimension (Objective Three). Top-loading of funding to Objective One continues, at about 70 per cent of the total, with the number of beneficiary regions reduced in all member states, save Greece. Up to 60 per cent of the ESF is to be invested in pursuing the employability goal, as defined in the European Employment Strategy. As a consequence of growing criticism about the unwieldy number of earmarked Community Initiatives, it was decided that, henceforth, only four would be funded. Among them are *EQUAL*, primarily to develop anti-discrimination measures in the labour market, and a new round of *URBAN*, its survival owing much to pressures from the European Parliament. In addition, the Commission is also promoting actions to reward 'best models' by means of a special funding allocation.

The four continental case studies are currently in receipt of Objectives Two and Three funding and – varyingly – the Community Initiatives. However, the only case-study area to be nominated for *URBAN2* is the Genovese Centro Storico. Genoa was also awarded 'European City of Culture' status for 2004. Other examples of funding include the St Pauli neighbourhood of Hamburg which, through Objective Two, is developing an ongoing partnership programme for local economic development. This is being complemented by ESF monies for youth and long-term unemployment measures (Kuhlmann, 2001).

Once again, Liverpool is the only case study to be included in an Objective One region and among the targeted areas is its inner city. Initial calculations estimated that Merseyside would receive 1.3 billion euros in the funding period extending to 2006. Taking all sources of matched funding and private leverage into account, the total inflow was expected to be in the region of 3.3 billion (Evans, 2002). When compared to its predecessor, *Merseyside 2000*, the 'conversion plan' is more streamlined. It specifies four overarching objectives: developing business; potentialising the sub-region's population; local area development; and targeted interventions among 'pathway' communities. More detailed operational goals include further action in expanding the contribution of IT to the sub-regional economy, refining equal opportunity measures, as well as greater attention to ensuring sustainability. Among specific actions attracting subsidies are continuing the redevelopment of the city centre and waterfront, in part through expanding cultural, leisure and tourism facilities. Local socio-economic development projects have been formulated for neighbourhoods such as Vauxhall, Everton, Granby and Dingle (Government Office for the North West, 1999; Liverpool Vision, 2000). Again, in comparison to *Merseyside 2000*, the plan has a stronger entrepreneurial focus. It also attaches greater importance to human capital development and the quality of the skills base, in particular through measures to combat the chronically low educational attainment on Merseyside. Whilst the community participation 'pathways' strand is maintained, there is to be a more robust attempt to direct it towards local economic development. The *Merseyside Special Investment Fund*, created for the first round of Objective One (see Chapter 4), proved too small-scale in impact and, accordingly, the current programme introduces a 'champion fund' which will adopt a more sectoral approach. Overall, Evans (2002) calculates that there has been a considerable revision of funding priorities in comparison with the first round of funding. Almost 40 per cent of total outlays are now earmarked for development, whilst the equivalent community pathway element is to receive 13 per cent. He also notes the significant role played by the then recently established regional development agency in the finalisation of the document and its strong influence over furthering the scope of sub-regional partnership in delivering objectives. Finally, Liverpool is also to follow Genoa as a 'City of Culture' – in 2008 – with the object of levering major private funding from what amounts to peppercorn outlays by the EU and other public sources. The city council has announced ambitious projections of increased tourism and associated job creation, although an independent study it commissioned set out a more modest scenario (ERM Economics, 2003).

URBAN2

In line with the general Structural Funds and the other Community initiatives, *URBAN2* seeks to reduce the population it embraces and to concentrate resources in order to maximise impact. As a result, in the new round, funding is restricted to 70 projects, compared to well over 100 in the first. They have been selected according to deprivation indices produced by the Urban Audit (see Appendix). This time there is no restriction on city size, although the targeted neighbourhoods are expected to have a population of at least 10,000. An EU budget of a little over 725 million euros has been allocated, about 45 per cent of the total projected outlays accruing. An agenda of subsidising measures for employment, education, crime prevention, and so forth, is continued. But, in this round, there is a stronger focus on information technology and sustainability in energy and transport use and – emblematic of the post-Agenda 2000 priorities – there is a dedicated allocation for . benchmarking and networking. Monies have also been directed towards the subsequent formation of *URBACT*, as discussed earlier. The regional fund (ERDF) will contribute up to 75 per cent of total outlays in the new Objective One regions and half elsewhere. On average, 40 per cent of spending will be reserved for physical and environmental regeneration, and roughly one-fifth each for social inclusion measures and for employment. The intent is to employ a single budgetary envelop in order to avoid the duplication of procedures and the heavy bureaucracy associated with *URBAN1* (European Commission, 2002a). Centro Storico is currently a participant, having received a budget of about 11 million euros, almost two-thirds of which is to be disbursed for physical regeneration.

From small beer to gravy train?

The determined effort on the part of the larger – and richer – member states to strongly resist expansion of the EU budget, by holding it at 1.27 per cent of the Union's GDP, has forced consistently greater attention towards ensuring efficiency of disbursement, particularly with regard to concentration of effort and added value. These concerns were growing against a background of castigations on the part of the European Court of Auditors that, in the late 1990s, prior to their reform, the administration of the Structural Funds was still indulging a widespread 'spending culture'. Yet, perceptions of ground-level recipients – especially those denied Objective One privileges – can be quite different. For them, the typical allocations at their disposal have amounted to small beer: cheese-paring, short term and small-scale. Moreover, these niggardly outlays have sometimes imposed an agenda subverting locally established priorities and incurring many hidden costs. It is partly for these reasons that respondents in some of the cities reported that, on occasions, EU monies were returned to Brussels, owing to a reluctance on the part of local authorities to allocate the required matched funding. Or, projects might be selected on the principle of easy disbursement rather than the most pressing need.

Mindful of these reservations, in the reforms instigated since the 1990s, there has been a pronounced move towards longer-term programmatic commitments, as too, an incorporation of qualitative as well as quantifiable sustainable effects (e.g. Bramezza, 1998). As multi-level urban governance has matured, so has the scope afforded to integrated complementarity, as opposed to a narrow preoccupation with parallel 'additionality' characteristic of the early phase of the 'planning system'. This arena demands sensitive negotiation and management, combining as it does a greater admixture of scales of interventions – neighbourhood, city-wide, sub-regional and regional – as well as cross-sectoral actions where competences mainly lie at EU or national level (see Schwarz, 1999; Atkinson, 2002). The ongoing political accommodation required is being advanced through a multiplicity of partnerships at all levels. Yet, in terms of the overall urban project, this diffusion of disparate networks – within and between regional and city regeneration – carries the risk of entrenching distinctly protective interest formations that may undermine a wider vision of socio-economic cohesion strategies (see Anderson, 1995; Atkinson, 2001).

Current EU actions, of varying scope and impact, extend into many areas now conventionally regarded as the remit of urban policy. Apart from a limited, but expanding, set of measures to ameliorate the problems of crime, drugs and other manifestations of urban deprivation, consolidation of the agenda has been the most advanced in the case of employment. As discussed earlier, a catalyst has been provided by the negotiation of the European Employment Strategy in 1997 and the accompanying national action plans. Ongoing work aims to achieve a closer integration of the Strategy's specific targets with broad objectives for economic and social cohesion. One resulting guideline, to which member states committed in 2000, is the pursuit of an overall employment rate of 70 per cent in the EU by 2010. Within the policy nexus, the Structural Funds are to be put towards greater efforts in stimulating firmer inward investment and demonstrating a direct effect on job creation. But, there is recognition that mere growth has not filtered down to a core of people excluded from labour markets. Thus, an important part of the associated strategy to promote social inclusion, which the member states agreed later in the same year, supports multi-dimensional flanking measures. Adopting the 'open method of coordination', among the eight action areas are child-care support, housing access, rights to work, education, measures to guarantee adequate income, as well as further interventions in urban regeneration. Finally, current employment guidelines propose a simplified catalogue of operational priorities, with emphasis on local economic development and stronger governance of the EES through closer involvement of local and regional actors and bottom-up partnerships (European Commission, 2003).

In comparison, the 'bricks and mortar' element of urban policy – at least in terms of housing – remains external to the EU remit. This being said, some physical enhancements of neighbourhood milieu have been subsidised which clearly may have spill-over effects on propensities to upgrade the housing stock (Barlow, 1998; Kleinman, 2002). Other EU policies may also demonstrate more widespread impact on the housing system and its rehabilitation. Priemus and colleagues (1994), for example, argue that housing investment is at the heart of urban regeneration and, in this regard, the Maastricht Treaty convergence criteria imposed serious restrictions on public budgetary allocations available for new house-building, maintenance and improvements. On the other hand, the deregulation of housing finance markets, dictated by the Single Market, creates a single 'mortgage space', although in practice there are still many constraints on its effective operation, not least emanating from continuing divergent legal systems (Kleinman, 1998).

Are we now in a better position to answer the question posed by Chapman (1995) as to the appropriateness of claiming a 'Europeanisation' of urban policy – one that is capable of efficiently integrating the actions of supranational, national and sub-national players? The award of a more comprehensive remit to EU institutions would require revision of the treaties and, as Atkinson (2001) argues, it is simply not in prospect. This being said, have the 'policy bridgeheads' identified by Levin (1997) – a tactic reliant on 'purposeful opportunism', as Cram (1993) puts it – now, at least, matured into a substantial and coherent output – a critical 'policy mass'? Certainly, with regards to the growing perception of a common problematic, there is a considerable literature supporting 'institutional learning' (see, for example, Paraskevopoulos, 2001). Such learning has been productive of a convergence in metaphor and discourse employed in addressing urban questions, as MacGregor (1993) already discerned over 10 years ago. Since then, this has filered through to much of the policy agenda. Yet, this apparent consensus has come about as a result of a somewhat uncomfortable fusion of continental social catholic and social democratic predilections and anglo-saxon neo-liberalism. It must be said, though, that the latter has been the more dominant. No doubt, the embrace of partnership, networking, benchmarking and dissemination of 'good practice' and the like are assisting practical application of these shared views. The resulting policy context is one where pro-active and tighter integration of investment in human capital and physical infrastructure is seen as paramount.

Yet, outside Objective One regions, the practical agenda for (inner city) regeneration at EU-level has not strayed too far from relatively 'small beer' gestures, so typical of much of the *acquis* to date. In any case, there are those who remain sceptical of the feasibility of 'one-size-fits-all' supranational approaches, not least due to pressing north–south differences in the urgency of presenting problems and governance capacities (Tosi, 2000; Chorianopoulos, 2002). On the other hand, EU activity in combating inner city and wider urban deprivation, at the very least, is now an accepted element of the accumulation of what Faist (2001) defines as 'nested citizenship', with its resolution between Union and lower-tier instances being continually negotiated.

7

The Inner City: Regulating Regeneration, Combating Social Exclusion

> Poverty is a great cutter-off... and riches a great shutter-off (Lawrence Durrell, *Justine*. Faber and Faber, 1968, p. 148).

This investigation concludes with some general reflections about the regeneration agenda in inner city Europe and the styles of governance adopted in its prosecution. Some of the socio-economic effects of rejuvenation policy, discussed earlier, are returned to. Then follows an examination of the changing role of professions, public institutions, markets and communities in emerging regeneration regimes. Finally, there is a brief speculation about convergent tendencies within the EU.

The 'laver of regeneration'?

In all five cities the cumulative lessons learned over the study period call into question many of the old premises about urban renewal. Here discussion is limited to a few points on each of the main dimensions.

First, regarding the scale of intervention: a proliferation of isolated, small-scale projects long held sway, in terms of design, funding commitments and quality of integration into mainstream programmes. Indeed, it is noticeable that respondents in the sampled cities reported a shared tendency for what were often cheese-paring dedicated outlays to be siphoned off from general allocations. Net gains in terms of finance were therefore often far more modest than what was being claimed by higher-tier government. To this must be added the pressure of hasty implementation, with little possibility of carefully planned lead-in time, entry and exit strategies. Especially prior to 1990, projects were too frequently sub-optimal, out for the 'quick fix' with scant regard for longer-term effects or sustainability and, significantly, detached from general socio-economic strategies. In several of the cities, all that began to change by the mid-1980s. A decade later, the need for 'joined-up', integrated approaches with longer-term input was universally acknowledged, if not always practised. Thus, concerns about appropriate policy mix became paramount. This was manifest in a policy demarche directed towards aspirations for harmonised, multi-level and cross-sectoral governance. The 'balkanisation' of projects and implementing agents operating independently was progressively eschewed officially. Yet, so too was a monolithic focus: in the post-modernist era, there is – it is claimed – less popularly shared support for many of the old overarching principles on which a comprehensive *Gesellschaftspolitik* could be based. Rather, a 'patchwork quilt' of rejuvenation is now the convention: one which, in variegated ways, seeks to integrate people and place, community and economy, neighbourhood and city, and city and sub-region (for further discussion, see Dangschat, 1993, 1999; Healey *et al.*, 1995; Power, 1997; Madanipour, 1998; Atkinson, 2000a). Central to the design of this patchwork is the determination of the appropriate balance between area and client-targeted interventions and general programmes. There are many salutary warnings in the literature about the pitfalls in erroneously delimiting these policy boundaries. Over the long pull there is, though, a consistent agreement that commitment to greater across-the-board redistribution has to underpin any supplementary positive discrimination (see, for example, Punter, 1981; Atkinson, 2000b). Education and employment are the cases that most readily spring to mind, despite the current fashion, in the latter, for localised economic development (see Musterd & de Winter, 1998).

Reviewing policy evolution in the UK, Glennerster and colleagues (1999) opine that area-targeting has enjoyed mixed fortunes in the allure it offers to policy-makers. It is currently in fashion, although one would have to say it has enjoyed more consistent appeal *outre Manche*. On the other hand, as discussed in Chapter 1, Spain occupies a somewhat interstitial position. In many parts of Germany the approach was embraced sometime later, although it has subsequently proved a pioneer in local economic development. In comparison, in Italy – outside housing rehabilitation – area-based interventions in social policy were long held in suspicion. But, in the converging policy discourse about regeneration, what now seems uncontroversial is that a concentration of presenting problems in clearly delimited spaces is a *sine qua non* as a justification, in order to maximise efficiency (e.g. Edwards, 1989; Smith, 1999). These decisions are highly sensitive to location and context. Whilst, in some cities and regions, there may be a high spatial density of problematic attributes, in many others the hallmarks of deprivation are too geographically diffuse to permit such fine-tuning of focus (for further discussion, see Office of the Deputy Prime Minister, 2003). Even when significant concentration is established, a frequent observation is that many of those most in need reside elsewhere, and are excluded as beneficiaries in contradistinction to those more privileged who otherwise would not qualify for policy input, but for mere place of residence. The outcome is that an element of 'deadweight loss' may have to be tolerated. The negative consequences derived from upgrading in terms of a variety of displacement effects have also been cited at several points earlier in the book. All these factors raise important questions about the compatibility of social and territorial justice, and suggest that a notional shadow-costing should be applied in the planning of projects as a matter of routine, in order to establish a truer input–outcome audit.

As methods fit for purpose, how area approaches may garner advantages has been well-aired in the literature and there is no space for an exposé here (see Geddes, 1997; Kürpick & Weck, 1998; Madanipour, 1998; Parkinson, 1998a; Amin et al., 2000; Born, 2001; MacGregor, 2001). It has to be said that conclusions are mixed. Among them, there remains a complaint about poor specificity of objectives and effective integration with wider strategies. Not least, this arises from the fact that the causes of multiple deprivation and the means for its resolution, all too often, remain speculative. For instance, urban exclusion has proved intransigent in many 'economically redundant' neighbourhoods of even the most booming cities – something, moreover, which has persisted in an environment where overall inequality has been decreasing (see Amin & Thrift, 1995; Skifter Andersen, 2003). At the end of the day, as Meegan and Mitchell (2001) insist, area-targeting is more a political than a technical decision and may be most indicated, albeit as a *faute de mieux* tactic, particularly when preventive measures to stem early signs of exclusion are judged as taking precedence over remedying its effects, once chronically entrenched (Skifter Andersen, 2002).

Turning now to the sectoral focus of intervention: any naïve presumption that investment in physical infrastructure can be a one-off exercise is now discredited. There is a superabundance of evidence that same neighbourhoods – especially when dogged by grave socio-economic problems – have consistently been the most prominent targets. Over-sanguine projections in the 1970s and 1980s not infrequently emanated from the temptation to achieve rapid demonstration effects by starting with the more easily retrievable areas or by reliance on single grand acts of salvation activism. Whilst both are a necessary input in order to generate momentum, they are never sufficient. Furthermore, they have artificially stimulated adoption of unrealistically brief planning horizons (for further discussion, see Carley et al., 2000). Other consequences can ensue. Poorer cities, for instance – desperate for investment to get rejuvenation off the ground – have tolerated low-quality urban design or have opted for the architectural fashions of the moment, which run the risk of rapidly going out of favour. Alternatively, they have fallen foul of the temptation to indulge in hastily implemented projects, with little regard to how they complement longer-term ambitions (these points are taken up in Office of the Deputy Prime Minister, 2003). Moreover, in the rush to steal a march on competitors, there has been a noticeable return in the 1990s to the larger-scale, iconic *grand projet* (e.g. *HafenCity* in

Hamburg; *Euroméditerranée* in Marseilles). All these trends prompt questions about how appropriate it is always to impose a primacy of competitiveness and sustainability over more 'welfarist' objectives. Important lessons, too, stem from the experiences of attempting economic regeneration. One, as discussed earlier, is how crucial it is to achieve effective management of macro-, meso- and micro-level interventions. Compartmentalised bureaucratic and professional preferences for one over the other compromise the extent to which an effective integrated blueprint is produced and, equally importantly, implemented. Whilst, the quality of local leadership has proved a vital ingredient in marshalling economic relaunch, it has to be admitted that the more successful examples among the sample have also benefited from external windfalls, as in Barcelona (with EU entry) and Hamburg (with the fall of the Wall). By comparison, in the poorest agglomerations – as respondents to this study insisted – it is low aggregate demand that has proved chronically problematic (see also Geddes, 2000). It is here that flanking 'welfarist' supports for labour market developments are most urgent, whether they take the form of structured assistance in negotiating job search or prior compensatory measures such as child care facilities for those most at risk of exclusion from work (see Hall, 1997). Furthermore, 'place marketing' and reliance on economic 'niches' may reap only ephemeral gains in an environment of increasingly footloose capital where what were once location-fixed, quality brand names have been transferred elsewhere in the world (for instance, as witnessed in the growing volume of pottery proclaiming to be '*of* Staffordshire' that is no longer produced *in* that county) (see also Graham, 1995; Lovering, 1995).

The interactive impacts of the decisions of individual actors, social institutions and market forces on what are sometimes cyclical processes of commodification, de-commodification and re-commodification, that bear marked socio-spatial attributes, have increasingly occupied the interests of researchers of the post-Fordist city. It was noticeable in several of the cities how social uses and users varied intensely over even relatively confined spaces. European research has plotted how housing, planning and welfare institutional practices have reinforced 'rewarding–penalising' propensities against a background of growing urban differentiation, although it has mostly stopped short of supporting depiction of the situation in terms of the harsh ghettoisation of an 'underclass', described in the case of USA by Wilson (1987). Sometimes the result in the EU is a close propinquity of self-selected, exclusive and 'other'-imposed, exclusionary segregation. Although this fragmentation has so far generally been confined to socio-spatial segmentation, a more scalar polarisation is evidenced in some cities – areas such as Granby-Toxteth, Prè and Belsunce spring readily to mind – and, moreover, it has assumed a more pronounced ethnic dimension (further discussion is contained in Vieillard-Baron, 1990; Hamnett, 1998; Skifter Andersen, 2003). On the other hand, the idea of a simplistic and highly polarised 'dual city' has long been discounted as over simplistic (Marcuse, 1989). More sensitised portrayals offer greater mileage. Thus, citing the collusion of the planning system, Fusero and colleagues (1991) outline a four-stage model of spatial differentiation based on their analysis of Genoa's Centro Storico. Its evolution begins with 'perimetration', continues with 'peripheralisation' and 'segregation', and ends in 'marginalisation'. 'Broken windows' and 'contagion' are among the many analogies implicated in this spiral of decline (Wilson & Kelling, 1982; Froessler, 1994; Alisch, 1998). More parsimonious still is the two-dimensional model developed by Musterd and Ostendorf (1998) specifying segregation/ inequality based on income and ethnicity, although this could be too limiting for cities where other segregating effects (e.g. based on religion) are more at play.

At the beginning of the 1990s, MacGregor (1992) alluded to a nascent dialogue about urban deprivation that owed much to the notion of core–periphery and reflected sharper horizontal cleavages, something that had also been taken up by those seeking to explain post-Fordist socio-economic transformations in terms of insider–outsider divisions (see, for example, van Parijs, 1986). Subsequently, theorising has crystallised around the concept of 'social exclusion' and its dynamic and interactive elements: disaffiliation, disengagement, consumption deficits, and social disqualification manifest in deficient participation and negation of worth as full citizens (see Castel, 1995; Allen, 1998; Bauman, 1998b; Vobruba, 1999). Its attractions lie in its more encompassing and less victim-blaming implications when compared to 'underclass', but its formulation remains inchoate, although EU-funded panel surveys are now being applied in the refinement of the range of indicators to be conventionally applied in its specification.

The selective process of spatial revaluation ('re-commodification', if you will) in the form of directly or indirectly subsidised 'gentrification' has been relatively well-documented cross-nationally. Here both pressures and speeds of impact have varied enormously among the case cities and sometimes they can be reversed – the immediate aftermath of urban riots being a case in point. As we have seen, gentrification implies a reasonably sophisticated initial risk assessment by 'pioneers', either as investors or as incoming residents, of the benefits of speculative retrieval activity. What is of import are perceived existing and, even more so, potentially accumulating rent gaps (the gap between actual and potential ground rents) accruing from 'selective re-quartering' (see Smith, 1986; Blasius & Dangschat, 1990; Dangschat, 1991b; Mangen, 1993). Here, anticipated housing demand and supply trends are determinant, as Power (2000) has argued in relation to abundant supply in the Liverpool housing market which, across many income groups, renders risk-taking unnecessary. Nor does 'pioneering' necessarily lead to immediate upgrading: there is evidence in some cities – again Liverpool provides an example – of speculative decay by investors in the hope of maximising future returns, when a change of planning regulation is anticipated. In conclusion, despite the potential advantages of gentrification in terms of arresting degradation, and improving local economies and fiscal bases, all too often the general observation has been that existing communities are least likely to benefit. Indeed, they may be exposed to displacement or be the object of negative impacts such as rent hikes and increased surveillance. Factors of this order frequently result in an intensification of local conflicts (see Busse, 1991; Foelsch, 1994).

Professions, social institutions and management of inner city spaces

The institutions which comprise broad welfare regimes and the professions they engage each set the operational arena in which the rules of the game governing inclusion and exclusion are played out over space and clientele. There has been a tendency in all welfare systems progressively to introduce elements of socio-spatial policy that are more conditional – and often more exclusionary. This being said, there are substantial cross-national differences in how public agencies shape the life chances of inner city and other deprived populations, not least in the way in which front-line social assistance operates and in the availability of social housing (see Naroska, 1989; Murie, 1998; Vobruba, 2001 for further discussion).

A literature relating to professional cultures has been developing, especially in terms of the ways in which socio-urban problems are defined and solutions specified. Of course, professions and the institutions which employ them are not monoliths and different 'policy networks' may be at play in various parts of the agenda. Furthermore, EU states now, at least nominally, espouse multi-disciplinary practice. On the other hand, there remain significant differences in influence over the urban policy agenda – and in the parts of the administration to which they are accountable – between those professions primarily privileging form and space (architects, engineers and planners) and those privileging community and economic development. Critically, these within-country differences extend to the level of connexion to wider international practice communities and, thereby, to what informs policy learning. Substantial differences in funding horizons and compartmentalised administrative cultures were cited on many occasions by respondents as posing constraints on the degree to which, in practice, multi-disciplinary work was facilitated. In Hamburg, for example, different parts of the city administration retained distinct operational preferences, not least in terms of the scale of intervention. Some departments were more committed to local economic development and the sponsoring of small and local firms, whilst others remained sceptical and heavily prioritised sub-regional strategies (see González & Hermman, 2001; Breckner *et al.*, 2002). Among professions, even the apparent 'near-neighbour' may uphold significantly different focuses. Those in neighbourhood management, for instance, have more typically worked within relatively short timescales demanding the speedy formulation of entry and exit strategies, whereas colleagues in community development have benefited from resort to more sustained engagement (see Born, 2001; von Kietzell, 2001). Different tactical styles have also been reported. Social workers, for example, may perceive that advantages to the locality accrue from highlighting disadvantages; in comparison, those occupied in neighbourhood economic development have tended to view that this could perpetuate a negative image, denting potentials for inward investment (see Smith, 1999; Allen & Cars, 2002).

Between-country variations are of a more substantial order and originate in the specificities of functional specialisms, professional hierarchies and lines of accountability. The extent to which practitioners are engaged as public employees or operate as semi-autonomous agents is also important. Among the many instances depicted in the literature are the southern European heritage of clientelistic practice in public administration, which has long influenced the exercise of professional discretion (e.g. Leontidou, 1993). Differences in the distribution of central and local government competences may also be at play. Le Galès and Harding (1998) cite the example of France where, they argue, the combating of urban deprivation is primarily seen as a national remit, permitting local professional strategies to develop in other directions. Such factors pose serious questions about cross-national, functional and contextual equivalence, since what superficially can appear as the same professional group may operate according to distinct practice and value sets, as Hatton (2001), among many others, recounts in relation to divergences in social work traditions. Differences in professional prestige, often accompanied by resistance to cede ground, was also a factor respondents identified as shaping the realities of a multi-disciplinary practice sometimes radically departing from the rhetoric. The elite status of architects in several of the member states investigated – together with over-production of their number – had the effect of their colonisation of adjacent spheres of action, particularly in housing and neighbourhood development. In this regard, Avarello and Ricci (2000) express their regrets that higher education authorities in Italy have rigidly embedded traditional training practices and, as a result, are not adequately preparing professionals for the new fields of action emerging.

The salience of strongly organised traditional professions does not, of course, necessarily imply absence of innovative dynamism in implementing regeneration. Administrative reforms, creating new opportunities must be taken into account. As material in Chapter 1 indicates, urban remits in major EU states are constantly being revised, entailing new departmental couplings, and so forth (see also Van den Berg *et al.*, 1998). For example, 'spaces' have been created through the instigation of area management by some of the German Länder, as well as in the ongoing federal programme (Alisch, 1998; Koller-Tejeiro, 1998). Still better surveyed, in terms of associated practitioner innovations, has been the evolution of the French *Politique de la Ville* (Le Galès & Mawson, 1994; Pitts, 1998), although its wider effective implementation has also encountered resistance on the part of some powerful professional blocks. Body-Gendrot (2000b), for example, recounts that among the ranks of the police, there has been a not infrequent interpretation of moves towards community-oriented styles as entailing demotion to less pressing, lower-status work. These kinds of problems can also be attributed to the fact that new practice trajectories, and their associated reward structures, may be relatively flat in terms of career progression, so that advancement might require a later re-insertion into more conventional hierarchies.

Turning to the formal political level, several investigations have documented how local elites have long colluded in sanctioning exclusionary segregation (e.g. Herrmann *et al.*, 1987; Arvati, 1988; Moore, 1997; Preteceille, 2000; Fitzpatrick, 2001). Planning policies they approve may expedite this process, by helping shape the contours of abandonment through toleration of poor-quality urban design or by providing poor inputs of public services which, in turn, influence private investment decisions (Madanipour, 1998; Caesperlein & Gliemann, 2001; Boddy, 2002). As discussed earlier in this book, official tolerance of degradation, in what may be viewed as 'superfluous spaces', might continue until neighbourhood compliance, manifestations of which include low electoral turnouts, evaporates into support for the far right or – more threateningly – urban riots. More generally, attempts to infuse greater responsiveness have derived from the dictates of 'new public management'. In this operational scenario, administrative discretion has been pruned back and wider partnership institutionalised. These new forms of contractual, 'networked' collaboration are fuelled by performance-led auditing (Lane, 2000; Bailey, 2001; Taylor, 2002). What these crosscutting changes represent is the strongest demonstration of international policy-borrowing in contemporary Europe. Among others, the 'Tilburg' model of contracting-out, privatisation and the introduction of flatter, decentralised hierarchies in this Dutch town has been an influential exemplar (Koller-Tejeiro, 1998; Stratmann, 1999).

Partnership

Vertical – and, even more so – horizontal partnership is central to new urban regimes evolving in Europe, and beyond (see Jewson & MacGregor, 1997). Varyingly depicted as 'networked governance' (Rhodes, 1997) or a new manifestation of what, in many cases, is a long tradition of 'corporatist localism' (Geddes, 1997, 2000), it is part and parcel of attempts by the central and local state to 'steer more and row less' (Body-Gendrot, 2001). As an analytical tool, though, there is a danger of 'conceptual stretching', given its variegated forms between policy sectors, even within a country. There is no space here to catalogue the diversity of partnership styles (see Hall & Mawson [1999] for analysis of typologies according to degree of positive engagement). Suffice it to repeat the important point made by Geddes and Le Galès (2001) that their feasibility, with regard to urban regeneration, is contingent on the effectiveness of overarching welfare and associated statutory institutions.

The abundant evaluative literature on partnership in different international arena, at least, allows for broad conclusions. The remedying of democratic deficits – if widely recruited – stimulation of innovation and collaboration, the encouragement of local identification and best practice, empowerment and – through use of new technologies – new *guichets* of access to decision-making have all been proposed as advantages (e.g. Geddes, 1998; Vogt, 1998; Parkinson, 1998a; Kedadouche, 2003; DIFU, 2003). Conversely, the conditionality of engagement has been stated as constituting an important constraint on the degree to which partnership contributes to stable alliances, capable of sustaining new urban policy regimes. Here, the private sector has tended to be the more contingent partner, particularly when negotiating with poorer municipalities desperate for inward investment. The influences on local politics of peak organisations like chambers of commerce have been relatively well treated. On the other hand, as Stoker and Mossberger (1994) complain, there are still sound reservations whether the kinds of individual enterprises participating in a non-contingent way are capable of parsimonious classification. What we know in general is that private-sector participatory propensities are a function of the degree of perceived risk (projects ensuring safer options being preferred) – particularly in respect of larger financing institutions – benefits of scale, trade-offs in terms of relaxation of strict environmental stipulations, and so on (see, for example, Harvey, 1973; Punter, 1981; Robson, 1988; Avarello & Ricci, 2000).

Sustained community participation may also be highly conditional. Some accounts have suggested that this may perhaps be more likely the case in southern states, where from an authoritarian past vestiges of distrust of officialdom remain. This being said, as argued in the case of Spain, the democratic transition unleashed innovative community mobilisation. However, model regeneration projects in Italian inner cities would not have been possible without active neighbourhood support. Crude north–south dichotomies in terms of quality of such variables as 'social capital', 'civil society' and 'civic community' have proved highly artefactual and fail to take sufficient account of cultural differences in the forms of associationism that are most popularly valued (Diamond, 1997; Maloney *et al.*, 2000; Mangen, 2001). Nonetheless, as a general consideration, contingency is an important possible effect that must be borne in mind: it can accentuate the classic double-bind of 'no success, no participation – no participation, no success'. Furthermore, there is a danger that it may result in 'shopping lists' of immediate demands on the part of community representatives, to their neglect of a longer-term, structured agenda (see Born, 2001; Skifter Andersen, 2003) .

Undoubtedly, a naïve assumption has been entertained that, with a modicum of encouragement by political actors, an acceptable level of community engagement can be readily generated and, moreover, that this will remain a dependable asset over time (see Atkinson, 2000b). But, frequently, input of the populace has been confined to consultation – to the lower rungs of the 'ladders of citizen participation' described by Arnstein (1969), whereby institutional control ensures that what results is token presence rather than effective voice. In the present study, a frequent complaint made by respondents was that, all too often, officials were primarily motivated by the desire merely to convey an impression of keeping faith with the community, in the interests of professional legitimisation – that what formal agents solicited was the opportunity to absorb information rather than radiate it (see also Davoudi & Healey, 1995; Allen, 1998; Herrmann, 1998). There is a well-represented argument that official overtures to the community are many times driven by attempts to manage disaffection and protest, through co-opting the more vociferous elements of urban social movements. This is substantiated by evidence from several countries. As a result, more radicalised community energies may be diverted to other causes (see Lowe, 1986; Beazley *et al.*, 1997; Body-Gendrot, 2000a; Font, 2003). Possibilities for this kind of manipulation are increased by the fact that the generation of effective community leadership and the time or skills possible recruits have to invest may not be a reliable resource; neither, in a context of rapid population turnover, is the stability of the community (see European Commission, 1996; Carley *et al.*, 2000; Body-Gendrot, 2000b; Purdue, 2001; Office of the Deputy Prime Minister, 2003). Pressures for heavier official supervision of community engagement are all the stronger when the stakes are high in terms of devolved administration of complex projects attracting major funding that, of necessity, is subject to tight auditing and accountability lines. In this regard, Foley and Martin (2000) are surely correct to question whether current administrative cultures, with implicit intolerance of failure, sit well with the necessary risks involved in adopting more 'bottom-up' implementation styles.

Some investigators discerned that, in the past decade, a more conservative-inspired agenda has tended to mobilise communities in Europe, one that privileges local economic growth alliances over the interests of collective consumption or environmental concerns (e.g. Roth, 2000; Mayer, 2000b). While this may provide greater scope for routine and pacific collaboration between public authorities and the populations they serve, a danger is that propensities for unrepresentative and skewed articulation pathways may be exacerbated, thereby favouring the more privileged, particularly when neighbourhoods face intense competition for resources (see Collinge & Hall, 1997; Dettmer & Kreutz, 1999). A much cited outcome is that it is the most deprived who are denied voice, but there may also be conscious desires to exclude other unfavoured groups, as reviewed earlier in this book in terms of ethnic and sexual minorities (see also Geddes, 2000; Mayer, 2000a). This form of community mobilisation, acting in local partnership with commercial and public actors, creates what could be termed corporatist 'insider power clubs' (for further discussion, see Healey, 1998; Stratmann, 1999; Coates *et al.*, 2001; Potts, 2002).

Irrespective of the benefits, local partnership in the planning and delivery of urban and social programmes cannot be afforded a monopoly, to the extent that it crowds out democratic control and accountability. Besides, the need for continued official input to guarantee sustained engagement may impose high transaction costs. On the basis of survey evidence, Geddes (2000) recorded a general tendency for public actors in the EU states to dominate, with varying strengths of input from the private sector and trade unions, and disparate styles of recruitment for community engagement. He shares with Parkinson (1998a) a concern about a common failure to invest sufficient resources in capacity-building and concludes that local partnerships are seldom a sufficient vehicle for the sustained tackling of urban social exclusion. Perversely, when they fail to deliver, they entrench demoralisation still further and can deepen feelings of resentment and suspicion among targeted communities.

Regeneration regimes

As consistently argued here and elsewhere, cross-national variations in the quality of horizontal partnerships – as a central element of evolving regeneration regimes – remain one of the most salient features of the urban renewal agenda in the EU. Similarly, vertical partnership and the role of state institutions in supporting horizontal collaboration assume diverse forms, although in general public actors remain the vital overseers of cooperative urban renewal structures, even in countries most robustly prosecuting the privatisation route (Harding, 1994; Bagnasco & Le Galès, 2000). Within broad transformations from urban managerialism towards entrepreneurialism, adumbrated by Harvey (1989), there remain important divergences in the conditions of 'new localism' imposed by the pressures of globalisation not only internationally, but also nationally (Le Galès, 2000). Even within cities, highly localised growth coalitions may be operating – with significantly different agenda – with consequences for the derivation of a coherent city-wide focus (see Hennings & Kunzmann, 1993; Newman & Thornley, 1996).

The conceptualisation of urban regimes has attracted growing research interest. Although essentially context-dependent, the principal ideal-types have been reasonably well-specified (see, for example, DiGaetano & Klemanski, 1993; Stoker & Mossberger, 1994). In terms of inner city rejuvenation, the regimes encountered in this study straddle several of the proposed categories:

among them, 'symbolic' or 'image-building' formations; those also pursuing a prestige maintenance or conservation agenda on several fronts; instrumental, change-promoting regimes; and those motivated, in part, by social reform and 'opportunity expansion'. What stands in sharper contrast among the sampled cities is a division between those having built rather tighter forms, in terms of funding packages and collaborative strengths, particularly with regard to incorporation of community and informal actors (Liverpool, Barcelona and Hamburg), and the somewhat looser cooperative networks operating in Centro Storico and the central arrondissements of Marseilles. This being said – irrespective of the different scales of interventions and inevitable cross-national variations – all the regeneration regimes have been unequivocally minded to invest in more careful management of economic growth. Public-led regimes were the rule, albeit with varying co-option of informal agents. In general, market-led regimes were primarily in operation in the *grand projet*, although, again, cross-national variations were pronounced.

Collaborative, cross-sectoral and multi-level governance, as a contested arena, is constantly being negotiated. The requirement to incorporate broad coalitions of state, market and other actors and, moreover, to sustain them sets the parameters (see Collinge & Hall, 1997; Boland, 2000; Benington, 2001). In this connexion, Amin and Thrift (1995) propose the attractive concept of 'institutional thickness' embracing such factors as 'institutional learning', knowledge capacities, flexibility, stability and trust. A combination of multiple path-dependent policy evolutions sustains it albeit – confronted by change-demanding events – punctuated by major strategic revisions (Baumgartner & Jones, 1993). How equilibrium is achieved is a function of the ease of accommodation between old and new, a policy *bricolage*, as Götting and Lessenich (1999) alluringly put it.

In essence, one traces in the formation of regeneration regimes something of a reversal of the neo-liberal critique about the welfare state that insists that the pressures of competitiveness demand a 'rush to the bottom'. Rather, in order to exploit the potential of the 'entrepreneurial city' and, within it, the inner core, what is argued is the case for a 'rush to the top', with cities competing to provide the highest quality infrastructural and social investment. Of course, the urban playing field is far from level; poorer cities are not best placed to commit to high-risk strategies for, despite a welter of programmes, all too often further economic decline has outpaced rejuvenation dividends (Taylor, 2002). For them, enticingly 'glocalised' rapid pro-growth options may entail surrender of the social dimensions of planning gain (Keating, 1991; Swyngedouw,1992; DiGaetano and Klemanski, 1993). Accordingly, as Jessop (2000) among others notes, it is not by chance that risk avoidance is often the order of the day – witness the plethora of copycat 'prestige' dockland re-developments. Some sort of negotiated 'urban settlement' is required: Begg and his colleagues (2002) conclude that competitive city entrepreneurialism is urgently in need of overarching management, lest the European urban order descend into a destructive free-for-all re-positioning.

Towards convergence?

The protean nature of the inner city condition has stimulated accelerating evolution of policy. In the space of three decades, a circumscribed physical agenda centred on public governance has been discarded in favour of an expanded ambit on all fronts, although the pace of this change does vary across countries. To be sure, international lesson-learning has stimulated a measure of convergence. What can be readily discerned among strategies formulated is a shared, irresistible temptation to resort to over-varnished, not to say meretricious, vocabulary reminiscent of the Pauline allusion to the 'laver of regeneration'. Opportunistic tactics and organisational delivery styles are converging (see Jewson & MacGregor, 1997). However, it would be going too far to argue that this is tantamount to crude standardisation. Most cross-national policy-borrowing veers towards the lighter end of the spectrum: its strongest incidence is among nearest neighbours, typically bringing forward what might, in any event, have occurred. Even here, undiluted replication is rare (for further discussion, see Ward, 2000). In other contexts, it might be easier to create room for independent innovation; and in many other cases, a contextually dependent 'mirroring' is more typical than a direct 'transplant'.[1]

What are the implications for the common development of professional and administrative practices? My conclusions, derived from extensive field-work is that – in these five cities at least – there has been relatively little exploitation of the 'freedom of movement' opportunities offered by EU membership, as far as international interchange of staff is concerned. On the other hand, the growing volume of cross-national research, together with dissemination and exchange of experiences the Union offers, is gradually permeating through to training, although, as argued earlier, some of the relevant professions are more exposed to these influences than others.

To end on a positive note, comparative research of the life chances and repertoire of coping strategies adopted by deprived urban communities is reaping evident dividends. What is being stressed, in sensitised analysis, is the intimate interactive effects of market exchange, communal reciprocity and state redistribution on the lives of many within the inner city. Here, mention should be made of the work of Moser (1996), who has developed one of the more culturally-grounded comparative paradigms. Empirical advances in depicting the importance of specific milieu, especially regarding the interaction of formal and informal economies, have been made by authors such as Kesteloot (1998) and Williams and Windebank (2000), who portray how communities survive – or go under. As for policy challenges, the nature of inner city problems demands, as always, a great degree of tenacity in the quest to reconcile solidarity-focussed and competition-motivated policy directions, in order to temper the interests of the 'commercial' with those of the 'social' city.

Note

1. I am indebted to Ana Guillén and Denis Bouget, my colleagues in the *Cross-National Research Group*, for these perspicacious comments.

Appendix: Statistical Audit

The statistics presented here should be seen as broad indicators that do not take into account changes in definitions of key terms or boundaries at local or city level. Where available, they refer to the entire study zone, but where there are variations they are indicated. Averages for the study zones can hide enormous variations within the neighbourhoods enclosed, this being especially the case in relation to housing tenures and presence of ethnic minority populations. Where percentage distributions do not total 100 this is due to non-recording.

Beyond the crude population statistics, there are considerable divergences in the quality and the range of the material conventionally available that should caution against other than a broad-brush impression. In this regard, the EU-funded Urban Audit represents a considerable dividend: the available survey includes city and sub-city data for 58 locations and work currently in progress extends this to 180.

The study zones are:

Barcelona – *Ciutat Vella*: the four neighbourhoods (*barris*) of Barceloneta, Barri Gòtic, Casc Antic and Raval.

Genoa – *Centro Storico*: the three neighbourhoods (*sestieri*) of Prè, Molo and Maddalena between the modern city centre and the old port.

Hamburg – *Innenstadt*: the core of the central borough (*Bezirk*) of Mitte (*Kerngebiet*) and three adjacent localities in the borough of Altona (Altstadt, Nord and Ottensen): a total of 12 neighbourhoods.

Liverpool – *Inner City*: the wards of Vauxhall, Everton, Smithdown, Kensington, Granby, Dingle and Abercromby enclosing the commercial city centre.

Marseilles – *Centre-Ville*: the local administrative districts (*arrondissements*) 1, 2 and 3 to the west and (mostly) north of the old harbour.

Table A.1

	Ciutat Vella	Barcelona
Population		
Population	177,544 (1970)	1,745,142 (1970)
	117,768 (1981)	1,752,627 (1981)
	90,612 (1991)	1,643,542 (1991)
	88,793 (2001)	1,505,325 (2001)
Percentage change 1970–2001	−50.0	−13.7
Population under 15 (%) (2001)	9.9	11.6
Population over pensionable age (%) (2001)	24.6	22.0

		44.5 (1970)
Housing		
Tenure type: owner-occupied (%)	39.2 (1985)	59.2 (1985)
	43.2 (1996)	67.1 (1996)
		62.3 (1970)
Tenure type: rented (%)	57.3 (1985)	38.4 (1985)
	54.4 (1996)	30.2 (1996)
Unoccupied housing (%) (1991)	22.4	10.4
Housing standards (% with hot running water) (1996)	76.3	95.7
Employment		
Percentage of occupied adults of working age	58.7 (1981)	58.4 (1981)
	46.8 (1996)	47.9 (2001)
		16.2 (1981)
Unemployment rates (%)	21.3 (1981)	13.7 (1991)
	20.3 (1991)	10.6 (2001)
Youth unemployment rate (under 25) (%)	20.0 (1985)	16.3 (1985)
		13.9 (1996)
Ethnic minority		
	7.6 (1981)	
Resident population (%)	22.7 (2000)	7.2 (2000)
Education statistics		
Educational attainment: percentage of adult illiteracy (2000)	0.6	0.2
Social indicators		
Per capita disposable family income (1985) ratio of city average	81	100
Health and social services		
Standard mortality ratios per 1000 population	169 (1991)	86 (1970)
	147 (2000)	95 (1991)
		103 (2000)
Crime statistics		
Total recorded crimes per 1000 population (1996)		22.8
Victimisation surveys ('index' percentage of annual victimisation among adults) (2000)	24.3	16.4

Table A.2

	Centro Storico	Genoa
Population		
Population	31,105 (1971)	816,872 (1971)
	26,935 (1981)	762,895 (1981)
	22,303 (1991)	678,771 (1991)
	23,216 (2000)	632,366 (2000)
Percentage change 1971–2000	–25.4	–22.6
Population under 15 (%) (2000)	9.6	10.2
Population over pensionable age (%) (2000)	17.1	24.9
Housing		
Tenure type: owner-occupied (%) (1991)	51.6	63.4
Tenure type: rented (%) (1991)	48.4	32.8
Unoccupied housing (%) (1991)	22.1	9.3
Housing standards: housing in 'very bad' condition (%) (1991)	78.2	38.6
Housing Standards: units without sole access to toilet (%)	0.9 (1991)	22.4 (1971) 5.4 (1991)
Employment		
Percentage of occupied adults	46.5 (1981)	52.0 (1981)
	46.5 (1991)	52.6 (1991)
		9.4 (1981)
Unemployment rates (%)	14.2 (1981)	15.2 (1996)
Youth unemployment rate (under 25) (%)	14.7 (1991)	3.7 (1991)
Ethnic minority		
		2.4 (1981)
Resident population 'foreigners' (%)	16.7 (1991)	3.3 (1991)
	19.9 (2000)	4.4 (2000)
Education statistics		
Educational attainment levels (illiteracy rate, adult population)	7.6 (1981) 3.1 (1991)	0.9 (1981) 0.8 (1991)
Health and social services		
Standard mortality ratios per 1000 population		127 (1981) 133 (2000)
Crime statistics		
Total reported punishable offences per 1000 population (1998)		86.7

Table A.3

	Innenstadt	Hamburg
Population		
Population	182,284 (1975)	1,717,383 (1975)
	182,609 (1990)	1,652,363 (1990)
	176,331 (2001)	1,710,932 (2001)
Percentage change 1975–2001	–3.2	–0.4
Population under 18 (%) (2001)	12.6	16.1
Population over pensionable age (%) (2001)	13.0	17.2
Housing		
Tenure type: owner-occupied (% of occupied units, 1987)	2.4	17.3
Tenure type: all rented (% of occupied units, 1987)	97.6	82.7
Tenure type: socially rented (%) (1987)	33.8	38.6
(2001)	12.4	17.6
Housing standards (% units without bath or toilet facilities internal to accommodation) (1987)	7.5	3.7
Employment		
(% adults statutorily socially insured and employed) (2001)	49.8	49.4
Unemployment rates (%)	17.5 (1987)	11.6 (1987)
	8.8 (2001)	6.5 (2001)
Youth unemployment rate (under 25) (%) (2001)	6.2	4.9
Long-term unemployment (1 + years, 1998, second trimester)	34.2	37.4
Ethnic minority		
Resident population (% of 'foreigners')	26.0 (1975) (St Georg only)[a]	6.8 (1975)
	28.6 (2001)	15.7 (2001)
Education statistics		
% of population over 18 without general school matriculation (1987)	14.5	17.5
Recipients of social assistance (%) (2001)	8.1	6.9
Crime statistics		
Total reported punishable offences per 1000 population, 2001	1080	186

[a] St Georg was rated the second highest of the 12 neighbourhoods in 2001 in terms of the percentage of 'foreign' population.

Table A.4

	Inner City	Liverpool
Population		
Population	138,621 (1971)	610,114 (1971)
	101,344 (1981)	516,700 (1981)
	81,856 (1991)	474,522 (1991)
	77,900 (2001)	439,473 (2001)
Percentage change 1971–2001	−43.8	−28.0
Population under 15 (%) (2001)	19.9	20.0
Population over pensionable age (%) (2001)	17.3	20.0
Housing		
	15.4 (1971)	31.7 (1971)
Tenure type: owner-occupied (%)	24.3 (1991)	51.1 (1991)
	29.2 (2001)	52.6 (2001)
	44.5 (1971)	36.2 (1971)
Tenure type: social housing (%)	59.7 (1991)	37.2 (1991)
	51.2 (2001)	40.9 (2001)
	40.1 (1971)	32.1 (1971)
Tenure type: privately rented (%)	14.4 (1991)	11.7 (1991)
	19.6 (2001)	15.2 (2001)
	3.7 (1971)	3.1 (1971)
Unoccupied housing (%)	7.7 (1991)	5.9 (1991)
Housing standards	39.7 (1971)	29.3 (1971)
(% without exclusive use of toilet and bath facilities)	1.4 (1991)	1.9 (1991)
	0.8 (2001)	0.5 (2001)
(% without central heating) (2001)	21.0	27.0
Employment		
Percentage adult-occupied population (2001)	38.6	48.9
	15.8 (1971)	10.6 (1971)
Unemployment rates (%)	35.4 (1991)	21.6 (1991)
	14.4 (2001)	8.7 (2001)
Youth unemployment rates (under 25) (%)	41.7 (1991)	31.2 (1991)
		31.0 (1996)
Long-term unemployment rate (1 + years) (%) (1999)	34.1	32.8
Ethnic minority		
Resident population (%)	9.4 (1991)	3.7 (1991)
	13.0 (2001)	5.7 (2001)
Education statistics		
Educational attainment levels (% post-A level qualifications)	6.3 (1991)	8.4 (1991)

Health and social services		
Standard mortality ratios per 1000 population (1998)	188	143
Crime statistics		
Total recorded crimes per 1000 population (1998/99)	370	136

Table A.5

	Centre-Ville	Marseilles
Population		
Population	125,230 (1975)	908,600 (1975)
	118,040 (1982)	870,851 (1982)
	104,727 (1990)	800,309 (1990)
	104,775 (1999)	797,491 (1999)
Percentage change 1975–1999	−16.3	−12.2
Population under 15 (%) (1999)	18.7	17.0
Population over pensionable age (%) (1999)	21.0	23.3
Housing		
Tenure type: owner-occupied (%)	27.0 (1975)	37.0 (1975)
	29.3 (1999)	43.9 (1999)
Tenure type: rented (%)	66.0 (1999)	51.7 (1999)
Unoccupied housing (%)		8.4 (1999)
Housing standards (percentage of units without sole access to shower or bath)	14.3 (1982)	4.9 (1990)
	2.8 (1999)	1.9 (1999)
Employment		
Percentage active population (includes employed, unemployed and the military)	50.0 (1999)	50.9 (1999)
Unemployment rates (%)	17.3 (1982)	14.5 (1982)
	26.9 (1990)	18.6 (1990)
	35.7 (1999)	23.2 (1999)
Long-term unemployment (1 + years)	56.2 (1999)	58.9 (1999)
Youth unemployment rates (under 25) (%)	45.8 (1999)	37.8 (1999)
Ethnic minority		
	13.6 (1975)	
Resident 'foreign' head households (%)	15.7 (1990)	6.9 (1990)
	15.6 (1999)	6.8 (1999)
Education statistics		
Educational attainment levels: percentage of students not completing compulsory education (1996)		9.7
Population over 15, not in education, without any form of matriculation (%) (1999)	31.4	23.7

Sources

Barcelona

Ajuntament de Barcelona. Departament d'Estadística (http://www.bcn.es/estadistica).
Ajuntament de Barcelona (1985) *Projecte Jove*. Barcelona, City Council. For 1985 youth unemployment statistics.
EU *Urban Audit Online* (see website below) for 1996 youth unemployment statistics and total recorded crime.
IEMB (1986) *Enquesta Metropolitana* 1986. Barcelona, Institut d'Estudis Metropolitans de Barcelona.
Social Indicators from: Soler, J., Sampere, E. & Ferrando, P. (1987) *Un Sistema de Indicadors Socials per a la Ciutat de Barcelona*. Barcelona, Ajuntament de Barcelona, Àrea de Serveis Socials.

Genoa

Belgiojoso, A. B. (1990) *Studio degli Itinerari Colombiano*. Genoa, Comune di Genova.
Comune di Genova (1994) *La Popolazione di Genova*. Genoa, City Council.
Comune di Genova (various years) *Anuario Statistico*. Genoa, City Council.
Comune di Genova (2000) *Genova Statistica*. Genoa, City Council.
Comune di Genova (2000) *Notiziario Statistico*. Genoa, City Council.
EU *Urban Audit Online* (see website below) for 1996 unemployment statistics.

Hamburg

Ambulante Hilfe (1989) 'Leitlinien und Perspektiven für die Wohnungspolitik der 90er Jahre in Hamburg'. *Praxis und Sozialplanung*. Vol. 3, Table A60, p. 116. For foreign resident population, St Georg, 1975.
Arbeitsamt (1998) *Bestand an Arbeitslosen nach Stadtteilen – Hamburg*. Long-term unemployed data supplied personally to author.
Podzuweit, U., Schütte, W. & Swierkta, N. (1992) *Sozialatlas – Datenbuch Hamburg*. Hamburg. Fachhochschule Hamburg, Fachbereich Sozialpädagogik.
Podzuweit, U. & Schütte, W. (1997) *Sozialatlas Hamburg: 1997*. Hamburg. Fachhochschule Hamburg, Fachbereich Sozialpädagogik.
Statistiches Landesamt (various years) *Hamburg in Zahlen*. Hamburg, Statistiches Landesamt.
Statistiches Landesamt (various years) *Statistisches Taschenbuch*. Hamburg, Statistiches Landesamt.
2001 data is from *Hamburg in Zahlen Online*: www.hamburg.de/fhh/behoerde_fuer_inneres/statistisches_landesamt.

Liverpool

EU *Urban Audit Online* (see website below) for Youth and Long-term unemployment statistics.
Liverpool City Council (1991) *Key Statistics: Liverpool Wards, 1971/81/91*. Liverpool, City Council, Central Policy Unit.
Long-Term Unemployment Rate, Standard Mortality Ratio and Recorded Crime 1998/9: statistics made available by the Central Policy Unit, Liverpool City Council.
2001 Census from *Neighbourhood Statistics Online*: www.neighbourhood.statistics.gov.uk/.

Marseilles

AGAM (various years) *Données Urbaines: Arrondissements 1, 2, 3*. Marseilles, Agence d'Urbanisme de l'Agglomération Marseillaise.

INSEE (1999) *Recensement de la Populaiton 1999: Exploitation Principale* (*Lieu de Résidence*). Marseilles, INSEE.

EU *Urban Audit Online* (see website below) for the adult population not completing formal education.

Urban audit online

http://europa.eu.int/comm/regional_policy/urban2/urban/audit/src/results.html.

Bibliography

Abella, M. (1999) 'Ciutat Vella: El Corazón Antiguo'. In Montaner, J. M. (ed.) *Barcelona 1979–2004: Del Desarrollo a La Ciudad de Calidad*. Barcelona, Ajuntament de Barcelona.

Action for Cities (1991) *Task Forces: What We Do*. London, Department of Trade and Industry.

Aden, H. (2001) 'L'État Protecteur, Mobilisation de Nouveaux Acteurs et Repli Sécuritaire: Les Politiques de Sécurité et de Prévention en Allemagne dans les Années 1990'. *Déviance et Société*, Vol. 25, 459–477.

AGAM (1987) *Portraits de Trois Cités*. Marseilles, Agence d'Urbanisme de l'Agglomération Marseillaise.

AGAM (1989) *Préparation du Xeme Plan: Document Cartographique des Quartiers Sensibles*. Marseilles, Agence d'Urbanisme de l'Agglomération Marseillaise.

AGAM (1990) *OPAH Canebière: Étude du Quartier Belsunce*. Marseilles, Agence d'Urbanisme de l'Agglomération Marseillaise.

AGAM (1993a) *Programme de Référence du Centre-Ville*. Marseilles, Agence d'Urbanisme de l'Agglomération Marseillaise.

AGAM (1993b) *Euroméditerranée – Dossier Documentaire de Presse, Références Bibliographiques*. Marseilles, Agence d'Urbanisme de l'Agglomération Marseillaise.

AGAM (1998) *Atlas du Parc Locatif Social de Marseille*. Marseilles, Agence d'Urbanisme de l'Agglomération Marseillaise.

AGAM (2000a) *Operation Euroméditerranée: Construction de Logement et d'Activités*. Marseilles, Agence d'Urbanisme de l'Agglomération Marseillaise.

AGAM (2000b) *Projet Centre-Ville et Politique de la Ville*. Marseilles, Agence d'Urbanisme de l'Agglomération Marseillaise.

AGAM (2000c) *Contrat de Ville: La Géographie d'Application du Contrat de Ville*. Marseilles, Agence d'Urbanisme de l'Agglomération Marseillaise.

AGAM (2000d) *Politique de la Ville: La Prévention de la Délinquance*. Marseilles, Agence d'Urbanisme de l'Agglomération Marseillaise.

Age Concern (2000) *Annual Report: 2000*. Liverpool, Age Concern.

Ahtik, V. & Sokoloff, B. (1990) *Social Revitalisation of the City Core: Two European Cases*. Paper Presented at the International Sociological Association World Congress, Madrid, 9–13 July.

Ajuntament de Barcelona (1988) *Proyecto Pauperisación y Prostitucóon en Districto No. 1 de Barcelona, 1988: Formacion e Insercion Sociolaboral*. Barcelona, City Council.

Ajuntament de Barcelona (1989a) *Rivitalització Urbana, Economica i Social*. Barcelona City Council, Procivesa agency for the Ciutat Vella.

Ajuntament de Barcelona (1989b) *A Ciutat Vella – Primer, la Gent – Resum d'Actuacións de l'Any 1989*. Barcelona, City Council, Districte Ciutat Vella.

Ajuntament de Barcelona (1990) *Barcelona 2000: Economic and Social Strategic Plan*. Barcelona, Ajuntament de Barcelona and the Executive Committee of 'Barcelona 2000'.

Ajuntament de Barcelona (1991) *Rivitalització Urbana i Social: Segones Jornades Ciutat Vella*. Barcelona City Council, Procivesa agency for Ciutat Vella.

Ajuntament de Barcelona (1993) *La Salut a Barcelona: 1991*. Barcelona, City Council, Institut Municipal de Salut Pública.

Ajuntament de Barcelona (1997a) *The Urban Renewal of the Ciutat Vella*. Barcelona, City Council.
Ajuntament de Barcelona (1997b) *Enquesta Reforma Urbanistica Ciutat Vella: Informe*. Barcelona, City Council.
Ajuntament de Barcelona (1999) *Urbanisme a Barcelona: 1999*. Barcelona, City Council.
Ajuntament de Barcelona (2000) *La Salut a Barcelona: 1998*. Barcelona, City Council, Institut Municipal de Salut Pública.
Ajuntament de Barcelona (2002) *La Salut a Barcelona: 1999*. Barcelona, City Council, Institut Municipal de Salut Pública.
Ajuntament de Barcelona (2003) *Precios de las Viviendas*. Barcelona, City Council, Institut Muncipal d'Hisenda.
Alabart, A., Aragay, J. & Sabaté, J. (1990) 'Encuesta de Victimicazión en los Comercios de Barcelona: Participación Ciudadana en la Politica de Seguridad'. *Prevenció*. No. 4.
Albert, C., Davia, M., Hernanz, V. & Toharia, L. (2002) 'Choosing between Education, Training and Labour Market Entry'. In Schömann, K. & O'Connell, P. (eds) *Education, Training and Employment Dynamics*. Cheltenham, Edward Elgar.
Alisch, M. (ed.) (1998) *Stadtteilmanagement; Voraussetzungen und Chancen für die soziale Stadt*. Opladen, Leske & Budrich.
Alisch, M. & Dangschat, J. (1991) *The Restructuring of Housing Supply as a Consequence of Demand Shifts: The Case of Hamburg*. Paper presented at the International Housing Research Conference, Oslo, 24–27 June.
Alisch, M. & Dangschat, J. (1994) 'Ziele und Strukturen einer Stadtentwicklung des Sozialen Ausgleiches in Hamburg'. In Froessler, R., Lang, M., Selle, K. & Staubach, R. (eds) *Lokaler Partnerschaften: Die Erneuerung benachteiligter Quartiere in europäischen Städten*. Basel, Birkhäuser.
Alisch, M. & zum Felde, W. (1991) 'Das gute Wohngefühl ist weg'. In Blasius, J. & Dangschat, J. (eds) *Gentrification*. Frankfurt, Campus.
Allen, J. (1998) 'Europe of the Neighbourhoods: Class, Citizenship and Welfare Regimes'. In Madanipour, A., Cars, G. and Allen, J. (eds) *Social Exclusion in European Cities: Processes, Experiences and Responses*. London, Jessica Kingsley.
Allen, J. & Cars, G. (2002) 'The Tangled Web: Neighbourhood Governance in a Post-Fordist Era'. In Cars, G., Healey, P., Madanipour, A. & de Magalhães, C. (eds) *Urban Governance, Institutional Capacity and Social Milieux*. Aldershot, Ashgate.
Alonso, C. & Castells, M. (1992) *Spain Beyond Myths*. Madrid, Alianza.
Ambler, A. (2001) 'Politics and Policy in Education'. In Guyomarch, A., Machin, H. & Hall, P. (eds) *Developments in French Politics 2*. Basingstoke, Palgrave.
Ambulante Hilfe (1989) 'Leitlinien und Perspektiven fuer die Wohnungspolitik der 90er Jahre in Hamburg'. In *Ambulante Hilfe Arbeitskreis Wohnraumversorgung in Praxis und Sozialplanung*. Vol. 3. Hamburg, Ambulante Hilfe.
Amin, A. & Thrift, N. (1995) 'Globalisation, Institutional "Thickness" and the Local Economy'. In Healey, P., Cameron, S., Davoudi, S., Graham, S. & Madanipour, A. (eds) *Managing Cities: The New Urban Context*. Chichester, Wiley.
Amin, A., Massey, D. & Thrift, N. (2000) *Cities for the Many Not for the Few*. Bristol, Policy Press.
Anderson, A. & Vieillard-Baron, H. (2000) *La Politique de la Ville: Histoire et Organisation*. Paris: Editions ASH.
Anderson, J. (1995) 'The Structural Funds and the Social Dimension of EU Policy: Springboard or Stumbling Block?'. In Leibfried, S. & Pierson, P. (eds) *European Social Policy: Between Fragmentation and Integration*. Washington, Brookings Institution.
Anselme, A. (1990) *Entre Logeurs et Logés*. Marseilles, CERFISE.

Antica, E. (1985) *Ricerca d'Informazioni ed Individuazione di un Progetto d'Intervento*. Genoa, City Council, Assessorato ai Servizi Sociali.

Apotheloz, C. & Lambert, E. (1994) 'Marseille – Le Frémissement'. *Marseille 94 – Le Nouvel Économiste*. No. 932.

Archivio de Studi Urbani e Regionali (1993) 'Genova: Opportunismo Istituzionale e Degrado'. *Archivio de Studi Urbani e Regionali*. No. 46, Editorial, 1–10.

Arcuri, C. (1987) 'Stranieri a Genova'. *Entropia*. No. 14, 1–15.

ARI (1999) *Memòria 1999: Ciutat Vella Rehabilitació*. Barcelona, Ajuntament de Barcelona.

ARI (2001) *Memòria 2000: Ciutat Vella Rehabilitació*. Barcelona, Ajuntament de Barcelona.

Arias Goytre, F. & Heitkamp, T. (2000) 'Distressed Urban Areas and Urban Renewal in Spain'. *Jahrbuch Stadterneuerung 2000*. Berlin, Technische Universität Berlin.

Arnstein, S. R. (1969) 'A Ladder of Citizen Participation'. *Journal of the American Institute of Planners*. Vol. 35, 216–224.

Arvati, P. (1988) *Oltre la Città Divisa: Gli Anni della Ristructurazione a Genova*. Genoa, Ed. Sagep.

Ascher, F. (1994) 'Le Partenariat Public–Privé dans le "Redéveloppement": Le Cas de la France'. In Heinz, W. (ed.) *Partenarists Public–Privé dans L'Aménagement Urbain*. Paris, Harmattan.

Ashton, J. (1991) 'The Origins of Health Cities'. In Ashton, J. (ed.) *Healthy Cities*. Milton Keynes, Open University Press.

ASJ-Foren (1990) *Mit der SPD die neunziger Jahre gestalten*. Hamburg, Arbeitsgemeinschaft Sozialdemokratische Juristen.

Associació Centre Solidari (1991) *Solidari Plà de Treball: Projecte de Dinamització Social Ciutat Vella*. Barcelona, Associació Centre Solidari Ciutat Vella.

Associazione 'Piazza delle Vigne' (1994) *Riepilo dei Soggetti tra'Associati in Casso di Adesione e di Possibile Involgimento*. Genoa, Associazione 'Piazza delle Vigne'.

Atkinson, J. & Gregory, D. (1986) 'A Flexible Future: Britain's Dual Labour Force'. *Marxism Today*. No. 4, 12–17.

Atkinson, R. (2000a) 'Narratives of Policy: The Construction of Urban Problems and Urban Policy in the Official Discourse of British Government 1968–1998'. *Critical Social Policy*. Vol. 20, 211–231.

Atkinson, R. (2000b) 'Combating Social Exclusion in Europe: The New Urban Policy Challenge'. *Urban Studies*. Vol. 37, 1037–1055.

Atkinson, R. (2001) 'The Emerging "Urban Agenda" and the European Spatial Development Perspective: Towards an EU Urban Policy?'. *European Planning Studies*. Vol. 9, 385–406.

Atkinson, R. (2002) 'The White Paper on European Governance: Implications for Urban Policy'. *European Planning Studies*. Vol. 10, 781–792.

Atkinson, R. & Moon, G. (1994) *Urban Policy in Britain: The City, the State and the Market*. Basingstoke: Macmillan.

Avarello, P. & Ricci, M. (eds) (2000) *Politiche Urbane: Dai Programmi Complessi alle Politiche Integrate di Sviluppo Urbano*. Rome, Istituto Nazionale di Urbanistica.

Bagnasco, A. & Le Galès, P. (2000) 'European Cities: Local Societies and Collective Actors?'. In Bagnasco, A. & Le Galès, P. (eds) *Cities in Contemporary Europe*. Cambridge, Cambridge University Press.

BAGS (1990) *Arbeit und Qualifizierung in Hamburg: Förderprogramme*. City State of Hamburg, Behörde für Arbeit, Gesundheit und Soziales.

BAGS (1991) *Zuwanderung nach Hamburg: Bestandaufnahme und Ausblick*. City State of Hamburg, Behörde für Arbeit, Gesundheit und Soziales.

BAGS (1993a) *Die Gesundheit älterer Menschen in Hamburg*. City State of Hamburg, Behörde für Arbeit, Gesundheit und Soziales.

BAGS (1993b) *Armut in Hamburg*. City State of Hamburg, Behörde für Arbeit, Gesundheit und Soziales.

BAGS (1994) *Hamburger Arbeitsmarktbericht: 1991–4*. City State of Hamburg, Behörde für Arbeit, Gesundheit und Soziales.

BAGS (1997) *Hamburger Arbeitsmarktbericht: 1997*. City State of Hamburg, Behörde für Arbeit, Gesundheit und Soziales.

BAGS (1998) *Armut in Hamburg: Beiträge zur Sozialberichterstattung*. City State of Hamburg, Behörde für Arbeit, Gesundheit und Soziales.

BAGS (2000) 'Tabellenanhang'. *Sozialhilfe-Report*. No. 17, 30–38. City State of Hamburg, Behörde für Arbeit, Gesundheit und Soziales.

BAGS (2001a) *Hamburger Arbeitsmarktbericht: 1997–2000*. City State of Hamburg, Behörde für Arbeit, Gesundheit und Soziales.

BAGS (2001b) *Stadtdiagnose 2: Zweiter Gesundheitsbericht für Hamburg*. City State of Hamburg, Behörde für Arbeit, Gesundheit und Soziales.

Bailey, C. (1991) *The Eldonians: Achievements of a Community in Vauxhall*. Liverpool, Eldonian Community Development Trust.

Bailey, N., Docherty, I. & Turok, I. (2002) 'Dimensions of City Competitiveness: Edinburgh and Glasgow in a UK Context'. In Begg, I. (ed.) *Urban Competitiveness: Policies for Dynamic Cities*. Bristol, Polity Press.

Bailey, S. (2001) 'Cities and Services: A Post-Welfare Analysis'. In Paddison, R. (ed.) *Handbook of Urban Studies*. London, Sage.

Ball, M. (2002) *RICS European Housing Review: 2002*. London, Royal Institute of Chartered Surveyors.

Barbieri, P., Paugam, S. & Russell, H. (2000) 'Social Capital and Exits from Unemployment'. In Gallie, D. & Paugam, S. (eds) *Welfare Regimes and the Experience of Unemployment in Europe*. Oxford, OUP.

Barcelona Activa (1999) *Pla d'Acció de Barcelona Activa: 1999–2003*. Barcelona, Barcelona Activa.

Barcelona Activa (various years) *Memòria d'Activitats*. Barcelona, Barcelona Activa.

Barcelona Economìa (1993) *Editorial* Barcelona Economia. No. 18.

Barcelona Economìa (2000) *Indicadors Econòmics de Barcelona I de la RegióMetropolitana*. No. 44.

Barcelona Societat (1999) *Barcelona Societat: Revista d'Informació I Estudis Socials*. No. 9. Barcelona, Ajuntament de Barcelona.

Barlow, J. (1998) 'Planning, Housing and the European Union'. In Kleinman, M., Matznetter, W. & Stephens, M. (eds) *European Integration and Housing Policy*. London, Routledge.

Barth, A. (1989) 'Kinder-Prostitution "Französisch 50, Verkehr 60" '. *Der Spiegel*. No. 44, 80–107.

Basile, M. (1999) 'Genova: Aree d'Ombra e Riuso'. *Urbanistica*. No. 111, 26–32.

Bauman, Z. (1998a) *Globalisation*. Cambridge, Polity Press.

Bauman, Z. (1998b) *Work, Consumerism and the New Poor*. Buckingham, Open University Press.

Baumgartner, F. & Jones, B. (1993) *Agendas and Instability in American Politics*. Chicago, University of Chicago Press.

Beazley, M., Loftman, P. & Nevin, B. (1997) 'Downtown Redevelopment and Community Resistance: An International Perspective'. In Jewson, N. & MacGregor, S.

(eds) *Transforming Cities: Contested Governance and New Spatial Divisions*. London, Routledge.

Begg, I., Moore, B. & Altunbas, Y. (2002) 'Long-Run Trends in the Competitiveness of Bristish Cities'. In Begg, I. (ed.) *Urban Competitiveness: Policies for Dynamic Cities*. Bristol, Polity Press.

Benfer, W. (1996) 'Orientations in Local Economic Development in the Federal Republic of Germany'. In Demazière, C. & Wilson, P. (eds) *Local Economic Development in Europe and the Americas*. London, Mansell.

Benington, J. (2001) 'Partnership as Networked Governance?'. In Geddes, M. & Benington, J. (eds) *Local Partnerships and Social Exclusion in the European Union*. London, Routledge.

Bensasson, S. & Teule, M. (2000) *Des Marges aux Interstices: Quelles Nouvelles Stratégies d'Acteurs sur le Marché de l'Habitat*. Marseilles, Centre d'Etudes, de recherche et de Formation Institutionelles du Sud-Est.

Ben-Tovim, G. (1983) *Equal Opportunities and the Employment of Black People: Ethnic Minorities on Merseyside*. Liverpool, Merseyside Association for Racial Equality in Employment & Merseyside Area Profile Group.

Ben-Tovim, G. (1988) 'Race, Politics and Urban Regeneration: Lessons from Liverpool'. In Parkinson, M., Koley, B. & Judd, D. (eds) *Regenerating the Cities: The UK Crisis and the US Experience*. Manchester, Manchester University Press.

Benyoussef, B. & Hayot, A. (1987) 'Tensions Inter-Ethniques ou Ville en Crise?: Le Centre de Marseille'. *Avis deRecherche*. No. 10.

Berger, O. & Schmalfeld, A. (1999) 'Stadtentwicklung in Hamburg zwischen "Unternehmen Hamburg" und "Sozialer Grossstadtstrategie"'. In Dangschat, J. (ed.) *Modernisierte Stadt: Gespaltene Gesellschaft*. Oplanden, Leske & Budrich.

Berkouche, P., Savy, M. & Veltz, P. (1988) *Metropôles en Europe: Gênes, Marseille, Barcelona*. Noisy-le-Grand, Ed Certes.

Bertoncello, B. & Rodrigues Malta, R. (2001) 'Euroméditerranée: Les Echelles d'un Grand Projet de Régénération Urbaine'. In Donzel, A. (ed.) *Métropolisation, Gouvernance et Citoyenneté dans la Région Urbaine Marseillais*. Paris, Maisonneuve et Larose.

Besio, M. (1999) *Dagli Parte degli Abitanti: Il Libro delle Vigne*. Turin, Allemandi & Co.

Best Value (2000) *Best Value Performance Plan: 2000–1*. Liverpool, Liverpool City Council.

BfA (1995) *Der Hamburger Arbeitsmarkt Jahresrückblick 1995*. Hamburg, Bundesanstalt für Arbeit, Arbeitsamt Hamburg.

BfA (1996) *Der Hamburger Arbeitsmarkt Jahresrückblick 1996*. Hamburg, Bundesanstalt für Arbeit, Arbeitsamt Hamburg.

BfA (2000) *Der Hamburger Arbeitsmarkt Jahresrückblick 2000*. Hamburg, Bundesanstalt für Arbeit, Arbeitsamt Hamburg.

Bianchini, F. (1990) 'Urban Renaissance? The Arts and the Urban Regeneration Process'. In MacGregor, S. & Pimlott, B. (eds) *Tackling the Inner Cities*. Oxford, Clarendon Press.

Bianchini, F., Dawson, J. & Evans, R. (1990) *Flagship Projects in Urban Regeneration*. University of Liverpool, Centre for Urban Studies, Working Paper No. 16.

Bier, A. G. (1980) *Crecimiento Urbano y Participación Vecinal*. Madrid, Centro de Investigaciones Sociologicas.

Birkhölzer, K. & Lorenz, G. (2001) 'Grass Roots Local Partnerships in the Federal Republic of Germany: Instruments for Social Inclusion and Economic Integration?' In Geddes, M. & Benington, J. (eds) *Local Partnerships and Social Exclusion in the European Union: New Forms of Local Social Governance?*. London, Routledge.

Bison, I. & Esping Andersen, G. (2000) 'Unemployment, Welfare Regime and Income Packaging'. In Gallie, D. & Paugam, S. (eds) *Welfare Regimes and the Experience of Unemployment in Europe*. Oxford, OUP.

Blanc, M. (1990) 'Du Logement Insalubre a l'Habitat Dévalorisé'. *Les Annales de la Recherche Urbaine*. No. 49, 38–48.

Blanco, I. & Rebollo, O. (2003) 'Community Planning in Trinitat Nova'. In Font, J. (ed.) *Public Participation and Local Govenance*. Barcelona, Institut de Ciències Politiques i Socials.

Blasius, D. & Dangschat, J. (eds) (1990) *Gentrification: Die Aufwertung innenstadtnaher Wohnviertel*. Frankfurt, Campus.

Boddy, M. (2002) 'Linking Competitiveness and Cohesion'. In Begg, I. (ed.) *Urban Competitiveness: Policies for Dynamic Cities*. Bristol, Polity Press.

Body-Gendrot, S. (2000a) 'Marginalisation and Political Responses in the French Context'. In Hamel, P., Lustiger-Thaler, H. & Mayer, M. (eds) *Urban Movements in a Globalising World*. London, Routledge.

Body-Gendrot, S. (2000b) *The Social Control of Cities*. Oxford, Blackwell.

Body-Gendrot, S. (2001) 'The Politics of Urban Crime'. *Urban Studies*. Vol. 38. 915–928.

Body-Gendrot & Duprez (2001) 'Les Politiques de Securité et de Prévention dans les Années 1990 en France: Les Villes en France et la Sécurité'. *Déviance et Societé*, Vol. 25, 377–402.

Boelhouwer, P., van der Heijden, H. & van de Ven, B. (1997) 'Management of Social Rented Housing in Western Europe'. *Housing Studies*. Vol. 12, 509–529.

Bohigas, O. (1986) *Reconstrucción de Barcelona*. Barcelona, Ajuntament de Barcelona.

Boland, P. (2000) 'Urban Governance and Economic Development: A Critique of Merseyside and Objective 1 Status'. *European Urban and Regional Studies*. Vol. 7, 211–222.

Bonoli, G. & Sarfati, H. (2002) 'Conclusions: The Policy Implications of a Changing Labour Market – Social Protection Relationship'. In Sarfati, H. & Bonoli, G. (eds) *Labour Market and Social Protection Reforms in International Perspective*. Aldershot, Ashgate.

Borja, J. (1977) 'Popular Movements and Urban Alternatives in Post-Franco Spain'. *International Journal of Urban and Regional Research*. Vol. 1, 153–160.

Born, L. (2001) 'Zwei Jahre Berliner Quartiersmanagement: Eine kritische Auseinandersetzung auch mit der Kritik'. *Jahrbuch Stadterneuerung 2001*. Berlin, Technische Universität Berlin.

Bou, L. & Pau, S. (1994) 'El Català, Garantia d'Igualtat?' *Avui*, 2 February, p. 6.

Bowpitt, G. (1993) *Faith in the City Revisited*. Paper presented at Social Policy Association Conference, July.

Boyle, M. & Rogerson, R. (2001) 'Power, Discourses and City Trajectories'. In Paddison, R. (ed.) *Handbook of Urban Studies*. London, Sage.

Bramezza, I. (1998) 'Italy'. In Van den Berg, L., Braun, E. & van der (eds) *National Urban Policies in the European Union*. Aldershot, Ashgate.

Breckner, I. & Herrmann, H. (2003) 'Socially Integrative City Programme: Hamburg-Lurup'. In Deutsches Institut für Urbanistik (eds) *Socially Integratie City*. Berlin, Deutsches Institut für Urbanistik.

Breckner, I., Herrmann, H., Gonzalez, T. & Läpple, D. (2002) *Endbericht der 'Programmbegleitung vor Ort' des Modellgebiets Hamburg-Altona-Lurup im Rahmen des Bund-Länder-Programms "Soziale Stadt"'*. Berlin, Deutsches Institut für Urbanistik.

Bremer, P. (1999) *Ausgrenzungsprozesse und die Spaltung der Städte*. Opladen, Leske & Budrich.

Bricocoli, M. (2001) 'Neue Wege der Stadterneuerung im italienischen Sozialen Wohnungsbau'. *Jahrbuch Stadterneuerung 2001*. Berlin, Technische Universität Berlin.

Brinkmann, M. (2003) 'Schule als positiver Standortfaktor für eine integrierte Stadtteilentwicklung'. *Soziale Stadt: Info 12*. pp. 14–15.

Buechler, H. (1983) 'Spanish Urbanization from a Grass-roots Perspective'. In Kenny, M. and Kertzer, D. (eds) *Urban Life in Mediterranean Europe: Anthropological Perspectives*. Urbana, USA, University of Illinois Press.

Burchard, D. (2000) 'Wieviel schwul verträgt St Georg?' *Hinnerk*. No. 11, 44–47.

Burton, P. & Boddy, M. (1995) 'The Changing Context for British Urban Policy'. In Hambleton, R. & Thomas, H. (eds) *Urban Policy Evaluation: Challenge and Change*. London, Paul Chapman.

Busquets, J. (1984) *Planning for the Ciutat Vella – A Functional Outline for its Restoration*. Barcelona, Ajuntament de Barcelona.

Busse, C. H. (1991) 'Gentrification: Stadtteile im Konflikt: Beispiel aus Hamburg'. In Blasius, J. & Dangschat, J. (eds) *Gentrification*. Frankfurt, Campus.

Caballero, F. (1982) 'Sociología Urbana de los Centros Historicos'. *Estudios Territoriales*. Vol. 6, 142–155.

Caesperlein, G. & Gliemann, K. (2001) 'Die zweite Perspektive der Einwanderung – überlegungen und Planungskonzepte auf Basis biographischer Interviews mit langjährigen Bewohner/innen von Einwanderungsstadteilen'. *Jahrbuch Stadterneuerung 2001*. Berlin, Technische Universität.

Calabi, D. (1984) 'Italy'. In Wynn, M. (ed.) *Planning and Urban Growth in Southern Europe*. London, Mansell.

Cameron, S. & Davoudi (1998) 'Combating Social Exclusion'. In Madanipour, A. Cars, G. and Allen, J. (eds) *Social Exclusion in European Cities: Processes, Experiences and Responses*. London, Jessica Kingsley.

Campagna, L. (1997) 'Normativa Regionale, Pianificazione Locale e Programmi'. In Latini, A. P. (ed.) *Programmi di Riqualificazione Urbana*. Rome, INU Edizioni.

Campagna, L. & Ricci, M. (2000) *Programma Urban-Italia: Europa, Nuove Politiche Urbane*. Rome, Ed INU.

Campani, G. (1993) 'Immigration and Racism in Southern Europe: the Italian Case'. *Ethnic and Racial Studies*. Vol. 16, 507–535.

Canepa, G. (1985) *Popolazione, Sistema Abitativo, Struttura Produttiva del Centro Storico di Genova*. Genoa, Istituto Ligure di Ricerche Economiche e Sociali.

Canepa, G., Gabrielli, B., Mollo, R., Seassaro, L. & Tirrelli, L. (1985) *Abitare in Liguria: Progetto e Primi Esiti dell'O.S.A.* Genoa, ILRES Studi e Notizie. No. 2.

Cappellin, R. & Orsenigo, L. (2000) 'The Territorial Dimension of Modern Industry and the Scope of Regional Industrial and Labour Market Policies'. In Klemmer, P. & Wink, R. (eds) *Preventing Unemployment in Europe*. Cheltenham, Edward Elgar.

Càritas (1993) *Pla d'Accions Socials, 1993*. Barcelona, Càritas Diocesana de Barcelona.

Càritas (2000) *Memória 1999 i Pla d'Accions Socials 2000*. Barcelona, Càritas Diocesana de Barcelona.

Carley, M., Chapman, M., Hastings, A., Kirk, A. & Young, R. (2000) *Urban Regeneration through Partnership: A Study of Nine Urban Regions in England, Scotland and Wales*. Bristol, Policy Press.

Carlota, S. (1987) *Els Treballadors Immigrants a Catalunya*. Barcelona, Centre d'Informació per a Treballadors Estrangers.

Carmona, S. (2000) 'Inmigración y Prostitución: El Caso del Ravel'. *Papers: Revista de Sociologia*. No. 60, 343–354.

Carrano, N. (1997) 'Gli Aspetti Negoziali e gli Strumenti di Contrattazione'. In Latini, A. P. (ed.) *Programmi di Riqualificazione Urbana*. Rome, INU Edizioni.

Carrer, F. (1988) 'La Police Italienne: Cinq Ans après la Loi de Reforme'. *Revue Internationale de Criminoligie et de Police Technique*. Vol. 1, 97–103.

Casas i Masjoan, X. (1994) *La Salut a Barcelona*. Ajuntament de Barcelona, Institut Municipal de la Salut.

Casier, D., Niekus, H. & Tews, K. (1991) *Hamburgische Wirtschaft: Wirtschaftsanalysen: 1990*. Hamburg, Hamburgische Landesbank.

Cassino, A., Cifatte, M. & Grossi, G. (1983) *Studio d'insieme del Centro Storico*. Genoa, Commune di Genova.

Castel, R. (1995) *Les Métamorphoses de la Question Sociale*. Paris, Ed. Fayard.

Castells, M. (1989) *The Informational City*. Cambridge, Oxford.

Castells, M. & Godard, F. (1974) *Monopolville: L'Entreprise, L'Etat, L'Urbain*. Paris, Ed. Mouton.

Castles, S. & Miller, M. (1998) *The Age of Migration: International Population Movements in the Modern World*. New York, Guildford Press.

CCOO (1990) *Dossier Rau i Solidaritat: 1990*. Barcelona, Confederació Sindical de la Commissió Obrera Nacional de Catalunya.

CDS (1985) *From Year to Year*. Liverpool, Cooperative Development Service.

CDS (1987) *Building Democracy: Housing Cooperatives on Merseyside*. Liverpool Cooperative Development Service. Revised Edition.

CDS (1994) *Building Democracy: Housing Cooperatives on Merseyside*. Liverpool Cooperative Development Service. Revised Edition.

CDS (1999) *The Friary Project: Building on Success*. Liverpool, Cooperative Development Service.

CDS (2000) *Celebrating 25 Years of CDS: 1975–2000*. Liverpool, Cooperative Development Service.

Centre de Serveis (2000) *Informe d'Activitat: 2000*. Barcelona, Centre de Serveis de Promoció Econòmica I Ocupació de Ciutat Vella (Barcelona Activa).

Centre Social Belsunce (1991) *Rapport d'Activités: 1990–1*. Marseilles, City Council.

Chapman, M. (1995) 'Urban Policy and Urban Evaluation: the impact of the European Union'. In Hambleton, R. & Thomas, H. (eds) *Urban Policy Evaluation: Challenge and Change*. London, Paul Chapman.

Cheshire, P. (1990) 'Explaining the Recent Performance of the European Community's Major Urban Regions'. *Urban Studies*. Vol. 27, 311–333.

Cheshire, P. & Hay, D. (1989) *Urban Problems in Western Europe*. London, Unwin Hyman.

Chorianopoulos, I. (2002) 'Urban Restructuring and Goverance: North–South Differences in Europe and the EU URBAN Initiative'. *Urban Studies*. Vol. 39, 705–726.

Cifatte, C. (1993) 'Le Proposte dell'Ufficio per il Centro Storico del Comune di Genova – Un Quadro degli Interventi in Alto e Programmati con una Verifica Critica'. *Controspazio*. No. 1.

Cinieri, M. (1990) *Per una Scuola sense Esclusioni*. Paper presented at a conference, Genoa, Istituto Ligure di Ricerche Economiche e Sociali, 26–27 October.

CITE (1993) *Recull Annual sobre Immigració: 1992*. Barcelona, Centre d'Informació per a Treballadors Estrangers.

Clark, D. (1989) *Urban Decline*. London, Routledge.

Clasen, J. (1999) 'Unemployment Compensation and Other Labour Market Policies'. In Clasen, J. (ed.) *Comparative Social Policy*. Oxford, Blackwell.

Clos, J. (1991) 'Ciutat Vella, The Decisive Moment'. *Barcelona: Metropolis Mediterranea*. No. 18, 1–12.

Coates, A., Farnsworth, K. & Zulauf, M. (2001) *Social Exclusion and Inclusion: Partnerships for Neighbourhood Regeneration in London*. London, South Bank University, Faculty of Humanities and Social Sciences.

Colla, L. & Germani, P. (1989) *Decentramento e Participazione a Genova*. Genoa, Ed. Marietti.

Collinge, C. & Hall, S. (1997) 'Hegemony and Regime in Urban Governance: Towards a Theory of the Locally Networked State. In Jewson, N. & MacGregor, S. (eds) *Transforming Cities: Contested Governance and New Spatial Divisions*. London, Routledge.

Colmenares, M. (1999) 'Educational Action in the Ciutat Vella'. In *Barcelona Societat: Revista d'Informació I Estudis Socials*. No. 9, 31–35. Barcelona, Ajuntament de Barcelona.

Comune di Genova (1979) *Progetto Genova: Piano Programma 1978–81*. Genoa, City Council.

Comune di Genova (1983) *Studio Organico di Insieme del Centro Storico: Titolo IV – Le Grandi Funzioni*. City of Genoa, Servizio Urbanistica – Ufficio Centro Storico.

Comune di Genova (1991) *Programma Organico di intervento Zona Porta Soprana, San Donato Sarzano – Programme di Regia-Concessionaria Porta Soprana s.c.p.a.* Genoa, City Council, Servicio Edilizia Residenziale – Recupero Centri Storici.

Comune di Genova (1992a) *Genova verso il 1992*. Genoa, City Council, Assessorato all' Urbanistica.

Comune di Genova (1992b) *Civis Sistema*. Genoa, City Council.

Comune di Genova (1994a) *Civis Ambiente*. Genoa, City Council.

Comune di Genova (1994b) *Projetto Zenit: Zona Ecoligca di Nuove Infrastrutture e Techologie*. Genoa, City Council.

Comune di Genova (1997) *Civis Ambiente: Rapporto Finale*. Genoa, City Council.

Comune di Genova (2000) *Piano degli Interventi*. Genoa, City Council.

Comune di Genova (2002) *Il Voto a Genova (1946–2001)*. Genoa, Unità Organizzativa Statistica.

Condro, S. & Vitale, P. (2001) 'Évaluer la Politique de la Ville ou Sisyphe Revisité'. In Donzel, A. (ed.) *Métropolisation, Gouvernance et Citoyenneté dans la Région Urbaine Marseillaise*. Paris, Maisonneuve et Larose.

Contardi, L. (1999) 'Il Senso della Qualità nell'Integrazione: Prime Esperienze di un Altro Approccio'. In Contardi, L., Moscato, M. & Ricci, M. (eds) *Programmi di Riqualificazione Urbana: Azioni di Programmazione Integrata nell Città Italiane*. Rome, INU Ed.

Cooperative Development Services (undated) *Information about West Everton*. Liverpool, Cooperative Development Services.

Coriminas, X. (1994) 'La Policía de Catalunya'. *Prevenció*. No. 10, 29–31.

Corolleur, F. & Pecqueur, B. (1996) 'Local Economic Policy in France in the 1980s'. In Demazière, C. & Wilson, P. (eds) *Local Economic Development in Europe and the Americas*. London, Mansell.

Costa, J. (1991) 'Barcelona'. In Ashton, J. (ed.) *Healthy Cities*. Milton Keynes, Open University Press.

Cottle, S. (1993) *TV News, Urban Conflict and the Inner City*. Leicester, Leicester University Press.

Couch, C. & Dennemann, A. (2000) 'Urban Regeneration and Sustainable Development in Britain: The Example of the Liverpool Ropewalks Partnership'. *Cities*. Vol. 17, 137–147.

Couch, C. & Wynne, S. (1986) *Housing Trends in Liverpool*. Liverpool, Liverpool Council of Voluntary Service.

Cousins, L. (1980) *Merseyside in Crisis*. Liverpool, Mersyside Socialist Research Group.

Coym, J. & Schmid, H. (1985a) *Einkommen im Alter: Ein sozialempirischer Beitrag zur Lebenssitutation alterer Menschen in Hamburg.* City State of Hamburg, Behörde für Arbeit, Gesundheit und Soziales.

Coym, J. & Schmid, H. (1985b) *Wohnen im Alter: Ein sozialempirischer Beitrag zur Lebenssitutation alterer Menschen in Hamburg.* City State of Hamburg, Behörde für Arbeit, Gesundheit und Soziales.

Cram, L. (1993) 'Calling the Tune without Paying the Piper?: Social Policy Regulation in the Role of the Commission'. *Policy and Politics.* Vol. 21, 135–146.

Crawford, A. (2002) 'The Growth of Crime Prevention in France as Contrasted with the English Experience'. In Hughes, G., McLaughlin, E. & Muncie, J. (eds) *Crime Prevention and Community Safety: New Directions.* London, Sage.

Crick, M. (1986) *The March of Militant.* London, Faber.

Crowther Hunt, E. & Billinghurst, L. (1990) *Inner Cities: Inner Strengths.* London, Industrial Society Press.

Cruz-Castro, L. & Conlon, G. (2001) *Initial Training Policies and Transferability of Skills in Britain and Spain.* Madrid, Instituto Juan March de Estudios e Investigaciones. Working Paper No. 162.

CURS (1999) *Measuring the Sustainability of Neighbourhoods in Liverpool.* University of Birmingham, Centre for Urban and Regional Studies & Liverpool First.

Dalby, S. (1990) 'Heseltine's Vision of Land Regeneration Takes Shape'. *Financial Times.* 30 October, p. VI (Supplement on 'Urban Development in the Thatcher Era').

Dangschat, J. (1990) 'Population, Economy and Politics as Reasons for Increasing Socio-Spatial Disparities: the case of Hamburg in the mid 1980s'. In Villadsen, S. (ed.) *Big City Politics.* Roskilde, Forlaget for Samfundsokonomi og Planloegning.

Dangschat, J. (1991a) 'Welche Zusammensetzung der Wohnbevölkerung is erhaltenswert? Kommentar zur Anwendung der Milieuschutzsatuzung aus soziologischer Sicht'. In Dohrendorf, R. (ed.) *Die Soziale Erhaltungssatzung und ihre Bedeutung für die Stadterneuerung und Stadtentwicklung.* Hamburg, STEG.

Dangschat, J. (1991b) 'Gentrification in Hamburg'. In Van Weesep, J. & Musterd, S. (eds) *Urban housing for the Better Off: Gentrification in Europe.* Utrecht, Stedelijke Netwerken.

Dangschat, J. (1992) 'Konzeption, Realität und Funktion "neuer" Standortpolitik: am Beispiel des "Unternehmen Hamburg"'. In Heinelt, H. & Mayer, M. (eds) *Politik in europäischen Städten.* Basel, Birkhäuser.

Dangschat, J. (1993) 'Conceptualising Urban Space in Germany'. *Cross-National Research Papers,* Third Series, No. 2, 23–43.

Dangschat, J. (1999) 'Regulation, Nach-Fordismus und Global Cities: Ursachen der Armut'. In Dangschat, J. (ed.) *Modernisierte Stadt: Gespaltene Gesellschaft.* Oplanden, Leske & Budrich.

Dangschat, J. & Ossenbrügge, J. (1990) 'Hamburg: Crisis Management, Urban Regeneration and the Social Democrats'. In Judd, D. & Parkinson, M. (eds) *Leadership and Urban Regeneration.* London, Sage.

Dauge, Y. (1991) *Riots and Rising Expectations in Urban Europe.* Proceedings of a lecture given at the University of London, School of Economics and Political Science, 6 March.

Davia, M., García-Serrano, C., Hernanz, V., Malo, M. & Toharia, L. (2001) 'Do Active Labour Market Policies Matter in Spain?'. In de Koning, J. & Mosley, H. (eds) *Labour Market Policy and Unemployment.* Cheltenham, Edward Elgar.

Davoudi, S. (1995) 'Dilemmas of Urban Governance'. In Healey, P., Cameron, S., Davoudi, S., Graham, S. & Madanipour, A. (1995) (eds) *Managing Cities: The New Urban Context.* Chichester, Wiley.

Davoudi, S. & Healey, P. (1995) 'City Challenge – A Sustainable Mechanism or Temporary Gesture'. In Hambleton, R. & Thomas, H. (eds) *Urban Policy Evaluation: Challenge and Change*. London, Paul Chapman.

Dawson, J. (1990) *Urban Development Corporations and the Grassroots: A Model for Community Regeneration*. University of Liverpool, Centre for Urban Studies, Working Paper. No. 15.

Dawson, J. & Parkinson, M. (1991) 'Merseyside Development Corporation: 1981–1989'. In Keith, M. & Rogers, A. (eds) *Hollow Promises: Rhetoric and Reality in the Inner City*. London, Mansell.

Dawson, J. & Parkinson, M. (1992) *Urban Development Corporations: The Merseyside Experience 1981–90*. University of Liverpool, Centre for Urban Studies, Working Paper No. 13.

Deakin, N. & Edwards, J. (1993) *The Enterprise Culture and the Inner City*. London, Routledge.

De Koning, J. & Mosley, H. (2002) 'How can Active Policies be made more Effective?'. In Schmid, G. & Gazier, B. (eds) *The Dynamics of Full Employment*. Cheltenham, Edward Elgar.

Delgado, D. (1989) *Belsunce: d'Hier et d'Au'jourdhui*. Marseilles, CERFISE.

Delgado, J. (1994) 'Un Nuevo Sistema de Seguridad para Catalunya'. *Prevenció*. No. 10, 7–19.

Dematteis, G., Governa, F. & Rossignolo, C. (1999) *The Impact of European Programmes on the Governance of Italian Local Systems*. Paper presented at the EURA Conference *European Cities in Transformation*. Paris, 22–23 October.

Department of the Environment (1994a) *Assessing the Impact of Urban Policy: Inner Cities Research Programme*. London: HMSO.

Department of the Environment (1994b) *Merseyside Special Allocation: The Government Response*. London, Department of the Environment.

Derogy, J. & Pontant, J.-M. (1984) *Enquete sur les Mysteres de Marseille*. Paris, Editions Robert Laffont.

DETR (Department of the Environment, Transport and the Regions) (2000) *Our Towns and Cities: The Future: Delivering an Urban Renaissance* (Urban White Paper). London, Department of the Environment, Transport and the Regions.

Dettmer, J. & Kreutz, S. (1999) 'Quartierserneuerung als interkommunaler Wettbewerb'. *Jahrbuch Stadterneuerung 1999*. Berlin, Technische Universität Berlin.

Detzel, P. & Rubery, J. (2002) 'Employment Systems and Transitional Labour Markets: A Comparison of Youth Labour Markets in Germany, France and the UK'. In Schmid, G. & Gazier, B. (eds) *The Dynamics of Full Employment*. Cheltenham, Edward Elgar.

Deutsche Städtetag (1990) *Statistisches Jahrbuch der deutschen Gemeinden*. Cologne, Deutsche Städtetag.

Diamond, L. (1997) *Civil Society and the Development of Democracy*. Madrid, Instituto Juan March de Estudios e Investigaciones, Working Paper No. 101.

Dickens, P. (1990) *Urban Sociology*. London, Harvester Wheatsheaf.

Diesner, C., Pfadt, A., Reich, M. & Seifert, S. (1994) *Integriertes Handlungs und Massnahmenkonzept für den Stadtteil Hamburg St. Georg – Endbericht*. Hamburg, Stadtentwicklungsbehörde – Amt für Stadterneuerung.

DIFU (2003) *Good Practice in Altbau – und gemischten Quartieren*. Berlin, Deutsches Institut für Urbanistik, Arbeitspapiere zum Programm Soziale Stadt, Vol. 10.

DiGaetano, A. & Klemanski, J. (1993) 'Urban Regimes in Comparative Perspective'. *Urban Affairs Quarterly*. Vol. 29, 54–83.

Direcció General d'Arquitectura I Habitatge (1988) *Memòria sobre els Ajuts per a la Rehabilitació d'Habitatges.* Generalitat de Catalunya, Departament de Política Territorial i Obres Públiques.

Dohrendorf, R. (1990) *Soziale Brennpunkte und Stadterneuerung.* Hamburg, Stadtentwicklungsbehörde.

Dohrendorf, R. (ed.) (1991) *Die Soziale Erhaltungssatzung und ihre Bedeuting für die Stadterneuerung und Stadtentwicklung.* Hamburg, Stadtentwicklungsbehörde.

Domingo I Clota, M. & Bonet I Casas, M. (1998) *Barcelona I Els Moviments Socials Urbans.* Barcelona, Ed. Mediterrània.

Donzel, A. (1988) 'Comportements Politiques et Immigration – Le cas de Marseille'. In Institut de Recherches et d'Études sur le Monde Arabe et Musulman (eds) *Des immigrants et des Villes – Mobilité et Insertion.* Paris, Institut de Recherches et d'Études sur le Monde Arabe et Musulman.

Donzel, A. (1990) 'Regeneration in Marseilles: The Search for Political Stability'. In Judd, D. & Parkinson, M. (eds) *Leadership and Urban Regeneration: Cities in North America and Europe.* Urban Affairs Annual Reviews. Vol. 37. Newbury Park, Sage.

Donzel, A. (1991) *Urbanisation et Fonctions des Villes: Le Cas de Marseille.* Marseilles, École des Hautes Études en Sciences Sociales. Unpublished.

Donzel, A. (1993) 'Suburban Development and Policy Making in France: The Case of Marseilles'. *Cross-National Research Papers*, Third Series. No. 2, 44–53.

Donzel, A. (1998) *Marseille: L'Expérience de la Cité.* Paris, Ed. Anthropos.

Donzel, A. (2001) 'Le Projet Civique Marseillais et la Construction de l'Espace Métropolitain'. In Donzel, A. (ed.) *Métropolisation, Gouvernance et Citoyenneté dans la Région Urbaine Marseillais.* Paris, Maisonneuve et Larose.

Donzel, A. & Guilhaumou, J. (2001) 'Les Acteurs du Champs d'Exclusion à la Lumière de la Tradition Civique Marseillaise'. In Schnapper, D. (ed.) *Exclusion au Coeur de la Cité.* Paris, Ed. Anthropos.

Donzel, A. & Hayot, A. (1989) 'Intervention Marseille: L'Effet Vigouroux – Tradition Historique et Recomposition Politique'. *Avis de Recherches et Interventions.* No. 17.

Drewe, P. (2000) 'European Experiences'. In Roberts, P. & Sykes, H. (eds) *Urban Regeneration: A Handbook.* London, Sage.

Dubouchet, L. & Mekboul, S. (1992) *Diagnostic Securité Marseille: Rapport Intermédiaire.* Marseilles, Ville de Marseille.

Duffy, K. (1995) 'A Local Partnership Approach to Social Policy: The Experience of Poverty 3'. In Duffy, K. (ed.) *Partnership and Participation: The Experience of Poverty 3 in the UK.* London, HMSO.

Duffy, K. & Breitenbach, E. (1995) *Building Local Partnerships Against Poverty: Issues and Questions for Discussion.* London, HMSO.

EBNSC (1997) *Partners in Corporate Initiatives: Stimulating Job Growth, Improving Employability and Tackling Social Exclusion.* Brussels, European Business Network for Social Cohesion.

École Normale Supérieure de Fontenay (1988) *Les Immigrés et l'École: Une Course d'Obstacles'.* Paris, Ed. Harmattan.

Economic Development Strategy Forum (1991) *Economic Development Plan: 1992–3.* Liverpool, City Council.

Edou, E. (1998) *Les HLM.* Paris, Edition Economica.

Edwards, J. (1989) 'Positive Discrimination as a Strategy against Exclusion: The Case of the Inner Cities'. *Policy & Politics.* Vol. 17, 11–24.

Edwards, J. (1995) 'Social Policy and the City'. *Urban Studies.* Vol. 32(4), 695–712.

El País (1991) 'Los Inmigrantes Ilegales en España Ocilan entre 72,000 y 124,000 segun un Estudio'. *El País*, 18 March.

Emms, P. (1990) *Social Housing: A European Dilemma?* Bristol, School for Advanced Urban Studies.

ERM Economics (2003) *European Capital of Culture 2008: Socio-Economic Impact: Assessment of Liverpool's Bid*. Manchester, ERM Economics.

Esping-Andersen, G. (1990) *The Three Worlds of Welfare Capitalism*. Cambridge, Polity.

Esteban, J. (1999) *El Projecte Urbanístic: Valorar la Perifèria i Recuperar el Centre*. Barcelona, Aula.

Estivill, J. (2001) 'A New Approach to Partnership: The Spanish Case'. In Geddes, M. & Benington, J. (eds) *Local Partnerships and Social Exclusion in the European Union: New Forms of Local Social Governance?*. London, Routledge.

Estivill, J. & de la Hoz (1993) *Reparacion Interior de Viviendas de Gente Mayor sin Recursos Economicos*. Barcelona, Gabinet d'Estudis Socials.

Europe Innovation (2001) *Territorial Employment Pacts: State of Play*. Europe Innovation, 2000. http://www.inforegio.cec.eu.int/pacts.

European Commission (1991) *Europe 2000: Outlook for the Development of the Community's Territory*. Luxembourg, Office for Official Publications.

European Commission (1992) *Social Europe: Urban Social Development*. Brussels, Commission of the European Communitie, Social Europe Supplement No. 1/92.

European Commission (1994) *Europe 2000+: Cooperation for European Territorial Development*. Luxembourg, Office for Official Publications.

European Commission (1996) *Social and Economic Inclusion through Regional Development: The Community Economic Development Priority in European Structural Fund Programmes in Great Britain*. Luxembourg, Office for Official Publications.

European Commission (1998) *Sustainable Urban Development in the EU: A Framework for Action*. COM (1998) 605 final. Brussels, Commission of the European Communities. 28 October.

European Commission (1999a) *Better Management through Evaluation: Mid-Term Review of Structural Funds Programmes (1994–9)*. Luxembourg, Commission of the European Communities.

European Commission (1999b) *Second Interim Progress Report on the Territorial Employment Pacts*. Commission Staff Working Paper.

European Commission (2000) *Promoting Employment Locally: A Local Dimension for the European Employment Strategy*. Brussels, Commission of the European Communities.

European Commission (2002a) *The Programming of the Structural Funds: 2000–2006: An Initial Assessment of the URBAN Initiative*. Brussels, Commission of the European Communities.

European Commission (2002b) *The URBACT Programme: 2000–2006*. Decision 2002 EU 16 0 PC 001. 20 December.

European Commission (2003) *The Future of the European Employment Strategy*. Brussels, Commission of the European Communities. COM (2003) 6 final.

European Court of Auditors (2001) *Special Report No 1 Concerning the Urban Community Initiative*. Brussels, Official Journal OJ C 124, 25 April.

Eurostat (2002) 'Public Expenditure on Labour Market Policies in 1999 Varied Greatly among Member States'. *Statistics in Focus: Population and Social Conditions: Theme 3*. No. 12.

Evans, R. (1990) *Training and Enterprise Councils: An Initial Assessment*. Liverpool, Centre for Urban Studies Working Paper No. 17.

Evans, R. (2000) *Governance, Competitiveness and Social Exclusion: The Merseyside Objective 1 Programme*. Liverpool John Moores University, European Institute for Urban Affairs.

Evans, R. (2002) 'The Merseyside Objective One Programme: Exemplar of Coherent City-Regional Planning and Governance or Cautionary Tale?' *European Planning Studies*. Vol. 10, 495–517.

Faist, T. (2001) 'Social Citizenship in the EU: Nested Membership'. *Journal of Common Market Studies*. Vol. 39, 37–58.

Federazione Regionale Solidarietà Lavoro (2000) *Progetto 'Oltre la Strada'*. Genova FRSL.

Feldblum, M. (1993) 'Paradoxes of Ethnic Politics: The Case of Franco-Maghrebis in France'. *Ethnic and Racial Studies*. Vol. 16, 52–74.

Ferracci, M.-F. (1983) *Histoire et Invertissements Symboliques de l'Espace du Panier*. Marseilles, Université de Provence, UER de Sociologie.

Ferras, P. (1977) *Barcelone: Croissance d'une Metropole*. Paris, Ed. Anthropos.

Fitzpatrick, T. (2001) 'New Agendas for Social Policy and Criminology: Globalisation, Urbanism and the Emerging Post-Social Security State'. *Social Policy & Administration*. Vol. 35, 212–229.

Foelsch, P. (1994) 'Die Aufwertung innenstadtnäher Ortsteile in Hamburg von 1968 bis 1987 – Zusammenfassung einer Arbeit zum Tema "Gentrifizierung"'. *Hamburg in Zahlen*. June Issue.

Foley, P. & Martin, S. (2000) 'A New Deal for the Community? Public Participation in Regeneration and Local Service Delivery'. *Policy & Politics*. Vol. 29, 479–492.

Font, J. (2003) 'Local Participation in Spain: Beyond Associative Democracy'. *BCN Political Science Debates*. No. 1, 43–64.

Forschung & Beratung (1997) *Evaluation der Massnahmen zur Armutsbekämpfung als Bestandteil sozialer Stadtentwicklung*. Hamburg, Bürgerschaftsdrucksache 15/7778.

Foster, J. (1990) *Villains: Crime and Community in the Inner City*. London, Routledge.

Foundation for Civil Society (2000) *The Somali Community in Liverpool*. Birmingham, Foundation for Civil Society.

Fourest, A. (1989) *Gérer Marseille Aujourd'hui: Mission impossible?* Marseilles, CERFISE.

Fox-Przeworski, J. (1991) 'New Roles for Local Governments: Mobilization for Action'. In Fox-Przeworski, J. Goddard, J. & de Jong, M. (eds) *Urban Regeneration in a Changing Economy: An International Perspective*. Oxford: Clarendon.

Freie und Hansestadt Hamburg (1989a) *Mietspiegel 1989*. Hamburg, Baubehörde.

Freie und Hansestadt Hamburg (1989b) *Mitteilungen des Senats an die Burgerschaft: Finanzielle Förderung von ABM-Projecten und Initiativen aus Haushaltsmitteln*. Hamburg, Senate.

Freie und Hansestadt Hamburg (1990) *Kinder sind die Zukunft*. Hamburg, Amt für Stadterneurung.

Freie und Hansestadt Hamburg (1991) *Die Wirtschaft in Hamburg: Jahresbericht 1991*. Hamburg, Behörde für Wirtschaft, Verkehr und Landwirtschaft.

Freie und Hansestadt Hamburg (1992) *Bericht über Massnahmen zur Verbesserung der Stadtteilentwicklungen*. Hamburg, Senate.

Freie und Hansestadt Hamburg (1993) *Analyse der Hamburger Wahlen am 19. September 1993*. Hamburg in Zahlen, October Issue. Hamburg, Statistisches Landesamt.

Freie und Hansestadt Hamburg (1999) *Stadtentwicklungskonzept*. Hamburg, Stadtentwicklungsbehörde.

Fribourg, A.-M. (1999) 'Strategies and Policies for Urban Renewal and Housing Rehabilition in France'. In Skifter Andersen, H. & Leather, P. (eds) *Housing Renewal in Europe*. Bristol, Policy Press.

Friedrichs, J. (ed.) (1985) *Die Städte in den 80er Jahren*. Opladen, Westdeutscher Verlag.

Friedrichs, J. (1993) 'A Theory of Urban Decline: Economy, Demography and Political'. *Urban Studies*. Vol. 30, 907–917.

Friedrichs, J. (1998) 'Social Inequality, Segregation and Urban Conflict: The Case of Hamburg'. In Musterd, S. & Ostendorf, W. (eds) *Urban Segregation and the Welfare State*. London, Routledge.

Froessler, R. (1994) 'Integrierende Politik: Aufgaben, Inhalte und Formen staatlicher Programme zur Erneuerung benachteiligter Quartiere'. In Froessler, R., Lang, M., Selle, K. & Staubach, R. (eds) *Lokaler Partnerschaften: Die Erneuerung benachteiligter Quartiere in europäischen Städten*. Basel, Birkhäuser.

Froessler, R. (2000) 'Britische Erfahrungen mit der Erneuerung benachteiligter Stadtquartiere: Ein überblick über Programme und Politiken der Quartierserneuerung in Grossbritannien' *Jahrbuch Stadterneuerung 2000*. Berlin, Technische Universität Berlin.

FRSL (1994) *Relazione sulla Federazione Regionale Solidarietà e Lavoro*. Genoa, Federazione Regionale Solidarietà e Lavoro.

Furbey, R. (1999) 'Urban "Regeneration": Reflections on a Metaphor'. *Critical Social Policy*. Vol. 19, 419–445.

Fusero, P., Gabrielli, B., Gazzola, A. & Seassaro, L. (1991) 'Il Centro Storico di Genova'. *Archivo di Studi Urbani e Regionali*. No. 40, 85–107.

Fyfe, N. (1995) 'Policing the City'. *Urban Studies*. Vol. 32, 759–778.

Gabrielli, B. (1987) 'Gênes Exemplaire'. In CERFISE (ed.) *Gérer les Crises Urbaines*. Actes du Colloques de Marseille. Marseilles, CERFISE.

Gabrielli, B. (1989) 'Tanti Progetti, Nessun Progetto'. *Urbanistica*. Vol. 95, 102–103.

Gallén, A. (1999) 'Las Actuaciones de Mejora en Los Barrios'. In Montaner, J.-M. (ed.) *Barcelona 1979–2004: Del Desarrollo a La Ciudad de Calidad*. Barcelona, Ajuntament de Barcelona.

Gallie, D. & Paugam, S. (2000) *Welfare Regimes and the Experience of Unemployment in Europe*. Oxford, OUP.

Gallo, A. & Scaltritti, F. (1994) *Progetto Sperimentale Finalizzato al Contenimento delle Diffusione del Virus HIV ma i Tossicodipendenti del Centro Storico di Genova*. Genoa, Lega Italiana Per la Lotta contro l' AIDS di Genova.

García, M., O'Neany, M. & Lopez, A. (1989) *Els Avis del Casc Antic: Estudio Socioligico*. Barcelona, Ajuntament de Barcelona.

García, S. (1991) 'Barcelona'. In European Commission (ed.) *The Future of Port Cities*. Brussels, European Commission, Directorate General 16.

García, S. (1993) 'Big Events and Urban Politics: Barcelona and the Olympic Games'. In Haußermann, H. & Siebel, W. (eds) *Festivalisierung der Stadtpolitik: Stadtentwicklung durch große Projekte*. Opladen, Westdeutscher Verlag.

García, S., Gazzola, A., Dangschat, J. & Parkinson, M. (1992) *Metropôles Portuaires en Europe*. Les Chaiers de la Recherche Architecturale. Special Issue, Nos. 30/1.

Garofoli, G. (2002) 'Local Development in Europe: Theoretical Models and International Comparisons'. *European Urban and Regional Studies*. Vol. 9, 225–239.

Gasparrini, C. (1997) 'La Formazione del Quadro Legislativo di Riferimento'. In Latini, A. P. (ed.) *Programmi di Riqualificazione Urbana*. Rome, INU Edizioni.

Gausa, M. (1999) 'A Leap in Scale: From Urban to Metropolitan Barcelona'. In Diputació de Barcelona (ed.) *1856–1999: Contemporary Barcelona*. Barcelona, Institut d'Edicions.

Gazzola, A. (1982) *Genova: Dinamiche Urbane e Devianza*. Milan, Ed. Unicopli.

Gazzola, A. & Carminati, M. (1991) 'Le Città Portuali in Europa: Il Caso di Genova'. *Les Cahiers de la Recherche Architecturale*. Special Issue, Nos. 30/1, 1–19.

Gazzola, A. & Seassaro, L. (1988) 'Le Centre Historique de Gênes: Répresentation et Attenes'. *Les Cahiers de l' Anah*. Special Issue, 24–36.

Geddes, M. (1997) 'Poverty, Excluded Communities and Local Democracy'. In Jewson, N. & MacGregor, S. (eds) *Transforming Cities: Contested Governance and New Spatial Divisions*. London, Routledge.

Geddes, M. (1998) *Local Partnership: A Successful Strategy for Social Cohesion*. Dublin, European Foundation for the Improvement of Living and Working Conditions, Dublin.

Geddes, M. (2000) 'Tackling Social Exclusion in the European Union?: The Limits to the New Orthodoxy of Local Partnership'. *International Journal of Urban and Regional Research*. Vol. 24, 782–800.

Geddes, M. (2001) 'Local Partnerships and Social Exclusion in the UK: A Stake in the Market?' In Geddes, M. & Benington, J. (eds) *Local Partnerships and Social Exclusion in the European Union: New Forms of Local Social Governance?* London, Routledge.

Geddes, M. & Benington, J. (2001) 'Social Exclusion, Partnership and Local Governance – New Problems, New Policy Discourses in the EU'. In Geddes, M. & Benington, J. (eds) *Local Partnerships and Social Exclusion in the European Union*. London, Routledge.

Geddes, M. & Le Galès, P. (2001) 'Local Partnerships, Welfare Regimes and Local Governance'. In Geddes, M. & Benington, J. (eds) *Local Partnerships and Social Exclusion in the European Union: New Forms of Local Social Governance?* London, Routledge.

Generalitat de Catalunya (1987) *Estructura del Mercat Residencial a Barcelona-Ciutat*. Barcelona, Generalitat de Catalunya, Dirreció General d'Arquitectura i Habitat.

Generalitat de Catalunya (1990) *Educació Compensatoria: Memoria 1989–90*. Barcelona, Generalitat de Catalunya, Departament d'Ensenyament.

Generalitat de Catalunya (1996a) *Programa d'Educació Compensatoria a Catalunya*. Barcelona, Generalitat de Catalunya, Departament d'Ensenyament.

Generalitat de Catalunya (1996b) *Educació Intercultural*. Barcelona, Generalitat de Catalunya, Departament d'Ensenyament.

Generalitat de Catalunya (2000a) *Estadístiques sobre el Mercat d'Habitatges de Lloguer a Catalunya*. Barcelona, Generalitat de Catalunya, Direcció General d'Arquitectura I Habitatge.

Generalitat de Catalunya (2000b) *Estadístiques de la Construcció d'Habitatges a Catalunya*. Barcelona, Generalitat de Catalunya, Direcció General d'Arquitectura I Habitatge.

Generalitat de Catalunya (2000c) *Dades Estadístiques sobre Població Escolar*. Barcelona, Generalitat de Catalunya, Departament d'Ensenyament.

GEWOS (1982) *Verbreitende Untersuchengen: Hamburg St. Pauli-Nord, Schulterblat – Teil A*. Hamburg, GEWOS.

GEWOS (1989) *Grundlagendaten für den Hamburger Mietspiegel, 1989*. Vol. 2. Hamburg, GEWOS.

Ghirardelli, R., Ratti, D., Proface, A. & Rosso, A. (1991) *Le Tossicodipendenze in un Centro Urbano Metropolitano: Indagine sull' Incidenza della Tossicodipendenza nella Città di Genova*. Genoa. Regione Liguria, Servizi di Salute Mentale, XII U.S.L.

Gifford, A. (1989) *Loosen the Shackles: First Report of the Liverpool 8 Inquiry into Race Relations in Liverpool*. London, Karia Press.

Giraud, O. (2002) 'Firms' Further Training Practices and Social Exclusion'. In Schömann, K. & O'Connell, P. (eds) *Education, Training and Employment Dynamics*. Cheltenham, Edward Elgar.

Glennerster, H. (2001) *United Kingdom Education, 1997–2001*. London, London School of Economics, Centre for Analysis of Social Exclusion. CASE Paper No. 50.

Glennerster, H., Lupton, R., Noden, P. & Power, A. (1999) *Poverty, Social Exclusion and Neighbourhood: Studying the Areas Bases of Social Exclusion*. London, London School of Economics, Centre for Analysis of Social Exclusion. CASE Paper No. 22.

Comà, R. & Brugue, J. (1994) *Public Participation in a Decentralised City: The Case of Barcelona*. Barcelona, Institut de Ciències Politiques i Socials, Working Paper No. 84.

Comà, R. & Rosetti, N. (1999) 'Ciutat Vella: Degradation, Crisis and Regeneration'. *Barcelona Societat: Revista d'Informació I Estudis Socials*. No. 9, 58–79. Barcelona, Ajuntament de Barcelona.

González, T. & Herrmann, H. (2001) 'Soziale Stadtentwicklung in Hamburg-Altona-Lurup: Voraussetzungen und Handlungsperspektiven in einer Großwohnsiedlung am Rande der Stadt'. *Jahrbuch Stadterneuerung 2001*. Berlin, Technische Universität Berlin.

Götting, U. & Lessenich, S. (1999) 'Sphären sozialer Sicherheit: Wohlfahrtsstaatliche Regimeforschung und gesellschaftliche Transformation'. In Lessenich, U. & Ostner, I. (eds) *Welten des Wohlfahrtskapitalismus*. Frankfurt, Campus.

Goul Andersen, J. & Bendix Jensen, J. (2002) 'Different Routes to Improved Employment in Europe'. In Sarfati, H. & Bonoli, G. (eds) *Labour Market and Social Protection Reforms in International Perspective*. Aldershot, Ashgate.

Governa, F. & Salone, C. (2002) 'Territorial Recomposition and Development Strategies: Lessons from Italian Urban and Territorial Policies'. Paper presented at the EURA Conference. *Urban and Spatial European Policies: Levels of Territorial Government*. Turin, 18–20 April.

Government Office for Merseyside (1994) *Merseyside 2000: European Community Objective One: Regional Conversion Plan for Merseyside*. Liverpool, Government Office for Merseyside.

Government Office for the North West (1999) *Merseyside Objective 1 Programme: 2000–6*. Single Planning Document. Liverpool, Government Office for the North West.

Graham, J. & Bennett, T. (1995) *Crime Prevention Strategies in Europe and North America*. Helsinki, European Institute for Crime Prevention and Control.

Graham, S. (1995) 'The City Economy'. In Healey, P., Cameron, S., Davoudi, S., Graham, S. & Madanipour, A. (eds) *Managing Cities: The New Urban Context*. Chichester, Wiley.

Granados-Cabezas, V. (1995) 'Another Mythology for Local Development? Selling Places with Packaging Techniques: A View from the Spanish Experience on City Strategic Planning'. *European Planning Studies*. Vol. 3, 173–187.

Granby-Toxteth Task Force (1991) *Action Plan: 1991–2*. Liverpool, Granby-Toxteth Task Force.

Granby-Toxteth Task Force (1993) *Action Plan: 1993–4*. Liverpool, Granby-Toxteth Task Force.

Granby-Toxteth Task Force (1994) *Action Plan: 1994–5*. Liverpool, Granby-Toxteth Task Force.

Green, H. & Booth, P. (1995) 'Urban Policy in England and France'. In Hambleton, R. & Thomas, H. (eds) *Urban Policy Evaluation: Challenge and Change*. London, Paul Chapman.

Griffiths, R. (1993) 'The Politics of Cultural Policy in Urban Regeneration Strategies'. *Policy & Politics*. Vol. 21, 39–46.

Guelfi, G.-P. (1999) 'Le Strategie della Citta' di Genova e I "Dannati della Terra"'. *La Repubblica*, 15 May.

Guelfi, G.-P., D'Alessandro, R. & Gagliardi, A. (1990) *Il Buon Uso della Legge sulla Droga*. Genoa, Unità Sanitaria Locale 11, Servizio Salute Mentale.

Hackett, K. (1993) *Draft Paper for the Merseyside Forum: Objective One Status and Political Campaigning*. Liverpool, Merseyside Forum.

HafenCity (2000) *HafenCity Hamburg: Der Masterplan*. Hamburg, Hamburg Port Area Development Corporation.

Hall, P. (1997) 'Regeneration Policies for Peripheral Housing Estates: Inward- and Outward-Looking Approaches'. *Urban Studies*. Vol. 34, 873–890.

Hall, S. & Mawson, J. (1999) *Challenge Funding, Contracts and Area Regeneration*. Bristol, Policy Press.

Hambleton, R. & Thomas, H. (1995) (eds) *Urban Policy Evaluation: Challenge and Change*. London, Paul Chapman.

Hamburger Abendblatt (2001a) 'Anwohner in Karolinenviertel wehren sich: Roma sollen nicht an den Knochen ziehen'. *Hamburger Abendblatt*. 17 June, p. 3.

Hamburger Abendblatt (2001b) 'Weniger Wohnungen frei – Mieten steigen jetzt wieder'. *Hamburger Abendblatt*. 19 March, p. 11.

Hamnett, C. (1998) 'Social Polarisation: Economic Restructuring and Welfare State Regimes'. In Musterd, S. & Ostendorf, W. (eds) *Urban Segregation and the Welfare State*. London, Routledge.

Hanhörster-Schiewer, H. (1999) 'Konflikt und Integrationsräume in benachteiligten Stadtteilen'. *Jahrbuch Stadterneuerung 1999*. Berlin, Technische Universität Berlin.

Hantrais, L. (2000) *Social Policy in the EU*. Basingstoke, Palgrave. 2nd Edition.

Harding, A. (1994) 'Urban Regimes and Growth Machines: Towards a Cross-National Research Agenda'. *Urban Affairs Quarterly*. Vol. 29, 356–382.

Harrison, P. (1983) *Inside the Inner City*. Harmondsworth, Penguin.

Hart, T. & Johnston, I. (2000) 'Employment, Education and Training'. In Roberts, P. & Sykes, H. (eds) *Urban Regeneration: A Handbook*. London, Sage.

Harvey, D. (1973) *Social Justice and the City*. London, Edward Arnold.

Harvey, D. (1989) 'From Managerialism to Entrepreneurialism: The Transformation of Urban Governance in Late Capitalism'. *Geografiska Annaler, Series B*, Vol. 17B, 3–17.

Hatton, D. (1988) *Inside Left: The Story So Far*. London, Bloomsbury Press.

Hatton, K. (2001) 'Translating Values: Making Sense of Different Value Bases – Reflections from Denmark and the UK'. *International Journal of Social Research Methodology*. Vol. 4(4), 265–278.

Healey, P. (1998) 'Institutionalist Theory, Social Exclusion and Governance'. In Madanipour, A., Cars, G. and Allen, J. (eds) *Social Exclusion in European Cities: Processes, Experiences and Responses*. London, Jessica Kingsley.

Healey, P., Cameron, S., Davoudi, S., Graham, S. & Madanipour, A. (1995) (eds) *Managing Cities: The New Urban Context*. Chichester, Wiley.

Healey, P., Cars, G., Madanipour, A. & de Magalhäes, C. (2002) 'Transforming Governance, Institutionalist Analysis and Institutional Capacity'. In Cars, G., Healey, P., Madanipour, A. & de Magalhäes, C. (eds) *Urban Governance, Institutional Capacity and Social Milieux*. Aldershot, Ashgate.

Hebenton, B. & Thomas, T. (1995) *Policing Europe: Cooperation, Conflict and Control*. London, Macmillan.

Heidensohn, F. & Farrell, M. (eds) (1991) *Crime in Europe*. London, Routledge.

Heinz, W. (1994) 'Partenarists Public-Privé: La Perspective Allemande'. In Heinz, W. (ed.) *Partenarists Public-Privé dans L'Aménagement Urbain*. Paris, Harmattan.

Held, G. (1992) 'Barcelona 2000: Locale Politik als Internationale Strategie?' In Heinelt, H. & Mayer, M. (eds) *Politik in Europäischen Städten*. Basel, Birkhäuser.

Held, G. (1994) 'Partenariats Public-Privé dans le Redéveloppement Urbain en Espagne'. In Heinz, W. (ed.) *Partenarists Public-Privé dans L'Aménagement Urbain*. Paris, Harmattan.

Hennings, G. & Kunzmann, K. (1993) 'Local Economic Development in a Traditional Industrial Area: the Case of the Ruhrgebiet'. In Meyer, P. (ed.) *Comparative Studies in Local Economic Development*. Westport, Connecticut, Greenwood Press.

Herrmann, H. (1998) 'Institutionalisierte Öffentlichkeit, Bewohnerbeteiligung oder Alibi?' In Alisch, M. (ed.) *Stadtteilmanagement; Voraussetzungen und Chancen für die soziale Stadt*. Opladen, Leske & Budrich.

Herrmann, M., Lenger, H., Reemtsma, J. & Roth, K. (1987) *Hafenstrasse: Chronik und Analysen eines Konflikts*. Hamburg, Verlag am Galgenberg.

Hetherington, P. (1996) 'Mersey Upbeat'. *The Guardian*. 25 April, p. 4.

Hibbitt, K., Jones, P. & Meegan, R. (2001) 'Tackling Social Exclusion: The Role of Social Capital in Urban Regeneration on Merseyside: From Mistrust to Trust?' *European Planning Studies*. Vol. 9, 141–161.

Higgins, M. (1991) *Final Report: Anglican Cathedral Area*. Liverpool, Liverpool Information Service for Merseyside Police Authority.

Hinrichs, G. (1990) *Situation der ausländischen Bevolkerung in Hamburg*. Hamburg, Burgerschaft der freien und Hansestadt Hamburg.

Hoffmann-Martinot, V. (1992) 'Municipal Employees and Personnel Policies: A Comparison of Seven Countries'. In Mouritzen, P. E. (ed.) *Managing Cities in Austerity: Urban Fiscal Crisis in Ten Western Countries*. London, Sage.

Hohaus, G. (1992) 'Das Heroin treibt Marlis vier Tage nach der Entbindung auf der Strich'. *Der lachende Drache*. No. 5.

Hooper, J. (1986) *The Spaniards: A Portrait of the New Spain*. Harmondsworth, Viking Press.

Huggins, R. (2002) *The State of Urban Britain*. London, Robert Huggins Associates.

Hugon, M.-A. (1983) 'Les Textes Officiels'. In Collection Cresas (eds) *Écoles en Transformation: Zone Prioritaires et Autres Quartiers*. Paris, Ed. Harmattan.

Hutchinson, J. (2000) 'Urban Policy and Social Exclusion'. In Percy-Smith, J. (ed.) *Policy Responses to Social Exclusion: Towards Inclusion?* Buckingham, Open University Press.

Ibáñez, S. G. V. (1998) *La Rehabilitación Urbanística*. Pamplona, Ed. Aranzadi.

Il Laboratorio (1991) *Cooperativa di Servizi 'Il Laboratorio'*. Genoa, Consiglio di Circonscrizione.

ILRES (1988) 'Caratteristiche, Componenti ad Aspettative dei Residente e degli Operatori Economici del Centro Storico di Genova'. *Les Cahiers de l'ANAH*. Special Issue.

ILRES (1989) *Lo Raporto sullo Stato della Sanità in Liguria*. Genoa, Istituto Ligure di Ricerche Economiche e Sociali.

ILRES (1991) *Immigrati Extracomunitari in Liguria*. Genoa, Istituto Ligure di Ricerche Economiche e Sociali.

ILRES (1994) *I Fondi Strutturali in Liguria*. Genoa, Istituto Ligure di Ricerche Economiche e Sociali.

INSEE (1995) *Les Bas Revenus à Marseille*. Marseille, 1995.

INSEE (1999) *Les Bas Revenus dans les Bouches-du-Rhône*. Marseille, 1999.

Institut für Landes- und Stadtentwicklungsforschung des Landes Nordrhein-Westfalen (2000) *Evaluation of Local Socio-Economic Strategies in Disadvantaged Urban Areas*.

Dortmund, Institut für Landes- und Stadtentwicklungsforschung des Landes Nordrhein-Westfalen.

ISTAT (1995) *Stranieri a Genova*. Genoa, ISTAT Regional Office.

Jack, I. (1987) *Before the Oil Ran Out: Britain 1977–86*. London, Flamingo.

Jacobs, B. & Dutton, C. (2000) 'Social and Community Issues'. In Roberts, P. & Sykes, H. (eds) *Urban Regeneration: A Handbook*. London, Sage.

Jacquier, C. & Laino, G. (2002) *Ex Ante Evaluation of the URBACT Programme*. Grenoble, CERAT.

Jahrbuch Stadterneuerung (2000) *Jahrbuch Stadterneuerung 2000*. Dedicated Issue on the German Federal Neighbourhood Regeneration Programme. Berlin, Technische Universität Berlin.

Jauhiainen, J. (1995) 'Waterfront Redevelopment and Urban Policy: The Case of Barcelona, Cardiff and Genoa'. *European Planning Studies*. Vol. 3, 3–23.

Jessen, J. & Neumann, W. (1999) 'Stadtpolitik in Frankreich'. *Jahrbuch Stadterneuerung 1999*. Berlin, Technische Universität Berlin.

Jessop, B. (2000) 'Globalisation, Entrepreneurial Cities and the Social Economy'. In Hamel, P., Lustiger-Thaler, H. & Mayer, M. (eds) *Urban Movements in a Globalising World*. London, Routledge.

Jewson, N. & MacGregor, S. (eds) (1997) *Transforming Cities: Contested Governance and New Spatial Divisions*. London, Routledge.

Jodogne, S. (1991) *Dynamiques urbaines et Metropoles: Gênes – Analyse de Processus de Mutation*. University of Lille-Flandre-Artois, Dissertation for Maitrise de Sciences et Techniques.

Johnson, L. (2001) 'Crime, Fear and Civil Policing'. *Urban Studies*. Vol. 38, 959–976.

Johnson, N. (1999) *Mixed Economies of Welfare*. London, Prentice Hall.

Jorzich, P. (1993) *Quartiersbezogene Handlungsansätze im Rahmen einer sozialen Großstadtstrategie*. Hamburg, Steg.

Judd, D. & Parkinson, M. (1990) 'Urban Leadership and Regeneration'. In Judd, D. & Parkinson, M. (eds) *Leadership and Urban Regeneration*. London, Sage.

Karolinen-Poker (1984) *Sanierung*. Hamburg, Karolinen-Poker (Community Newsletter).

Keating, M. (1991) *Comparative Urban Politics: Power and the City in the United States, Canada, Britain and France*. Aldershot, Edward Elgar.

Keating, M. (2001) 'Rethinking the Region'. *European Urban and Regional Studies*. Vol. 8, 217–234.

Kedadouche, Z. (2003) *Synthèse du Rapport sur la Participation des Habitants dans les Opérations de Renouvellement Urbain*. Paris, Inspection Générale des Affaires Sociales.

Keim, K.-D. (2000) 'Gewalt, Kriminalität'. In Häußermann, H. (ed.) *Großstadt: Soziologische Stichworte*. Opladen, Leske & Budrich.

Keith, M. & Rogers, A. (1991) (eds) *Hollow Promises: Rhetoric and Reality in the Inner City*. London, Mansell.

Kellas, J. (1991) 'European Integration and the Regions'. *Parliamentary Affairs*. Vol. 44, 226–239.

Keller, C. (1999) *Armut in der Stadt*. Opladen, Westdeutscher Verlag.

Kennett, P. (2001) *Comparative Social Policy*. Buckingham, Open University Press.

Kenny, M. & Knipmeyer, M. (1983) 'Urban Research in Spain: Retrospect and Prospect'. In Kenny, M. and Kertzer, D. (eds) *Urban Life in Mediterranean Europe: Anthropological Perspectives*. Urbana, USA, University of Illinois Press.

Kesteloot, C. (1998) 'The Geography of Deprivation in Brussels'. In Musterd, S. & Ostendorf, W. (eds) *Urban Segregation and the Welfare State*. London, Routledge.

Kinsey, R. (1984) *Merseyside Crime Survey: First Report*. University of Edinburgh, Centre for Criminology.

Kleinman, M. (1998) 'Western European Housing Policies: Convergence or Collapse?'. In Kleinman, M., Matznetter, W. & Stephens, M. (eds) *European Integration and Housing Policy*. London, Routledge.

Kleinman, M. (2002) 'The Future of European Union Social Policy and its Implications for Housing'. *Urban Studies*. Vol. 39, 341–352.

Kleinman, M. & Piachaud, D. (1993) 'European Social Policy: Conceptions and Choices'. *Journal of European Social Policy*. Vol. 3, 1–20.

Koller-Tejeiro, Y. (1998) 'Sozialplanung: Zaubermittel oder zahnloser Tiger'. In Alisch, M. (ed.) *Stadtteilmanagement; Voraussetzungen und Chancen für die soziale Stadt*. Opladen, Leske & Budrich.

Korte, W., Zimmermann, I. & Freigang, M. (1999) 'Kinder, Gesundheit und Armut aus Sicht der Gesundheitsberichterstattung in Hamburg'. *Sozialhilfe-Report*. No. 16, 4–11. Hamburg, Behörde für Arbeit, Gesundheit und Soziales.

Kreibaum, J. & Mutschler, R. (1990) 'Wohnungsversorgung in Hamburg als soziales Problem – Ein Überblick'. In Fachhochschule Hamburg: Fachbereich Sozialpädagogik (ed.) *Standpunkt: Sozial – Wohnungsnot und Wohnraumversorgung in Hamburg*. Vol. 1.

Kuhlmann, M. (2001) *Local Partnerships and Neighbourhood Management to Combat Social Exclusion*. Hamburg, Daniel Lawaetz Foundation.

Kunze, R. & Schubert, D. (2001) 'Einführung in den Schwerpunkt: Stadtteile mit besonderem Entwicklungsbedarf: Soziale Stadt'. *Jahrbuch Stadterneuerung 2001*. Berlin, Technische Universität.

Kunzmann, K. R. (1998) 'Germany'. In Van den Berg, L., Braun, E. & van der Meer (eds) *National Urban Policies in the European Union*. Aldershot, Ashgate.

Kürpick, S. & Weck, S. (1998) 'Policies Against Social Exclusion in Germany'. In Madanipour, A., Cars, G. and Allen, J. (1998) *Social Exclusion in European Cities: Processes, Experiences and Responses*. London, Jessica Kingsley.

Lanaspa, L., Pueyo, F. & Sanz, F. (2003) 'The Evolution of Spanish Urban Structure during the Twentieth Century'. *Urban Studies*. Vol. 40, 567–580.

Landeskriminalamt (1989) *Kriminalitätslage Hamburg: Überblick und Polizeiliche Kriminalstatistik 1989*. Hamburg, Landeskriminalamt.

Landeskriminalamt (1991) *Kriminalitätslage Hamburg: Überblick und Polizeiliche Kriminalstatistik 1991*. Hamburg, Landeskriminalamt.

Landeskriminalamt (1992) *Sozialer und Medizinischer Hintergrund des Drogentodes*. Hamburg, Landeskriminalamt.

Landeskriminalamt (2000) *Kriminalitätslagebericht für Hamburg*. Hamburg, Landeskriminalamt.

Lane, J.-E. (2000) *New Public Management: An Introduction*. London, Routledge.

Lang, M. (1994) 'Neue Hanlungsansätze zur Erneuerung benachteiligter Stadtquartiere in Deutschland'. In Froessler, R., Lang, M., Selle, K. & Staubach, R. (eds) *Lokaler Partnerschaften: Die Erneuerung Benachteiligter Quartiere in Europäischen Städten*. Basel, Birkhäuser.

Läpple, D. (2000) 'Ökonomie der Stadt'. In Häußermann, H. (ed.) *Großstadt: Soziologische Stichworte*. Opladen, Leske & Budrich.

Läpple, D., Deecke, H. & Krüger, T. (1994) *Strukturentiwicklung und Zukunftsperspecitven der Hamburger Wirtschaft unter raümlichen Gesichtspunkten* (unpublished).

Latini, A. P. (1997) (ed.) *I Programmi di Riqualificazione Urbana*. Rome, INU Edizioni.

La Vanguardia (1991) 'No es bueno para Cataluña que su Presidente se arriesgue tanto con preferencias partidistas'. *La Vanguardia*. 28 April, 19–20 (Rafael Jorba & Marta Ricart).

Lawaetz Stiftung (1991) *Information über den Fonds zur Förderung von örtlichen Beschäftingungsinitiativen in Hamburg*. Hamburg, Lawaetz Stiftung and Behörde für Arbeit, Gesundheit und Soziales.

Lawaetz Stiftung (1993) *ESF Programmkoordination: Sachbericht 1993*. Hamburg, Johann Daniel Lawaetz Stiftung.

Lawless, P. (1989) *Britain's Inner Cities*. London, Paul Chapman (2nd Edition).

Le Galès, P. (1998) 'Regulations and Governance in European Cities'. *International Journal of Urban and Regional Research*. Vol. 22, 482–506.

Le Galès, P. (2000) 'Private-Sector Interests and Urban Governance'. In Bagnasco, A. & Le Galès, P. (eds) *Cities in Contemporary Europe*. Cambridge, Cambridge University Press.

Le Galès, P. & Harding, A. (1998) 'Cities and States in Europe'. *West European Politics*. Vol. 21, 120–145.

Le Galès, P. & Loncle-Moriceau, P. (2001) 'Local Parterships and Social Exclusion in France: Experiences and Ambiguities'. In Geddes, M. & Benington, J. (eds) *Local Partnerships and Social Exclusion in the European Union: New Forms of Local Social Governance?* London, Routledge.

Le Galès, P. & Mawson, J. (1994) *Management Innovations in Urban Policy: Lessons from France*. London, Local Government Management Board.

Legge, I. & Bathsteen, M. (1996) *Lokale Sicherheitsdiagnosen für Vier Stadtteile*. Hamburg, Landeskriminalamt, Kriminologische Regionalanalyse Hamburg. Vol. 2.

Legge, I. & Bathsteen, M. (2000) *Einfluss des Methadonprogramms auf die Delinquenzentwicklung polizeibehutsamer Drogenkonsument*. Hamburg, Landeskriminalamt.

Legge, I., Bathsteen, M. & Harenberg, R. (1994) *Kriminologische Regionalanalyse Hamburg-Altona: Methodologische Grundlagen Lokaler Sicherheitsdiagnosen*. Hamburg, Landeskriminalamt.

Lehto, J. (2000) 'Different Cities in Different Welfare States'. In Bagnasco, A. & Le Galès, P. (eds) *Cities in Contemporary Europe*. Cambridge: Cambridge University Press.

Leontidou, L. (1993) 'Postmodernism and the City: The Mediterranean Versions'. *Urban Studies*. Vol. 30, 949–965.

Leroy, M. C. (1990) 'Quartiers Fragiles en Europe'. In *Quartiers Fragiles et Développment Urbaine*. POUR, No. 125/6, 45–55.

Leutner, B. (1990) *Wohnungspolitik nach dem 2. Weltkrieg* Bonn, Bundesminister für Raumordnung, Bauwesen und Städtebau. Schriftenreihe Forschung No. 482.

Levin, P. (1997) *Making Social Policy*. Buckingham, Open University Press.

Lhermite, M. (2000) 'Urbanisme Rime avec Infrastructures'. *TPBM*. No. 319, 12–13.

LHT (2000) *LHT Annual Reports 1998–2000*. Liverpool, Liverpool Housing Trust.

Lindbeck, A. & Snower, D. (1989) *The Insider–Outsider Theory*. London, MIT Press.

Liverpool Black Caucus (1986) *The Racial Politics of Militant in Liverpool*. London, Runnymede Trust.

Liverpool Central and Southern Community Health Council (1990) *Annual Report*. Liverpool, Central and Southern Community Health Council.

Liverpool City Council (1985) *Housing Investment Programme, Submission for 1985/6*. Liverpool City Housing Department.

Liverpool City Council (1986a) *Urban Decline and Deprivtion: Liverpool's Relative Position*. Liverpool, City Council.

Liverpool City Council (1986b) *The Urban Programme: Urban Regeneration Strategy, Annual Report*. Liverpool, City Council.

Liverpool City Council (1987a) *An Economic Development Strategy for Liverpool: The Framework*. Liverpool, City Council.

Liverpool City Council (1987b) *The Urban Programme: Urban Regeneration Strategy*. Liverpool, City Council.

Liverpool City Council (1988a) *Poverty in Liverpool*. Liverpool, City Council.

Liverpool City Council (1988b) *The Urban Development Programme*. Liverpool, City Council.

Liverpool City Council (1989) *Merseyside Into the 1990s*. Liverpool, City Council.

Liverpool City Council (1990) *Economic Initiatives*. Liverpool, City Council.

Liverpool City Council (1991) *The Urban Programme: 1990/91*. Liverpool, City Council.

Liverpool City Council (1992) *Housing Policy Statement: 1992/3*. Liverpool, City Council.

Liverpool City Council (1993a) *The Liverpool Quality of Life Survey No. 22*. Liverpool, City Council.

Liverpool City Council (1993b) *Housing Investment Programme: Strategy and Submission, 1994–9*. Liverpool, City Council, Housing and Consumer Services Directorate.

Liverpool City Council (1993c) *Housing Investment Programme: Strategy and Submission: 1994–9*. Liverpool, City Council, Housing and Consumer Services Directorate.

Liverpool City Council (1994a) *Economic Development Plan 1994/5–1996/7*. Liverpool, City Council.

Liverpool City Council (1994b) *City Challenge 1994/5: CityCentre East: Action Plan – Making the Difference*. Liverpool, City Council.

Liverpool City Council (1994c) *Liverpool Public Health Annual Report 1994*. Liverpool, Public Health Department.

Liverpool City Council (1994d) *The Objective One Programme: 1995 Proposals*. Liverpool, City Council.

Liverpool City Council (1995a) *Liverpool Public Health Annual Report 1995*. Liverpool, Public Health Department.

Liverpool City Council (1995b) *The City of Liverpool Housing Investment Programme: 1996/7*. Liverpool, Housing & Consumer Services Directorate.

Liverpool City Council (1996) *Liverpool Unitary Development Plan*. Liverpool, City Council.

Liverpool City Council (1997) *Poverty Digest 1997: The Extent of Poverty in Liverpool*. Liverpool City Council, Anti-Poverty Team.

Liverpool City Council (1999a) *Poverty Digest 1999: The Extent of Poverty in Liverpool*. Issue 2. Liverpool City Council, Research & Development Team.

Liverpool City Council (1999b) *Housing Strategy Statement: 1999–2002*. Liverpool, Housing and Consumer Services Directorate.

Liverpool City Council (2000) *Liverpool Public Health Annual Report 2000*. Liverpool, Public Health Department.

Liverpool FHSA (1991a) *Deprived Areas Strategy*. Liverpool, Family Health Services Authority.

Liverpool FHSA (1991b) *Vauxhall Health Report*. Liverpool, Family Health Services Authority.

Liverpool First (2000) *Liverpool First: The Prospectus*. Liverpool, Liverpool Partnership Group.

Liverpool New Deal for Communities (2000) *Pathfinder Delivery Plan: 2000–2010*. Liverpool, Liverpool Partnership Group.

Liverpool Partnership Group (2000) *City Regeneration Strategy*. Liverpool, Liverpool City Council.

Liverpool Vision (2000) *Liverpool Vision: Strategic Regeneration Framework*. Liverpool, Liverpool Partnership Group.

Loh Lynn, I. (1982) *The Chinese Community in Liverpool*. Liverpool, Merseyside Area Profile Group (Department of Sociology, University of Liverpool).

Lorrain, D. (1992) 'The French Model of Urban Services'. *West European Politics*. Vol. 15, 77–92.

Lovering, J. (1995) 'Creating Discourses rather than Jobs: The Crisis in the Cities and the Transition Fantasies of Intellectuals and Policy Makers'. In Healey, P., Cameron, S., Davoudi, S., Graham, S. & Madanipour, A. (1995) (eds) *Managing Cities: The New Urban Context*. Chichester, Wiley.

Lowder, S. (1980) 'The Evolution and Identity of Urban Social Areas: The Case of Barcelona'. Glasgow University, Geography Department, Occasional Papers. No. 4.

Lowe, S. (1986) *Urban Social Movements: The City After Castells*. Basingstoke, Macmillan.

MacFarlane, R. & Laville, J.-L. (1992) *Developing Community Partnerships in Europe*. London, Directory of Social Change and Calouste Gulbenkian Foundation.

MacGregor, S. (1990) 'The Inner-City Battlefield'. In MacGregor, S. & Pimlott, B. (eds) *Tackling the Inner Cities*. Oxford, Clarendon Press.

MacGregor, S. (1992) 'Poverty, Marginalisation and Dualism: A Commentary'. *Cross-National Research Papers*. Second Series. No. 7, 1–11.

MacGregor, S. (1993) 'The Semantics and Politics of Urban Poverty'. *Cross-National Research Papers*. Third Series. No. 2, 65–78.

MacGregor, S. (2001) 'Social Policy and the City'. In Paddison, R. (ed.) *Handbook of Urban Studies*. London, Sage.

Maclennan, D., Stephens, M. & Kemp, P. (1996) *Housing Policy in the EU Member States*. University of Glasgow, Report to the European Parliament.

Madanipour, A. (1998) 'Social Exclusion and Space'. In Madanipour, A., Cars, G. and Allen, J. (eds) *Social Exclusion in European Cities: Processes, Experiences and Responses*. London, Jessica Kingsley.

Malara, L. (1991) 'Il Caso di Genova: frá Declino e Asfissia'. *The Future of Port Cities*. Paper presented at the Conference. Marseilles, 26–28 September.

Maloney, W., Smith, G. & Stoker, G. (2000) 'Social Capital and Urban Governance: Adding a more Contextualised "Top Down" Perspective'. *Political Studies*. Vol. 48, 802–820.

Mangen, S. (1989) 'The Politics of Reform: Origins and Enactment of the "Italian Experiment" '. *International Journal of Social Psychiatry*. Vol. 35, 7–19.

Mangen, S. (1992) 'Marginalisation and Inner City Europe'. *Cross-National Research Papers*. Second Series. No. 7, 55–72.

Mangen, S. (1993) 'Urban Polarisation in Europe: Contexts and Concepts'. *Cross-National Research Papers*. Third Series. No. 2, 1–12.

Mangen, S. (2001) *Spain After Franco: Regime Transition and the Welfare State*. Basingstoke, Palgrave.

Mangin, D. & Panerai, P. (1999) *Projet Urbain*. Marseille, Editions Parenthèses.

Manzanera, R., Torralba, L., Brugal, M., Armengol, R., Solanes, P. & Villalbi, J. (2000) 'Afrontar los Estragos de la Heroína: Evaluación de Diez Años de un Programa Integral en Barcelona'. *Gac Sanit*. Vol. 14, 58–66.

Maragall, P. (1986) *Referent Barcelona*. Barcelona, Ed. Planeta.

Marcelloni, M. (1992) 'La Crisis de las Ciudades Italianas'. *Estudios Territoriales*. No. 39, 181–196.

Marcuse, P. (1982) 'Determinants of State Housing Policies in West Germany and the United States'. In Fainstein, N. & S. (eds) *Urban Policy Under Capitalism*. Beverly Hills, Sage.

Marcuse, P. (1989) 'Dual City: A Muddy Metaphor for a Quartered City?' *International Journal of Urban and Regional Research*. Vol. 13, 697–708.

Marks, D. & Couch, C. (1991) *Renewal Areas in North West England*. Liverpool, Liverpool Polytechnic.

Marseille, Aménagement (2000) *Les Périmètres de Restauration Immobilière: Panier, Centre Ville/Thubaneau*. Marseilles, Marseilles City Council.

Marseille Habitat (1992) *Revitalisation du Centre Ville de Marseille*. Marseilles, Marseille Habitat.

Marshall, T. (1996) 'Barcelona – Fast Forward?: City Entrepreneurialism in the 1980s and 1990s'. *European Planning Studies*. Vol. 4, 147–165.

Marti i Jusmet, F. (1990) 'La Seguridad Ciudadana'. In Borja, J., Castells, M., Dorado, R. & Quintana, I. (eds) *Las Grandes Ciudades en los Noventa*. Madrid, Ed. Sistema.

Martin, S. & Pearce, G. (1995) 'The Evaluation of Urban Policy Project Appraisal'. In Hambleton, R. & Thomas, H. (eds) *Urban Policy Evaluation: Challenge and Change*. London, Paul Chapman.

Martínez Veiga, U. (1997) *La Integración Social de los Inmigratnes Extranjeros en España*. Madrid, Ed. Trotta.

Masllorens, A. (1992) *Acollir l'Immigrant es un Acte de Justicia: Curs de Promoció per a Dones Maroquines*. Càritas Diocesana de Barcelona.

Matthews, H. (2001) *Children and Community Regeneration*. London, Save the Children Fund.

Mattina, C. (2001) 'Des Médiateurs Locaux: Les Présidents des Comités d'Intéret de Quartier autour de la Rue de la République'. In Donzel, A. (ed.) *Métropolisation, Gouvernance et Citoyenneté dans la Région Urbaine Marseillais*. Paris, Maisonneuve et Larose.

Mawby, R. (1992) 'Comparative Police Systems: Searching for a Continental Model'. In Bottomley, K., Fowles, T. & Reiner, R. (eds) *Criminal Justice: Theory and Practice*. London, British Society of Criminology.

Mawby, R. (2001) 'The Impact of Repeat Victimization on Burglary Victims in East and West Europe'. In Farrell, G. & Pease, K. (eds) *Repeat Victimization*. New York, Criminal Justice Press.

Mawby, R. (2003) 'Models of Policing: Stability or Change?'. In Newburn, T. (ed.) *A Handbook of Policing*. Cullompton, Willan Publishing.

Mayer, M. (1995) 'Urban Governance in the Post-Fordist City'. In Healey, P., Cameron, S., Davoudi, S., Graham, S. & Madanipour, A. (1995) (eds) *Managing Cities: The New Urban Context*. Chichester, Wiley.

Mayer, M. (2000a) 'Social Movements in European Cities: Transitions from the 1970s to the 1990s'. In Bagnasco, A. & Le Galès, P. (eds) *Cities in Contemporary Europe*. Cambridge, Cambridge University Press.

Mayer, M. (2000b) 'Urban Social Movements in an Era of Globalisation'. In Hamel, P., Lustiger-Thaler, H. & Mayer, M. (eds) *Urban Movements in a Globalising World*. London, Routledge.

Mayhew, P. & van Dijk, J. (1997) *Criminal Victimisation in Eleven Industrialised Countries*. The Hague, Wetenschappelijk Onderzoek-en-Documentatiecentrum.

Mayo, M. (1997) 'Partnerships for Regeneration and Community Development'. *Critical Social Policy*. Vol. 17, 3–26.

Mayor of London (2002) *London Divided: Income Inequality and Poverty in the Capital*. London, Greater London Authority.

Mazauric, A. (1990) 'Remous autour d'une Mosquée'. *Les Cahiers de l'Orient*. No. 16, 35–44.

Mazzella, S. (1996) 'Le Quartier Belsunce à Marseille: Les Immigrés dans les Traces de la Ville Bougeoise'. *Annales de la Recherche Urbaine*. Vol. 72, 122–143.

McClain, P. (2001) 'Urban Crime in the USA and Western Europe: A Comparison'. In Paddison, R. (ed.) *Handbook of Urban Studies*. London, Sage.

McDonald, A. (1986) *The Weller Way: The Story of the Weller Street Housing Cooperative*. London, Faber & Faber.

Meegan, R. (1994) 'A "Europe of the Regions"?: A View from Liverpool on the Atlantic Arc Periphery'. *European Planning Studies*. Vol. 2, 59–80.

Meegan, R. & Mitchell, A. (2001) 'It's not Community round here, It's Neighbourhood: Neighbourhood Change and Cohesion in Urban Regeneration Policies'. *Urban Studies*. Vol. 38, 2167–2194.

Mellor, R. (1997) 'Cool Times for A Changing City'. In Jewson, N. & MacGregor, S. (eds) *Transforming Cities: Contested Governance and New Spatial Divisions*. London, Routledge.

Mény, Y. (1984) 'Decentralization in Socialist France: The Politics of Pragmatism. *West European Politics*. Vol. 7, 65–79.

Merrifield, A. (1995) 'Social Justice and Communities of Difference: A Snapshot from Liverpool'. In Merrifield, A. & Swyngedouw, E. (eds) *The Urbanization of Injustice*. London, Lawrence & Wishart.

Merseyside Development Corporation (1981) *Initial Development Strategy*. Liverpool, Merseyside Development Corporation.

Merseyside Development Corporation (1993) *The New Wave*. Liverpool, Merseyside Development Corporation.

Merseyside's Health 2000 (2000) *Merseyside's Health 2000*. Liverpool, Merseyside's Public Health Officers.

Merseyside Improved Housing (1992) *MIH Yearbook*. Liverpool, Merseyside Improved Housing.

Merseyside Improved Housing *Annual Reports 1994–2000*. Liverpool, Merseyside Improved Housing /Riverside Housing Association.

Merseyside Police (1986) *Responsible Demand Enforcement: A Survey*. Liverpool, Merseyside Police Authority.

Merseyside Police (1990) *Form 104: Active Prostitutes A2 Subdivision*. Liverpool, Merseyside Police Authority, Copperas Hill Station.

Merseyside Police (1991) *Community Liaison Committee*. Liverpool, Merseyside Police Authority.

Merseyside Police (1993) *Residents' Attitudes to the Police: Research by MORI for Merseyside Police Authority*. Liverpool, Merseyside Police Authority.

Merseyside Police (2002) *How are We Doing?: Chief Constable's Report for the Year Ending March 31st 2002*. Liverpool, Merseyside Police Authority.

Merseyside Task Force (1991) *MTF Newsletter*. Autumn Edition.

Miguet, A. (2002) 'The French Elections of 2002: After the Earthquake, the Deluge'. *West European Politics*. Vol. 25, 207–220.

Mingione, E. (1995) 'Social and Employment Change in the Urban Area'. In Healey, P., Cameron, S., Davoudi, S., Graham, S. & Madanipour, A. (eds) *Managing Cities: The New Urban Context*. Chichester, Wiley.

Mission Centre Ville (1990) *Marseille Centre – Politique Urbaine.* Marseilles, Ville de Marseille.

Monteverde, F. (1989) 'Dossier Genova'. *Entropia: Crisi e Trasformazione.* Supplement to No. 16.

Mooney, J. (1997) ' Violence, Space and Gender: The Social and Spatial Parameters of Violence Against Women and Men'. In Jewson, N. & MacGregor, S. (eds) *Transforming Cities: Contested Governance and New Spatial Divisions.* London, Routledge.

Moore, D. (2001) 'Marseille: Institutional Links with Ethnic Minorities and the French Republican Model'. In Rogers, A. & Tillis, J. (eds) *Multicultural Policies and Modes of Citizenship in European Cities.* Aldershot, Ashgate.

Moore, R. (1994) 'Crisis and Compliance: The Liverpool Non-Discrimination Notice, 1989–1994'. *New Community.* No. 20, 581–602.

Moore, R. (1997) 'Poverty and Partnership in the Third European Poverty Programme: The Liverpool Case'. In Jewson, N. & MacGregor, S. (eds) *Transforming Cities: Contested Governance and New Spatial Divisions.* London, Routledge.

Morén-Alegret, R. (2001) 'Tuning the Channels: Local Government Policies and Immigrants' Participation in Barcelona'. In Rogers, A. & Tillie, J. (eds) *Multicultural Policies and Modes of Citizenship in European Cities.* Aldershot, Ashgate.

Moscato, M. (2000) 'Urban-Italy, the Complex Programmes and Negotiated Programming: A Reference Framework in Evolution'. In Campagna, L. & Ricci, M. (eds) *Programma Urban-Italia: Europa, Nuove Politiche Urbane.* Rome, Ed INU.

Moser, C. (1996) *Confronting Crisis: A Comparative Study of Household Responses to Poverty and Vulnerability in Four Urban Communities.* Washington, International Bank for Reconstruction and Development.

Mosley, H. & Schütz, H. (2001). 'The Implementation of Active Policies in the German Regions: Decentralization and Co-operation'. In de Koning, J. & Mosely, H. (eds) *Labour Market Policy and Unemployment.* Cheltenham, Edward Elgar.

Mourtizen, P. E. & Nielsen, K. H. (1992) 'Was There a Fiscal Crisis'. In Mouritzen, P. E. (ed.) *Managing Cities in Austerity: Urban Fiscal Crisis in Ten Western Countries.* London, Sage.

Müller, T. (1994) 'Jetzt is Ensemblegeist gefordert: Wir brauchen ein Bündnis gegen die Armut'. *Standpunkt: Sozial – Stadtentwicklung und soziale Politik.* No. 1, 1–15.

Murie, A. (1998) 'Segregation, Exclusion and Housing in the Divided City'. In Musterd, S. & Ostendorf, W. (eds) *Urban Segregation and the Welfare State.* London, Routledge.

Musterd, S. & de Winter, M. (1998) 'Conditions for Spatial Segregation: Some European Perspectives'. *International Journal of Urban and Regional Research.* Vol. 22, 665–673.

Musterd, S. & Ostendorf, W. (1998) 'Welfare State Effects on Inequality and Segregation: Concluding Remarks'. In Musterd, S. & Ostendorf, W. (eds) *Urban Segregation and the Welfare State.* London, Routledge.

Nahr, H. (1999) 'Das Programm der "Sozialen Stadtteilentwicklung" '. *Sozialhilfe-Report.* No. 16, 18–21. Hamburg, Behörde für Arbeit, Gesundheit und Soziales.

Naroska, H.-J. (1989) 'Urban Underclass und "neue" soziale Randgruppen im städtischen Raum'. In Friedrichs, J. (ed.) *Soziologische Stadtforschung.* Opladen, Westdeutscher Verlag.

National Audit Office (1990) *Regenerating the Inner Cities.* London, HMSO.

Naylon, J. (1981) 'Barcelona'. In Pacione, M. (ed.) *Urban Problems and Planning in the Developed World.* London, Croom Helm.

Nebot, M. & Farré, M. (1991). *Estudi de la Fecunditat en Adolescents a Barcelona: 1979–88.* Barcelona, Ajuntament de Barcelona, Institut Municipal de la Salut.

Negre i Rigol, P. (1988) *La Prostitucion Popular: Relatos de Vida*. Barcelona, Fundacio Caixa de Pensions, 1989.

Neild, L. (1991) 'Police Tighten Curbs on Kerb Crawlers'. *Liverpool Echo*. 12 March, p. 6.

Neild, L. & Elias, R. (2002) 'Bettison Under Fire'. *Liverpool Daily Post*. 18 January, p. 1.

Nel.lo, O. (1998) 'Spain'. In Van den Berg, L., Braun, E. & van der Meer (eds) *National Urban Policies in the European Union*. Aldershot, Ashgate.

Nel.lo, O., Recio, A., Solsona, M. & Subirats, M. (1998) *Enquesta de la Regió Metropolitana: La Tansformació de la Societat Metropolitana*. Barcelona, Institut d'Estudis Metropolitans.

Nelson, U. (1985) *Les Pistoles: Insertion d'un Bâti Neuf dans un Quartier Ancien: Le Panier*. Marseilles, UAP Marseille-Luminy.

Nevin, B. & Lee, P. (2000) *Developing a Housing Investment Framework for the Inner Core of Liverpool*. University of Birmingham, Centre for Urban and Regional Studies.

Newburn, T. (2001) 'The Commodification of Policing: Security Networks in the Late Modern City'. *Urban Studies*. Vol. 38, 829–848.

Newburn, T. (2002) 'Community Safety and Policing'. In Hughes, G., McLaughlin, E. & Muncie, J. (eds) *Crime Prevention and Community Safety: New Directions*. London, Sage.

Newman, P. & Thornley, A. (1996) *Urban Planning in Europe*. London, Routledge.

Niemeyer, R. (1990) 'Jugendbildungsstätte des DGB-Berufsfortbildungswerkes'. *Standpunkt Sozial*. No. 3, 82–84.

Nispel, A. (2000) *Offen für Migrantinnen?* Freie und Hansestadt Hamburg, Senatsamt für die Gleichstellung.

Nixdorf, C. (1989) 'St Georg: ein Kreuz für jeden Drogentoten'. *Mopo*. 8 November, p. 4.

North West Network (1994) *Building the Pathways to Integration – Approaches to Developing Self-help for Merseyside Neighbourhoods*. Liverpool, North West Network.

Northern Housing (2000) *A Turning Tide for Liverpool*. Liverpool, Liverpool Partnership Group.

Nuvolati, G. (2002) 'Urban Development Programmes in Italy'. Paper presented at the EURA Conference. *Urban and Spatial European Policies: Levels of Territorial Government*. Turin, 18–20 April.

Oatley, N. & Lambert, C. (1995) 'Evaluating Competitive Urban Policy: The City Challenge Initiative'. In Hambleton, R. & Thomas, H. (eds) *Urban Policy Evaluation: Challenge and Change*. London, Paul Chapman.

Obadia, Y., Viau, A. & Campocasso, J. (1989) *L'État de la Santé dans les Bouches du Rhone*. Marseilles, Observatoire Régional de la Santé.

Oberti, M. (2000) 'Social Structures in Medium-Sized Cities Compared'. In Bagnasco, A. & Le Galès, P. (eds) *Cities in Contemporary Europe*. Cambridge, Cambridge University Press.

OECD (1983) *Managing Urban Change: Policies and Finance*. Paris, OECD.

OECD (1986) *Economic Survey: Spain, 1985/6*. Paris, OECD.

OECD (1989) *Economic Survey: Spain, 1988/9*. Paris, OECD.

OECD (1998) *Integrating Distressed Urban Areas*. Paris, Organisation for Economic Co-operation and Development.

Office of the Deputy Prime Minister (2003) *The Effectiveness of Government Regeneration Initiatives*. London, House of Commons, Housing, Planning Local Government and the Regions Committee: Seventh Report of Session 2002–3. Vol. 1.

ORS (1998) *Evaluation du Dispositif des Automates Échangeurs-Distributeurs de Seringues a Marseille*. Marseilles, Observatoire Régional de la Santé.

PACA (1992) *Quartiers de Marseille*. Marseilles, Région Provence Alpes Côte d'Azur.

PACT (1990) *Contrat de Plan Etat-Région 1989–1993*. Convention d'Execution État-Région.

Pain, R. (2001) 'Gender, Race, Age and Fear in the City'. *Urban Studies*. Vol. 38, 899–913.

Palermo, P.-C. (2000) 'An Opportunity to Reflect on Urban Policies'. In Campagna, L. & Ricci, M. (2000) *Programma Urban-Italia: Europa, Nuove Politiche Urbane*. Rome, Ed INU.

Palumbo, M. (1997) *Liguria Obiettivo Lavoro: Un Futuro Possible*. Milan, Angeli.

Paniagua, J. (1950) 'La Vivienda en España'. In Instituto Sindical de Estudios (ed.) *Reflexiones sobre Política Economica*. Madrid, Ed. Popular.

Pannella, R. (1980) 'Centro Storico e Centro Città'. In Ciardini, F. & Falini, P. (eds) *I Centri Storici*. Milan, Ed Mazzotta, 2nd Edition.

Paraskevopoulos, C. (2001) *Interpreting Convergence in the EU: Patterns of Collective Action, Social Learning and Europeanization*. Basingstoke, Palgrave.

Pareja, M. & San Martín, I. (2002) 'The Tenure Imbalance in Spain: The Need for Social Housing Policy'. *Urban Studies*. Vol. 39, 283–295.

Parkinson, M. (1988) 'Liverpool's Fiscal Crisis: An Anatomy of Failure'. In Parkinson, M., Koley, B. & Judd, D. (eds) *Regenerating the Cities: The UK Crisis and the US Experience*. Manchester, Manchester University Press.

Parkinson, M. (1990) 'Leadership and Regeneration in Liverpool: Confusion, Confrontation, or Coalition?'. In Judd, D. & Parkinson, M. (eds) *Leadership and Urban Regeneration*. London, Sage.

Parkinson, M. (1994) *Social Exclusion in European Cities*. Liverpool John Moores University, European Institute for Urban Affairs.

Parkinson, M. (1998a) *Combating Social Exclusion: Lessons from Area-Based Programmes in Europe*. Bristol, Policy Press.

Parkinson, M. (1998b) 'The United Kingdom'. In Van den Berg, L., Braun, E. & van der Meer (eds) *National Urban Policies in the European Union*. Aldershot, Ashgate.

Parkinson, M. & Evans, R. (1989) 'Urban Development Corporations'. In Campbell, M. (ed.) *Local Economic Policy*. London, Cassell.

Parkinson, M. & Harding, A. (1993) 'European Cities Towards 2000: Problems and Prospects'. *Polarisation and Urban Space*. Cross National Research Papers. Third Series, 13–22.

Parkinson, M. & Russell, H. (1994) *Economic Attractivenss and Social Exclusion: The Case of Liverpool*. Liverpool, John Moores University, European Institute for Urban Affairs.

Pascual i Esteve, J.-M. (1999) *La Estrategia de las Ciudades*. Barcelona, Diputació de Barcelona.

Paugam, S. (1991) *La Disqualification Sociale*. Paris, Presses Universitaires de France.

Paulus, S. (2000) 'URBAN': A Critical Case Study of the Formulation and Operationalisation of a Community Initiative*. London School of Economics, PhD Thesis.

Peraldi, M. (2001) 'La Métropole Déchue (Belsunce Breakdown)'. In Donzel, A. (ed.) *Métropolisation, Gouvernance et Citoyenneté dans la Région Urbaine Marseillais*. Paris, Maisonneuve et Larose.

Pescaglia, C. & Seassaro, L. (1995) *Il Mercato Abitativo Ligure Attorno alla Meta degli Anni 1990*. Genoa, ILRES, Report No. 42.

Petsimeris, P. (1998) 'Urban Decline and the New Social and Ethnic Divisions in the Core Cities of the Italian Industrial Triangle'. *Urban Studies*. Vol. 35, 449–465.

Pfadt, A. (1996) *Zwanzig Jahre Stadterneuerung in St George*. Hamburg, STEG.

Pfadt, A. (2000) *Aufwertung in St Georg: Folge der Sanierung?* Hamburg, ASK (unpublished).

Pfotenhauer, E. (2000) 'Stadterneuerung-Sanierung'. In Häußermann, H. (ed.) *Großstadt: Soziologische Stichworte*. Opladen, Leske & Budrich.

Piaggio, F. (1997) *Requalificazione Urbana di un Tessuto Storico: Modalità di Intervento per il Caso Genovese*. Genoa, Università degli Studi di Genova, Facoltà di Architettura, Dottorato di Ricerca in Recupero Edilizio ed Ambientale.

Pindado Sánchez, F. (2000) *La Participación Ciudadana en la Vida de las Ciudades*. Barcelona, Eds. del Serbal.

Pinson, D. & Bekkar, R. (1999) 'Urban Renewal, Ethnicity and Social Exclusion in France'. In Khakee, A., Somma, P. & Thomas, H. (eds) *Urban Renewal, Ethnicity and Social Exclusion in Europe*. Aldershot, Ashgate.

Pitts, J. (1998) 'The French Social Prevention Initiative'. In Marlow, A. & Pitts, J. (eds) *Planning Safer Communities*. Lyme Regis, Russell House Publishing.

Pla Estratègic (2000) *Diez Años de Planificación Estratégica en Barcelona: 1988–98*. Barcelona, Pla Estratègic de Barcelona.

Poal, G. (1989) *El Pla Integral de Roguetes: Un Impuls per un Barri*. Barcelona, Ajuntament de Barcelona.

Podzuweit, U. (1994) 'Die Soziale Frage als Herausforderung städtscher Politik'. In Fachhochschule Hamburg: Fachbereich Sozialpädagogik (ed.) *Standpunkt: Sozial – Stadtentwicklung und soziale Politik*. No. 1.

Podzuweit, U., Schütte, W. & Swierkta, N. (1992) *Sozialatlas – Datenbuch Hamburg*. Hamburg. Fachhochschule Hamburg, Fachbereich Sozialpädagogik.

POI (1998) *Programma Organico d'Intervento dei Giustiniani*. Genoa, Commune di Genova.

Pol, F. (1989) 'Le Politiche di Recupero dei Centri Storici nella Spagna degli anni Ottanta'. *Urbanistica*. No. 94, 53–71.

Pomrehn, W. (1998) 'Wirtschaftspolitik zurückholen'. In Alisch, M. (ed.) *Stadtteilmanagement; Voraussetzungen und Chancen für die soziale Stadt*. Opladen, Leske & Budrich.

Potts, G. (2002) 'Competitiveness and the Social Fabric: Links and Tensions in Cities'. In Begg, I. (ed.) *Urban Competitiveness: Policies for Dynamic Cities*. Bristol, Polity Press.

Potz, P. (1998) 'Sostenibilità Urbana'. *Jahrbuch Stadterneuerung 1998*. Berlin, Technische Universität Berlin.

Power, A. (1997) *Estates on the Edge: The Social Consequences of Mass Housing in Northern Europe*. New York, St Martin's Press.

Power, A. (2000) *Poor Areas and Social Exclusion*. London, London School of Economics, Centre for Analysis of Social Exclusion. CASEpaper No. 35.

Pressestelle (2000) *Für den Ottensener Spritzenplatz wird keine soziale Erhaltungsverordnung erlassen*. Freie und Hansestadt Hamburg, 9 May.

Preteceille, E. (2000) 'Segregation, Class and Politics in Large Cities'. In Bagnasco, A. & Le Galès, P. (eds) *Cities in Contemporary Europe*. Cambridge, Cambridge University Press.

Prevenció (1989) Special Edition on Urban Security in Barcelona. *Prevenció*. No. 3.

Priemus, H., Kleinman, M., Maclennan, D. & Turner, B. (1994) 'Maastricht Treaty: Consequences for National Housing Policies'. *Housing Studies*. Vol. 9, 163–182.

Princes Park Health Centre (1991) *Public Health Nurse Project*. Proceedings of Meeting, 30 October.

Priore, M. & Marcaccini, G. (1989) *Relazione Progetto Inserimento Lavorativo: Anno 1989*. Genoa, Regione Liguria: Coordinamento Inserimento Lavorativo Minori in Difficultá.

PROCIVESA (1989) 'Revitalització Urbana, Economica i Social'. *Primeres Jornades Ciutat Vella*. Barcelona, 6–10 November.

PROCIVESA (1991) 'Revitalització Urbana i Economica'. *Segones Jornades Ciutat Vella*. Barcelona, 2–4 December.

Prono, M. (1989) *La Production des Catégories de Pauvreté en Situation d'Interaction*. Marseilles, École des Hautes Études en Sciences Sociales.

PRUSST (1999) *Programma di Riqualificazione urbana e Sviluppo Sostenible del Territorio*. Genoa, Commune di Genova.

PSS (1994) *PSS Yearbook: 1993–94*. Liverpool, Personal Social Services.

PSS (1995) *PSS Yearbook: 1994–95*. Liverpool, Personal Social Services.

Public Health Sector (2000) *Ethnicity Profiling in Primary Care: The Princes Park Health Centre Model*. Liverpool, John Moores University, School of Health and Human Sciences.

Pullen, D., Hatton, D., Jackson, K., Maher, C. & Murphy, E. (1975) *Towards a Realistic Community Development Plan*. Liverpool, City Council, Community Development Committee.

Punter, L. (1981) *The Inner City and Local Government in Western Europe*. Reading, College of Estate Management, CALUS Research Report.

Purdue, D. (2001) 'Neighbourhood Governance: Leadership, Trust and Social Capital'. *Urban Studies*. Vol. 38, 2211–2224.

Quartiersnachrichten (2001) 'Kein Crack'. *Quartiersnachrichten*. No. 26, p. 8. Hamburg, STEG.

Radtke, F.-O. (2003) 'Lokales Bildungs- und Integrationsmanagement'. *Soziale Stadt: Info 12*. 9–10.

Ramon, S. & Giannichedda, M.-G. (eds) (1991) *Psychiatry in Transition: The British and Italian Experiences*. London, Pluto Press. 2nd Edition.

Ratcliffe, P. (1997) '"Race", Housing and the City'. In Jewson, N. & MacGregor, S. (eds) *Transforming Cities: Contested Governance and New Spatial Divisions*. London, Routledge.

Raventós, F. (2000) *La Col.laboració Publicoprivada*. Barcelona, Aula.

Recasens i Brunet, A. (2001) 'Politiques de Sécurité et Prévention dans l'Espagne des Années 1990'. *Déviance et Societé*. Vol. 25, 479–497.

Redempteur, N. (1987) 'Faut-il Venfdre Marseille?' *Avis de Recherche*. No. 11, p. 31.

Rex, J. (1984) 'Disadvantage and Discrimination in Cities'. In Benyon, J. (ed.) *Scarman and After*. Oxford, Pergamon.

Rhodes, R. (1997) *Understanding Governance: Policy Networks, Governance, Reflexivity and Accountability*. Buckingham, Open University Press.

Rhodes, R., Bache, I. & George, S. (1996) 'Policy Networks and Policy Making in the EU: A Critical Appraisal'. In Hooghe, L. (ed.) *Cohesion Policy and European Integration*. Oxford, Clarendon.

Ricci, M. (1999) 'PRUSST: al di là dei Programmi di Riqualificazione Urbana'. In Contardi, L., Moscato, M. & Ricci, M. (eds) *Programmi di Riqualificazione Urbana: Azioni di Programmazione Integrata nell Città Italiane*. Rome, Ed INU.

Richardson, L. & Hills, J. (eds) (2000) *View of the National Strategy for Neighbourhood Renewal*. London School of Economics, Centre for Analysis of Social Exclusion.

Rieper, A. (1992) *Stadtische soziale Bewegungen als Reaktion auf Stadtentwicklungsplanung und Stadtteilveränderung*. University of Hamburg, Diploma Dissertation.

Riez, U. (2000) 'Schwerpunkte der Hamburger Arbeitsmarktpolitik vor dem Hintergrund der Sozialen Stadtteilentwicklung'. *Sozialhilfe Report*. No. 17, 9–11. Hamburg, Behörde für Arbeit, Gesundheit und Soziales.

Ripol-Millet, A. (1994) *Revitalisation of the Ciutat Vella, Barcelona*. Barcelona, Ajuntament de Barcelona.

Riverside Housing (1999) *Annual Report*. Liverpool, Riverside Housing Association.

Robson, B. (1988) *Those Inner Cities: Reconciling the Economic and Social Aims of Urban Policy*. Oxford, Clarendon.

Robson, B., Harrison, E. Parkinson, M., Evans, P., Garside, A., Harding, A. & Robinson, F. (1994) *Assessing the Impact of Urban Policy*. London, Department of the Environment.

Robson, B., Parkinson, M., Boddy, M. & Maclennan, D. (2000) *The State of English Cities*. London, Department of the Environment, Transport and the Regions.

Roca, J. (1988) 'El Planeamiento Municipal y la Recuperación de la Ciudad Historica'. *Estudios Territoriales*. Vol. 27, 119–140.

Rodgers, G. (1995) 'The Design of Policy against Exclusion'. In Rodgers, G., Gore, C. & Figueiredo, J. (eds) *Social Exclusion: Rhetoric, Reality, Responses*. Geneva, International Labour Organisation.

Rodríguez, J. (1990) 'La Política de Vivienda en España: Una Aproximación a los Principales Instrumentos. In Borja, J., Castells, M. Dorado, R. & Quintana, I. (eds) *Las Grandes Ciudades en la Decada de los Noventa*. Madrid, Ed. Sistema.

Rodríguez, J. & Lemkow, L. (1990) 'Health and Social Inequities in Spain'. *Social Science and Medicine*. Vol. 31, 351–358.

Romani i Alfonso, O. (1989) 'El Proceso de Modernisación, Cultural Juvenil y Drogas'. In Rodríguez Gonzalez, F. (ed.) *Comunicación y Lenguaje Juvenil*. Alicante, Instituto de Estudios Juan Gil-Albertmadrid, Fundamentos.

Röseler, S. & Vogel, D. (1993) *Illegale Zuwanderer: ein Problem für die Sozialpolitik*. Bremen, Zentrum für Sozialpolitik Arbeitspapier No. 1.

Roth, R. (2000) 'New Social Movements, Poor People's Movements and the Struggle for Social Citizenship'. In Hamel, P., Lustiger-Thaler, H. & Mayer, M. (eds) *Urban Movements in a Globalising World*. London, Routledge.

Roulleau-Berger, L. (1997) 'De La Socialisation des Jeunes en Situation Précaire: Le Cas des Espaces Intermédiaires à Lyon et à Marseille'. In Martens, A. & Vervaeke, M. (eds) *La Polarisation Sociale des Villes Européennes*. Paris, Anthropos.

Ruben, S. (1990) 'The Implications for Drug Dependency Clinics'. In Henderson, S. (ed.) *Women, HIV, Drugs: Practical Issues*. London, Institute for the Study of Drug Dependence.

Russell, H. (1997) *Liverpool City Challenge: Final Evaluative Report*. Liverpool, European Institute for Urban Affairs, John Moores University.

Russell, H. (2001) *Local Strategic Partnerships: Lessons from New Commitment to Regeneration*. Bristol, Policy Press.

Russo, R. (1993) 'La Valorizzazione del Centro Storico di Genova'. *Urbanistica: AL*. No. 29, 6–11.

Sabaté, J. & Aragay, J. M. (1995) *La Delinqüència a Ciutat Vella: Realitat I por: Dotze Anys d'Enquestes de Victimització 1984–1995*. Barcelona, Institut d'Estudis Metropolitans de Barcelona.

Sabaté, J., Aragay, J. M. & Torrelles, E. (1999) *Delinqüència I Seguritat a Ciutat Vella*. Barcelona, Institut d'Estudis Metropolitans de Barcelona.

Sabaté, J., Aragay, J. M. & Torrelles, E. (2001) *Delinqüència I Seguritat l'Any 2000 (Primers Resultats)*. Barcelona, Institut d'Estudis Metropolitans de Barcelona.

Safer Merseyside Partnership (1994) *Safer Merseyside Partnership Programme 1995–2002*. London, Safer Merseyside Partnership.

Sallez, A. (1998) 'France'. In Van den Berg, L., Braun, E. & van der Meer (eds) *National Urban Policies in the European Union*. Aldershot, Ashgate.

Sanmarco, P. & Morel, B. (1985) *Marseille: L'Endroit du Décor*. Aix, Edisud.

Sarfati, H. (2002) 'Labour Market and Social Protection Policies: Linkages and Inter-actions'. In Sarfati, H. & Bonoli, G. (eds) *Labour Market and Social Protection Reforms in International Perspective*. Aldershot, Ashgate.

Sauter, M. (2001) 'Verstetigung- aber wie?. Integrierte Stadtteilentwicklung zwischen Sonderprojekt und Regelaufgabe der kommunalen Verwaltung'. *Jahrbuch Stadterneuerung 2001*. Berlin, Technische Universität.

Schmid, G. (2002) 'Employment Systems in Transition: Explaining Performance Differentials of Post-Industrial Economies'. In Schmid, G. & Gazier, B. (eds) *The Dynamics of Full Employment*. Cheltenham, Edward Elgar.

Schmid, G., Speckesser, S. & Hilbert, C. (2001) 'Does Active Labour Market Policy Matter? An Aggregate Impact Analysis for Germany'. In de Koning, J. & Mosley, H. (eds) *Labour Market Policy and Unemployment*. Cheltenham, Edward Elgar.

Schmid, J. & Roth, C. (2000) 'European Labour Market Policy and National Regimes of Implementation'. In Klemmer, P. & Wink, R. (eds) *Preventing Unemployment in Europe*. Cheltenham, Edward Elgar.

Schmid-Hopfner, S. (1988) 'Gesundheitsindikator untergewichtiger Lebendgeborenen: zeitliche Entwicklung und räumliche Verteilung in Hamburg'. *Hamburg in Zahlen*. No. 7.

Schmitz, L. (2001) 'Quartiersentwicklungskonzepte in Hamburg'. *Soziale Stadt: Info 6*. 10–12.

Schömann, K. (2002) 'Training Transitions in the EU: Different Policies but Similar Effects?' In Schömann, K. & O'Connell, P. (eds) *Education, Training and Employment Dynamics*. Cheltenham, Edward Elgar.

Schömann, K. & Becker, R. (2002) 'A Long Term Perspective on the Effects of Training in Germany'. In Schömann, K. & O'Connell, P. (eds) *Education, Training and Employment Dynamics*. Cheltenham, Edward Elgar.

Schubert, D. (1990) 'Gretchenfrage Hafenstrasse – Wohngruppeprojekte in Hamburg'. *Forschungsjournal Neue soziale Bewegungen*. 3–10 April.

Schubert, D. (1993) 'Soziale Grossstadtstrategie in Hamburg: neue Planungstruktur oder intelligenteres Krisenmanagement'. *Jahrbuch Wohnpolitische Innovationen*. Darmstadt, VWP.

Schubert, D. (1994) '"Soziale Brennpunkte" und "vernachlässigte Gebiete" – Mit einer "Sozialen Grossstadtstrategie" zur neuen Planungskultur?' In Fachhochschule Hamburg: Fachbereich Sozialpädagogik (ed.) *Standpunkt: Sozial – Stadtentwicklung und soziale Politik*. No. 1.

Schubert, D. (1998a) 'Vom Stanierenden Wiederaufbau zur Nachhaltigen Stadterneuerung: Kontinuitäten und Paradigmenwechsel'. *Jahrbuch Stadterneuerung 1998*. Berlin, Technische Universität Berlin.

Schubert, D. (1998b) 'Revitalización de Zonas Portuarias y Ribereñas de Hamburgo: Realidad, Proyectos, Visiones'. *Ciudad y Territorio*. Vol. 30, 65–84.

Schubert, D. & Harms, H. (1993a) 'Schickimickies oder Sozialmieter: Wohnen am Hafen in den 90er Jahren – zwischen Aufwertung, Verdrängung und Vernachlässigung'. In Schubert, D. & Harms, H. (eds) *Wohnen am Hafen*. Hamburg, VSA Verlag.

Schubert, D. & Harms, H. (1993b) 'Von der Hafenstadt zum Dienstleistungszentrum mit Zukunft'. In Schubert, D. & Harms, H. (eds) *Wohnen am Hafen*. Hamburg, VSA Verlag.

Schütte, W. (1993) *Soziale Grossstadt: Strategien in Hamburg*. Hamburg, Fachhochschule Hamburg, Fachbereich Sozialpädogik.

Schütte, W. (1994) 'Armutsentwicklung und Stadtentwicklung in Hamburg'. *Standpunkt*. No. 1, 1–7.

Schwarz, J. (1999) 'Gründe für einen Perspecktivenwechsel'. *Jahrbuch Stadterneuerung 1999*. Berlin, Technische Universität Berlin.

Scott, G., Campbell, J. & Brown, U. (2002) 'Child Care, Social Inclusion and Urban Regeneration'. *Critical Social Policy*. Vol. 22, 226–246.

Seassaro, L. (1991) 'Genoa between Relaunch and Decline: The Hope for Reindustrialisation and the Redevelopers Role'. *Housing Policy as a Strategy for Change*. Conference, Oslo, 24–27 June.

Seassaro, L. (1993) 'Politiche Della Casa Tra Istanze Sociali ed Economiche'. *Recuperare*. No. 8, 642–648.

Seassaro, L. (1995) 'Nature, History, Culture as Active Factors in Urban Change: Long-Term Evolution and Recent Changes in the Housing System of the Genoa Metropolitan Area'. In Padovani, L. (ed.) *Urban Change and Housing Policies: Evidence from Four European Countries*. Venice, Daest Collana Ricerche.

Seassaro, L. (1999) 'Al di là della Riqualificazione Urbana: Piani ma anche Programmi e Interventi di Area Vasta'. In Contardi, L., Moscato, M. & Ricci, M. (eds) *Programmi di Riqualificazione Urbana: Azioni di Programmazione Integrata nell Città Italiane*. Rome, INU Ed.

Seassaro, L. (2000) 'La Ragionevole Aspirazione a Mettere a Sistema Piani, programmi e Azioni secondo una Visione di Medio Termine'. *Urbanistica a Genova: Nuovi Piani, Nuove Politiche: Urbanistica Dossier 28*. Supplement to *Urbanistica Informazioni*. No. 169.

Seassaro, L. & Pescaglia, C. (1993) *Il Fabbisogno Abitativo 1992–7 a Genov: Elementi di Stima per il Dimensionamento del PPP*. Genova, ILRES Report No. 37.

Seassaro, L. & Sola, G. (1992) *Il Sistema Abitativo nella Area Metropolitana Genovese*. Genoa, Banca Carige.

Segnalini, O. (1997) 'I Programmi di Riqualificazione Urbana delle Grandi Città'. In Latini, A. P. (ed.) *Programmi di Riqualificazione Urbana*. Rome, INU Edizioni.

Serra, N. & Maragall, P. (1990) *Barcelona: La Ciutat i el 1992*. Barcelona, Institut Municipal de Promoció Urbanistica.

Serra, P. (1989) *Jornades Ciutat Vella: Las Actuaciones sobre Ciutat Vella – El Programa ARI*. Barcelona, Ajuntament de Barcelona.

Serra, P. & Gausa, M. (1995) 'Ciutat Historica versus Ciutat Nova'. *Jornades Ciudad Vella: 1995*. Barcelona, Ajuntament de Barcelona, Area de Rehabilitació Integrada. Seminar Paper.

Sharples, J. (1991) *Report of the Chief Constable for the Year 1990*. Liverpool, Merseyside Police Authority.

Shennan, P. (1994) 'What a Waste'. *Liverpool Echo*. 4 September, p. 1.

Silverman, E. & Della-Giustina, J.-A. (2001) 'Urban Policing and the Fear of Crime'. *Urban Studies*. Vol. 38, 941–957.

Simey, M. (1988) *Democracy Rediscovered: A Study of Police Accountability*. London, Pluto.

Simmons, J. & Dodd, T. (eds) (2003) *Crime in England and Wales: 2002/3*. Home Office Statistical Bulletin 07/03. London, Home Office.

Sinounet, R. (1988) 'Le Nouveau Visage de Marseille'. *Le Moniteur des Travaux Publics et du Bâtiment*. 9 September, p. 4.

Skifter Andersen, H. (1999) 'Housing Rehabilitation and Urban Renewal in Europe: A Cross-National Analysis of Problems and Policies'. In Skifter Andersen, H. & Leather, P. (eds) *Housing Renewal in Europe*. Bristol, Policy Press.

Skifter Andersen, H. (2002) 'Can Deprived Housing Areas be Revitalised? Efforts against Segregation and Neighbourhood Decay in Denmark and Europe'. *Urban Studies*. Vol. 39, No. 4, 767–790.

250   *Bibliography*

Skifter Andersen, H. (2003) *Urban Sores: On the Interaction between Segregation, Urban Decay and Deprived Neighbourhoods*. Aldershot, Ashgate.

Smith, G. (1999) *Area-Based Initiatives: The Rationale and Options for Area Targeting*. London, London School of Economics, Centre for Analysis of Social Exclusion. CASEpaper No. 25.

Smith, N. (1986) 'Gentrification, the Frontier, and the Restructuring of Urban Space'. In Smith, N. & Williams, P. (eds) *Gentrification of the City*. Boston, Allen & Unwin.

Soho, M. (ed.) (1990) *Kein Ort für Ausländige Leute: St Georg – ein Lebenswerter Stadtteil*. Hamburg, VSA Verlag.

Sole, C. (1987) *Ells Treballadors Immigrants a Catalunya*. Barcelona, Centre d'Informació per a Treballadors Estrangers.

Soler, J., Sampere, E. & Ferrando, P. (1987) *Un Sistema de Indicadors Socials per a la Ciutat de Barcelona*. Barcelona, Ajuntament de Barcelona, Àrea de Serveis Socials.

SOMICA (1985) *Marseille: La Fonction Économique du Quartier Belsunce. Synthese*. Marseilles, SOMICA.

Somma, P. (1999) 'Ethnic Minorities, Urban Renewal and Social Exclusion in Italy'. In Khakee, A., Somma, P. & Thomas, H. (eds) *Urban Renewal, Ethnicity and Social Exclusion in Europe*. Aldershot, Ashgate.

Soziale Stadt (2003) Editorial. *Soziale Stadt: Info 12*. 1–2.

Sparkes, J. (1999) *Schools, Education and Social Exclusion*. London School of Economics, CASEbrief 12.

SPD (1992) *Konzept Soziale Brennpunkte*. Hamburg, SPD-Fraktion der Hamburgishcen Burgerschaft.

Stadtdialog (2001) *Stadtdialog Hamburg*. No. 13.

Stanghellini, S. (2000) 'Community Programmes and Town Planning'. In Campagna, L. & Ricci, M. (eds) *Programma Urban-Italia: Europa, Nuove Politiche Urbane*. Rome, Ed INU.

STEB (1999) *Soziale Stadtteilentwicklung: Das programm*. Hamburg, Stadtentwickungsbehörde.

STEB (2000a) *Perlenkette: Hamburgs Hafenrand*. Hamburg, Stadtentwickungsbehörde.

STEB (2000b) *Im Stadtteil Arbeiten: Beschäftigungswirkungen wohnungsnaher Betriebe*. Hamburg, Stadtentwickungsbehörde.

STEG (1993) *Stadterneuerung in Osterkirchenviertel*. Hamburg, Stadtentwicklungsgesellschaft.

STEG (1994) *Sanierungsblatt: Karolinenviertel. No. 5*. Hamburg, Stadtentwicklungsgesellschaft.

Stegmann, M. (1976) *Wem die Stadt gehört: Stadtplanung und Stadtentwicklung in Hamburg, 1965–1975*. Hamburg, Verlag Association.

Stewart, M. (1995) 'Public Expenditure Management in Urban Regeneration'. In Hambleton, R. & Thomas, H. (eds) *Urban Policy Evaluation: Challenge and Change*. London, Paul Chapman.

Stoker, G. & Mossberger, K. (1994) 'Urban Regime Theory in Comparative Perspective'. *Environment and Planning C: Government and Policy*. Vol. 12, 195–212.

Stratmann, B. (1999) *Stadtentwicklung in globalen Zeiten*. Basel, Birkhäuser.

Streff, N. (1989) *L'Operation 'Developpement Sociale' du Quartier Belsunce, 1984–5*. Marseille, DRASS.

Subirós, P. (1999) *Estratégies Culturals I Renovació Urbana*. Barcelona, Aula.

Süss, W. & Trojan, A. (1992) *Armut in Hamburg*. Hamburg, VSA Verlag.

Swyngedouw, E. (1992) 'The Mamon Quest: Glocalisation, Interspatial Competition and the Monetary Order: The Construction of New Scales'. In Dunford, M. & Kafkalas, G. (eds) *Cities and Regions in the New Europe*. London, Bellhaven.

Taboada, R. (1991) 'La Necessitat d'un Habitatge Popular'. *Ciutat Vella*. No. 5, 1–9.

Taylor, M. (2000) *Top Down Meets Bottom Up: Neighbourhood Management*. London, Joseph Rowntree Foundation.

Taylor, M. (2002) 'Is Partnership Possible? Searching for a New Institutional Settlement'. In Cars, G., Healey, P., Madanipour, A. & de Magalhäes, C. (eds) *Urban Governance, Institutional Capacity and Social Milieux*. Aldershot, Ashgate.

Tengeler, S. (2001) 'Soziale Stadt – meine Sicht'. *Soziale Stadt: Info 6*. 18.

Thomas, C. & Bromley, R. (2000) 'City Centre Revitalisation: Problems of Fragmentation and Fear in the Evening and Night-time City'. *Urban Studies*. Vol. 37, 1403–1429.

Thomas, M. & Lodge, G. (2000) *Radicals and Reformers: A Century of Fabian Thought*. London, Fabian Society.

Thornley, A. (1991) *Urban Planning Under Thatcherism: The Challenge of the Market*. London, Routledge.

Tizot, J.-Y. (2001) 'The Issues of Translation, Transferability and Transfer of Social Policies: French and British "Urban Social Policy": Finding Common Ground for Comparison'. *International Journal of Social Research Methodology*. Vol. 4, 301–317.

Tomann, H. (1990) 'The Housing Market, Housing Finance and Housing Policy in West Germany: Prospects for the 1990s'. *Urban Studies*. Vol. 27, 919–930.

Torkington, N. (1983) *The Racial Politics of Health: A Liverpool Profile*. Liverpool, Merseyside Area Profile Group.

Torkington, N. (1991) *Black Health: A Political Issue*. Liverpool, Catholic Association for Racial Justice and Liverpool Institute of Higher Education.

Torres i Carol, J. (1988) 'Una Politica de Seguretat Ciutadana'. *Prevenció*. No. 1, 5–11.

Torti, M.-T. (1992) *Stranieri in Liguria*. Genoa, Ed. Marietti.

Tosi, A. (2000) 'Urban and Social Policies'. In Campagna, L. & Ricci, M. (2000) *Programma Urban-Italia: Europa, Nuove Politiche Urbane*. Rome, Ed INU.

Tricart, J.-P. (1991) 'Neighbourhood Social Development Policy in France'. In Alterman, R. & Cars, G. (eds) *Neighbourhood Regeneration: An International Evaluation*. London, Mansell.

Trojan, A., Stumm, B. & Suss, W. (1993) *Gesundheitsförderung und Bürgerbeteiligung im Rahmen ökologischer Stadterneuerung*. Hamburg, University of Hamburg, Institut für Medezin-Soziologie.

Tudor Hart, J. (1971) 'The Inverse Care Law'. *Lancet*. Vol. I, 405–412.

Tulasne, E. (1994) 'Trois Décennies de Planification (1960–1990)'. In Bequart, D. (ed.) *Marseille: 25 Ans de Planification Urbaine*. Marseille, Eds de l'Aube.

Turok, I. & Edge, N. (1999) *The Jobs Gap in Britain's Cities*. London, Joseph Rowntree Foundation.

Turró, C. (1998) 'Los Consejos de Participación'. *Prevenció*. No. 14, 47–52.

Ulbrich, R. & Wullkopf, U. (1993) 'Housing Affordability in the Federal Republic of Germany'. In Hallett, G. (ed.) *The New Housing Shortage: Housing Affordability in Europe and the USA*. London, Routledge.

University of Liverpool (1991) *GranbyToxteth Community Project: Poverty 3*. Liverpool, University Race and Social Policy Unit.

Valls, X. (2001) *Quan l'Habitatge fa Ciutat*. Barcelona, Aula.

Van den Berg, L., Braun, E. & van der Meer, J. (1998) 'Synthesis'. In Van den Berg, L., Braun, E. & van der Meer, J. (eds) *National Urban Policies in the European Union*. Aldershot, Ashgate.

Van Dijk, J., Mayhew, P. & Killias, M. (1990) *Experiences with Crime Across the World: Results of the 1989 International Telephone Survey*. The Hague, Kluwer.

Van Hees, I. (1991) 'The Italian Housing Market: Its Failures and Their Causes'. *Urban Studies*. Vol. 28, 15–39.

Van Parijs, P. (1986) 'A Revolution in Class Theory'. *Politics and Society*. Vol. 15, 453–482.
Van Weesep, J. & Musterd, S. (eds) (1991) *Urban housing for the Better Off: Gentrification in Europe*. Utrecht, Stedelijke Netwerken.
Vieillard-Baron, H. (1990) Le Ghetto: Un Lieu Commun Impropre et Banal. *Les Annals de la Recherche Urbaine*. No. 49, 13–22.
Villalbi, J., Guarga, A., Pasarin, M., Gil, M., Borrell, C., Ferran, M. & Cirera, E. (1999) 'Evaluación del Impacto de la Reforma de la Atención Primaria sobre la Salud'. *Attención Primaria*. Vol. 24, 62–76.
Ville de Marseille (1985) *Le Rehabilitation du Panier: Histoires et Procedures*. Marseilles, Directorat de l'Habitat.
Ville de Marseille (1989) *Contrat de Plan État-Région: 1989–1993*. Marseilles, City Council.
Ville de Marseille (1990a) *OPAH Canebière – Étude du Quartier Belsunce*. Marseilles, City Council.
Ville de Marseille (1990b) *Contrat de Plan État-Région, 1989–93: Programme d'Aménagement Concerté*. Marseilles, City Council.
Ville de Marseille (1990c) *Contrat de Plan État-Région, 1989–93: Programme d'Action*. Marseilles, City Council.
Ville de Marseille (1990d) *Conseil Communal de Prévention de la Délinquance: Assemblée Plénière*. Marseilles, City Council, 10 December.
Ville de Marseille (1993) *Le PACT Politique Urbaine En Chiffres*. Marseilles, City Council.
Ville de Marseille (1995) *Belsunce Sainte Barbe – Données Operationelles, Analyse des Actions 1982–7, Evaluation d'un Programme 1988–95*. Marseilles, City Council.
Ville de Marseille (1996) *Projet de Développement de Site Centre Ville*. Marseilles, Direction Général de l'Urbanisme et de l'Habitat.
Ville de Marseille (2000) *Contrat de Plan: Etat/Region Provence-Alpes-Cotes d'Azure: Politique de la Ville: Contrat de Ville – 2000–2006*. Marseilles, City Council.
Vinci, I. (2002) 'Local Governance, Urban Regeneration and Planning Projects in Italy: The Process of Internalisation in the City of Palermo'. Paper presented at The EURA Conference. *Urban and Spatial European Policies: Levels of Territorial Government*. Turin, 18–20 April.
Vintró i Castells, E. (1989) 'Diferentes, pero no al Margen'. *Prevenció*, No. 3, 1–14.
Vintró i Castells, E. (1991a) 'Actituds dels Barcelonins envers els Immigrants Provinents d'altres Cultures'. In Ajuntament de Barcelona (ed.) *Barcelona som Tots: Tolerancia Social*. Barcelona, City Council.
Vintró i Castells, E. (1991b) 'Los Retos de la Politica de Bienestar Social'. *Prevenció*. No. 6, 1–11.
Vize, R. (1994) 'Urban Regeneration Bid faces the Axe'. *Local Government Chronicle*. 9 September, p. 5.
Vobruba, G. (1999) 'The End of the Full Employment Society: Changing the Basis for Inclusion and Exclusion'. In Littlewood, P., Glorieux, I., Herkommer, S. & Jönsson, I. (eds) *Social Exclusion in Europe: Problems and Paradigms*. Aldershot, Ashgate.
Vobruba, G. (2001) *Integration und Erweiterung: Europa im Globalisierungsdilemma*. Vienna, Passagen.
Vogt, A. (1998) 'Partnerschaftliche Stadtteilentiwcklung'. In Alisch, M. (ed.) *Stadtteilmanagement; Voraussetzungen und Chancen für die soziale Stadt*. Opladen: Leske & Budrich.
Von Kietzell, D. (2001) 'Gemeinwesenarbeit und Quartiersmanagement: Beide Dienste sind notwendig für die Entwicklung einer Sozialen Stadt'. *Jahrbuch Stadterneuerung 2001*. Berlin, Technische Universität Berlin.
Von Petz, U. & Schubert, D. (1998) 'Einführung zum Themenschwerpunkt Nachhaltige Stadtentwicklung'. *Jahrbuch Stadterneuerung 1998*. Berlin, Technische Universität Berlin.

Waldorf, B. (1990) 'Housing Policy Impacts on Ethnic Segregation Patterns: Evidence from Düsseldorf, West Germany'. *Urban Studies*. Vol. 27, 637–652.

Walklate, S. (2001) 'Fearful Communities?' *Urban Studies*. Vol. 38, 929–939.

Walton, F. (2000) 'Education and Training'. In Percy-Smith, J. (ed.) *Policy Responses to Social Exclusion: Towards Inclusion?* Buckingham, Open University Press.

Ward, S. (2000) 'Re-examining the International Diffusion of Planning'. In Freestone, R. (ed.) *Urban Planning in a Changing World*. London, Taylor & Francis.

Weck, S. (2000) 'Beschäftigungs- und Wirtschaftsförderung in der integrierten Stadtteilerneuerung'. *Jahrbuch Stadterneuerung 2000*. Berlin, Technische Universität Berlin.

West Everton Community Council (1991) *Housing Forum: Minutes*. 25 November.

White, P. (1984) *The West European City: A Social Geography*. Harlow: Longman.

Williams, C. & Windebank, J. (2000) 'Helping People to Help Themselves: Policy Lessons from a Study of Deprived Urban Neighbourhoods in Southampton'. *Journal of Social Policy*. Vol. 29, 355–373.

Williams, C. & Windebank, J. (2001) *Revitalising Deprived Urban Neighbourhoods*. Aldershot, Ashgate.

Wilson, A., May, T., Warburton, H., Lupton, R. & Turnbull, P. (2002) *Heroine and Crack Cocaine Markets in Deprived Areas: Seven Local Case Studies*. London School of Economics, CASE Report No. 19.

Wilson, J. Q. & Kelling, G. L. (1982) 'Broken Windown'. *Atlantic Monthly*. No. 3, 29–38.

Wilson, W. J. (1987) *The Truly Disadvantaged: The Inner City, the Underclass and Public Policy*. Chicago, University of Chicago Press.

Winchester, H. M. (1993) *Contemporary France*. London, Longman.

Wirtschaftsbehörde (1993) *Die Wirtschaft in Hamburg: Jahresbericht*. City State of Hamburg, Wirtschaftsbehörde.

Wohlert, F. (1991) *Anmerkung zur Ermittlung von sozialen Brennpunkten und Kleinräumingen Sozialplanung*. Hamburg, Behörde für Schule, Jugend und Berufsbildung.

Wohlfahrt, S. (1990) 'Bewohner und Bebauungsstruktur von Grosssiedlungen in Hamburg'. *Hamburg in Zahle*. No. 10.

Wolman, H., Goldsmith, M., Ercole, E. & Kousgaard, P. (1992) 'Fiscal Stress and Central–Local Relations: The Critical Role of Government Grants'. In Mouritzen, P. E. (ed.) *Managing Cities in Austerity: Urban Fiscal Crisis in Ten Western Countries*. London, Sage.

Woods, H. (1989) 'Working with Male Prostitutes in Liverpool'. *Aidslink*. No. 2. March.

Wynne, M. (1984) 'Spain'. In Wynn, M. (ed.) *Planning and Urban Growth in Southern Europe*. London, Mansell.

Young, A. (1995) 'Granby Toxteth Community Project'. In Duffy, K. (ed.) *Partnership and Participation: The Experience of Poverty 3 in the UK*. London, HMSO.

Zint, G. (1984) *Die weiße Taube flog für immer davon: Ein St Pauli-Bilderbuch*. Reinbek, Rowohlt.

6, Perry & Vidal, I. (eds) (1994) *Delivering Welfare*. Barcelona, CIES, 1994.

Index

Alisch, M., 63, 97, 154
Atkinson, R., 37, 192
Avarello, P., 187
Aznar, José-Maria, 32

Ball, M., 54
Ben-Tovim, G., 65, 66
Besio, M., 93
Blair, Tony, 38
  Blairism, 78, 99, 126, 151
  New Labour, 38–41, 105, 106
Body-Gendrot, S., 12, 153
Bohigas, Oriol, 85
Booth, P., 12
Brandt, Willy, 17
Breckner, I. *et al.*, 99
Brown, Gordon, 170

Castells, M., 6
Castles, S., 64
Central government
  France, 83, 110–11
  Germany, 18–20, 94, 97, 99
  Italy, 24–7, 90, 92–4
  Spain, 28, 39–43
  United Kingdom, 33–6, 38–41,
    73–4, 83, 99–105
Chapman, M., 192
Cheshire, P., 44
Chirac, Jacques, 14, 77, 112
Clos, Joan, 75
Conservative Party, 35–8, 100
coordination
  horizontal, 9, 17, 41, 112, 120
  vertical, 8, 42, 72–4, 90–1, 112,
    120, 152
Crawford, A., 152, 153
crime, 142–7
  area-targeted effects, 172–3
  Barcelona, 143
  drug-related, 145–6
  ethnic minorities, 143–5
  general attributes, 142–3
  Genoa, 143

Hamburg, 143–4
Liverpool, 144
Marseilles, 144–5
policing, 147–50; area-targeting,
  150–3; Barcelona, 148–9, 150;
  Genoa, 148; Hamburg, 149, 151;
  Liverpool, 149, 151–2;
  Marseilles, 150, 152–3
prostitution, 147

Dangschat, J., 3, 52, 56, 58, 60, 61,
  62, 63, 76, 97, 168, 169
Dawson, J., 103
de Gaulle, Charles, 10
de Winter, M., 36, 49, 71
Deferre, Gaston, 68, 73, 77, 109
Delors, Jacques, 183
demography, 49–54
Donzel, A., 12, 15, 46, 68, 71, 77,
  108, 109, 110, 111

economy, 45–9
  see also labour markets
education, 138–42
  area targeting effects, 173
  Barcelona, 138–9
  Genoa, 138, 139–40
  Hamburg, 139–40
  Liverpool, 138, 140–1
  Marseilles, 139, 141–2
ethnic minorities, 50, 52, 53, 63,
  64–71, 123, 125, 129
  Africans, 145
  Afro-Carribeans, 65
  Barcelona, 64–5, 66, 69
  Chinese, 66, 120
  Genoa, 65, 67, 69, 70
  Jews, 53
  Liverpool, 65–6, 67–8, 69
  Magrebin, 53, 54, 66, 68, 108, 120,
    139, 144, 146, 165, 166
  Marseilles, 53–4, 62, 66, 68, 70, 108
  pieds noirs, 50, 68, 165
  Romany, 66, 67, 139, 145

Somalis, 66
Spain, 66–7
Turks, 65, 67, 69, 145
European Commission, 23
  White Paper *Growth, Competitiveness and Employment*, 183
European Union, 177–93
  open method of coordination, 187–8, 192
  partnership approach, 180–1
  planning system, 177–8, 179–80
  Quartiers en Crise, 181–2
  sustainability, 179, 183–4, 187, 190
  Territorial Employment Pacts, 26, 188
  Third Poverty Programme, 182
  URBAN Community Initiatives: URBACT, 186–7; URBAN1, 26, 185–6; URBAN2, 186–7, 190–1
  Urban Pilot Projects, 25, 181
  see also structural funds
Evans, R., 190

Far right
  Front National, 14, 16, 68, 70
  other political parties, 70
Ferras, P., 6, 55, 146
Font, J., 159
Franco, Francisco, 28, 29, 86
Friedrichs, J., 75
Froesler, R., 17
Furbey, R., 5
Fusero, P. *et al.*, 198

Gateway cities, 44–9
Gaudin, Jean-Claude, 14, 77, 112
Geddes, M., 197, 201, 202, 204
Glennerster, H., 141, 195
Godard, F., 6
Gomà, R., 62
Gonzalez Felipe, 29, 30, 75
Green, H., 12

Hall, S., 37
Harding, A., 120–1
Harrison, P., 138
Hatton, Derek, 73
health services, 134–8
  area targeting, 136–8
  Barcelona, 136–7, 173
  ethnic minorities, 135, 136

general attributes, 134–6
general effects, 173
Genoa, 137
Hamburg, 137
Liverpool, 137
Marseilles, 137–8
rehabilitation, 166–8
social effects, 168–9
Heseltine, Michael, 73
Hibbitt, K. *et al.*, 185
housing, 54–61, 166–8
  amenity standards, 55–7
  Barcelona, 50–1, 55, 83, 166–7; Barcelona 2000, 88; clientelism, 58
  Bologna, 22
  EU competences, 192
  France: *co-proprieté*, 16, 113; ethnic minorities, 69; general issues, 83–5; *Habitat et Vie Sociale*, 10, 16, 165
  Genoa, 51–2, 55–6, 166–7; clientelism, 60; Porta Sorprana, 92, 160; Prè, 90–1, 160; Vigne, 93, 161
  Germany, 94–8
  Hamburg, 53, 56, 83, 94–5, 167
  Italy, 22–3, 25–6, 90
  Liverpool, 53, 56, 167–8; Urban Regeneration Strategy, 101–2
  Marseilles, 53–4, 56–7, 109–11, 112
  owner-occupation, 57–8
  private-rented, 60
  rehabilitation outcomes, 166–8
  shanty towns, 55, 66, 69, 166, 167
  social housing, 58–60
  Spain, 28–32, 88; Boyer Act, 30; Caritas, 28, 30, 133; Franco Rent Act, 30; United Kingdom, 33–6, 104–7
Hutchinson, J., 106

inner cities
  administrative reforms, 200–1
  Barcelona, 50
  conceptual and functional equivalence, 3
  general attributes, 3–7, 49–50, 199–200
  Genoa, 51–2
  Hamburg, 52–3
  housing, 54–61

inner cities (*Continued*)
Liverpool, 53
Marseilles, 53–4
national variation, 200

Jessop, B., 205
Jodogne, S., 9, 21, 71
Johnson, N., 150
joined-up-government, 19, 40, 98
Judd, D., 75

Keating, M., 12, 17, 178
Keith, M., 3
Kellas, J., 179
Kleinman, M., 178, 180
Klose, Hans-Ulrich, 76, 95
Kohl, Helmut, 18
Kuhlmann, M., 20
Kunze, R., 17

labour markets
Barcelona, 48, 118, 123–4, 171
ethnic minorities, 118–20
France: *régies des quartiers*, 130–1;
zones franches, 172
general attributes, 45, 99, 106–7,
116–18, 120, 123
Genoa, 48–9, 118, 124–5
Germany, 125–8; Alliance for Jobs,
19, 126
Hamburg, 46, 48, 119, 126–8
Liverpool, 47–8, 104, 119, 128,
129–30, 172
Marseilles, 49, 113, 120, 131–2, 171
regeneration of, 169–72
Spain, 123
unemployment, 62–4, 169–72
United Kingdom, 128–9;
Enterprise Zones, 172
Labour Party, 33, 78
Lang, M., 18
Latini, A. P., 24
Lawless, P., 34, 100, 129
Le Galès, P., 8, 202
Lee, P., 61, 169
Leroy, M., 12
Liberal Democratic Party, 78
local and regional government
Barcelona, 29, 45–6
ethnic minorities, 71

France, 10–11, 12, 68, 77
general attributes, 9, 202–3
Genoa, 77–8, 89–90
Germany, 17, 21
Hamburg, 18, 20, 76–7, 94–6
Italy, 23–4, 26
Liverpool, 99–100; Militant,
73, 78, 101–2
Marseilles, 109–11; clientelism, 77
Spain, 29, 75–6, 83, 85–9
United Kingdom, 38, 67–8, 78, 100–6

MacGregor, S., 198
Maclennan, D., 54
Major, John, 36
Maragall, Pasqual, 58, 72, 75, 86,
123, 159
Marshall, T., 87
Mawson, J., 37
Mayer, M., 8
Mény, Y., 11
migration, internal, 21
Barcelona, 21, 49–50
Genoa, 21, 52
Marseilles, 50
Miguet, A., 71
Miller, M., 64
Minford, Patrick, 185
Mitterand, François, 7, 11, 73,
109, 110, 141
Moon, G., 37
Moore, R., 8, 35
Musterd, S., 36, 49, 71

Nel.lo, O., 62
Nevin, B., 61, 169
new public management, 40, 76,
98, 120
Newburn, T., 150

Ossenbrügge, J., 3, 60, 62, 168

Pareja, M. I., 32
Parkinson, M., 8, 13, 16, 36, 38,
40, 47, 49, 65, 71, 75, 78,
103, 120–1, 135, 172, 204
participation, community, 157–66, 203
Centre-Ville, 165–6
Centro Storico, 160–1
Ciutat Vella, 158–9

Innenstadt, 161-3
Inner city Liverpool, 163-5
partnerships, 156-66, 202-4
    Barcelona, 158-9
    EU approaches, 180-1
    Genoa, 160-1
    Hamburg, 161-3
    Liverpool, 163-5
    local, 203-4
    Marseilles, 165-6
    regeneration policies, 205
    see also coordination
Paugam, S., 62
Pentopartitito, 78
Pericu, Giuseppe, 78, 125
Pfadt, A., 169
Pfotenhauer, E., 17, 18, 19
Piachaud, D., 178
Pol, F., 29
Pomrehn, W., 172
Power, A., 198
Priemus, H. *et al*., 192
Pujol, Jordi, 72, 86
Punter, L., 10, 23

Ratcliffe, P., 69
Raventós, F., 159
regeneration policies, 3-43,
    83-115, 116-53
    administration, 157-8
    Agenda 21, 19, 184
    Barcelona, 51, 72-3, 75, 85-9
    convergence, 206-7
    displacement effects, 6, 17-18,
        19, 30-1, 50, 89, 109, 197-8
    European Union, 177-93
    evaluation, 154-74
    France, 10-17, 107-14; *Banlieu 89*,
        11; *Contrats de Ville*, 11, 13-17, 77,
        109-13, 130, 131, 134, 138, 142,
        153, 165-6, 171, 186; *Demain la
        Ville*, 15; *Développement Social des
        Quartiers*, 7, 11, 12; *Développement
        Social Urbain*, 12; *Grands Projets
        de Ville*, 15; *Grands Projets Urbains*,
        8, 13; *Habitat et Vie Sociale*, 10,
        16, 165; *Loi sur la Solidarité et le
        Renouvellement Urbain*, 15; *Zones
        Urbaines Sensibles*, 16
    funding, 154-6

general evolution, 5-6, 7-41, 44, 84,
    114, 116, 174, 194-9, 204-6
    Genoa, 46-7, 51-2, 77, 89-94
    gentrification, 161, 163, 168-9, 198-9
    Germany, 17-21, 94-9; *Soziale Stadt*, 19,
        126; *Stadtbauförderungsgesetz*, 17
    Hamburg, 18, 52, 94-9
    Italy, 21-8, 89-94; Complex
        Programmes, 24; Integrated
        Programmes, 24; Neighbourhood
        Contracts, 26; PRUs, 25; PRUSST
        Programmes, 26
    Liverpool, 34, 100-7; Marseilles,
        107-14; regeneration regimes,
        204-6; Rio Summit, 19, 184;
        Spain, 28-33
    local governance, 74-8
    United Kingdom, 33-41, 99-107; City
        Challenge, 18, 36-8, 103-4, 128,
        152; City Grant, 34, 35; National
        Strategy for Neighbourhood
        Renewal, 40; New Commitment
        to Regeneration, 39; New Deal
        for Communities, 38-9; Single
        Programme Budget, 39-40; Single
        Regeneration Budget, 37-9; Urban
        Development Corporations, 8, 34;
        Urban Programme, 33, 36; Urban
        Regeneration Companies, 39;
        Urban White Paper, 39-40
Revenu Minimum d'Insertion, 11, 62, 130
Ricci, M., 27, 187
Riots, 8, 12, 33-4, 67, 100
    Scarman Report, 8
Robson, B., 34, 172
Roca, J., 85
Rodriguez, J., 30
Rogers, A., 3
Rosetti, N., 62
Runde, Ortwin, 77
Russell, H., 39, 49, 78, 103, 156, 172

San Martin, I., 32
Sansa, Adriano, 78
Sauter, H., 20
Schröder, Gerhardt, 18, 99, 126, 151
Schubert, D., 17, 21
Seassaro, L., 5, 22, 27, 71, 89-90, 91, 161
    see also social exclusion
Serra, Narcis, 75

Sheppard, David, 78
Skifter Anderson, H., 84
social exclusion
  case study cities, 61–4
  ethnic minorities, 64, 79, 84, 91
  national regeneration policies,
    11–12, 16, 19–20, 38–9
  poverty, 97–8, 127
social services, 132–4
  Barcelona, 132–3
  general attributes, 132
  Genoa, 133
  Hamburg, 133–4
  Liverpool, 134
  Marseilles, 134
Societés mixtes, 10
SPD, 76, 126
SPD-Green Coalition, 19
Streff, N., 165
structural funds, 178, 182–5,
  188–90, 192
  additionality, 180
  central governments, 179–80
  general, 178–81, 191–3
  Germany, 20
  Italy, 23, 24, 25–6
  Liverpool, 184–5, 189

Marseilles, 111
  partnership, 180–1
  reforms, 183–5, 187–8, 190;
    Agenda 2000, 188–9
  United Kingdom, 78, 104–5, 106–7,
    128, 129, 130, 172

Tapie, Bernard, 12
Thatcher, Margaret, 33–5, 73, 140
Thornley, A., 159
trickle-down effects, 6, 41

UDF, 77

Van Hees, I., 22
Vigouroux, Robert, 77, 110, 131
Vintró i Castells, E., 66
von Beust, Ole, 77
von Dohnanyi, Klaus, 76, 96, 126, 162
Voscherau, Henning, 76–7

Warlock, Derek, 78
White, P., 6, 22, 57, 68
Winchester, H., 10
Wolman, H. *et al.*, 11

zum Felde, W., 97

Printed in the United States
96057LV00002B/15/A